Education in the Emerging Indian Society

Education in the Emerging Indian Society

ISMAIL THAMARASSERI

KANISHKA PUBLISHERS, DISTRIBUTORS
NEW DELHI-110 002

KANISHKA PUBLISHERS, DISTRIBUTORS
4697/5-21A, Ansari Road, Daryaganj
New Delhi -110 002
Phones : 2327 0497, 2328 8285
Fax : 011-2328 8285
E-mail : kanishka_publishing@yahoo.co.in

Education in the Emerging Indian Society
First Published-2008
Edition-2016

PRINTED IN INDIA

Published by Madan Sachdeva for Kanishka Publishers, Distributors, 4697/5-21A, Ansari Road, Daryaganj, New Delhi-110 002, Typeset by Sunshine Graphics, Delhi, and Printed at Rajdhani Printers, Delhi.

Preface

Professional education of teachers is reaching new boundaries with the explosion of knowledge in the field of teacher education and explosion of expectations in other realms. The existing political, social and economic structures, reforms have their impacts on education as they give rise to many problems that become a challenge for education. For educating the prospective teachers, different Indian universities have been adopting divergent patterns of curriculum. The book 'Education in the Emerging Indian Society" caters to the need of the students of education in the various universities of India.

On this book, the author has necessarily drawn materials and data from various sources—such as, standard works, government publications and URL's, the names of which have been duly incorporated in the bibliographies given towards the close of the portions of the work. The author expresses his gratitude to the writers and publishers of all these works. The authors shall ever remain obiiged to his teachers, parents, friends and family members for their directions and guidance. All the colleagues also encouraged the author by giving due recognition to his book. Besides the trainees/ students of the several years deserve special thanks. The author is also great thankful to M/s Infratec Computer Systems, Calicut University, for the type setting of the work. To them all, the author offers his grateful thanks to M/s Kanishka Publishers, Distributors, New Delhi who came forward willingly to undertake the publishing of this book at a short time.

ISMAIL THAMARASSERI

Contents

1
Introduction to Education

EDUCATION MEANING AND DEFINITIONS

Human life is two aspects the biological and the sociological. While the biological aspect of human life is maintained and transmitted by nutrision and reproduction, the social aspect of human life is maintained and transmitted by education. Man is distinguishable from the lower animals because of his educatieable ability. He is endowed with intelligence; he wants to remain active, energetic and even original. The list of human achievements is very big. How has all this been done? through education.

The concept of education is like a diamond which appears to be of a different colour (nature) when seen from different angles (point of view or philosophy of life). The reason for different interpretations/ definition to education, are:

- The complex nature of human personality
- Complex nature of environment
- Different philosophies of life
- Different educational theories and practices.

The Education Commission (1964-66), the very amptly began its report with these words, "the destiny of India is now being shaped in her classrooms." The NPE (1986) also observed, "The country has reached a stage in its economics and technical development when a major effort must be made to derive the maximum benefit from the assets already created and to ensure that the fruits of change reach all sections. Education is the high way to the goal."

According to thinkers in ancient India, vidya/knowledge/learning/education was considered the 'third eye' of man, which gives him on insight in to all affairs and teaches him how to act; it leads as to our salvation in the mundane sphere, it leads us to all round progress and prosperity.

Definitions of Education

1. *Building of human mind and spirit*
—Sri. Aurobindo Ghosh (1872-1950)
2. *Development of the whole man*
—Confucious (551-478 BC) A Chinese scholar
3. *Formation of character*
—Swami Dayananda (1824-1883)
4. *All round drawing out of the best*
—Gandhiji (1869-1948)
5. *Helping the individual to flower greatly in love and wisdom*
—Jidhu Krishnamurti
6. *Making a young man an embodiment of the finest in his culture*
—Jawahar Lal Munshi (1887-1974)
7. *Enabling the individual to be a producer as well as a good citizen*
—Jawahar Lal Nehru (1889-1964)
8. *Enabling an individual to win victory over the five enemies—lust, anger, greed, infatuation and ego,* (Kam, Krodh, Lobh, Moh, Ahankar)
—Guru Nanak (1469-1539)
9. *Training the intellect refinement of the heart and discipline of the spirit.*
—Dr. S. Radhakrishnan (1888-1975)
10. *Purification of the mind and the heart*
—Rama Krishna Paramahamsa (1836-1886)
11. *Noble thoughts coming from every side*
—Rigveda 3000 BC
12. *Helping the mind of the educand to realize absolute moral and intellectual value*
—Dr. Zakir Hussain (1897-1969)
13. *Manifestation of the perfection already in man*
—Swami Vivekananda (1863-1902)

14. *Leading from the unreal to the real, from darkness to light, from death to immortality*

—Brihadars Upanishad (1000 BC)

15. *Making life in harmony with existence*

—Rabindra Nath Tagore (1861-1941)

16. *Realisation of the self and attainment of Moksha (salvation)*

—Sankaracharya (788-820)

Some Great Western Thinkers of Education

1. *Dispelling error and discovering truth*

—Socrates (469-399 BC)

2. *Preparing for complete living*

—Herbert Spencer (1820-1903)

3. *An advocate of freedom in learning*

—Count Leo Nikolayevich Tolstoy (1828-1910)

4. *Learning to be an active assimilation of general ideas which could be applied to life'* —Afred North Whitehead (1861-1947)

5. *Enabling the child to sense eternal realities*

—M.L. Jacks

6. *Enabling the child full participation in the richest available group life*

—William Heard Kilpatrick (1871-1925)

7. *Attainment of a sound mind in a sound body*

—John Locke (1632-1704)

8. *Educating children in the great eternal principle of justice and might which underline the entire length of human existence*

—Horace Mann (1796-1859)

9. *Fitting a man to perform justly, skillful and magnanimously all the official,. both private and public, of peace and war'*

—John Milton (1608-1674)

10. *Cultivating manners, behaviour and judgement than bare and mere liberal learning*

—Michel Eyquem De Montaigne (1533-1592)

11. *Helping in the complete unfolding of the child's individuality*

—Maria Montessori (1870-1952)

12. *Complete development of the individuality of the child so that he*

can make an original contribution to human life according best of his capacity

—T. Percy Nunn (1870-1944)

13. *Realization of all the possibilities of human growth*
—Francis Wayland Parker (1837-1902)
14. *Natural, harmonious and progressive development of men's innate powers*
—Johann Heinrich Pestalozzi (1746-1827)
15. *Developing the body and the soul of all the perfections which they are capable of* —Plato (427-347 BC)
16. *Character as the end of Education*
—Quintilian (38-86 AD)
17. *Development from within* —Jean Jacques Rosseau (1712-1778)
18. *Developing physical health, manual and moral training*
—John Ruskin (1819-1900)
19. *Developing four qualities in child-courage, intelligence, sensitiveness and vitality* —Bertrand Russell (1872-1970)
20. *Providing liberal education to a minority and teaching of three R's for the masses* —Santayana (1863-1952)
21. *Education as a process of emotional development*
—Friedrich Schiller (1759-1805)
22. *Creation of a sound mind in a sound body*
—Aristotle (384-322 BC)
23. *Development of the whole man*
—John Amos Comenius (1592-1670)
24. *Increasing Social Efficiency*
—John Dewey (1859-1952)
25. *Controlling the mind*
—Ralph Waldo Emerson (1803-1882)
26. *Developing real wisdom* —Desiderius Erasmus (1466-1536)
27. *Leading and guiding for peace and unity with good*
—Friederich Wilhem Auguste Froebel (1782-1852)
28. *Preparing the individual for the reciprocal union with society*
—William T. Haris (1835-1928)
29. *Developing morality* —Johann Friedrich Herbart (1776-1841)

30. *Adjusting with the ultimate nature of the cosmos*
—H.H. Horne (1874-1946)

A review of these definitions reveals that the definition given by Gandhi is the best. Gandhi remarked, "By education I mean all-round drawing out of the best in the child and man-body, mind and spirit. Literacy is neither the end of education nor even the beginning. It is one of the means whereby man and women can be educated. Literacy in itself is no education."

Functional and Operational Definition of Education

Education is a process which draws out the best in the child with the aim of producing well-balanced personalities cultural refined, emotionally stable ethically sound mentally alert morally upright, physically strong, socially efficient spiritually upright vocationally self-sufficient and internationally liberal.

Narrower Meaning of Education

S.S. Mackenzi, "In narrow sense, education may be taken to mean any consciously directed effort to develop and cultivate our powers."

Prof. Drever, "Education is a process in which and by which knowledge, character and behaviour of the young are shaped and moulded."

G.H. Thompson, "The influence of the environment on the individual with a view to producing a permanent change in his habits of behaviour, of thought and attitude."

The wider meaning of education includes the following:

1. The process of education is a lifelong process from infancy to old age or from 'womb to grave'.
2. It includes experiences gained through the various formal and informal agencies of education. We learn from home, school, church, cinema, club, press, travel, medias, physical and social environment.
3. We receive education many a time when we are not conscious of the fact.
4. All experience is said to be educative.

Narrow meaning of education includes—

1. Such a type of education is imparted in planned institutions like schools.
2. It is a deliberate, conscious and systematic influence exerted

by the mature person i.e., the teacher, on the immature person i.e., the child.

3. It is limited to the teaching of ready-made material.
4. This type of education is intentional rather than incidental.
5. Knowledge is considered as the accumulated experience of the human race.
6. Education is regarded as synonymous with instruction.

Wider Meaning of Education

M.K. Gandhi, "By education, I mean the alround drawing out of the best child and man-body, mind and soul."

Dumville, "Education in its widest sense includes all the influences which act upon an individual during his passage from cradle to the grave."

S.S. Mackenzi, "In the wider sense, it is a process that goes on throughout life, and is promoted by almost every experience in life."

Analytical Meaning of Education

- Education is not limited to knowledge imparted in schools.
- Education as the development of child's innate power.
- Education as a dynamic process.
- Education as a Bipolar process (*Adams*)—Teacher and Child.
- Education as a Tripolar process (*John Dewey*)—Teacher, Child and Society.

Etymological Meaning of Education

Etymologically, the word 'education' is derived from some Latin words which are explained as under:

1.	Education	The act of teaching
2.	Educare	To lead out or to draw out
3.	Educare	To bring up, to train, to nourish
4.	Educo	To lead forth, to extract out.

Thus education implies;

1. Act of drawing out
2. Act of extracting out
3. Act of leading forth
4. Act of leading out
5. Act of teaching
6. Act of training

Characteristic of Education

- Education – A lifelong process. 'Womb-to tomb'
- Education – A bipolar process (*John Adams* and *John, S. Ross*)
- Education – A tripolar and multipolar process (*Gandhi, Dewey*)
- Education – A deliberate process, i.e., the process of education is not only conscious but also deliberate.
- Education – A psychological process.
- Education – A sociological process.
- Education – A child centred process.
- Education is an attempt to develop the man.
- Education means the modifications of behaviour.
- Education is an act of training.
- Education is direction.
- Education is integrated growth.
- Education is continuous re-organization and integration of activities and experiences.
- Education is empancipation from ignorance.
- Education is the influence of the environment upon the individual.

Ingredients of Education

According to John Dewey, education is a tripolar process. It has three important ingredients:

1. The teacher,
2. The learner, and
3. The curriculum.

Education and Instruction

"Instruction ends in the classroom but education ends with life."

—F.W. Roberston

A UNESCO publication 'Learning to be' (1975) has preferred the term lifelong education in place of instruction. In instruction as observed by Bertrand Russell, "the School has the opportunity of instilling certain mental habits." In education, this just forms a part of education. Education is not instruction. The field of instruction is narrow in comparison with education.

Table—1.1
Comparison between Education and Instruction

Aspects	*Education*	*Instruction*
Field	Wide	Narrow
Place of child	Central, pivotal and prime	Secondary
Role/place of teacher	Subsidiary	Central
Interests/abilities of the child	Gives full attention	Neglecting
Preparation	Prepares the child for real life	Prepares to pass an exam
Nature of learning	Self-learning	Cramming/pre-determined dozes or knowledge

Old and Modern Concept of Education

Table—1.2
Old and Modern Concept of Education—A Comparison

Sl. No.	*Aspects of Education*	*Old Concept of Education*	*Modern Concept of Education*
1.	Meaning	Instruction	Development
2.	Aims	Knowledge	1. Development of Total Personality 2. Social efficiency
3.	Curriculum	Subject centred	Activity/social centred
4.	Methods	Rote memorization	Learning by doing/ project
5.	Discipline	Rigid, Repressionistic	Self-discipline
6.	Examination	Essay type	Objective type
7.	Agencies	Formal (school)	Both formal and informal
8.	Teacher	Instructor	Friend, philosopher and guide, scafolder
9.	Child	Passive recipient	Active/dynamic
10.	School	Teaching shops	Miniature of society

Educations is not Information or Knowledge

As observed by A.N. Whitehead, "A merely well-informed person is the most useless bore on earth." Education is not synonymous with information and knowledge. The child's mind is not be stuffed with all kinds of knowledge. Teachers are not information mongers and walking encyclopaedias. Information and knowledge must lead to constructive thinking and wisdom.

Education as Teaching

Education has a much wider scope than teaching. Teaching is primarily and basically concerned with the knowledge of school subjects. It is on account oF reason that the terms 'Teaching'/ 'Training' replaced by 'Education'. Teaching involves at least two persons, that is the teacher and the taught but education can be self-education.

Education and Literacy

Literacy is concerned with the traditional 3 R's that is reading, writing and arithmetic. It is related to acquiring knowledge of some subjects. Education, on other hand, is related to 7 R's, that is reading, writing, arithmetic, rights, responsibilities and their relationships and recreation.

Educational and Schooling

Table—1.3
Education and Schooling—Comparison

Education	*Schooling*
1. Education has three aspects formal, informal and non-formal	1. In schooling though formal aspect assumes the most importance
2. Field of education is very broad	2. It is a part of the field of education
3. A natural process	3. Artificial
4. Continues and lifelong process	4. Within a limited/predetermined period

Dimensions of the Education Process

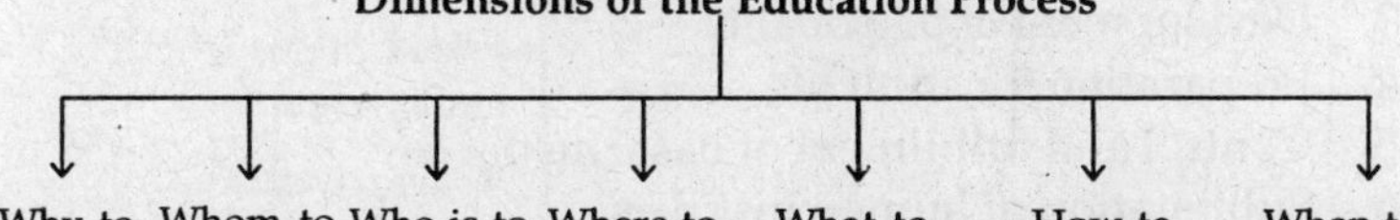

Functions of Education

In meanings we discuss, "What education is?" in function we discuss, "What education does?" In the words of M.L. Jacks, if we "believe in the doctrine of original sin..." there is plenty of work for education to do, its prime task is to transform original evil in to acquired good." Education according to him must enable the child to think for himself, to respect hardwork, to have good fellowship, to have taste and sense of eternal realities.

Daniel Webster said that through education, "The feelings are to be disciplined, the passions are to be restrained, true and worthy motives are to be inspired, a profound religious feeling is to be instilled and pure morality is to be inculcated under all circumstances."

To plato, the business of education is to be "discover aptitudes and progressively to train them for social use." There is no doubt that the task of the school is to provide a special environment for the young. This type of environment simplifies, purifies and balance the environment of man as he naturally grows. It equips children to cope with the emergencies of changing order and to keep them into relationship throughout with the human, social process. Education enables a person to make a choice of values. It presents the desirable and also tells the undesirable, thus leaving a man to choose whatever he likes. Selection of desirable and rejection of undesirable requires knowledge and insight and these two are supplies by right type of education. It also helps a person to have keen observation, reflective thinking and strong will. In the words of John Dewey, "The function of education is to help the growing of a helpless young animal in to a happy moral and efficient if he recognizes the fundamental truths of life and practices of higher values of life." In short, the important functions of education are:

1. Development of natural abilities.
2. Character building.
3. Development of personality.
4. Preparation for adult life.
5. Control and fulfillment of basic instincts.
6. Sublimation of human instincts.
7. Creation of useful citizens.
8. Development of a sense of community.
9. Protection through culture and civilization.
10. Encouragement to social welfare.
11. National development.
12. Use of leisure time properly.

13. Increase of consciousness of other culture.
14. Improvement of emotional unity.
15. Development of International feeling.

Aims and Objectives of Education

Education is necessary for the survival of the society. What is that the education should be trying to do? What are its goals? Aims? Objectives? Without determining the aims of education, it is not possible to plan the curriculum and methods of imparting that curriculum. Aims enables us to act with meaning. "It gives direction to the activity." Absence of an aim in education makes it a blind alleg.

The aims of education are determined by human life.

Aims of Education in Human Life

Human beings always live in groups because they cannot fulfill many of their needs alone. Social life of some kind is essential for everyone. The aims of education are intimately connected with human life. The following points can be made in this connection:

1. Livelihood.
2. Development of personality.
3. Intellectual development.
4. Physical development.
5. Moral development.
6. Aesthetic development.
7. Social development.
8. Cultural development.
9. Spiritual development.
10. Total development.
11. Training for civil life.
12. Training in international living.

Vocational Aims of Education

John Dewey commended that education is meaningful only when it aims at some vocation or employment. Economic independence is essential in the present day world, and for this reason parents arc determined to educate their children. This aim also called 'bread and butter aim'. Mahatma Gandhi says, "True education ought to be for them (boys and girls) a kind of insurance against unemployment." William Godwin wrote, "The true object of education is the generation of happiness." Man is really happy when he is adjusted to his occupation.

Advantages

- Solution of economic problems.
- Dynamism – i.e., the principle of activity applies to the vocational aim of education.
- Moral, intellectual and cultural-development.

Disadvantages

- Absence of liberal education.
- One sided attitude.
- Materialism.

Character Formation Aim of Education

The philosopher plato, Aristotle, Herbert and Pestalozzi are considered character formation, as one of the most important aim of education. But it must be remembered that no two thinkers have defined character in the same way. Character formation is an important objective of education, but by no means the only one.

On being asked, "What is your goal in education?" Gandhiji replied, "character building, I would try to develop courage, strength, virtue, the ability to forget oneself in working towards great aims. I should feel that if we succeed in building the character of the individual, society will take care of itself."

In the words of Raymont, "The teacher's ultimate concern is to cultivate, not wealth of muscle, nor fullness of knowledge, not refinement of feeling, but strength and purity of character." According to Herbert, "The whole problem of education may be comprised in a single concept morality."

Education Leisure

Some educationists are of the opinion that the best education is the one which teaches the educand many ways of spending his leisure usefully and constructively. The various objects of culture, such as literature, music, art, religion and philosophy are the creation of leisure.

What is leisure? According to dictionary meaning it is "free and un occupied time." But here free and un occupied time doesn't mean a time when one is doing nothing but a time when one is not doing something of the nature of bread-earning pursuit. It is a time which we can use in any way we like. It is a time, which away from daily toils, is given to the freedom of the inner life of man.

In order to achieve the goal of education for leisure "the school should undertake

1. to set up standards and develop tastes which will help to determine the choice of proper forms of recreation and pleasure.
2. to develop habits which will continue to give enjoyment and recreations in leisure hours in mature life." Interest in reading should be created by making the students library-minded.

Education for Culture/Cultural Objective of Education

The first factor in the cultural objective of education is the transmission of the social heritage from one generation to the next. Education aims at imparting the values, traditions, customs, patterns of life, etc., of the particular social group to the child, so that he can conform to these patterns and make his own contribution to the cultural development of his group. But the possession of a degree certificate is no guarantee of culture. A cultured person is expected to:

1. appreciate ideas and art,
2. have broad human interests,
3. have social efficiency and socially acceptable behaviour, and
4. understand the best thoughts of the community.

Complete Living Aim/Education for Complete Living

Herbert Spencer believed that the general aim of education was training for complete living. Spencer uses the term 'life' to imply five kinds of activities:

1. the action of self-defence,
2. the action of aparently protecting life,
3. the action of protecting one's progeny,
4. the action of safe guarding society, and
5. the action of spending one's leisure.

Education must aim generating proficiency in each one of these activities. Education tells a person how "to play the game of life wisely and well on three grounds – the playground of the senses, the playground of the skills and the playground of the soul."

Harmonious Development Aim

The harmonious development of the various aspects of human beings is the aims of education suggested by some philosophers.

The human personality is made up of many aspects, such as the physiological the mental etc. In addition to this, each individual is born possessed of certain instincts, education, according to this approach, must aim at a harmonious development of these aspects and instincts. Such a development amounts to a balanced development, which precludes the possibility of the greater development, of anyone aspect at the expense of another. Hence, it leads to the creation of a balanced personality.

Self-Realization

Self-realization the great aim of education according to idealism. It is not merely the manifestation of one's self but the complete development of the individual. Individualism shouldn't be considered a contradiction of the social environment because the social aspect cannot be separated from human nature.

In fact, the concept of a spiritual personality comprehends both the social and the individual aims of education. As J.S. Ross has argued, "The only meaning of the individual aim in education that is worthy of our acceptation is the development of valuable personality and spiritual individuality." Both social and individual aims can be synthesized in this goal of self-realization (Moksha). This aim of education is supported by modern sociology, psychology, ethics and democratic principles.

Education for Knowledge

"Knowledge is power by which things are done", said Socrates. The educators those who advocate the knowledge aim believe that "every advance in knowledge has a practical bearing on life, either on the material or on the mental side." It is knowledge that has enabled humanity to make progress. Human greatness is measured by power of thought. Both Fransis Bacon and John Amos Comenious wanted "all knowledge for all." Education is training for life for complete living. To live life well, it is essential to know life first of all. Knowledge of life comes through intellectual training, which results in power to understand the world. Man becomes resourceful through knowledge. It fits the mind for anything, everything and all things. Socrates said, "One who had true knowledge could not be other than virtuous." It is knowledge which makes a realist a visionary. It is knowledge which ensures success in any profession/vocation. In fact, whatever the sphere of life physical, social, moral, spiritual and economic knowledge is sine qua non.

Education for Spiritualism

"The aim of education is neither national efficiency nor world solidarity, but making the individual feel that he has within himself something deeper than intellect, call it spirit if you like." Said Dr. Radhakrishnan while emphasizing education for spiritualism. For the extreme idealist the only aim of education is to develop the spiritual side of an individual. Since times immemorial our great saints and sees have emphasized the spiritual values.

Individual Aims in Education/Education for Individual Development

Development of the individuals personality was an accepted aim of education both in Ancient Greece and India. "Individuality is the ideal of life", thus observed Sir Percy Nunn and added that "A scheme of education is ultimately to be valued by its success in fostering the highest degree of individual excellence." Exalting the 'individual development' as the aim of education, Sir Percy Nunn believes, "That nothing good enters into the human world except in and through the free activities of individual man and women, and that educational practice must be shaped to accord with that truth."

All the developments in the individual can take place by two processes.

1. Self-realization, and
2. Self-expression.

It must be admitted that the individual cannot grown in vaccum. He is a social animal. In all walks of life he is influenced by all those who surround him. He cannot escape from the influence of the society.

Education for Social Efficiency/Social Aims of Education

Man is a social animal. Without society, either he is a beast or an angel. Since he is neither of the two but a rational social being, the aim of the education should be social efficiency. Social efficiency implies,

- Social awareness,
- Economic productivity, and
- Cultural and moral refinement.

Social awareness will produce in the mind of the child, a sense of fairness in dealing with others, open mindedness and the ability to follow and lead as the situation warrants. Economic independence will help him to pull his own weight, and he will not be a parasite or a drag on society. Cultural and moral refinement means that he will have a spirit of social service and self-sacrifice.

According Lycurgus (the great spartan), a citizen should have no wish for himself but for his country. That is why the Sparta man "was born not for himself but for his country. Their whole education was an exercise of obdiance."

In the broader sense social aim of education enables a person to utilize one's development for the corporate and co-operative life. One must use one's capacities and abilities in social occupations. Education "is directed in a broader sense to the good of the community." Education for social aim is 'education for social service' and education for citizenship.

FORMAL, INFORMAL AND NON-FORMAL EDUCATION

Formal Education

Formal education is provided in educational institutions according to a particular pattern. In the school, the educator educates the educands according to a specific programme aiming at particular goal. He/she follows a pre-determined syllabus. In this formal kind of education, the time and place of teaching are fixed and the educand has to arrive at that place and at that specific time to receive education. The length is also fixed. So it is synonymous with educational institutions.

Characteristics of Formal Education

- Deliberately planned, purposive.
- Age specified.
- Rigid time schedule.
- Rigid rule for admission.
- Promotion and attendance.
- Pre-designed fixed curriculum.
- Direct schooling and tution.
- Guided and supervised by persons.
- Limited to a period of being taught.
- Generally not integrated with work.
- Has fixed point of entry and exist.
- In it the 'giver' dominates and the 'receiver' is rather passive.
- Geared to knowledge acquisition.
- Fosters on uncritical obedience.

- Works within a fixed social frame.
- Associated with traditional schooling, schooling confined to a school or a college etc.
- Rigid with regard to various aspects of education, i.e., admissions, curriculum, place of instruction, mode of instruction, the time and duration of instruction.

Informal Education

Informal education complements the formal education outlined above, without which formal education remains incomplete. Education of this kind has no specific time or place at which it is provided. Even the educator is not fixed. All fixed syllabi, rules, formalities are absent from it. Education of this kind is the education one receives while playing in field, talking to family members in the house, roaming around some where, in fact, everywhere. This kind of education never comes to an end, and it teaches the individual more than he can ever learn through is formal education.

Characteristics of Informal Education

- Incidental education received by living with others.
- Not provided deliberately.
- Free and uncontrolled environment.
- Neither fixed location nor fixed duration of time.
- Lifelong education.
- No limitations for curriculum.
- No guidance and supervision.
- It is un planned.
- Non-purposive.

Table—1.4

Comparison between Formal and Informal Education

Sl. No	*Formal Education*	*Informal Education*
1.	It is planned, purposive, organized and systematic educational activity.	Unplanned, non-purposive un-organized and unsystematic.
2.	It has some pre-determined aim	No pre-determined definite aim
3.	It starts and ends at a particular stage	It is a lifelong process
4.	It is imparted through formal lessons lessons	Not imparted through any formal

(Contd.)

Sl. No	Formal Education	Informal Education
5.	There is a definite course to be covered during a definite period	No such definite course and period
6.	The taught is aware of the process, through which education is imparted	Taught is not aware of the process
7.	It puts some mental strain both on the teacher and the taught	Being natural, it doesn't strain any body
8.	It is organized by some agency	No organized body is usually behind the process

Non-Formal Education

Non-Formal Education is an arrangement where in flexibility is the key word. Such a system is an open one with regards to various aspects of education i.e., admissions, curriculum, place of instruction, mode of instruction and the time and duration of instruction. Various examples of such a system are the open school and open university, open learning and the correspondence courses.

Non-formal education includes adult education, continuing education and on the job-education, etc. Philip Coombs and Ahmed (1974), "Any organized, systematic educational activity carried on outside the framework of the formal system to provide selected types of learning to particular sub-groups in the population, adults as well as children."

Characteristics of Non-Formal Education

- It is flexible.
- It is open ended.
- It has flexible points of entry and exist.
- It has diversified flexible curriculum.
- It is a process of sharing and exploring together with full learner participation.
- It permits any one willing and desirous of sharing knowledge, ideas and skills etc., with others to impart instruction.
- It is a process of meeting the individuals own needs.
- It doesn't emphasize on examination and certification.
- It is motivated by the need for individual.
- It is participatory.

Advantages of Non-Formal Education

- Universalization of education.
- Eradication of adult illiteracy.
- Meeting the omissions of formal education.
- Meeting the enormous and imperative challenges of democratic set-up.
- Enabling the people to learn and earn.
- Enabling those students to study who had to discontinue formal education owing to pecuniary and other circumstances.
- Enabling the students in geographically remote areas to get education because the formal education cannot be within their easy reach.
- Enabling individuals to refresh and update their knowledge.
- Rectifying the educational imbalance between those who live in villages and those live in towns.
- Providing educational facilities to socially and economically neglected sectors of society.

Functions of Non-Formal Education

- Universalize education.
- Eradicate adult illiteracy.
- Meet the omissions of formal education.
- Meet the challenges of the complex society.
- Enable pupils to learn and earn simultaneously.
- Enable 'drop-outs' to continue studies.
- Make education accessible to hill tribes and others isolated geographical barriers.
- Enable peoples to refresh knowledge.
- Maintain balance between villagers and town men.
- Provide educational facilities to neglected sectors.

Objectives of Non-Formal Education

- The removal of illiteracy.
- The application of 'new' knowledge to resolve economic culture and social problems.
- To provide for lifelong education.

Types of Non-Formal Programmes

- Adults functional literacy programmes.
- Correspondence courses.

- Open school studies.
- Satellite instructional Television Programmes.
- Programme for dropouts in the age group 6-14.

Persons Benefits by Non-Formal Education

- People of all ages
- Students
- Learners
- Labourers
- Educated unemployed
- Graduates, professionals and intellectuals.

Agencies of Non-Formal Education

1. Institutions for formal education.
2. Special agencies for non-formal education such as Nehru Yuva Kendra Sangathan (NYK), training centres in factories, public libraries, centres of correspondence education, extension centres of universities/ colleges etc.
3. Voluntary NGO's like clubs and societies.
4. Radio and Television.

Formal v/s Non-Formal Education

Table—1.5
Formal and Non-Formal Education

Sl. No	*Formal Education*	*Non-formal Education*
1.	Limited to a period of being taught	Lifelong and not limited to any period of being taught.
2.	Generally not integrated with work	Integrated with work.
3.	Has fixed points of entry and exist	Has flexible points of entry, exist re-entry and re-exist. In fact, it continues throughout the life span of the individual.
4.	Has fixed curriculum	Has diversified and varied curriculum.
5.	In it the 'giver' dominates and the 'receiver' is rather passive	A process of sharing, exploring, analyzing and judging together.
6.	Geared to knowledge acquisition	A process of enabling the individual understand his needs, the environmental situation and mutual relationships.

(Contd.)

Sl. No	*Formal Education*	*Non-formal Education*
7.	Fosters an uncritical obedience	An open-end process of education which develops self-reliant awareness.
8.	Works within a fixed social frame	Anticipates and prepares for change.
9.	Associated with traditional schooling-schooling confined to a school or a college, etc.	Not confined to any educational set up.
10.	Rigid with regard to various aspects of education i.e., admissions, curriculum, place of instruction, mode of instruction, the time and duration of instruction	Very flexible in regard to various aspects of education.

Factors Influencing Education

Economic Factors

Formal education is possible where production exceeds consumption. This may be the result of tremendous industrial development or favourable natural circumstances. This will depend upon the fertility of the soil, abundant mineral deposits and proper climate conditions for work. Such conditions provide men with leisure to pursue education. Where there is a subsistence economy, it is a far cry to afford time for formal schooling. This is the reason why poorer and undeveloped countries have a minimum education for their children while industrially advanced countries keep nearly all their children at school and for a longer time.

Education is the result of economic development. It is true in all its aspects. The quality of education is also decided by economic development of the society. A poor country cannot provide for all its citizens costly educational facilities. It is applicable in the case of a family also.

The type of education is also determined by the economic condition. The education needed by an agrarian and an industrialized communities/countries will be different.

Philosophical Factors

Philosophy influences every aspect of education namely the aim, content, method and discipline. It is philosophy which determines whether the aim of education should be intellectual, spiritual, liberal, aesthetic, moral or vocational. For example, the Hindu philosophy in ancient India resulted in the evolution of the Gurukula system of education. The militant philosophy ancient Sparta gave rise to the regimental system of education. The Nazism of Germany gave rise to the Fantic, anti-jewish system of education.

Philosophy influences the methodology too. Naturalistic philosophy emphasizes paido-centric (child-centred) methods, idealism emphasis socratic and lecture methods. Pragmatism emphasis the project method.

In the case of curriculum, naturalists start with present experiences and interests of children. Idealists stress the study of religion, culture ethics and literature. Pragmatists advocate the study of functional subjects which have utility value.

Philosophy influences the discipline in education. Autocratic philosophy leads to repressionism, idealism leads to impressionism, naturalism leads to emancipation and modern pragmatism leads to free discipline.

The teacher must possess a sound philosophy of life. He/she must be a lover of wisdom, a seeker of knowledge and a man/women of virtues/values. Then only he/she can bring about desirable changes in his pupils.

Social Factors

Education reflects the social pattern of society. The tremendous explosion of science and technology has shaken the old leisurely outlook on life and has created intricate problems of social adjustment. A new emphasis has been placed on literacy. A growing interest is shown in re-organizing the curricula at all stages. The new forces in the social structure of the Indian society have provided a fresh incentive for educationists to pattern the educational system.

Education will be different in different kinds of society since total way of life of a society influence education. Even the same society, education provided at different time spans will be different. Although it is said that education is one of the causes in social change, it could be seen that in most cases educational change trends to follow rather than initiate social changes. Educational institutions and other organizations are inter-related with the rest of the social structure. A.K.C. Ottaway stated, "Education is an activity which goes on in a society and its aims and methods depend on the nature of the society in which it takes place."

Cultural Factors

Culture and education are initially and integrally connected. Hence the cultural pattern of a country conditions its educational pattern. For example—a society based on the spiritual pattern of culture emphasis the attainment of moral and eternal values—truth, goodness and beauty- of life through education. At the same time a society based on materialistic pattern emphasis the attainment of material values through education. Culture influences aims of education, curriculum, methodology, discipline and textbooks.

Political Factors

Political ideologies go a long way in determining the aims and the system of education. Different political ideologies like totalitarian or fascist communist or socialist and democratic will call for different systems of education. Political philosophy of a nation has great influence on its education. Today we have different forms of political systems. They are totalitarianism, communism and democracy.

A totalitarian state will assume complete control of the educational system. The rulers will prescribe curriculum, syllabi, textbooks. Education will be directed to secure mechanical discipline, duty and unquestioned obedience. There will be no room for community participation. For example—education in ancient Sparta.

Communism conceives education as one of the principle instruments for economic advancement and social progress. State produce textbooks and they conduct training in order to attain the goal of socialism. Education will be a national concern. Individuals will have only limited freedom in educational sector. Education will be free at all levels.

In a democratic set-up education under the control of society. The powers and resources age distributed between Central and State Governments. The state provide educational facilities. A kind of participatory approach and de-centralized planning is adopted here. Universal education is a matter of social necessity in a democratic society. Education aims at improvements in vocational and practical efficiency. Significant place is given to the total development of each individual. The schools indicate respect for the national flag and national anthem. Exceptional children/poor/disadvantaged are given special consideration. Education of ancient Athens up to an end this kind.

The ruled nations had a different educational system than their rulers as they were being exploited by their rulers. The system of British education was implanted in this country from purely political motives.

Historical Factors

History of a nation must influence the education of that country. History of a nation includes, its past politics, culture, social system and economy etc. Thus, influence of any of the above factors will influence education also. For example—Still we following British system of education.

If a nations history was full of wars, the education in that nation will give much importance to training of troops and developing modern ammunitions/weapons. If a nation was under the rule of some other nation, its education will be influenced by the culture, politics and social system of that ruling nation. Definitely education in present will be influenced by history.

Religious Factors

The influence of religion is very powerful as it penetrates the emotional depth of human nature. The Brahmanic system of education, the Buddhist education, medieval Islamic education were dominated by religion. In Europe, the protestant countries were wedded to the education of the masses and the catholic countries to the education of the classes.

MODEL QUESTIONS

1. Distinguish between non-formal and information education.
2. Which type do you support between formal and non-formal education? Give reasons.
3. How do political factors influence education?
4. What is education? Explain it meaning and functions. How far, we have succeeded in achieving its objectives?
5. What do you mean by education? Differentiate between wider and narrower meanings of education.
6. State important definitions of education.
7. What are the aims of education?
8. What are the functions of education?
9. Differentiate between education and training.
10. What is the difference between education and schooling?

REFERENCES

1. Aggaral, J.C. (2003). *Teacher and Education in a Developing Society.* Vikas Publishing House (P) Ltd., New Delhi.
2. Chakraborty, A.K. (2003). *Principle and Practice of Education,* R. Lal Book Depot, Meerat.
3. Taneja, V.P. (2003). *Educational Thought and Practice,* Sterling Publishers (P) Ltd., New Delhi.

2

Introduction to Educational Philosophy

INTER-DEPENDENCE OF PHILOSOPHY AND EDUCATION

The chief task of philosophy is to determine 'what constitutes a life worth living.' The chief task of education is 'to make life worth living.' Therefore the relationship between philosophy and education is very close. Philosophy tells the goal and essentials of good life. Education tells the means to achieve those goals and learn those essentials of good life. Philosophy deals with abstract; education deals with the concrete. All great philosophers are great educators.

Fichte, "The art of education will never attain complete clearness without philosophy." James Ross, "Education is the dynamic side of philosophy." John Dewey, "Philosophy is the theory of education in its most general phases."

Philosophy and Aims of Education

Aims, goals, ends or objectives of education are the first essentials of any educational system. Without them the whole educative process would be meaningless. Aims of education depend on the philosophy that prevails at the time of determining the aims of education. That is why they have been charging with the changing philosophy of life. 'No System of education', says Acharya J.B. Kripalini, the noted Gandhian philosopher, "Can be properly appraised, and appreciated, unless it is studied in connection with the ideas and ideals which it represents."

Aims in Primitive Time

In ancient times men needed training in the use of bows and arrows for their safety. Their needs were simple and a few. The process of

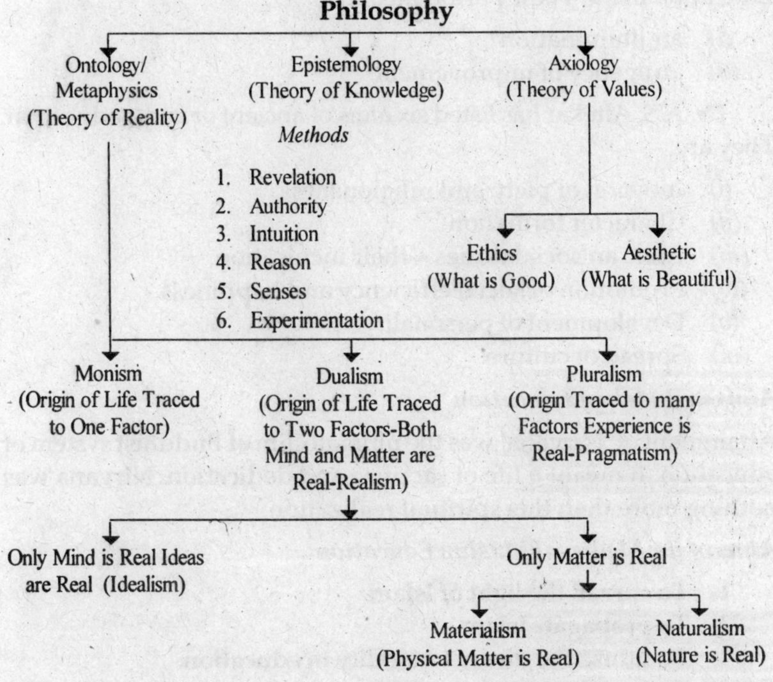

Illustration 2.1: Diagrammatic Presentation of Philosophy.

production, consumption, distribution and exchange was quite simple. Thus, the educative needs were also simple and could be met by a process of education which was also very simple.

Education in Ancient India

Education in Ancient India was mostly dominated by the religions considerations. Learning was considered as a means of salvation or self-realization, 'Mukti' or emancipation has been the highest ends of life.

Aims of Vedic/Brahmanical Education

- Emphasis upon knowledge and experience.
- Sublimation of instincts.
- Spirituality.
- Growth of character and personality.
- Fulfillment of duty.
- Protection of culture.

Education in the Vedic period meant,

(i) an illumination.
(ii) an agency of improvement.

Dr. A.S. Altekar has listed six aims of ancient or vedic education. They are:

(i) Infusion of piety and religiousness.
(ii) Character formation.
(iii) Civic an social duties – their inculcation.
(iv) Promotion of social efficiency and happiness.
(v) Development of personality.
(vi) Spread of culture.

Aims in Buddhist Education

Attainment of 'Nirvana' was the ultimate aim of Buddhist system of education. It meant a life of sacrifice and dedication. Nirvana was nothing more than this spiritual realization.

Aims of the Medieval Muslim Education

1. To spread the light of Islam.
2. To propagate Islam.
3. To infuse the distinct morality in education.
4. To attain material prosperity.
5. To spread the light of learning and to illuminate the minds of followers of Islam.

Aims Under British Rule

The Charter Act of 1813 made in English East India Company to accept the responsibility of educating the Indians. Aims mainly was

1. proselytization.
2. produce faithful servants.
3. missionary works.

Aims of Education in Free-India

Four aims of education stated by the Secondary Education Commission (1952-53).

1. Development of democratic citizenship.
2. Improvement of vocational efficiency.
3. Development of personality.
4. Development of qualities for leadership.

Education Commission (1964-66) on the Objectives of Education

1. Relating education to productivity.
2. Strengthening social and national integration through educational programmes.
3. Consolidation of democracy through education.
4. Development of social, moral and spiritual values.
5. Modernization of society.

Some of the Recognized Aims of Education

1. *Knowledge Aim*: Knowledge lays the foundation of any time of education. Most of the educators in olden days held knowledge as the supreme aim of education.
2. *Vocational Aim*: Education should prepare a child for a calling or profession, enabling him to earn his livelihood. Vocational aims are essential for leading a worthy life. A liberal education without vocational education is useless.
3. *Harmonious Development Aim*: Pestalozzi and Gandhiji have emphasized 'harmonious development' as an intrinsic quality of any good system of education. Pestalozzi, "Education as the harmonious development of the heart, head and hand." Gandhiji, "all-round drawing out of the best in the child and man-body, mind and spirit."
4. *Complete Living Aim:* Herbert Spencer, "To prepare us for complete living is the function which education has to discharge, and the only mode of judging any educational causes, is to judge in what degree it discharges such function."
5. *Religious Aim:* "Faith in the fatherhood of god and brotherhood of man is the essence of all religion and all religious education."
6. *Moral Aim:* Herbert, "The one and the whole problem of education may be summed up in a single concept-morality."
7. *Individual Aim:* Sir Percy Nunn, "The central aim of education is the autonomous development of the individual," "Nothing good enters into the human world except in and through the free activities of individual men and women. Educational practice, therefore, must be shaped to accord with the truth."
8. *Social Aim:* Raymont, "The isolated individual is a figment of imagination." Bagley and Dewey are important advocates

of the social aim of education. According to them education should aim at making each individual socially efficient.

Aims of Education in a Totalitarian State

J.F. Brown, "Education in any country and at all periods reflects on the ruling class." The aim of education are determined by the political ideologies.

1. Each individual must be trained to subordinate his interests to the interests of the state.
2. Every child must undergo a rigorous code of discipline.
3. Thinking along the lines approved by the authorities is stressed-very little independent thinking is allowed.
4. Physical education and military training are given great importance.
5. The student is made to realize the value and importance of obedience and conformity.

Aims of Education in a Democratic Set-up

1. It should develop a wide range of whole some interest in each pupil by providing for learning through co-operative work.
2. It should develop social outlook.
3. It should develop ability to constructive and independent thinking.
4. It should develop the capacity of the pupil to different truth from falsehood, fact from propaganda, and to reject the dangerous appeal of fanaticism and prejudice.
5. It should provide for training dignity of labour.
6. It should provide equal opportunities to all.
7. It should develop love and respect for others.
8. It should develop human relations.
9. It should cater to the individual difference of children and teach them accordingly. No attempt should be made towards uniformity.
10. It encourages originality and inventiveness.
11. Vocational choices are broad based.

Idealism and Aim of Education

1. Exaltation of human personality.
2. Universal Education.
3. Development of inventive and creative powers.

4. Acquisition and enrichment of culture environment.
5. Self-realization.
6. Development of moral sense.
7. Self-realization.

Naturalism and Aims of Education

1. Self-expression.
2. Autonomous development of individuality.
3. Improvement of racial gains.
4. Preparation of the struggle for existence.

Aims of Education in Pragmatism

1. Social efficiency.
2. Change with changing times.
3. More and more education and continues growth.
4. Adaptation to environment.

Realism and the Aims of Education

1. Complete living.
2. Understanding of human society.
3. Adjust himself in the environment.
4. Develop upto utmost perfection.

Philosophy and Curriculum

The need of philosophy of education felt very seriously in the area of curriculum planning. The philosophical approach to life is the guiding factors in the choice of students to be included in the curriculum.

Meaning of Curriculum

The curriculum is the sum total of the schools efforts to influence learning, whether in the classroom or in the playground, or out of school: K.G. Saiyidain, "The curriculum is primarily an aid in the process of adjusting the child to the environment in which he functions from day-to-day and in the environment in which he will have to organize his activities late."

The concept of the curriculum differs with different schools of philosophy.

Idealism and Curriculum

1. It lays stress on nature of the child.
2. Curriculum should emphasize the higher values.

3. Curriculum provides humanities a place of prominence.
4. Ethics, religion and arts find an important place.
5. Importance to physical education, hygiene, philosophy, physical skills, gymnastics and athletics.

Ross summarizes from Rusk a Shame for a complete and generous education.

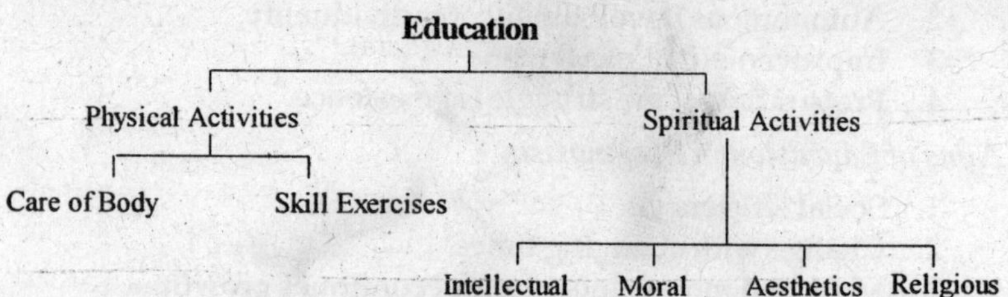

Naturalism and Curriculum

1. It is based on the nature of the child, his interests.
2. It lays stress on subjects that are helpful in self-preservation.
3. It stresses basic sciences.
4. It emphasis physical and health education.

Pragmatism and Curriculum

1. Pragmatism stresses experience curriculum.
2. Pragmatism regards utility as the prime mover in the determination of curriculum.
3. Pragmatism assigns due place to the interests of the child.
4. Pragmatism provides for problem-solving activities.
5. Pragmatism emphasis subjects and studies like physical training, hygiene, social studies, maths and science.

Realism and the Curriculum

The realist gives a high priority to subjects like physical sciences and mathematics. Modern languages may find a place in the curriculum because they enable one to read, write and conduct all types of social intercourse; but literature, as such will find no prominent place because the realist believes that it is out of touch with the real line of human advance.

Philosophy and Methods

Methodology of teaching establishes a contact of the teacher, the taught and the subject. It raises many problems. All such questions and the problems that arise in the classroom techniques are satisfactorily tackled by philosophy.

Idealism and Method of Teaching

1. Learning through reading.
2. Learning through lecturing.
3. Learning through memorization and discussion.
4. Learning through imitation.
5. Socratic method/Dialectics (*Plato*).

Naturalism and Method of Teaching

1. Learning by doing.
2. Learning through experience.
3. Learning through observation.
4. Learning through heuristic method.

Pragmatism and Method of Teaching

1. Project method—(*Dr. Kilpatrick*)
2. Learning by doing 'sine qua non'—(*John Dewey*)
3. Learning through creative activities.
4. Learning through purposeful activities.
5. Learning through experiences.

The Method of Instruction and Sarvodaya Philosophy

Sarvodaya—a socialist philosophy, is a culmination of Indian idealistic thought. Its foundation have deep roots in the Indian soil, but it is different from Indian philosophies. Our philosophies were individualistic. Sarvodaya—its basis in the socio-economic conditions of the present day world, is aimed at the 'good of all' presents a synthesis of all good points in different Indian and western philosophies of life. "Correlation of studies" is the main principle of Sarvodaya method. It develop an integrated personality.

The Philosophical Methods

The philosophical method is not absolutely different from scientific method. Philosophical problems have much in common with the scientific problems. The philosopher utilizes the same method of induction and deduction as used by scientist.

Induction: The principles of different sciences are arrived at by means of inductive process. The philosopher utilizes concepts and propounds new theories. For Example—materialism, idealism etc. and then he tries to explain his experiences satisfactorily on the basis of these theories.

Deduction: Deduction is the process to arrive at certain particular prepositions from a general prepositions.

Dialectical method: This is the natural method of philosophical thinking. This is a common place experience that when we think over a problem we arrive at certain positive facts. That is *thesis*. Now after sometimes we came to know some facts which are contradictory to thesis that is *anti-thesis*. This thesis and anti-thesis cannot live together for a long, hence they are synthesized into a *synthesis*. This synthesis arrived through anti-thesis is more comprehensive than the original thesis. Thus, knowledge grows in a dialectical process through thesisà anti-thesisà synthesis. This method was developed by Hegal.

Analysis: Analysis means the process of distinction between different elements evolved in a particular state of experience, so that, they might be more clear. Realistic philosophers have emphasized this procedure while absolutists have advanced arguments against it.

Synthesis: This method involves connecting together the scattered elements in a particular experience which brings into light new patterns and facts. The idealist philosophers have laid emphasis on synthesis.

Nature of Philosophy

Whenever, it is asked regarding a science as to what is its nature, it is said that it is scientific. Nature of philosophy is philosophical. In order to understand the scientific nature of a science we have to understand scientific method, scientific attitude, scientific problems and scientific activities. Similarly, in order to explain that the nature of philosophy is philosophical, we will have to explain the philosophical problems, philosophical attitude and philosophical activities, etc. Philosophical problems are the general problems of different philosophical sciences. In its critical and synthetic aspects, the problems of philosophy are the examination and synthesis of the postulates and conclusions of different sciences. Philosophical attitude is reflective, curious, tolerant, guided by experience and reasoning and a persistent effort to reach the truth through never in a hurry to arrive as final conclusions.

Philosophical methods includes induction, deduction, analysis, synthesis and dialectical method, philosophical activity begins in wonder, curiosity and discontentment at the existing order of things.

This activity may be individual as well as social, alone as well as in group. The aim of this activity is to present a total world-view. Different philosophers arrive at different conclusions through philosophical methods. However, different these conclusions might be, they are different from scientific conclusions as a class by the very virtue of the fact that they are philosophical. The philosophical nature philosophy shows the effect on the individual, group and community.

In brief, the philosophical problems, philosophical attitude, philosophical method, philosophical activity, philosophical conclusions and their effect on the individual and society show that the nature of philosophy is philosophical. It follows that when we say that the nature of philosophy is philosophical we mean all these problems, methods, attitude, activity, conclusions and effects characteristic of philosophy.

Functions of Philosophy

The speculative function of educational philosophy is, therefore, closely related to its function of determining the values which education ought to pursue. Taken together, these aspects of educational philosophy would seem to indicate that it has a prospective reference and that it anticipates and directs practices. While there are many who agree that philosophy should provide certain ideas at which teachers should aim, there are others who take a less ambitious view of educational philosophy. Philosophy is retrospective rather than prospective in character.

Normative Philosophy

Normative philosophers advocates the aim of education as follows, "The prime goal of education is the conquest of internal and spiritual freedom to be achieved by individual persons." Normative philosophers stresses to three things:

1. What human dispositions are excellences and worthy at cultivation, they will show,
2. Why these dispositions are to be considered as excellence, and they may also discuss, and
3. How these excellence are to be cultivated.

   Plato (*Republic*) one of the normative philosopher.

Analytical Philosophy

Analytical endeavour in crucial in philosophy. Concepts control in important lines of enquiry have been clarified. The validity of argument have been assessed, and hidden assumptions have been exposed. Plato in 'Republic' to clarity the concept of justice, he depicted the Socrates as taking pains to copose weakness of counter argument at in the dialogue. Contemporary philosophers have attempted to clarify concepts such as 'equity', teaching, learning, punishment, indoctrination, intelligence and education itself. (*International Encyclopedia of Education*, Vol. 7, pp. 3860-61)

Scope of Educational Philosophy

The concept of education and philosophy from the basis of arriving at the definition of philosophy of education. Thus philosophy of education is essentially a method of approaching educational experience rather than a body of conclusions. It is the specific method which makes it philosophical. Philosophical method is critical, comprehensive and synthetic. Therefore, philosophy of education is the criticism of the general theory of education. Clarification of the definition of education will be further clarified by a discussion of scope and nature of philosophy of education.

The traditional concept of philosophy has been developed for ages with reference to metaphysics. It deals with the knowledge of the universe, the ultimate reality and its source or origin. Thus philosophy directs its enquiry in to life in its totality. It also deals with the aim and purpose as well as some other relevant issues and problems around life. The task of philosophy is also to unfold the mystery behind creation and the creater.

Philosophy is a term which is based on the concept of life and knowledge. It is an attempt to understand the world of experience in different perspective. "The nature and functions of philosophy itself a kind of philosophical problem over which there have always been controversies" says Reid. Philosophy is lone of wisdom needed most in our life. A philosopher is the lover of wisdom who can see life steadily as a whole. O'conner believes, that is a mistake to assume that philosophy is a sort of superior and profounder science. Metaphysics has emerged as a separate branch of knowledge to explain life and its purpose. Philosophy helps man to attain a clear and consistent conception of world system.

The scope and function of philosophy are no doubt, limited. The primary responsibility is to understand the nature of reality in all its dimensions. All the sciences started as branches of philosophy in a very general sense to cover all enquiries. In the past, philosophy was regarded as a specialized decipline relevant to education. This approach has been modified in recent years.

The moral and spiritual values and the relevant problems have been the topics for discussion in the area of philosophy. The basic assumption is that people must live in happiness with a purpose. With a view to ensuring this the following must be considered:

(a) The existence of the individual and individualism.
(b) Understanding the need for love, kindness and acceptance.
(c) Cultivation of capabilities and right frame of attitude.

Thus philosophy has also the following roles to enrich human life;

(d) Creating a self concept.
(e) Learning certain human relations.
(f) Inclusion of positive attitudes, human dignity, etc.
(g) Learning of cultural sets.

Besides, the philosophers have undertaken the challenging task of generating values. Educational philosophy emerged as a concept for dealing with the philosophical issues and problems in educational perspectives.

Education is the core of almost all the social sciences. This is a purposive activity, a process and not a product. One can ask if education should have some ultimate objectives. The basic query is whether education should have a philosophy. It does not mean that it should be bound by some set of values. Philosophy provides a vision and a wide perspective.

To Dewey, education is life itself, and it is as dynamic as living. As we live, we learn and educate themselves. This is a pragmatic view of Dewey. Various schools of philosophy have emerged with their distinct bearing on education. It appears that education should be consistent with certain fundamental value in life. The question arises whether these dimensions of life, can be reached through education. It is obvious that goodness and truth cannot be divorced from beauty and happiness. Education for happiness is the ultimate concern of all.

Plato provides us with the psychology of education. Plato does not forget that life has more than single purpose which a man may consciously pursue. As there are in main reason, spirit and desire, each of these must be developed by training and education. Life in order to have meaning and direction should be guided by philosophy.

Philosophy as a vision helps us to look at life and creation in wider perspectives. Metaphysics in the opinion of Ewing, helps one to make genuine discoveries of truth.

In short, philosophy of education is the application of philosophy and its methods in the field of education. Education is a purposive activity towards the objectives determined primarily by philosophy.

It is a process of enabling one not merely to line but to live adequately. There are various aspects of education, academic, aesthetic, moral, physical, social and spiritual. Theories of education have been formulated and different values emphasized. It is not very difficult to trace the evolution of educational theories.

The scope of philosophy of education is concerned with the problems of education. These problems are general in nature, such as the interpretation of nature, the world and the universe, explanation of aims and ideals, the relationship of the various constituents of the field of education. The main problems of philosophy of education include aims and ideals of education, analysis of human nature, relationship of education and state, educational values, theory of knowledge and its relationship to education, economic system and education the place of school in educational system the curriculum and process of education, and finally the relationship of education and social progress.

Problems of philosophy of education constitute its scope and clarity its nature. Philosophy of education aims at presenting a synthesis of various aims and ideals of education. Value is typically a philosophical subject since it is more substract than concrete, mental than physical, integral than one-sided, universal than particular. Educational values was determined by philosophical values.

Philosophy of education is an important branch of applied philosophy of the three divisions of philosophy, meta physics, epistemology and axiology, philosophy of education falls in the third. It is, therefore, mainly concerned with educational values. As a branch of philosophy it utilizes philosophical methods for the solution of philosophical problems with a philosophical attitude to arrive at philosophical conclusions. In this comprehensive process it includes facts concerning education and synthesis them with values.

Conclusion

The horizon of education is gradually expanding the modern movement in education is concerned with the child and its development in relation to his life and environment. Some amount of idealism underlying the philosophy of new education. Today education has become experimental as a science in the laboratory of human life. Principles underlying all the educational behaviour are derived from philosophy of education. In the words of John Dewey, "Whenever philosophy has been taken seriously. It has always been assumed that it signified achieving a wisdom that would influence the conduct of life."

Philosophy, life and education are intimately linked with one another. They are also related to time and space. If we consider 'what', 'how' and 'where' to teach, we shall be discussing the subject-matter, methods of education and human relations in schools. All these aspects of education are not fixed. They change according to the social and economic needs and concept of social sciences prevailing in our at the particular time. The same type of training and the same modes of behaviour which were considered to be most essential in ancient society, are out of date in modern society. The needs of our present day society are not the same as those of ancient society.

BRANCHES OF PHILOSOPHY

Epistemology

The most important branches of philosophy are metaphysics, epistemology and axiology.

Epistemology is concerned with the discussion of the problems concerning knowledge. It is analysis of the nature of knowledge. Epistemology or the theory of knowledge has often been thought to be at the heart of the philosophical enterprise.

Etymologically, epistemology means, the logic of understanding (episteme) i.e., the origin, nature and validity of knowledge.

If you have to know that you have good reasons for a belief before you claim knowledge then it seems that the definition is question-begging. We have two ways for accepting this definition:

1. asking questions, and
2. justification of questions.

While most beliefs have to be justified by other beliefs there must be some basic, foundational beliefs which do not stand in need of justification. Epistemology as a distinct branch of philosophy developed out of the growth of individualism.

Epistemology is the branch of philosophy which is concerned with the discussion of the problems concerning knowledge. Its main problems are:

1. What is the relation between the knower and known?
2. Is the content of knowledge identical with the external object or is it different from it?
3. How can we know that our knowledge is real knowledge of the object?
4. What are the limits of knowledge?
5. What are the sources of knowledge? etc.

Besides, the epistemologist raises certain other questions such as: What is knowledge? How can we distinguish between true an false knowledge? What is ignorance? Is it a form of knowledge or different from it? What is the process of knowledge? What is the meaning of forgetting of knowledge? What are the errors possible in the process of knowledge? How is it that some beliefs are considered to be more valid than others? What are the distinctions between different types of knowledge? What are the relations of knowledge with science and philosophy?

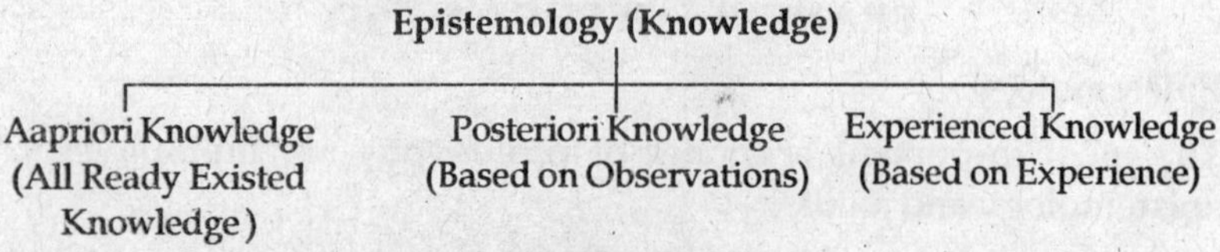

Epistemology (Knowledge)

Aapriori Knowledge (All Ready Existed Knowledge)	Posteriori Knowledge (Based on Observations)	Experienced Knowledge (Based on Experience)

Epistemology and Education

Epistemology is the philosophical discussion of problems related to knowledge. It uses the philosophical methods of induction and deduction, synthesis and analysis. One finds different conclusions presented by different epistemologists regarding epistemological problems.

According to the realist philosophers, knowledge is the knowledge of objects, idealists define it as the knowledge of ideas.

Some epistemologists think that the presence of object is necessary for knowledge, and therefore, every knowledge is a knowledge of both knower and known; others think that the knowledge of known is different from the knowledge of knower. About the possibility of knowledge, one finds different approaches such as agnostic, septic and mystic. All these approaches have thrown light on different aspects of knowledge.

This explanation shows the importance of epistemology for education. Empiricist school of philosophy discussed the methods and value of empirical knowledge. Its opposite rationalist school pointed out how some of the knowledge is innate. Scepticism shows the limits of knowledge. David Hume pointed out that certainty can be possible only in mathematics and not in the field of sciences. Agnosticism shows the relativity of human knowledge. Criticism shows that knowledge is synthetic, requiring sensibility, understanding and reasoning. Intuitionism shows that intellect and intuition are complementary. Mysticism shows the value of spirital experience in the field of religion. Instrumentalism points out that reason is an instrument for the satisfaction of human needs. Humanism shows that the criterion of all knowledge is man himself and there is no ultimate knowledge. Experimentalism and relativism points out that knowledge is experimental and relative. This all the schools of epistemology show the methods, limits and value of knowledge. They supply the necessary foundation for all knowledge, scientific and otherwise.

Knowledge

Human knowledge as it exists today broadly consists of facts and theories. New facts, new concepts, and new ways of doing things increased its quantum with the passage of time. This knowledge enables us to understand, comprehend, explain, control, predict or cope with a given situation. The sources from which we obtain knowledge range from those that are highly reliable to those that are completely unreliable. The knowledge obtained from the unreliable sources is based on assumptions, beliefs and untested generalizations. Such generalizations are usually accepted on faith, tradition, or authority and no effort is made to verify their validity. In contrast, reliable knowledge is based on objective verification of generalizations.

The acquisition and expansion of knowledge is not an automatic and self-perpetuating process. On the contrary, it requires constant and planned effort by intelligent and highly trained people. The present level of knowledge is an outcome of the various methods adopted by man over a period of several centuries.

The word "know" is slippery. It is not always used in the same way. Sometimes when we take about knowing, we are referring to acquaintance of some kind. For example, "Do you know Vinod Kumar?" means approximately the same as "Are you acquainted (familiar) with Vinod Kumar?" You might know him, in the sense of acquaintance, without knowing much about him.

Sometimes we speak of knowing how: Knowing how is an ability—we knowhow to rich a horse if we have the ability to ride a horse, and the test of whether we have the ability is whether (in the appropriate situation) we can perform the activity.

The word know is most frequently used in the prepositional sense. For example—I know that I am an American citizen where the word "that" is followed by a proposition.

Methods of Acquiring Valid Knowledge

We are now ready to consider some aspects of knowledge. A proposition may be true although one does not know it to be true. By what means, then, do we come by knowledge? What are the avenues by means of which we are enabled to know propositions to be true? Let us now consider some alleged.

Sense-Experience

You can know many things about the world by seeing, hearing, touching, smelling and testing. It is primarily through seeing about touching that we know 'that' physical thing exists. We see the chair and then we sit on it. But all our senses on various occasions inform us of 'what' the thing's characteristics are: we can see the colour and feel the texture of the chair.

Sometimes we have sense experience when there is nothing at all to be perceived: We may be having a hallucination, such as when we are thirsty and think we see water and trees in the desert.

Sometimes, what we see is really there, but we think it has one characteristic when it really has another example. In the darkness we mistake donkey for a horse. If we are colour blind, we think it is gray when it is black/brown.

These are all perceptual errors. The existence of perceptual errors shows that our senses are fallible. When we make a perceptual error owing to incomplete or fragmentary sense-experiences, it is always further sense experience that lead us to discover our error.

Before being embodied into knowledge all sense-experiences require judgement. You must first judge that this is a chair, this is a book and so on. The sense experience itself is neither true or false, it merely exists or occurs. We get information about the outside world- through 'external senses'.

There are 'internal senses' acquainting us with our own internal states. (feeling, attitudes, moods, pains and pleasures). As well as our own mental operations such as thinking, believing and wandering. In these cases, we do not have sense organs. We are entitled to state certain prepositions on the basis of certain experiences.

Example—I am thinking about next summer's vacation
I am having a toothache.

Reasoning

Reasoning is one source of knowledge. It is the degree of ability to engage in thinking. If we could not think, we could not acquire any knowledge. This ability is indispensable to having knowledge of any sort, including knowledge acquired through sense-perception. People are engaged in reasoning when they take certain statements as the basis for making one or more other statements.

(a) Deductive Reasoning

The most familiar kind of reasoning which is often taken as the model for all reasoning, is deductive reasoning. In a deductive argument, the conclusion must logically follow from the premises. If the premises of argument are true, the conclusion must be true. For example,

All dogs are mammals.
All mammals are animals.
All dogs are animals is a valid deductive argument.

The following argument, however though its proponent may claim it to be a deductive argument is not valid.

All dogs are mammals.
All cats are mammals.
Therefore, all dogs are cats.

This is not a valid argument. Some arguments are valid and others are not. Invalid argument, the premises need not be true: it is only required that the conclusions follow logically from the premises, i.e., if the premises are true, then the conclusion must be true. But in the above argument they are false.

(b) Inductive Reasoning

We also argue inductively: we may know the truth of the premises, but we still do not know the conclusion is true—the premises provide evidence for the conclusion, but not complete evidence.

In inductive reasoning a conclusion is reached by observing all instances and generalizing from instances to the whole phenomena. In order to attain inductive conclusion, all instances must be observed. It is perfect induction. To examine all the instances of a phenomenon under study is not practical; one may arrive at a generalization by observing only some instances that make up the phenomenon. This is known as imperfect induction.

Although imperfect induction does not help man to arrive at infallible conclusions. It can provide him reliable knowledge upon which he makes reasonable decisions.

Authority

The statements we hear or read would require years of investigation before their truth could be ascertained. So as a practical expedient, we usually take the author's word. The modern man seeks advice from authorities for the solution of the problem faced by him. The authorities may be the persons who have had long experience with the problem and who have studied and thought much about it.

When factual evidences cannot be obtained to solve a problem, one may have to rely upon authoritative opinion temporarily as the only possible method for arriving at a solution. In such a solution care must be employed in choosing authorities and evaluating their claims to knowledge. One should check not only the credentials of authorities but also the arguments and evidence upon which they base their judgements.

The precautions for selecting authority are:

1. The person whose word we take as authority must really be an authority, one who is a specialist in his field of knowledge.
2. Whenever one accepts another person's statement as

authority, he should be able to find out whether the authority's statement is true, if he were to take the time and trouble.

Intuition

The word intuition is verbally indefinable. The word in its most limited sense is merely the label for a certain kind of experience, one that is not easily described. A conviction of certainty comes upon quite suddenly, like a 'light' going on inside or like a 'flash'. The existence of intuition as an experience can hardly be doubted, doubtless we all have had experiences that we would call intuitions. It is noted that much of what we claim to know by intuition is actually not this, but through sense-experience. i.e., intuition with knowledge. If you say "I know by intuition", this really doesn't explain how you know you may arrive at a correct conclusion and not knowhow you come by it. This is simply a cover up term for our ignorance, revealing only that we do not know how he was able to do this.

Revelation

Sometimes one claims to know something by means of revelation. When a person had some experience, he calls it as 'a revelation from God'. Whenever something is revealed through a sacred book, the revelation is form God, but through a book. The book is sacred because the author of the book claims that it is true. There are competing candidates for the position of true revelation – The Bible, The Quran and numerous other works. If the claims made are such that sense – experiences or reason could substantiate them, then it is because of this we believe that the claims are true, but we could never verify them.

Experience

Our own personal experience or that of others is the most primitive and yet the most familiar and fundamental source of knowledge. In ancient times, nomads and various tribes from their personal experience remembered that certain wild fruits always made them ill, that grains ripened at particular times of the year etc. When confronted with a problem, modern man often tries to seek its answers from his own personal experience or from others who are familiar with the problem. Children often consult their teachers, parents or even their old siblings to derive answers to their questions.

Let's concluding, true knowledge was due to the operation of stable, universal, self-consistent being, falsity to an intermixing of becoming non-being, particularly and mere potentiality. All portions of modern philosophy which discuss the possibility, nature and limits of knowledge or the basis of these presuppositions constitutes epistemology.

Methaphysics

Basically, we can say that philosophy is attempt to explain and appreciate life as a whole. Therefore, the outlook of a philosopher, is far wide and comprehensive. Philosophy is the corner stone of the foundation of education. Philosophy should be interpreted as a vision in wider perspective. This being so, education should be wedded to some philosophy in general.

The most important of philosophy are:

1. *Metaphysics*—study of the nature of ultimate reality.
2. *Epistemology*—theory of knowing and knowledge.
3. *Axiology*—concerned with value, theory and prescribes what is good and rights conducts.

Metaphysics is the branch of philosophy which deals with the problems of reality. Traditionally metaphysics has been sub-divided into three branches.

1. *Cosmology*—which deals with the nature and origins of universe.
2. *Ontology*—which is concerned with different theories of being.
3. *Theology*—which is concerned with the nature of properties of god and divine creatures.

Metaphysics (Reality)

Cosmology (Which Deals with Nature and Origin of Universe)	Ontology (Which is Concerned with Different Theories of Being/Science of Reality)	Theology (Concerned with the Nature and Properties of God and Divine Creatures)

Origin of Metaphysics

The name "metaphysics" was designating philosophy of someone of its branches arose from a misunderstanding of an accidental way of describing certain writings of Aristotle, namely those coming after the physics. This was shortly taken to mean the things that lie beyond the physical, that are above the natural conception which medieval thought identified with the supernatural. This long remained the popular signification, so that Shakespeare, for example, refers to ghosts as metaphysical.

Aristotle himself in the body of his teatise supplied some ground for identifying his discussions with theology. His formal designation is first philosophy and this he says has for its objects a descriptive definition of being as being or existence as existence. Each branch of science considers the traits of some set or class of existences, but no science considers the traits that all existences alike possess. Hence they leave room for and indeed require a more general in formal science to take up the matter they leave untouched. So far there is no ground for referring first philosophy or anything transcending the subject of the sciences. But in the course of his discussions, Aristotle is led to discriminate grades of being and to conclude that only pure actually or god is completely real, or can be said be without qualification. Hence metaphysics appears as a science of the highest or more real modes of being.

Throughout the eighteenth and earlier ninetieth centuries "metaphysics" was loosely used to denote inquiries concerned with mind, what would now generally be called psychology and also to denote any inquiry of an ultimate sorts. In the later sense, it was generally divided into ontology or inquiry into being and epistemology or inquiry into the nature and limits of knowing. At presents, there is a tendency to revert to the more limited Aristotelian sense, though the terms is still widely used as a generic name to cover all sorts of inquiries that do not seem to fall within the scope of any of positive or mathematical sciences.

Metaphysics and Education

The most important branches of philosophy are metaphysics, epistemology and axiology. Again, the relationship of philosophy and education should be sought in different fields of education such as the aims and ideals, the methods of teaching, the curriculum, the school administration, discipline and finally evaluation. All these branches of education are based upon philosophical foundations.

Aristotle developed the study of metaphysics to the studied after physics. While physics studies the laws of the external form of existence, metaphysics thinks over the real essence of things. Its main problems are: What is the nature of existence? What is reality? What is birth? What are its different forms? Is the world one or many? What is time? What is substance? What is casuality? What is fact? What is the purpose or aim? What is change? What is novelty? What is similarity? Who am I? Is there a purpose in creation? Is the world determined or free? Is there a god? Has the world progressed? etc. Thus, the subject-matter of metaphysics includes the self, the world and the god. Its scope includes ontology. Philosophy of self, cosmology and theology. Ontology is the science of reality.

Metaphysics in brief deals with reality in man, world and hereafter. This has a close learning upon the aims and ideals of education. The metaphysical attitude provides the educationists the proper perspective for devising aims ideals of education. What we want to make out of man depends upon his nature and place in the universe. Again, the concept of self is the basis of the developments of character, the central aim of education, know thyself and be thyself is the universally acknowledged aim of education. The concept of world is directly concerned with the individual's relationships with society and nature. While Indian philosophy emphasizes harmony between man and the world, the western philosophers have made too much of man's desire to overpower nature. While the former philosophy has been the foundation of educational institutions like Vishwabharati or Sri Aurobindo's International University, the other approach is the philosophy behind the technological and scientific education of today. In fact, the more integral is the world-view the more multi-sided will be the education based upon it. In the end, moral and religious education is based upon it in the end, moral and religious education is based upon the metaphysical concept of god. This does not mean that moral education must necessarily be linked to religious education. It only shows that our explanation of the ultimate reality or the total reality, call it god or anything else, has important bearing upon education particularly its aims and ideals and therefore its means and plans.

The most important metaphysical theories which have influenced education are Naturalism, Idealism, Pragmatism and Realism. Naturalism has been manifests in different types of theories such as atomic naturalism. Scientific naturalism, mechanistic and historical naturalism. The most important metaphysical theory in the field of education is idealism. Idealism has been subjective, objective, phenomenalistic and absolute. The most influential metaphysical theory in today's field of education, however is pragmatism. This is closely linked to instrumentalism and humanism. In the end, the metaphysical theory known as Realism is very much influenced by education concerning science and technology.

Some Metaphysical Problems

The problems of metaphysics and epistemology are inextricably interwoven. Indeed the distinction is not always easy to draw metaphysical problems have to do with "what is", whereas epistemological problems have to do with "our knowledge of what is." Not all problems about "what is" are metaphysical problems. Those "what is" problems that could, in principle at least, be resolved by empirical means alone are scientific ones, and those that could be solved by mathematical means alone are mathematical ones; the remainder are metaphysical ones.

There are problems which appear to resist empirical attempts at solution. Into what classes or categories, for example, reality is to be divided-temporal v/s non-temporal, material v/s non-material, mental v/s non-mental is an issue left to metaphysics. It is wider even than empirical science, which normally treats only of the physical. Metaphysicians world insist that they are concerned with factual issues, but they would then divide issues into two kinds, empirical and non-empirical metaphysical issues would belong to the latter. They would them consider issues of fact but facts that cannot be settled by the usual empirical means but only by the systematic exercise of the understanding.

Basically the metaphysical problems, are categorized into three heads. They are:

1. Substance and Universals.
2. Matter and Life.
3. Mind and Body.

Substance and Universals

(a) *The Problem of Substance*: The world contains many things or substances. These substances are of many different kinds—wood, chalk, granite and so on—but their constituents of these various kinds are relatively small in numbers.
Each substances has many different properties or characteristics. If we removed one or more of the defining characteristics, we would have left some substance or other. Suppose if we removed all the properties, wouldn't we then

be left with nothing at all? We would be inclined to say that it would not only no longer be the substance, it wouldn't be anything. There would be no properties left and no "if" to have the properties. Substances are simply the sum of their properties. On the contrary there can be no properties unless there is first a thing or substances that has them. Matter is the principle of individuation. It is substance—not qualities, that distinguishes one thing from another thing.

(b) *The Problem of Universals:* The problem of universals is a very complex one, which many philosophers believe to be the central problem of metaphysics. Since the word 'universal' is not ordinarily used as a noun in our language. It is difficult to convey briefly, a conception of what the problem is.

Here are a number of blue things—this shirt, that chair, the ocean, the sky. They are different in many ways but they are all alike in being blue. They all have a common characteristic: blueness. Now, the blue things are particular (individual things in the world in space and time), but the property blueness which they all share is a universal one.

Matter and Life

Among the vast magnitude of inorganic objects that constitute the earth, the other planets and the stars and galaxies, there are objects that are 'conspicuously different from the rest: They are living organisms.

There are two opposite points of view, known as mechanism and vitalism to explain. The distinguishing points between living and non-living things. Mechanism emphasizing the continuity and likeness between living and non-living things and vitalism the discontinuity and differences.

Let us consider several of the ways in which it is possible to state the issue between mechanism and vitalism.

(a) *Non-Material Life Force:* According to vitalism there is a non-material life-force which is present in living things but not in living things.
Mechanist's are objects this view saying that there should be some empirical evidence for the reasoning.

(b) *Emergence:* It is said that vitalism asserts that the

characteristics of living things are emergent while mechanism denies it.

(c) *Reducibility:* Here mechanism and vitalism differ in the concept of reducibility. For example: "Is biology reducible to physics and chemistry? If it is mechanism is true and if is not, vitalism is a true.

Mind and Body

The Body

The physical events we are concerned with in the mind-body problem are all events in the history of physical object, the body. The body is a physical thing, like chair and trees, occupying space, having mass etc, like every other physical thing. Physical objects are collections of molecules constituting it are primarily organic molecules.

One can control only his own body directly or without any command or force. A person's influence on the outside world is always by means of his body.

The Mind

Just as physical events occur in the history of physical objects (including human bodies), so mental events occur in the history of minds. The mind is that in which mental events occur just as the body in which physical events occur. Physical events are parts of the history of physical bodies and mental events are parts of the history of mind.

In historical succession, mind follows upon life. Just as life did not occur on our planet until inorganic matter assumed form of great of complexity, so mind did not arise until organic matter had reached a still further degree of complexity, involving sense-organs, nerves and brain. It is often said, that within the realm of the empirical we find three level: matter, life and mind.

Axiology

> "Philosophy is a collection of sciences such as theory of knowledge, logic cosmology, ethics and aesthetics, as well as a unified survey."
>
> – *Roy Wood Sellers*

In its most general term, philosophy is the human beings attempt to think most speculatively, reflectively and systematically about the universe and the human relationship to that universe. As a subject of paramount importance in education, the learner should know the various branches of philosophy and then study their relationship with education to get a precise idea regarding the close relationship of philosophy and education. The relationship of philosophy and education should be sought in different fields of education such as the aims and ideals, the methods of teaching, the curriculum, the school administration, discipline, evaluation etc. The most important branches of philosophy are:

Metaphysics – (Study of the nature of ultimate reality),

Epistemology – (Theory of knowing and Knowledge), and

Axioloty – (Concerned with value theory and prescribes what is good and right conduct).

Axiology is concerned with value theory and attempts to prescribe what is good and right conduct. The sub-divisions of axiology include three normative sciences. They are:

1. Logic,
2. Ethics, and
3. Aesthetics.

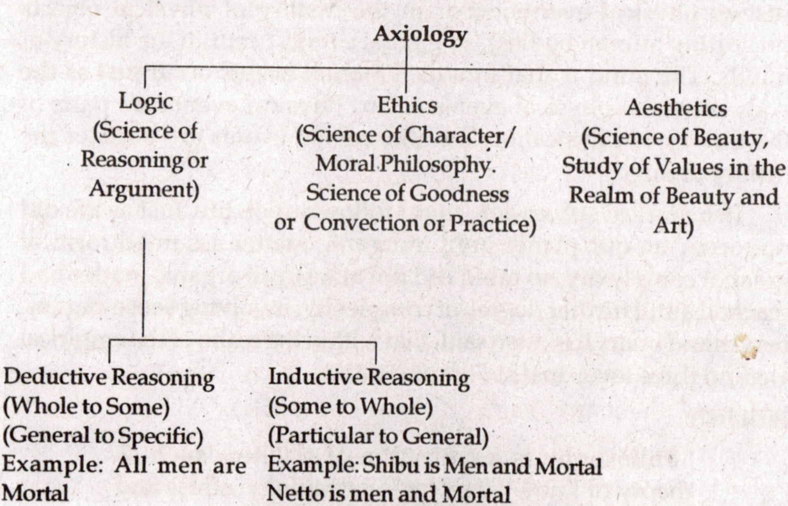

Logic and Education

The term logic is derived from the Greek word 'logos', which means reason or expression of reason in words. Thus, the etymological meaning of logic is the science of reasoning or argument. According to Dewey and Stebbing, reasoning is reflective thinking and reflective thinking is a process of finding ways out of some difficulty or problem by weighing the evidences on the basis of a tentative hypothesis and thereby reaching a conclusion. Thus, logic is concerned with the rules or patterns of correct and valid thinking and it examines the rules of valid inferences that enables us correctly to frame our propositions and arguments. In logics, inorder to form a conclusion or valid inference inductive reasoning and deductive reasoning is used. Inductive reasoning moves from particular to generalizations and deductive reasoning moves from general statements or principles to particular instances and application. In logic, we study the general principles governing both inductive and deductive reasoning. In short, logic is the basic of all knowledge and it studies various intellectual processes such as thinking, reasoning and judgement. The knowledge of logic helps us in avoiding error and arriving at correct generalizations in every field of knowledge.

Ethics and Education

According to philosophy, the word ethics is derived from the word 'Ethos', which means character. In this way, ethics is the science of character, habits of activity or behaviour of human beings. Ethics is also called moral philosophy. The world 'moral' is a derivative form of the Latin word 'mores', which mean conventions or practice. Thus, literally the term ethics means the science of convention or practice. Ethics is also considered as the science of character or habit because habits and behaviour are related to the permanent peculiarities of human character and conduct is the mirror of character. Thus, ethics is the science of character or habit and ethics evaluates human habits, character and voluntary determinations and discusses their propriety (the state of being correct) or otherwise.

In a general way, 'Ethics' refers to the philosophic study of moral values and conduct. It consider the duty of human beings and pronounces ethical decision upon conduct. Therefore, ethics studies what is right and what is wrong in character. It studies the ideals of human life and shows what ought to be done and what ought not to be done. According to J.S. Mackenzie, "ethics can be defined as the study of what is right or good in conduct." In this definition, ethics has been accepted as the study of both right and good. But there is difference between right and good. The word right is derived from the Latin word 'Rectas' which means "straight or according to law" and the word 'good' is derived from German word 'gut' which means useful for the 'supreme good'. Thus ethics is the study of good behaviour which leads to supreme good.

As a sub-division of axiology, ethics-philosophical study of moral values and conduct—is not true from criticisms. A classical conflict in values between objective versus subjective value theory exists there. There who subscribe to an objective value theory assert that what is good is rooted in the universe itself and is applicable everywhere for all time. In contrast, subjectivists asserts that values are personal preferences—likes or dislikes—that depend on particular circumstances, time and places. For them, values are not universally valid but are relative and depend on particular situations.

The most widely accepted aim of education is man making. According to J.S. Mackenzie, the study of ethics is classified into four divisions, such as;

1. Psychology of ethical consciousness,
2. Sociology of an ethical life,
3. Theories of ethical criterion, and
4. Application of ethical criterion in ethical life.

These four divisions of ethics are the foundation of all education. As the science of character, ethics analyses the psychology of ethical consciousness. It shown how different moral norms evolve in different circumstances and examines the validity of these norms and provides solid basis for social ethics of the educant. Ethics also examines the theories of moral standard and helps in the application of moral principles in actual life. Ethical activities are accompanied by vice and virtue and ethics details the criterion for this vice and virtue. The scope of ethics include the description of good qualities and bad qualities. Due to the relation of good and bad to every human activity, the field of ethics includes the conclusions of other successes and acts. In this way, many psychological, political, economical, sociological, religious and philosophical problems come to be included in the field of ethics.

Aesthetics and Education

The aim of education is to realize all-round development of the educant. In this development, moral and aesthetic developments occupy foremost place. Aesthetics is concerned with the study of values in the realm of beauty and art. It is the science of beauty, as logic is the science of truth and ethics is the science of good. In the broadest sense, aesthetic theory refer to the cultivation of taste and a feeling for that which is beautiful. While moral development requires knowledge of ethics, aesthetics development training in aesthetics. Aesthetics is the basis of all literacy and artistic criticism and supplies the philosophical basis to literature and art. As literature and art contribute significantly to education, the value of aesthetics in education is clear and education seeks to realize the true, the good and the beautiful. In short, aesthetic theory is not only concerned with the human attempt to objectify insights and feelings in various art forms but also equally concerned with the cultivation of persons whose live are harmonious, balanced and beautiful.

Let's concluding, the most widely accepted aim of education is man making and character building and the basis problem of education is to secure man's fullest development. For this, it is necessary to know what is man, his nature, his sociability etc. The social philosophy analyses human nature and finds out how far man is naturally social and how far not. The social philosophy examines the basic principle of human behaivour and supreme values of human life. Thus, it is the philosophical foundation which provides a solid ground for the educational system.

EDUCATIONAL PHILOSOPHY – SIGNIFICANCE FOR TEACHER

Why should a Teacher Study Educational Philosophy?

Philosophy has great influence on the teacher both in the area of thinking and behaving. Teacher himself should have an educational philosophy and influence children accordingly. He must keep in mind that his own beliefs, ideology and principles of behaviour have a powerful impact on the development of children. Hence he/she must posses a good understanding of all educational philosophies and chooses good and wholesome elements from them. The philosophy of the teacher effect the various problems of education – the educand, the aims and their realization, social organization in the school, its general tone curriculum, the discipline, the method the employs etc. So a teacher should study educational philosophy.

Uses of Philosophy of Education for the Teachers

1. *Theory of Education*: According to John Dewey, philosophy of education is not an external application of ready-made ideas to a system of practice having a radically different origin and purpose, it is only an explicit formulation of the problems of the right mental and moral attitudes in respect to the difficulties of contemporary social life. The most penetrating definition of philosophy of education which can be given is, then, that it is the theory of education in its most general phases.
2. *Teaching Methods*: Teaching methods are very much concerned with the philosophy of education the teacher holds. According to Spencer, only a true philosopher may give a practical shape to education. How he behaves with the students and how he communicates depends very much on low he defines the educands. Different philosophical systems of education have explained human nature in widely different ways. This very much governs the teachers attitude to the method of teaching.

   In the words of Bertrand Russell, "Philosophy is to be studied not for the sake of any definite answers to the questions, but rather than the sake of questions themselves; because the questions enlarge our conception of what is possible, enrich our intellectual imagination and diminish the dogmatic assurance which closes the mind against speculation but above all because through the greatness of the universe which philosophy contemplates, the mind also is rendered great and becomes capable of that union with the universe which constitutes its highest good."
3. *Aims and Ideals of Education:* The most important contribution of the philosophy of education to the teacher is, however, concerned with the aims and ideals of education. Without philosophy of education the teacher will not have any sense of purpose in his teaching. This is not possible by science; however, we may eulogies the role of science in the present day education. In fact, while science supplies the means,

only philosophy supplies the ends. In the words of John Dewey, "philosophy is concerned with determining ends of education, while the science of education determines the means to be used."

4. *Curricula*: Again, philosophy of education helps the teacher in the determination of the curricula of education. Plato said, "He who has a taste for every sort of knowledge and who is curious to learn and is never satisfied may be justify termed a philosopher." Philosophy provides a comprehensive and total view of educational situation. It leads to an integral approach. It is a total view point.

MODEL QUESTIONS

1. Why is an understanding of education philosophy essential for school teachers?
2. 'Education is the dynamic side of philosophy'—James Ross. Discuss.
3. 'Education and Philosophy use like two sides of the same coin'. Elucidate.
4. What is the meaning of epistemology?
5. Why is the study of philosophy important to education?

REFERENCES

1. Aggarwal, J.C. (1992). *Theory and Principles of Education*, Vikas Publishing House (P) Ltd., New Delhi.
2. Bourai, H.H.A. (1993). *Indian Theory of Education*, B.R. Publishing Corp., New Delhi.
3. Chandra, S.S. & Sharma, R. (1996). *Philosophy of Education*, Atlantic Publishers, New Delhi.
4. Chaube, S.P. & Chaube, A. (1987). *Foundations of Education*, Vikas Publishing House (P.) Ltd., New Delhi.
5. Conner, D.J.O. (1957). *An Introduction to the Philosophy of Education*, Routledge Kegan Paul, London.
6. Gerald, C. G. *Philosophical and Ideological Perspectives of Education.*
7. Hospers, John (1953). *An Introduction to Philosophical Analysis*, Prentice Hall, London.
8. Koul, Lokesh (1997). *Methodology of Educational Research*, Vikas Publishing House, Pvt. Ltd., New Delhi.
9. Monroe, Paul (2001). *Encyclopaedia of Philosophy of Education*, Cosmo Publications, New Delhi.
10. Murty, S.K. (1992). *Contemporary Problems and Current Trends in Education*, Parkash Brothers, Ludhiana.
11. Robert, R. Rusk. *The Philosophical Base of Education*, University of London Press.

12. Sharma, R. (2000). *Textbook of Educational Philosophy*, Kanishka Publishers, New Delhi.
13. Srinibas Bhattacharya (1996). *Foundation of Education*, Atlantic Publishers, New Delhi.
14. Taneja, V.R. (1987). *Educational Thought and Practice*, Sterling Publishers (P) Ltd., New Delhi.
15. Venkateswaran, S. (1993). *Principles of Education*, Vikas Publishing House (P) Ltd., New Delhi.

3
Introduction to Educational Sociology

INTRODUCTION

The man is born in the society and he has to pass his life in the society. Different types of influences fall upon him in the society and he also influences the society. In this way, the individual and the society both react upon each other and both of them have a mutual relationship. It is on account of this mutual relationship that this interaction becomes an important topic of study in the domain of education. Thus, sociology, is a subject which studies the interaction of the individual and the society.

MEANING OF SOCIOLOGY

Etymologically, the word sociology is derived from two words – 'Societies' and 'Logus' which mean 'Society' and 'study or science' respectively. Thus, the term *sociology* means the study of society or science of society. The word sociology is first used by 'Aaguste Comte' – the father of sociology – in his 'positive philosophy' published in 1938. Sociology is the study of human society and social behaviour. It is concerned with social interaction. It studies all those things which exercise some sort of influence upon human behaviour, social heritage, problems related with customs, traditions, legends, myths, mythological, religion and social institutions, classifications of casts, effects of geographical conditions, crimes, evolution of human beings and similar other problems. Thus, "Sociology is that science which explains, studies and analyses the mutual interaction which are born of contact with each other and all the relationships between the individual and the society, may they be in the nature of very simple influences as when the social custom, tradition and norms and unhesitatingly accepted and obeyed or quiet complex as when the individual not merely accept the social order but make efforts to re-orient reform or re-build the society in accordance with there own interpretations of the desirable social order."

Definitions

1. "The subject-matter of sociology is the interaction of human minds." —*L.T. Hobhouse*
2. "Sociology is the science that deals with social groups; their internal forms or modes of organization, the process that tend to maintain or change these forms of organization and relation between groups." —*H.M. Johnson*
3. "Sociology is a body of learning about society. It is a description about ways to make society better. It is social ethics, a social philosophy. Generally, however, it is defined as science of society." —*W.F. Ogburn*
4. Sociology asks what happens to men and by what rules they behave, not insofar as they unfold there understandable individual existence in their totalities, but insofar as they from groups and determined by their group existence because of interaction." —*Simmel*
5. "Sociology is the science if collective behaviour." —*R.E. Park and F.W. Buruess*
6. "Sociology in its broadest sense may be said to be the study of interactions arising from the association of living beings." —*Gillin and Gillin*
7. "Sociology deals with the behaviour of men in groups." —*Kimball Young*
8. The chief interest of sociology is the people, the ideas, the customs, the other distinctively human phenomenon which surrounds man and influence him, and which are, therefore, part of his environment. Sociology also devotes some attention to certain aspects of the geographical environment and to some natural as contrasted with human phenomena, but this interest is secondary to its pre-occupation with human beings and the products of human life in association. Our general field of study is man as he is related to other man and to the creation of other men which surrounds him." —*M.E. Jones*
9. Sociology seeks to discover the principles of cohesion and of order within the social structure, the ways in which it roots

and grows within an environment, the moving equilibrium of changing structure and changing environment, the main trends of the incessant change, the forces which determine its direction at any time, the harmonious and conflicts, the adjustment and maladjustments within the structure as they are revealed in the light of human desires, and then the practical application of means to end in the creative activities of social man." —*Mac Iver*

10. "Sociology is the synthesizing and generalizing science of man in all his social relationships." —*Arnold Green*
11. "Sociology is the scientific study of social relationships, their variety, their forms, whatever affects them and whatever they affect." —*T. Abel*
12. "Sociology is a special social science concentrating on inter human behaviour on processes of sociation, on association and dissociation as such." —*Wan Wiese*
13. "Sociology is the study of relationship between man and his human environment." —*H.P. Fairchild*
14. "Sociology may be defined as a body of scientific knowledge about human relationship." —*I.F. Cubar*
15. "General sociology is on the whole the theory of human beings living together." —*Ferdinand Tonnies*
16. "Sociology is the science which attempts the interpretive understanding of social action." —*Max Weber*
17. "Sociology is the scientific study of structure of social life." —*Young and Mack*
18. "Sociology is the science of the structure and functions of social life." —*John. W. Bennet*
19. "Sociology is a generalizing science of a socio-cultural phenomena viewed in their generic form, types and manifold interconnections." —*Pitrim A. Sorokin*
20. "Sociology may be defined as the study of the ways in which social experiences function in developing, maturing and repressing human beings through inter-personal stimulation." —*E.B. Bogardus*

IMPORTANCE OF SOCIOLOGY

The importance of sociology are:

Sociology Makes a Scientific Study of the Society

Before the emergence of sociology, the study of society was carried on in an unscientific manner and society had never been the central concern of any science. It is through the study of sociology that the truly scientific study of the society has been possible. Sociology has its bearing on many of the present day problems and scientific knowledge about society is pre-requisite to any marked improvement in the state of human affairs.

Sociology Studies the Role of Institutions in the Development of the Individual

It is through sociology that the scientific study of the great social institutions and the relation of the individual to each is being made. The institution through which the society functions are home and family, school and education, church and religion, the state and government, industry and work, community and association etc. Sociology studies these social institutions and their role in the development of the individual and suggest suitable measures for re-strengthening them with a view to enable them to serve the individual better.

The Study of Sociology is Indispensable for Understanding and Planning of Society

Society is a complex phenomena with a multitude of intricancies. It is not possible to understand and solve various problems of the society without the study of sociology. A certain amount of knowledge about the society is necessary before any social policy can be carried out became no real effective social planning would be possible without the investigation cawed on by sociology. It helps us to determine the most efficient means for reaching the goals agreed upon.

Example: The policy of decreasing birth rate is desirable. The best mean for achieving this goals cannot be determined in exclusively economic terms because matter of family organization, custom and traditional values must be taken into account and these require a sociological type of analysis.

Sociology is of Great Importance in the Solution of Social Problems

The present world is suffering from many problems which can be solved only through the scientific study of the society. The social evils do not just happen and everything has its due causes. The task of sociology is to study the social problems through the methods of scientific research and to findout solutions for them. The study of human affairs will ultimately provide the body of knowledge and principles that will enable us to control the conditions of social life and improve them.

Sociology has Drawn our Attention to the Intrinsic Worth and Dignity of Man

Sociology has been instrumental in changing our attitude towards human beings. In a highly specialized and developed society, we are limited as to the amount of whole organization and culture that we can experience directly and we can hardly know the people of other areas intimately. The knowledge of sociology is essential to have an insight into and appreciation of motives by which other live and conditions under which they exist. The knowledge of sociology helps us to realize the intrinsic worth of man and hollowness of the difference of cast, colour, creed and other factors.

Sociology has Changed our Outlook with Regard to the Problems of Crime etc.

It is through the study of sociology that the outlook of man on various aspects of crime has changed. As a result of the development of sociology, criminals are no longer treated as degenerated beasts, but they are regarded as human beings suffering from mental deficiencies and efforts are accordingly made to rehabilitate them as the useful members of the society. The sciences of criminology, penology, sociology work and social therapy are rendering commendable services in understanding social institutions and solving individual problems are handmaids of sociology.

Sociology has Made Great Contribution to Enrich Human Culture

Human culture has been made richer by the contribution of sociology. Sociology has given as training to have rational approach to question concerning one self, one's religion, customs, morals and institutions. It has further taught us to be objective critical and dispassionate. Sociology enables man to have a better understanding of himself and others and a comparative study of societies and groups other than his own, he is able to see many things as relevant to this existence. Sociology also impresses upon us the necessity of overcoming narrow personal prejudices, egoistic ambitions and class hatred. In short, the findings of sociology stimulate every person to render a full measure of service to every other person and to the common good.

Sociology is Useful as a Teaching Subject

The subject, sociology is becoming popular as a teaching subject also. It is being accorded an important place in the curriculum of colleges and universities because, the teacher need not only know the subject and his pupils as individuals but also understands the group life of which he is fitting them. By diffusing knowledge about society, socialized thinking will emerge, socialized behaviour will develop, social planning will be furthered and a new social order will be evolved. It is also felt that, without the study of sociology, the training and knowledge of the candidate aspiring to hold a high post in the administrative set up—such as IAS, IFS etc—of his country will be incomplete and imperfect.

Sociology as a Profession

As a profession, the students of sociology can get jobs in the fields of:

(a) In factories and government as a labour welfare officer, human relations officer, personal officer.

(b) In the field of reformation of criminals as probation officers, superintendents of juvenile homes, reformatory schools etc.

(c) In the field of social welfare as social welfare officer, youth welfare officer, rural welfare officer, child welfare officer, harijan welfare officer, tribal welfare officer etc.

(d) In the field of social education and adult education as social education officer and adult education officer.

(e) In the homes established for the welfare of the old, disabled as their superintendents.

(f) In the field of family planning on social worker or researcher.

PRACTICAL VALUES OF SOCIOLOGY

Sociology Studies the Organic Relation of Nature of Human Society

Sociology studies not only the material aspects of nature as environment but also the power of nature can laws and the processes and the relation of these laws and processes to human nature. Sociology studies the natural ecology and heritage of the people. Thus, it seeks to understand the efforts of mankind to search of an enduring balance and equilibrium between man and society.

Sociology Studies the Culture and its Relation to Total Human Society

Sociology studies the whole evolutionary process of the development of culture, the role of race and folk in culture, the relation of culture to national and regional environment.

Sociology Studies Civilization and its Relation to Total Human Society

Sociology studies the universal attributes of civilization such as urbanism, technology, intellectualism, centralization, power and totalitarian etc. It also studies the development of technology and the accelerating effects of science and invention upon cultural development. Thus, sociology not only describes what is happening but also describes how it is happening.

Sociology Studies People and their Relation to Total Human Society

Sociology explore more realistically the individual and the society and studies the socially behaving individual and his nature together with his environmental, cultural and hereditary influences which leads to individual difference. Thus, sociology studies the problem of social control.

Sociology Studies Modern Civilization with its Complicated Problem of Adjustment and Maladjustment with Reference to Social Change

Sociology studies the problems of values, institution, planning and development. Sociology utilizes these problems and situation to study human behaviour so as to provide knowledge useful to find their solutions.

Sociology Utilizes the Literature of History of Society, Social Thought and Social Philosophy for Understanding Modern Society

In this way sociology tries to synthesis the result of practical and empirical studies to social theories and test them by mean of their practical application to social situation. Thus, sociology enquires into the natural basis of culture and seeks to understand all that can be learned about social process, social organization and social control and tries to measures all these in the laboratory of human society.

Sociology Wishes Various Scientific Methods for Studying Social Phenomena

Sociology seeks to discover and make available other emerging methods to provide an increasingly unified body of knowledge gathered through them and to make it accessible both to the student and to the public. It seeks to utilize its knowledge not only for the understanding of the society but also for the improvement of education, enrichment of literature and art and the upliftment of mankind. These methods are social surveys, different types of observation, case study, interview and statistical method.

To sum up, the value of sociology lies in the fact that it keep us to update on modern-situation, it contribute in making good citizens, it contribute to the solution of community problems, it adds to the knowledge of the society; helps the individual to find his relation to society; it identifies good government with community and it helps one to understand cause of things and so on. In short, "economics tells us how to get things we want have, sociology tells us how to become what we want to be." —*Prof. Giddings*

EDUCATIONAL SOCIOLOGY

Development of Educational Sociology

Sociology is in itself a new subject but development of educational sociology as a branch of sociology has started only years bank. George Payne, who is credited with giving birth to the subject is called the father of educational sociology. In 1928, George Payne wrote a book named "The principles of educational sociology" in which he regarded the study of knowledge of social reaction as an essential part of the social progress. In his book, "The School and Society" and "Democracy and Education" Dewey emphasis that the complete development of education is possible only when the individual takes part in the social consciousness of the community. He writes, "All education proceeds by the participation of the individual in the social consciousness of the community. He writes, "All education proceeds by the participation of the individual in the social consciousness of the real." In India also the importance of sociology in increasing day-by-day in the field of education.

Definition of Educational Sociology

Brown, "Educational Sociology is the study of the interaction of the individual and his cultural environment including other individuals, social groups and patterns of behaviour."

Cook and Cook, "Educational Sociology is the study of human factors in the educative process, with the aim to improve teaching and learning in all types of educational systems."

Ottaway: "Educational sociology is the scientific study of the relationships between education and society."

Gene Payne: "By educational sociology we mean the science which describes and explains the institution, social groups and social process, that is the social relationship in which or through which the individual gains and organizes his experiences. These relationships are further more regarded particularly in relation to the educational system in its evolution and changing functions."

Scope of Educational Sociology

Educational sociology studies the social activity on education and the effect of education on social reactions. Thus, the scope of educational sociology is very wide. In brief following important specific problems are the essential parts of the educational sociology.

1. Place of Education in society.
2. Mutual relation between teacher and the student.
3. Problems, requirements and inspiration of the society.
4. Small units of the society and their mutual relations.
5. Effect of social life on individual and school.
6. Contracts between local social institution and schools.
7. Encouragement of best-education and democratic feelings in schools.
8. Suitable changes in the curriculum for the development of the individual as well as the society.

Educational Sociology and Sociology of Education

Angell in 1928 expressed the view that "educational sociology is merely a branch of the pure science of sociology." (Robert Cooley, Angell: "Science, sociology and education", *Journal of Educational Sociology*, 1, 1921, 406-413).

Sociology of education may be defined as the scientific analysis of the social processes and social patterns involved in the educational system. Brookover and Gottlieb consider that "This assumes that education is a combination of social acts and sociology is the analysis of human interaction." (Willbur B. Brookover and David Gottlieb: *A Sociology of Education*, New York: American Book Co., 1964, p. 6.)

Florian Znaniecki Syas, "Educational Sociology like to educational psychology, evolved as a discipline designed to prepare educators for their future tasks. It uses the results of sociological research in planning educational activities and in developing effective methods ore realizing these plans." (Florian Znaniecki: *The Scientific Function of the Sociology of Education, Educational Theory*, 1, 2, 1951.) On the other hand, we may describe sociology of education as that branch of knowledge which presents a sociological theory of education developed through the various analytical studies of the interactions between individuals in the formal school like educational situations or the other multiple informal educational institutions.

THE SOCIAL SYSTEM

Meaning of Social System

A social system represents one of the three aspects of social action. It consists of plurality individual actors who in a given situation interact with each other. According to Parsons, "A social system is a mode of organization of action elements relative to the persistence or ordered processes of change of the interactive patterns of a plurality of individual actor." It is therefore constituted by the actions of individuals. Its elementary unit is act, insofar as it is connected with the process of interaction.

Similar, according to Mclver and Page, "In every society there are two forces that bring about disorganization and organization. Both these forces are kept in balance. This keeping in balance is known as social system." In other words, social system is that state in which different constituent units of the society are inter-related with one another. They remain active and function in accordance to definite aims and objects.

Role and Status

Since a social system is a system of interaction, therefore, it involves participation of an actor in a process of interactive relationships. This participation, as parsons observes, involves two principal aspects namely the 'positional aspect' and the 'processual aspect.' The positional aspect indicates the location of an actor in a social system while the processional aspect represents the functional significance of an actor in relation to the social system. In other words, the positional aspect is called 'status' and the processual is called 'role'.

Status thus represents the position of an actor in a social system. On the one hand, it suggest the idea of rank while on the other it conveys the idea of a formalized behaviour. Thus an actor has a high and low status in a social system. He has to perform certain functions and a definite role to play. Therefore, when the behaviour of an actor is associated with a particular status, then that is called his role.

Status and role are not attributes of the actor but are the primary ingredients of a social system. Roles are differentiated within a social system and in turn are integrated together. A social system is firstly a system of differentiated role. Roles are assigned to different actors. This process of distribution according to Talcot Parsons is called 'allocation'.

Allocation is essentially an economic concept and denotes scarcity with respect to demand. Therefore, a social system is also confronted with the problem of allocation. In all societies role and status are assigned according to age, sex and birth. But besides this ascriptive mechanism, there are other methods known as 'Appointment' and 'competition'. The system of appointment depends on the explicit decision of other persons while competition is a selective process in which individuals attaining a certain position, are automatically selected.

The problem of allocation of role and status is associated with the problem of facilities. According to Parsons, "Facilities are possessions which are significant as means to further goals in complexes of instrumental orientation". In a social system 'power' occurs in two principal modes namely economic and political. These two types of power are integrated in a social system.

A social system is also associated with the problem of reward. Parson; "By reward we mean those transferable entities or possessions which are desired as objects to immediate gratification by actors."

Characteristics of Social System

1. Social system is connected with the plurality of individual actors.
2. Human interaction according to certain aims and objectives.
3. Order and pattern amongst various constituent units.
4. Functional relationship is the basis of unity.
5. Physical or environment aspect of social system.
6. Linked with cultural system.
7. Express and implied aims and objects.
8. Characteristics of adjustment.
9. Order, pattern and balance.

Elements of Social System

1. Faiths and Knowledge
2. Sentiments

3. Necessitics, Aims and Goals
4. Ideals and Norms
5. Statuses
6. Role
7. Power
   (a) Traditional
   (b) Legal
   (c) Charismatic
8. Sanctions
9. Privileges

Types of Social System

1. The particularistic ascriptive type.
2. The particularistic achievement type.
3. The universalistic achievement type.
4. The universalistic ascription type.

Maintenance of Social System

A social system is maintained by the various mechanisms of social control. These mechanism may be classified in the following categories:

1. Socialization.
2. Social control:
   (a) Institutionalization of Time Schedule.
   (b) Institutionalize Priorities.

SOCIAL INSTITUTIONS/AGENCIES OF EDUCATION

Family

According to McIver, "The family is a group defined by a sex relationship sufficiently precise an enduring to provide for the procreation and bringing of children."

Burgress and Locke; "A family is a group of person united by the ties of marriage, blood or adoption constituting a single household. Interesting and inter communicating with each other in their respective social role of husband, a wife, mother and father son and daughter, brother and sister creating and maintaining a command culture."

Home and family has been playing an important role in the training and education of a child. The family is expected to perform the following roles:

1. Proper physical development.
2. Proper moral environment.
3. Opportunities for participation in-house hold responsibilities.
4. Development of intellectual.
5. Understanding of the child's nature.
6. Understanding the importance of play in the education of the child.
7. Opportunities for self-expression.
8. Special responsibility for religious education.
9. Realization of the limitations of the school.

School

A school is a social institution set-up by the society to serve its ends. It is one of the formal agencies in education.

H.G. Wells has observed, "A world whose schools are unreformed in an unreformed world."

Nunn, "A nation's schools are an organ of its life, whose special function is to consolidate its spiritual strength, to maintain its historic continuity, to secure its past achievement, to guarantee its future ...."

The Kothari Commission (1964-66) observed that "the destiny of India is shaped in her classrooms."

Religion

McIver and Page, "Religion as we understand the term, implies a relationship not merely between man and man but also between men and same higher power. Hence, it normally invokes a sanction which may be called supra social, whether it be primitive ghost fear or the present worth of god or the penalties of an after life of torture in hell, merely the sense of being out of tune with infinite when its supposed laws disobeyed."

State

Prof. Hall, "State is a community permanently established for a political end, that is possesses a definite territory and that it is independent of external control."

Gettell, "Abstractly considered, the state is a judicial entity or person, concretely considered, it is the community the territory which is occupies and governmental organization through which it acts and wills.

Community – Role in Education

The school exists for the community without community a school will not have any existence. Hence, the community should provide adequate finance for the efficient conduct of the school. As an educated mass is the fundamental condition for a successful democracy. The government should see that the masses are educated. In our country both the Central and the State Governments are providing a large amount for the education of the masses. But the amount is not sufficient. Hence, the community must come forward to assist the school.

The responsibility of the community is not over once they provide financial support to education. The community must co-operate with the school in all its actively. It must provide the right ideals and values to the school, which are to be achieved through education.

Inter-relationship between School and Community

Education is closely related to society, and it is impossible to educate the children properly without the co-operation of the society. But this social interaction is not an one-way process. It is not a question of controlling the school by the society or helping the society by the school. It is a mutual interaction process, between the school and the society. Any mutual interaction, if it is to be carried on successfully, should be flexible. The school should be willing to take on and to drop off functions and services in the light of changing needs and developments within the community and resist becoming a static institution. Vested interests should have no part in determining its activities. The school should make use of community materials for the education process and vice versa.

Conclusion

Educational Sociology is the study of human relationships in the educative process. It is helpful processing society. Educational sociology aims at eliminating social evils through education. Sociology shapes education and forms a vital force in the entire framework of education. Society is dynamic, it grows and changes and as such these social changes must be affect it. It is only by connecting education with the general march of events that the school can lose its isolated character. "School must become the child's habitat to be a minimature community, an embryonic society."

MODEL QUESTIONS

1. Explain the linkage between education and sociology.
2. What is the role of community in education?
3. What you mean by sociology?
4. What is educational sociology? What are its implications?
5. Distinguish between Educational Sociology and Sociology of Education.

REFERENCES

1. B.C. Rai (1997). *Theory of Education-Sociological and Philosophical Bases and Education*, Prakashan Kendra, Lucknow.
2. *Encyclopaedia of Sociology* (Vol. I) – Laxmi Devi.
3. J.C. Aggarwal (1995). *Teacher and Education in a Developing Society*. Vikas Publishing House Pvt. Ltd., New Delhi.
4. Kamala Bhatia and Baldev Bhatia (1992). *The Philosophical and Sociological Foundations of Education*, Doaba House, New Delhi.
5. Mathur, S.S. *A Sociological Approach to Indian Education*, Vinod Pustak Mandir, Agra.
6. Roand Meigham, *A Sociology of Educating*.
7. *Sociology of Education* – B.D. Bhatt and S.R. Sharma
8. Srinibas Bhattacharya (1996). *Foundations of Education*, Atlantic Publishers, New Delhi.
9. Vidya Bushan and Sachdeva (1995). *An Introduction to Sociology*, Kitab Mahal, Allahabad.

4

National Goals and Education

NATIONAL GOALS EMBODIED IN THE CONSTITUTION OF INDIA

Pre-Amble of Indian Constitution

The preamble of the constitution is described as an identity card of the constitution. It contains the 'epitome' of the objectives to which the people of a country are permanently committed.

The preamble to the Constitution of India summarizes its aim and objectives. It reads as follows:

We the people of India, having solemnly resolved to constitute India into a Sovereign Socialist Secular Democratic Republic and to secure to all its citizens.

Justice, Social economic political.

Liberty of thought, expression, belief, faith and worship.

Equality of status and of opportunity, and promote among them all;

Fraternity assuring the dignity of the individual and the unity and integrity of the nation;

In Our Constituent Assembly this 26th day of November, 1949 do hereby adopt, Enact and Give to Ourselves this constitution.

Note: Three new terms-socialist, secular and integrity were added to the original text of the preamble when in 1976 the government passed the 42nd Amendment.

Education in the concurrent list—Till 1976 education was a state subject but with the 42nd Amendment to the constitution which received the president's assent on December 18, 1976. It was put on concurrent list.

Entry 25 of the concurrent list includes, "Education, including technical education, medical education and universities subject to entries 63, 64, 66 of list 1, vocational and technical training of labour."

The Significance of Preamble of Indian Constitution

The preamble of Constitution of India prescribes that the people of the country would try to secure,

1. Social, economic and political justice.
2. Liberty of thought, expression, belief, faith and worship.
3. Equality of status and of opportunity.
4. A sense of fraternity to assure the dignity of the individual and the unity of the nation.

Importance of the Preamble

Even preamble is not the part of constitution it has special significance. It sets forth the source from which the constitution draws its inspiration. It shows that the authority originates from the people of India. No individual or a class of individuals can claim to be the source of authority in India. The Government of India must be carried on by the elected representatives of the people. The head of the state must be an elected president. It can help the judges to understand the general objects and intentions of the constitution or of any law, which has been passed under that provision.

DEMOCRACY: MEANING, PRESENT CONDITIONS AND IMPLICATIONS

Abraham Lincoln defined, "Democracy as the government of the people, by the people and for the people. But, based on our present experiences-communal riots, politics, red tapism, correption—we can change that definition to "Democracy as the government off the people, buy the people and fore/foray the people."

The word democracy derived from,

Demo = people

Kratia = power

Democracy has two aspects,

1. Democracy as a way of life (*John Stuart Mill*). That is, an attitude or life style from the angle of people.

2. Democracy as a machinery, from the view of ruling class/ government. In this dimension includes a 'power/control'.

In a comprehensive outlook, democracy is the emanicipation of man's liberation from all social bondages, like poverty, etc. The basis principles of democracy are, justice, liberty, equality and fraternity. William Kornblum defines, democracy. "A political system in which all citizens have the right to participate in public decision-making" (*William Kornblum, Sociology – The central questions*).

Education and Democracy

Democracy, we know it's a philosophy of modern life style and education is a tool to achieve modernization and social change. Therefore, there two must be highly connected. Prof: Dewey in his book 'Democracy and Education' has explained the relationship in these words, "an undesirable society is one which internally and externally sets up barriers to free inter-course and communication of experience. A society which makes provisions for participation in its good of all its members on equal terms and which secures flexible re-adjustment of its institutions through the interaction of the different forms of associated life is so far democratic, such a society must have a type of education which gives individuals a personal interest in social relationships and control and the habits of mind which secure social changes without introducing disorder."

EDUCATIONAL FOR DEMOCRACY

'Preparing students to democracy' are of the aim of education. For strengthening Indian democracy we must given importance to some aims of education for the same. The Secondary Education Commission (1952-53) has suggested the following aims of education of a democratic society:

1. Development of democratic citizenship.
2. Improvement of vocational efficiency.
3. Development of personality.
4. Development of qualities of leadership.

Education for democracy doesn't mean just providing of some facts on democracy but must acquire attitudes, interests, skills to assimilate that philosophy. Education for democracy is a kind of citizenship training. Who is a citizen? Any one born as a citizen? What is the difference between a citizen and a individual? Citizen was not born but made. How? 'Education!', the only answer. We can train students for better students in school society. It prepares them to a citizen. He must aware about the fundamental duties and rights. Right implies duties. But now-a-days educated fellows even think about how save/escape from income-tax? In our beloved country there is no progress in social and economic democracy. But only political democracy we experience.

The theoretical study of rights and duties not made any effect in society. But we need the formation of democracy as a life style. For that our schools atmosphere must be democratic. Our nation, land of diversities, leads to issues problems. But everything can be solved through education for democracy.

Education Implications

Democracy is the result of education. Unless the principles of democracy are reflected in the aims and ideals of education, curriculum, methods of teaching, administration and organization, in discipline, in the atmosphere of the school and in the outlook of the teacher, democracy cannot grow. If democracy can catch roots anywhere, it is in the school, which is a very rich and fertile field for its growth and development.

Democratic Aims

The first goal in education in and for democracy is the full rounded and continuing development of the person.

Education in democracy must create democratic personality it must discover his potentialities and then enable him to realize them to the full by utilizing the facilities provided to the individuals. It must equip the individual with the power of judgement, scientific thinking and weighing the right and the wrong. The individual must be made aware of the ideals of life and he must grow in their context. Education must impart him correct knowledge of the political, social, religious and economic problems not only of his country but also of other countries. It must inculcate in his the spirit of tolerance for the views and modes of life of others and create in him a passion for social justice which should help him to have borad-mindedness and spirit of service. The individual's personality must have emotional balance. He must be mentally healthy, accept in himself, accept others and behave in a manner that he should be accepted by others.

Democratic aim in education does not mean passing the examination or gathering knowledge only but to enable the individual to have intellectual and moral qualities which must change his outlook.

Democratic Curriculum

Pragmatists say that children should learn what they are interested in this is an erroneous view. In fact, the children should be made interested to know what they need to know, though it is not always possible to interest all the children all the time in everything they need to know. But teachers, however, use motivation to interest the child in knowing what he should know.

Democratic curriculum should have variety and flexibility so as to be based upon the tastes and talents of children. The present higher secondary scheme is the vindication of this principle. Upto the 8th or 9th, the children are required to study a core curriculum or a knowledge which is essential and is fundamental for everyone to study irrespective of the role that he is to play in adult life.

Democratic curriculum is not subject curriculum alone. It includes every influence, every activity and every experience, which is educative. It is the total life and programme of the school, whether in classroom, in library or laboratory or in the play-field.

Democratic Methods and Techniques

New methods of instructions will produce citizens capable of accepting his challenges of the present and the future. Democrative teaching means a co-operative enterprise. Teaching, planning and execution of subject lessons and other educative activities are done by the pupils and the teachers together. It does not believe in the domination of the teacher or the textbook. Just stuffing information into the child is undemocratic and the negation of psychology. The teacher should not impose anything. He should encourage free enquiry and discussion. He should act as a guide, supervisor and inspirer. Group work, discussion, problem-solving, learning through experiences and group evaluation of results are the chief characteristics of democratic methods. Stress is on intelligence, learning, thinking and subjects of enquiry. It is in this sense that the new education advocates Dalton plan, Montessori system, Heuristic methods, socialized recitation etc., as methods which aim at purposeful study.

It is true that the school is a formal institution, but the methods of teaching should be most natural and informal. In the words of

Home "In the school the children should live and learn adequately, fully, richly, naturally, informally and creatively."

Democratic Administration and Organization

It is autocratic administration when the administrator thinks that he can sit by himself and see all angles of a problem. On the other hand, the democratic administrator realizes the potential powers of other brains and knows how to use them.

In a democratically administered school the students have the share in making the rules which relate to them. They have ample opportunities to shoulder responsibilities in running clubs, societies and associations and in organizing various functions in the school. Activities like organizing games, running the school store or school canteen, looking after the cleanliness of the school, bringing out a school journal, magazine or news bulletin should be left over to the managements of students. While the guidance and advice of teachers should be available, the students must enjoy powers to take their own decisions and show a sense of responsibility.

Democratic education must be well-planned, where in all the members work effectively, economically and harmoniously together to achieve a common purpose, where freedom is associated with responsibility. Democracy through co-curricular activities.

Co-curricular activities offer the pupils the best opportunity to manifest their self-reliance, qualities of leadership, initiative, co-operation, intelligent behaviour and responsible behaviour. They are the richest ground for the inculcation of democratic principles. One can learn to co-operate only by co-operating, to select leaders only by selecting leaders, to plan only by planning. In short, one can learn to live democratically only by living democratically.

Democratic Discipline

School is a laboratory in which children learn the arts and skills of democratic social living. Responsible co-operation and self-discipline or free-discipline should be two key notes of such a laboratory. Self-discipline develop through firm but kind discipline from others. In training our students for democracy, we should stimulate in them not—only willing subordination to the constituted authority, but also such desirable qualities as intellectual honesty, fearless reasoning and respect for order based on inner conviction and willing acquiescence. Love, sympathy, human relationship should be the bonds between the teacher and the taught. Sit still keep quiet and do as you are told. These commandments tend to create a graveyard discipline. There is no inner urge for obeying the laws and regulations of the school.

Discipline in democratic education is based on the conviction of doing the right thing in the right manner and at the right moment. It is based upon proper understanding of the nature of human relationships. Wherever, there is provision for self-development, there emerges an inner urge to obey the laws and regulations of the community.

Teacher in Democratic Education

A teacher in democracy should himself have adequate conceptual framework of democracy. If he wants to increase pupil's understanding in this area. To clarify the pupil's understanding the teacher should have proficiency in using such classroom management and teaching techniques as pupil-teacher planning, group work, discussions and problem-solving. (Besides giving children love and affection, the teacher must help to make them feel that they are important). Democracy and good citizenship come not from a course of studies but from a teacher, not from a curriculum but from a human soul.

The pre-requisite of a democratic teacher is that he should recognize that environment is more important than heredity, that every individual is different from every other individual, that every one is capable of making moral choices, of deciding what is true and false, good or bad, beautiful or ugly, that every child has a right to freedom, to think, to choose and equality of chances.

Democratic Atmosphere

It is the democratic environment which is congenial for the full flowering of human personality. Suppression and repression stifle the growth. An educational institution should be liberal and liberating institution. Equality of treatment should be the pervasive role. No pupil should be treated with Sarcasm or contempt. Snobbishness and selfishness should be discouraged. Everyone should know the efforts bring success and not the extraneous considerations. The atmosphere of strict adherence to tradition and blind loyalty will stop new ideas being tried and aired. The emphasis should be on constructive thinking. The headmaster should not turn a discouraging face on the teacher with a bright suggestion. Similarly the teacher should not pass off lightly what students have suggested. The head and staff should have profound respect for everyone.

Democratization of Education in India

The Acharya Narendra Dev. Committee in 1938, the Muthaliar Commission in 1952 and the Kothari Commission in 1966 have suggested a large number of measures for democritising education at various levels, the progress in the direction has not yet been satisfactory. K.G. Saiyidain said, "In India, the forms and institutions of political democracy have been established, but the spirit which gives them reality and meaning has yet to grow, for this purpose education should devote itself to the cultivation of the attitudes and ideals which are needed for the successful implementation of democracy."

The phenomenal expansion at all stages of education especially school education with the increase in the number of schools, teachers, pupils and expenditure therein, a large number of measures for improving the economic and social status of teachers, provision of multifarious incentives and facilities for the weaker and deprived sections of the community like free supply of textbooks and writing materials, free school uniforms, attendance scholarships, construction of quarters in tribal areas, establishment of textbook Banks etc., can undoubtedly be treated as clear indications of the landslide drift in the direction of democratization. The institution of various merit scholarships and loan scholarships provide educational opportunities to the deprived.

We have so far been trying to equalize educational opportunities through three main programmes: *(a)* expansion of faculties at all stages, *(b)* provision of free-education and *(c)* maintenance of low fees in higher education. These are the basic tools for the equalization of educational opportunities and this is the basic tenet in democratic education.

When functional democracy is established in the entire educational system, structure and institutions, democritisation is not only possible but also be stabilized.

ASPECTS OF DEMOCRACY

Political Democracy

Democracy is founded upon the principle of popular sovereignty, i.e., ultimate power resides in the citizens. An important principle of democracy is that all citizens have equal political privileges which only they can exercise and which they cannot transfer to any other persons. Another foundational principle is that rule of the majority shall prevail, this majority to be expressed by the citizens through direct voting or through their elected representatives. A third principle is that citizens can vote the government out of office.

Political democracy is that in which every adult has the right to govern the country. The rule does not lie "Into the hands of a small body of men or even into the hands of one class in the community." According to Dicey, "Democracy is a form of government in which governing body is comparatively larger fraction of the entire nation."

Economic Democracy

This is the second important aspects of democracy. Economic democracy means a democracy in which the economic resources or means are not monopolized by a few capitalists but economic power is in the hands of majority. Every individual will provided work according to his abilities and capabilities. This aspect of democracy is found only in a socialist country. There labour is honoured and given the best possible facilities. In India, we have achieved political freedom. No doubt, but economic freedom is still to be achieved and this can only be possible through increased production and economic democracy.

In a democracy, economic and social equality must flourish, "Without economic equality and equal opportunities, human energies are bound to be go waste and to rot; individual development and social progress are bound to be impossibilities with destruction and violence into the bargain."

Social Democracy

This aspects of democracy indicates, "All distinctions based on class, birth or possession of money" – must be done away with. There must not be any problem of caste and creed. Every man is born equal and has the equal status in the society.

IMPORTANCE OF EDUCATION IN DEMOCRACY

1. *Education for Citizenship*: The educational system must make its contribution to the development of habits, attitudes and qualities of character, which will enable the citizens to bear worthily the responsibilities of democratic citizenship and to counteract all those

tendencies which hinder the emergence of a broad, national and secular outlook.

2. *Education for Improving Productive Efficiency:* One of its most urgent problems is to improve productive efficiency to increase the national wealth and thereby to raise the standard of living.

3. *Stimulating of Cultural Renaissance:* As a result of the oppressive and widespread poverty, there is a serious lack of educational facilities and the bulk of the people are so obsessed with the problem of some sort of living that they have not been to give sufficient attention to cultural pursuits.

Views of Secondary Education Commission (1952)

The Commission discovered defects which were at the root of the prevailing system. The defects are as follows:

1. Education was too bookish and Mechanical, stereotypical and rigidily uniform and did not cater to the different aptitudes of the pupil.
2. The existing system did not develop the basic qualities of discipline, co-operation and leadership.
3. The stress on examinations, the over-crowded syllabus, the method of teaching an the lack of proper material amenities tended to make education a burden rather than a joyous experience to the youthful mind.
4. Rigid time-table, unsuitable textbooks, and unduly detailed syllabus.
5. Due to heavy strength, the classes suffer from the proper attention and guidance by the teacher.
6. The existing secondary education is isolated from life. After the youths come out of their school, they feel ill-adjusted. Their whole personality is not trained—their practical aptitudes, emotions, sense of appreciation and tasks are largely ignored.

Secondary Education Commission recommended that Secondary Education should aim at developing the following qualities in the future citizens:

Intellectual, Social and Moral Qualities

(*a*) To live with others and to appreciate the value of co-operation.

(*b*) He should have social awakening.

(c) Thinking and reasoning capacities should be cultivated.
(d) Ability to carry on one's burden.
(e) Ability and desire for social upliftment.
(f) The understanding in the intellectual integrity to shift truth from falsehood, facts from propaganda and to reject the dangerous appeal of fanaticism and prejudice.

Vocational Ability

(a) The pupils should be encouraged to acquire a yearning for the perfection and learn to take in doing everything.
(b) Craft education should be encouraged.
(c) Diversification of courses should be introduced.

To Create Means for a Harmonious Development of the Personality

(a) The children should be enabled to develop psychologically, socially and emotionally in accordance with their practical needs.
(b) The commission prescribed for the appreciation of the cultural-heritage and subjects like art, craft, and music.
(c) Hobbies should be developed.

Recommendation of Education Commission (1966)

The Education Commission under the leadership of Dr. D.S. Kothari submitted some important suggestions.

1. Re-organize our educational pattern, change our syllabi to improve our examination system.
2. Major improvement in the effectiveness of primary education.
3. Work experience as an integral element of general education.
4. Vocationalize secondary education.
5. Improve the quality of teachers at all levels and to provide teachers in sufficient strength.
6. Strengthen centres of advanced study and strive to attain, in some our universities at least, higher international standards; to lay special emphasis on the combination of teaching and research.
7. Pay particular attention to education and research in agriculture and allied sciences.

Functions of the School in a Democracy

1. To convey to the students the meaning of democratic values, ideals and principles and their implications for conduct in the various life situations.

2. To enable the students to incorporate these values, ideas and principles in their daily conduct, in and out of school.
3. A democratic school introduces radical changes in respects of methods, discipline and administration.

Methods of Educating the Students in a Democratic Way of Life

- Respect of individual personality.
- Introduction of self-government in schools.
- Provision for manual work.
- Equal opportunities for admission.
- Encouragement to group work.
- Democratic methods of teaching.
- Promotion of self-expression.
- Opportunities for social service.
- Vocational efficiency.
- Development of hobbies.
- Hostel life.
- Student parliament.
- Visits to legislature.

SECULARISM/EDUCATION FOR SECULARISM/ SECULARIZATION OF EDUCATION

Meaning

The meaning of secularism different to country to country. European secularism emerge as a protest against Christianity in 19th century. The meaning of secularism different in India and Europe. Webster says, "Secularism, a system of doctrines and practices that rejects any form of religious faith and worship." Gandhiji says, "We believe in *Sarva Dharma Samabhavana* having equal regard for all faith and greeds."

Dr. B.R. Ambedkar explains, "Secular state doesn't mean that it shall not take into consideration the religious sentiments of the people. All that secular state means is that this parliament shall not be competent to impose any particular religion upon the rest of the people. This is the only limitation that the constitution recognizes (*Parliamentary Debates, 1951, Vol-III, Part II*).

This term secularism incorporated in the constitution by 42nd Constitutional Amendment in 1976. But the constitutional frame-workers have a clear-cut idea regarding since constitution framing. We are not following western concept of secularism fully, we indianise it. Secularism is a attitude and belief. It is not anti-religious or irreligious. It doesn't rejecting any religion.

The Characteristics of a Secular State/Secularism as State's Policy

- The state as such has no religion of its own.
- It doesn't accord preferential treatment to the followers or any faith.
- It doesn't discriminate against any person on account of his faith.
- All citizens are eligible to enter government service irrespective of their faith.
- Consider religion as personal issues.
- State not support any religion and not controlled by any religion

Educational Implications of Education

In a multi-religious country like India, the spirit of secularism is to be developed in order to maintain the unity and integrity of the nation. Education should play a positive role in preparing people for a secular society and a purposeful life. We hope secularism will develop in to stronger force leading to the Social Unity of India. When institutionalized religions gradually lose their coersive hold on the younger generation. A process in which the dominance of religion over other institutions is reduced, is called secularization.

According to Brubacher secularism has "No religious point of view while it has a theory of moral education." Brubacher has also observed, "If the secularist has any religion at all it is likely that scientific doctrine constitutes the presuppositions of that religion and that scientists are its high priests."

Secularism is a philosophy of moral education. Secular behaviour springs in the school from the influence of the school, through the conduct and behaviours of the teachers themselves and little in the school community as a whole. All the activities and programmes of the schools must strive for the inculcation of values of love, truth and tolerance.

Religious and Moral Education in Secular India/Indian Constitution and Secularism

Article 19(1): "Subject to public order, morality and health and to other provisions of this part, all persons are equally entitled to freedom to conscience and the right freely to profess, practise and propagate religion."

Article 21: "No person may be compelled to pay any taxes, the proceeds of which are specifically appropriated in payment of expenses for the promotion or maintenance of any particular religion or religious denomination."

Article 22(1): "No religious instruction shall be provided in any educational institution wholly maintained out of state funds."

Provided that nothing in this clause shall apply to an education institution which is administered but has been established under an endowment or trust which requires that religious instructions shall be imparted in such institutions.

Article 22(2): No person attending any educational institution recognized by the state of receiving aid out of state funds shall be required to take part in any religious institution or to attend any religious worship that may be conducted in such institution or in any premises attached there to unless such person, or if such person is a minor his guardian has given his consent thereto."

Article 30(1): "All minorities whether based on religion or language, shall have the right to establish and administer educational institutions of their choice."

Article 30 (2): "The state shall not in granting aid to educational institutions, discriminate against any educational institution of the ground that it is under the management of minority, whether based on religion or language."

The Education Commission (1964-66) on Religious Education and Education About Religion

"We suggest that a syllabus giving all chosen information about each of the major religions should be included as a part of the course in citizenship or as a part of general education to be introduced in schools and colleges upto the first degree. It should be highlight the fundamental similarities in the great religions of the world and the emphasis they place the cultivation of certain broadly comparable moral and spiritual values."

SOCIALISM AND ITS EDUCATIONAL IMPLICATIONS

As an economic and political philosophy, socialism began as an attack on the concepts of private property and personal profit. These aspects of capitalism, socialists believed, should be replaced by public ownership of property and sharing profits.

Robert Owen in England, Henri de Saint Simon (France) and in 19th century Karl Marx (USSR) are the proponents of socialism. Karl Marx observed, socialist state must be controlled by working class.

Definitions

"An economic philosophy based on the concept of public ownership of property and sharing of profits, together with the belief that economic decision should be controlled by the workers."

– *William Kornblum, 1998*

Meaning

Socialism has its origin in Europe as a revolt against capitalism in the 19th century. Its salient ideas spread all over the world. These are different brands/forms or socialism especially those shared by Karl Marx Lenin in Russia, Mao in China and Gandhi in India.

In 1947 in an editorial under the caption 'who is a socialist' Gandhi wrote, "Under socialism all the members of the society are equal-none low, none high .....Even as members or the individual body are equal, so are the members of the society. This is socialism, under it, the prince and the peasant, the wealthy and the poor, the employer and the employee are all on the same level."

Socialism is a scheme of social organization, which places the means of production and distribution in the hands of the community. Socialism is part and parcel of the concept of the welfare state. By planning and fully utilizing all the resources available in the country, it seeks to provide maximum benefit to all the people."

Characteristics/Features

- Socialism aims at social justice.
- It aims at equality.
- It aims a class less society, free from exploitation, oppression and disparity.
- It pre-supposes public ownership of the means of production.
- It aims at active participation of the individual in the productive process of society.
- It aims at establishing a society based on mental co-operation and fellow feeling.
- It aims at abolishing the capitalist system.
- It aims at developing necessary skills and favourable attitudes towards work.

Indian Constitution and Socialism

Through the 42nd Constitutional Amendment on 1976 the term socialism included in our constitution. Upto that it implicit in 4th chapter, directive principles of state policy. Based on the implicit/ hidden one our parliament accept the idea of 'socialistic pattern of society' in 1954. In economy we stand between capitalism and socialism i.e., mixed economy. We aim a democratic socialist nation. We keep both socialist ideals and basic human rights.

Friends, but what's the present condition? Our great aim, a class less society still a myth even after 60 years of independence. Equality between man and man, is a far reaching objective. In democracy, we trying to uphold uniqueness. But it doesn't go parallel with universality/socialism. This conflict leads liberal democracy and extending freedom. Political parties and peoples misusing our freedom. 80 per cent wealth accumulated on 20 per cent of population. It's not only the issue of India but also all over the world. In our democracy, welfare of the majority is the welfare of the all, i.e., if 51 per cent of people have food, that equal to nation have food.

Educational Implications of Socialism

Aims of Education and Socialism, Emphasis on

(*a*) social development of an individual,
(*b*) education for citizenship, and
(*c*) socialization of the individual.

Contents/Curriculum

(*a*) More emphasis on core curriculum.
(*b*) Subject-matter stressing equality,
(*c*) Study of socialistic movements, and
(*d*) Socially useful productive work and work experience.

Methods of Teaching

(*a*) Socialized recitation techniques,
(*b*) Project method,
(*c*) Problem method, and
(*d*) Team teaching.

Educational Measures for Promoting a Socialist Society

Kothari Commission observed, "One of the important social objectives of education is to equalize opportunity, enabling the backward or under privilaged classes and individuals to use education as a lever for the improvement of their condition. Every society that values social justice and is anxious to improve the lot of the common man and cultivate all available talent, must ensure progressive equality of opportunity to all section of population. This is the only guarantee for the building up of an egalitarian and human society in which the exploitation of the weak will be minimized."

Teaching of Socialism

It is the responsibility of the educational institutions to bring about adequate awareness regarding socialism among the teachers and students so that the young people are armed with knowledge which will enable them to chart the course of the nation towards the goal of socialism. The following are three main ways in which a school can convey positive attitudes and values regarding socialism to students:

1. Direct teaching of socialism.
2. Living the values and attitudes to be learned through the organization of various activities.
3. Teachers becoming models embodying the desired values and attitudes.

Textbooks and Socialism

As an impact of socialism, textbooks at the school stage, by and large, have been nationalized. The contents of textbooks are oriented and regulated according to the national policy and ethos. Efforts are being made to keep the price range of textbooks within the easy reach of the parents.

EQUALITY OF OPPORTUNITY IN EDUCATION

The Kothari Commission observed, "On grounds of social justice as well as for the furtherance of democracy it is essential to make special efforts to equalize educational opportunities between these groups."

Ways and Means of Providing Equality of Opportunity in Education

- Tuition fee education to economically weaker sections of students.
- Free textbooks and informs to the weaker sections.
- Establishment of book banks.
- Award of scholarship.
- Granting of loans.
- Day-study centres and lodging houses.
- Earn and learn facilities.
- Special facilities for girls.

- Special stress on the education of the backward sections of societies – tribals, slum areas, hilly areas etc.
- Meeting the needs of slow learners and the handicapped.
- Running and maintenance and state/government schools.
- Equality of opportunity in admission.
- Common school system.

CONSTITUTIONAL PROVISIONS OF EDUCATION/ CONSTITUTIONAL GUARANTEE

Prior to 1947, education in India was conducted according to the educational system introduced by the British Government. By Government of India Act (1935) autonomous administration had come in to existence. It was at this time that education was given certain constitutional provisions. In 1944 after the victory of the Allies in the World War II, the British administration once again turned its attention to the development of education in the post-war period.

After winning independence, the problem of developing education confronted us. The education ministeries of the states and the Government of India devoted their best thought to facing the problem. On January 26, 1950, the people of India faithfully dedicated their constitution of themselves. Various provisions have been made for education in the constitution itself.

Article 30: The Right of Minorities to Set-up and Administer Educational Institutions

30 (1) All minorities based on religion or language will have the right to set up and administer institutions in their own interest.

30 (2) In giving aid to educational institutions, the government will not discriminate against any institution on the basis of its being set up and administered by the particular religious or linguistic minority.

The government will not foist any language of its own choice on any minority. The minority status of a group will be determined on the basis of its population. The reservation of particular groups not be considered as a violation of the constitution. No educational institution will be entitled to refuse admission to any child on the basis of religion, caste, creed or language.

Article 45: Provision for Free and Compulsory Education for Children

"The state shall endeavour to provide, within a period of ten years from the commencement of this constitution, for free and compulsory education for all children until they complete the age of fourteen years."

Amendment of the Constitution

The 86th Amendment (2002) inserts a new Article 21(A) to provide for a fundamental right to education to all children of 6-14 years. Also, it substitutes Article 45 in the directive principles by a new article providing for Early Child Care and Education to children below 6 years. By amending Article 51(A), a new fundamental duty is sought to be added for parents or guardians providing educational opportunities to children between the age of 6-14 years.

Article 46: Promotion of Educational and Economic Interests of the Scheduled Castes, Scheduled Tribes and Other Weaker Sections

The state shall promote with special care the educational and economic interests of the weaker sections of the people, and in particular, of the scheduled castes and the scheduled tribes, and shall protect them from social injustice and all forms of exploitation.

Article 28: Freedom as to Attendance at Religious Instruction or Religious Worship in Certain Educational Institutions

There are many religions in India, with very substantial numbers of followers. Though our country is itself a secular state, the constitution of our country has shown great awareness or that religious susceptibilities of the people.

28 (1) Any educational institution drawing its total financial assistance from the governments funds must not impart education of any religion.

28 (2) The condition is Part (1) shall not applicable to any educational institutions administered by the state but in the case of an institution established by a trust or a religious body, religious education may be carried on.

28 (3) Any educational institution which receives aid from the government funds shall not compel any individual admitted to that institution take part in any religious activities conducted in the institution or any place of

worship attached to it, as long as permission to do so has not been obtained from that individual, or if he is a minor from his guardians.

Article 29: Protection of Interests of Minorities

The most controversial part of the Indian constitution.

29 (1) The citizens in any part of the country having their own specific language, script and culture, will have the right to maintain these languages, scripts and cultures. The article clearly grants to the individual the right choose his own culture and language and it also clarifies that each state and its citizen will be to choose their own language and culture.

29 (2) No citizen shall be denied admission in to educational institution maintained by the state or receiving aid out of state funds on grounds only of religion, race, caste, language or any of them.

Article 27: Freedom as to Payment of Taxes for Promotion of Any Particular Religion

No person shall be compelled to pay any taxes, the proceeds of which are specifically appropriated in payment of expenses for the promotion or maintenance of any particular religion or religious denomination.

Article 350: Language to be Used in Representations for Redress of Grievances

Every individual has the right to give representation to an officer in state or central language.

350 (A) Facilities for Instruction in Mother Tongue at Primary Stage.

350 (A) Advise that education be imparted in the mother tongue, starting that if will be the endeavour of every state, and of every local official within the state to provide suitable facilities for providing education to the children of linguistic minorities in their mother tongue at the primary stage.

350(B) Special Officer for Linguistic Minorities.

350(1) *(a)* There will be a special officer appointed by the president of India for linguistic minorities.

350 (2) *(b)* It will be the duty of the special officer to conduct research or studies in to all subjects related to the notion of linguistic minorities as defined in this constitution, and to send suggestions to the president regarding these subjects.

351 Directive for Development of the Hindi Language.

It shall be the duty of the union to promote the spread of the Hindi language, to develop it so that it may serve as a medium of expression for all the elements of the composite culture of India and to secure its enrichment by assimilating without interfering with its genius, the forms, style and expressions used in Hindustani and in the other languages of India specified in the eight schedule, and by drawing, wherever necessary/ desirable for its vocabulary, primarily on Sanskrit and secondarily on other languages.

Indian Constitution Articles 345, 346, 347 dealing with regional languages.

- 345 – languages used for states purposes.
- 346 – the state language for communication between one state and another or between state and union.
- 347 – special provisions relating to a language spoken by a section of the population of a state.
- 343 – related official language of the union. Hindi in the Devanagri script, and use of international number system.

EDUCATION AS A FUNDAMENTAL RIGHTS

21(A) added as a new article by Constitution (86th Amendment) Act, 2002 provides for free and compulsory education for all children between the age of 6-14 years.

Fundamental Duties of Indian Citizen

(Part IV A – Article 51. A)

It is one of the valuable part of constitution and also most neglected.

The fundamental duties enshrined in Article 51(A) now are in consonance with Article 29(1) of the Universal Declaration of Human Rights which says: "everyone has duties to the community in which alone the free and full development of his personality is possible."

The new Part IV. A, Articles 51 A (a) to (j) laid down to constitution (86th Amendment) Act, 2002 added new clause (K) as the eleventh duty.

To Abide by The Constitution and Respect its Ideas and Institutions, The National Flag and The National Anthem

These are the very physical foundations of our citizenship. All of us are supposed to maintain the dignity of the constitution, by not indulging in any activities in violation of the letter of spirit of the constitution. Our is a vast country with many languages, sub-cultures, religions and ethnic diversities, but the essential unity of the country is epistomized in the one constitution, one flag, one people and one citizenship.

We are governed and guided by this constitution irrespective of caste, religion, race, sex etc. We must put the nation above our narrow personal interests and then only we will be able to protect our hard-earned freedom and sovereignty.

To Cherish and Follow the Noble Ideals Which Inspired Our National Struggle for Freedom

If we, the citizens of India, remain conscious of and committed to these ideals, we will fissiparous tendencies raising their ugly heads now and there here and there. Parties and politicians who use religion, casteism, separation etc., for political ends and for capturing power are clearly violating their fundamental duties under the constitution.

To Uphold and Protest the Sovereignity, Unity and Integrity of India

In a democratic system of governance, sovereignty lies with the people. To defend our sovereignity is our own responsibility. If the freedom and unity of the country are jeoponsibility. If the freedom and unity of the country are jeoparadized, the nation ceases to exist and if there is no nation, who lives?

To Defend the Country and Render National Service When Called Upon to do so

Civilians may be required also to take up arms in defence of the country, if the situation warrants it. By fighting to defend the country, the citizens are fighting only to defend their own liberty and that of their posterity.

To Promote Harmony and the Spirit of Common Brotherhood Amongst all the People of India Transcending Religious, Linguistic and Regional or Sectional Diversities to Renounce Practices Derogatory to the Dignity of Women

'Yatra Naristu Pujayanthe Ramanthe Thathra Devatha', (gods reside

where women are worshiped). That's our culture, India is a land diversities, we must keep a unity even the diversities.

To Value and Preserve the Rich Heritage of our Composite Culture

One of the most ancient civilizations of the world, India can take legitimate pride in having been a civilizational unity without a break for more than 5000 years. We all are the part of this great civilization and culture. Our contribution in the field of art, sculpture, architecture, mathematics, science, medicine etc., are well-known. Some of the oldest, deepest and most sublime philosophical thought and literature was born in India. We have several historical monuments or great archeological value spread over the entire country. These includes forests, palaces, temples etc. As to this territory had the honour of being the birth place of several great religions like Hinduism, Budhism, Jainism and Sikhism. Our past has shown us the path of peace, love, non-violence and truth. As citizens of this country, it is the responsibility of all of us to work for the preservation of this rich heritage and its cultural values and live in love and harmony.

The directive principles under Article 49 similarly enjoins, the state to protect monuments and places and objects of national, artistic or historical importance.

To Protect and Improve the Natural Environment Including Forests, Lakes, Rivers and Wild Life to Have Compassion for Living Creatures

In the face of menace of the increasing pollution and environmental degradation, it is the duty of every citizen to protect and improve natural environment including, forests, lakes, rivers and wild life and to have compassion for living creatures.

Earth is the common heritage of men and animals. We have no right to annihilate of drive away from their territory or natural habitat or the world denizens. '*Sarveshawam Santhir Bhavanthu*' (peace unto all living beings and entire environment), and '*Ahimsaparamo dharma, ahimsaparmo thapa*' (Non-violence is the greatest duty and the greatest penance).

To Develop the Scientific Temper, Humanism and Spirit of Inquiry and Reform

One of our great founding fathers, Nehru, always laid great emphasis on the need for Indian citizens developing a scientific temper and a spirit of inquiry – an inquisitiveness for learning from developments around the world. It is the bounden duty of every citizen to preserve and promote a scientific temper and a spirit of inquiry to keep pace with the fast changing world.

To Safeguard Public Property and to Abjure Violence

It is most unfortunate that in a country which preaches non-violence to the rest of the world, we see from time-to-time spectacles of senseless violence and destruction of public property indulged in by a few of its citizens.

To Strive Towards Excellence in all Spheres of Individual and Collective Activity, so that the Nation Constantly Rises to Higher Level of Endeavour and Achievement

To drive for excellence in all spheres of individual and collective activity is the demand of times and a basic requirement in a highly competitive world. Nothing, but the best would have survival potential in tomorrow's world. This would include respect for professional obligations and excellence.

Every Parent or Guardian to Provide Opportunities for Education to His Child or Ward Between the Age of 6-14 Years

The National Commission to Review the Working of the Constitution (NCRWC) had recommended making education a fundamental right for all children up to the age of 14.

The Constitution (86th Amendment) Act, 2002 however provided for free and compulsory education as a legally enforceable fundamental right for all children between the 6-14 years. To meet the criticism of not covering the children below 6 years, the Act amended directive principles to say that the state shall endeavour to provide Early Childhood Care and Education (ECCE) for all children below the age of six years. Also it added a new Clause (K) to Chapter IV A, Article 51 A to cast on parents and guardians a duty to provide opportunities for education to children between the age 6-14 years.

There is no provision in the constitution for direct enforcement of the fundamental duties enshrined in Article 51 A nor is there any provision to prevent or punish their violation.

The National Commission to Review the Working of the Constitution (2002–03, NCRWC) [appointed by President of India on 23rd February, 2000 and submitted its report on 31 March, 2002-

regarding the completion of constitution's 50 years. 1990-2000] recommended the following should be incorporated as fundamental duties in Article 51(A) of the constitution.

1. To foster a spirit of family values and responsible parenthood in the matter of education, physical and moral well-being of children.
2. Duty of industrial organizations to provide education to children of their employees.

FUNDAMENTAL RIGHTS

Part III – Articles 12-35

Six Broad Categories

1. *The Right to Equality:* Including the equality before law and the equal protection of laws (Article 14), prohibition of discrimination on grounds of religion, race, caste, sex or place of birth (Article 15), equality of opportunity in matters of public employment (Article 16) and abolition of untouchability and the system of titles (Articles 17, 18).
2. *The Right to Freedom:* Including the right to protection of life and personal liberty (21) and the right to freedom of speech and expression, assembly, association or union, movement and reside and settle in any part of India, and the right to practice any profession and occupation (Articles 19).

Right of Education

Article 21 (A) added as a new article by the Constitution (86th Amendment) Act, 2002 provides for free and compulsory education for all children between the age of 6-14 years. This included under right to freedom.

3. *The Right Against Exploitation:* Prohibiting all forms of forced labour, child labour and traffic in human beings (Articles 23, 24).
4. *The Right to Freedom of Conscience and Free Proession,* practice and propagation of religion (Articles 25 to 28).
5. *The Right of Minorities to Conserve Their Culture,* language and script and to establish and administer educational institutions of their choice (Articles 29, 30).
6. *The Right to Constitutional Remedies for the Enforcement of All These Fundamental Rights* (Article 32).

EDUCATION AS FUNDAMENTAL RIGHTS

Introduction

The conflict between man and the state is as old as human history. Although attempts have been made for centuries to bring about a proper adjustment between the competing claims of the state and the individual, the solution seems to be still far off. This is primarily because of the dynamic nature of human society where old values, ideas and forces constantly yield place to new ones. It is obvious that if individuals are allowed to have absolute freedom of speech and action, the result would be chaos, ruin and anarchy. Hence, the eternal problem that faced statesman and political scientists was how to make a proper adjustment between individual freedom and social control, the need for protecting personal liberty against governmental power and that of limiting personal liberty by governmental power. The problem assumes extreme difficulty only under a democratic system of government. A democracy aims at the maximum development of the individual's personality; and the personality of the individual is inseparably boand with his liberty. Only a free society can assure the progress of its members which ultimately helps the advancement of human welfare. Therefore, every democracy pays special attention to securing this basic objective to the maximum extent without, at the same time, endangering the security of the state itself. A common device that is adopted by most of them for this purpose is to incorporate a list of fundamental rights in their constitutions and guarantee them from violation by executive and legislative authorities. The theory of fundamental rights implies limited government.

The provisions of Part III of our constitution which enumerates the Fundamental Rights are more elaborate than those of any other Fundamental Rights, and cover a wide range of topics. The constitution itself classifies the fundamental rights under seven groups as follows:

(a) Right to equality,
(b) Right to particular freedom,
(c) Right against exploitation,
(d) Right to freedom of religion,
(e) Cultural and educational rights,
(f) Right to property (eliminated by 44th Amendment Act), and
(g) Right to constitutional remedies.

Education as a Fundamental Right

In order to fulfil the obligations enshrined in the preamble of the constitution, provisions are made in it in the form of article and the corresponding clauses. The various constitutional provisions regarding education in India are in accordance with our political, economic and cultural needs. These provisions regarding education in India aim at fulfilling the aspirations of the people through the medium of education.

The Constitution of India provides the following provisions relating to education in the country:

Article 45

Article 45 states, "The state shall endeavour to provide within a period of ten years from the commencement of this constitution, for free and compulsory education for all children until they complete the age of fourteen years."

Article 45 of directive principles of state policy includes the most important constitutional provision regarding Indian Education. It deals with free and compulsory primary education.

Baroda, a tiny state of India, introduced compulsory primary education in 1906. In 1911, Mr. Gopala Krishna Gokhale, a member of Imperial Legislature, moved a resolution in the council to make elementary education free and compulsory throughout the country, but it was rejected. It become reality in 1920 when all the provisional governments passed acts for introducing compulsory primary education in their provinces. Gandhiji's scheme of basic education (1937) also aimed at providing primary education to all children until they completed the age of 14 years. The Sargent report also recommended a universal system of primary education.

THE NORMS OF FUNDAMENTAL RIGHT OF EDUCATION

1. Provision of teachers in the ratio of 1:30 at primary and upper primary level and a provision of at least two teachers in every two primary schools.
2. Provision of a upper primary school for every two primary schools. This would entail establishment of more than 2.21 lack new upper primary schools.
3. Provision of primary school within one kilometer of every habitation. This would entail the establishment of nearly 1.84 lakh new primary schools.

4. Provision of classroom for every teacher and a separate Headmaster's room in upper primary school.
5. Provision of schools equipments to add proposed new primary schools and upper primary schools as per the operation black-boards norm of Rs. 10,000 per primary schools and Rs. 50,000 per upper primary school.
6. Provision for school uniform and scholarship to children below the poverty line. Provisions has been made for 50 per cent add the enrolled children in the 6-14 age group.
7. Provision of cooked meal/food grains to 50 per cent of the enrolled children which has been made though the final figure should be based on actual requirement and livelihood of success of the scheme.
8. Provision of free textbooks and stationary has been made for all the children at primary and upper primary levels as per norms given by the NCERT.
9. Establishment of new DIETS, Block Resource Centres and cluster resources centres have been made in uncovered regions.
10. Provisions for maintenance of school buildings and other school infrastructure and replacement of school equipments at primary and upper primary stage have also been made on regular basis.
11. For disabled children, an assessment of four per cent of the total children has been made and provisions made as per current norms in scheme for disabled persons four per cent incidence of disability has been taken on the basis of some current assessment in this regard.
12. Provision for teacher training, and community monitoring of elementary education projects and classroom observation by resource persons has also been made.
13. The 1993, all India educational survey provides basis for assessing educational facilities that were available to schools in 1993. Between 1993 and 1997-98, investments have been made by Central and State Governments.

Administration

Education was a state subject till 3rd January, 1977, when the 22nd Amendment to the constitution was made to bring education under concurrent list. The amendment cancelled (deleted) the 'entry' of the state list and enlarged the 'entry 25' in the concurrent list.

The entry 25 of the concurrent list how reads as, "Education, including technical education, medical education and universities subject to the provisions of entries 63, 64, 65 and 66 of list I, vocational and technical training of labour."

List I (Union List)

Entry 63: Universities and other institutions declared by parliament by law to be institutions of national importance.

Entry 64: Institutions for specific or technical education declared by parliament to be institutions of national importance.

Entry 65: Mentions union agencies and institutions for professional, Vocational or technical training for the promotion of special studies or research etc.

Entry 66: The co-ordination and determination of standards in institution for higher education, or research and scientific and technical institutions becomes the exclusive responsibility of the union.

Universal Primary Education

86th Constitutional Amendment (2002), Amending Articles 21, 51 (A) and 45.

Article 21 (A)

Article 21 states the fundamental rights of Indian citizens. It means that of enables the citizen to seek the enforcement of the right by way of resort to "write" under Articles 32 and 226 of the Constitution.

The new Article, Article 21 A says that "the state shall provide free and compulsory education to all children of the age six to fourteen years in such a manner as the state may, by law, determine."

By the 86th Constitutional Amendment Right to education, for children aged between 6 to 14 years had become the right of citizen under Article 21 which can be enforced through law. By this amendment, our 'rights' had increased from 6 to 7.

Article 51A (K)

Article 51A defines the fundamental duties of the citizens. The new clause to Article 51A (K) sates that "It shall be the duty of every citizen of India who is a parent of guardian to provide opportunities for education to his child or as the case may be, ward between the age of six and fourteen years."

Article 45

Article 45 says about education of children under age group 0-6 that is ECCE.

Criticism

Many legal experts, educationalists and voluntary organizations like National Alliance for the Fundamental Rights to Education (NAFRE) had criticized the amendment. A few most important among them are given below:

(a) The Guarantee of education for 6 to 14 years category is meaningless without the state taking responsibility for Early Childhood Care and Education (ECCE). The bill does not address the issue of making ECCE, a concept noted in the NPE, 1986 amendatory without which the complete enrolment of childrens especially of girls education, of the age group 6-14 to primary class will be difficult.

(b) According to D. Anil Sadgopal, former Dean and Head of the Department of Education, Delhi University, in the amendment, the element of enforcement had been taken out. The amendment is not attached with any financial provision and it shows the governments lack of commitment to the objective.

(c) Another feature of the Amendment which is criticized is the insertion of Clause 'K' under Article 51A. Under the clause there is a possibility of assment, by the authorities of parents who is not giving opportunities for education to their children due to financial or any such problem in which they have no contrast.

The NAFRE points out that between 1951 to 1971 at least 15 lakhs parents have been prosecuted under the State Compulsory Education Act, which was inforce in 19 states. The meaning of the term "opportunity for education" is also much criticized.

(d) It is also said that the government had diluted the objective of guaranteeing free and Universal Elementary Education (UEE) to all children by keeping 0-6 age group under the directive principles.

Conclusion

Here we can conclude that taking the rights guaranteed under religious, educational and cultural field as a whole, it will be noted that these are conched in the most comprehensive language and the maximum possible freedom is guaranteed to the minorities, religious and linguistics. The democratic basis of the constitution would have been lost if the minorities were not given adequate protection to preserve their religious beliefs, and institutions of education and culture.

MODEL QUESTIONS

1. List any two constitutional provisions on education in India.
2. Discuss the slogan "Education For All" (EFA) in the light of "Education as a fundamental right."
3. Discuss the salient features of education for democracy.
4. Explain the values laid down in the Indian constitution. How can they be realized through education.
5. Is secularism same as irreligion? Explain the difference.

REFERENCES

1. Basu, D.D. *Introduction to the Constitution of India.*
2. Kashyap C.S. (2005). *Our Constitution – An Introduction to India's Constitution and Constitutional Law,* National Book Trust, India, New Delhi.
3. Kornblum, William (1998). *Sociology the Central Themes.* New York: Harcourt Brace College Publishers.
4. Pylee, M.V. (2003). *Indian Constitution,* Bhasha Institute Thiruvananthapuram: Kerala.
5. Pylee, M.V. (2005). *An Introduction to the Constitution of India,* Vikas Publishing House (P.) Ltd., New Delhi.
6. Taneja, R.P. (2000). *Dictionary of Education,* Anmol Publishing (P) Ltd.

5

History of Education in Modern India

The contemporary education can find the right direction if education is studied from the historical perspective. Such perspective makes study of educational problems objective.

HISTORY OF INDIAN EDUCATION

- Education in Ancient India, 5000-650 AD
  - Vedic education,
  - Brahmanic education, and
  - Buddhist education.
- Education in Medieval Period, 650 AD-1700 AD
  - Medieval Hindu education
  - Medieval Muslim education.
- Education in Modern Period, 1700 AD +
  - Education under colonial rule
  - Education in independent India.

In India contrary to many other nations we have not borrowed education from the west. Instead we have our own traditions and a glorious history in this area, since vedic periods. India has been bestowed upon with the blessings of knowledge. In fact, we had a perfect education system in vedic age and Buddhist period and after the renaissance of the Brahmanism. This system was further polished and nourished by Arabs, Turks and Mughals who arrive this land as conquers but settled here.

Later came the British who reformed the traditional system and founded a modern education system in India. Following independence the Government of India rectified the faults and promoted a system to new heights. As a result the existing educational system in India is perfect and match any system in the developed world.

Changing Pattern

Portuguese Missionaries functioned here 4 kinds of institutions. They are:

1. Portuguese and Latin language primary schools attached to churches and missionary instruction.
2. Schools providing vocational and agricultural education along with traditional education, to the orphan children in India.
3. Jesuit schools for higher education.
4. Theological training centres for training paderes and missionaries.

The first Christian padere priest to take upon his shoulders the task of propagating both religious and education in India was St. Francis Xavier. He collaborated with St. Ignatius Loyloa in the establishment of a Jesus society.

St. Xavier made a practice of roaming from village-to-village with a book in one hand and a bell in the other.

Like Portuguese in South India, the Dutch were carrying on the work of religious conversion and education in Bombay. The French established educational institutions at Mahe, Yanam, Chandranagar, Karkil and Pondicherri.

British East India Company's Role

The BEIC established by a few Englishmen in 1599 for the purpose of trading with India. In 1660, it obtained the permission of Queen Elizabeth to trade with Eastern countries. This caused to Indian education,

- expand rapidly,
- financial position become strong,
- spread of religion,
- in addition to trading ambitious spreading to education also,
- sent few Indian to England 1614,
- Department of Arabic set up in Oxford University for training missionaries.

A Madrassa in 1780 at Culcutta and a Sanskrit college in 1791 at Benaras were established for pleasing the Muslim and Hindu population.

Westernization of Education – Mecaulay's Minutes

Thomas Babington Mecaulay solved the stagnation and problem by presenting the forceful minute. He rejected the claim of Sanskrit and Arabic on he following grounds:

- English is the key to modern knowledge.
- It stands eminent among the languages of the west.
- It would bring about renaissance in India.
- The natives are desirous of learning English.

Ways of Grant Utilization

- British Government's main aim is to spread European literature and science among Indians and so all the money granted for education will be spent for that purpose.
- Oriental institutions will not be closed and their teachers and students shall continue to receive their pay and scholarships as usual.
- Oriental literature will not be published in future as sufficient money had been spent on this item.
- The money, thus saved, will be spent in the spread of English literature and science among Indians through English medium.

'Contribution' of Lord Mecaulay to Indian Education

- Ending Anglicist orientalist (oriental *vs* occidental) controversy.
- Through English education he wanted to create, "A class of persons, Indians in blood and but English in taste, in opinions, in morals and in the intellect."
- He did create a groups of WOGs (Western Oriented Gestle-men).

In a letter to his father 1836 Mecaulay write, "Our English schools are increasing with leaps and bounds and now the condition has reached to a position that it has become difficult to accommodate the students... Hindus are much influenced with education. There is no Hindu, who may keep real faith in his religion after studying English. I have full confidence that if our education policy succeeds then no

Idolater will be left in Bangal. All this done naturally without any religious preaching and interference."

This clearly unreveals the motives of Macaulay.

Lord Willian Bentick accepted the arguments by Macaulay in support of his educational policy. He observe, "I give my entire concurrence to the sentiments expressed in this minute."

Changes Enforced in Indian Education

- European literature and science will be propagated among the Indians.
- Funds will be employed only for encouraging English education.
- Future allocation of funds to oriental students and teachers will be stopped.
- No funds will be available for printing of oriental works.
- The medium of education will be English.

Downward Filtration Theory

Filtration means coming of something to the bottom from the top. Coming down of education or knowledge from the top to the bottom, i.e., from the higher class people to the lower or the general people.

Education is to be filtered to the common people, drop-by-drop, the education should go to the common public so that at due time it may take the form of a vast stream which remained watering desert of the society for long times and high class of people should be educated and common people gain influence form them."

Characteristics

- To educate only the high class people in order to give them higher posts in the administration with view to strengthening the roots of British empire in the country.
- When the higher class people would receive English education their culture would be improved and the general public would accept them as their role models, as a result, the lower class people would also be educated after being influenced by the higher class people.
- In educate the higher class people who might undertake the responsibility of educating the general people.
- Mecaulay think "as such people connect a link between British East India Company and public."

Causes of Filtration Theory

- Need for Government Servants –
  They wanted to have cheap servants who work in different capacities. This aim could be fulfilled only by an educated higher class of people of India.
- No money for mass education.
- British belief, British rulers concluded that if the standard of living and ideas of the people of higher classes in society could be changed through English education then the people of the lower class will also be influenced and they shall be loyal to the British Government.
- Further expansion –
  In 1839, the general committee of public instruction again repeated the stand that education would be given only to the higher class people who should shoulder the responsibility of educating their country men.

Failure of the Theory

- The educated elite making themselves richer and richer. As a result education became concentrated only to those who had money.
- Too many English educated Indians came out in the field and it was not possible for the government to give them suitable employment, according to their expectations that leads to unemployment.
- It create a feeling of self-respect, national honour and independence in the English educated Indians. These re-awakened persons could not be tempted by government services and they took a vow to fight for national independence.

Policy of Lord Auckland

Lord Auckland Succeeded William Bendick as Governor-General. Supporters of Eastern education presented him with a representation opposing Macaulay's declaration. Lord Auckland agreed their demands. Increased the grant for Eastern education, increase the number of scholarships, made arrangements for printing and publication of oriental works.

Declaration of Lord Hardinge

Lord Hardinge encouraged education well. He opened 101 primary schools in Bombay in 1854. He gave financial grounds to primary schools and opened an Engineering Department in Calcutta Hindu College and opened Girls School in Calcutta.

In 1844, Governor-General Lord Hardinge declared that priority in employment in the British East Indian Companies organization would be given to those who had received English education, therefore demand for English education increased. Education directly linked with livelihood.

These improvements in the educational sphere were no more than a drop in the ocean.

19 years period between 1835-53 had been very important in Indian education. Education saw many upheals during this period and ultimately it was brought on a definite track.

Macualay has been criticized in India for his pride and fool hardiness. But this narrow-mindedness had ultimately helped. India towards its re-generation and national independence. Macualay's policy produced clerks on the one hand but it also produced great patriots on the other.

Thomas Babington Mecaulay died 140 years ago but in India he still widely remembered, still controversial. In his 4 years in India he made two notable contributions, i.e., draft of criminal procedure code and the minute. Why he come out to India, well-established at home, as a parliament member and highly regarded writer?

Woods Despatch (1953-54)

In 1853, when the British East India Company's charter again came up for review and modifications after 20 years the need for a permanent and comprehensive educational policy was felt. The British parliament asked the Select Committee to consider this question. A Committee was formed in 1854 for studying the problem of education. Chalse Wood, was its Chairman. He also the President of the British East India Company's Board of Control. He publish a new declaration in 1854 and it send to India.

This dispatch is to great important in the field of education for the country.

The dispatch contains 100 principal clauses. It give a clear direction to the company with regard the aims of education, medium of instruction, women education, vocational education, educational administration, grant-in-aid, curriculum, oriental studies and literature, indigenous schools and Indian Languages. Therefore, this called 'The Magna Carta of Indian Education'.

Three Englishmen – Marshman, Parry, Wilson – worked hard in preparing the dispatch.

Recommendations

- *The Aim of Education:* It should be to impart useful knowledge to the Indian people in such a way to raise their intellectual, moral and economic status in order that government might get efficient workers.
- *The Curriculum*: Sanskrit, Arabic and Persian should be included in the curriculum along with English education, western literature and science. Education in law also recommended.
- *The Medium of Instruction*: Along with English, Indian languages should also be accepted as the medium.
- *Department of Public Instruction* (DPI): It should be constituted in each province. The Director of Public Instruction should be the chairman of this department. A deputy-director and inspectors should be appointed under the director. Director was made responsible and he was to submit an annual report about education in the province. Five provinces – in India at that time are, Bangal, Madras, Bombay, North-western Province and Punjab.
- *University Education:* Three universities should be established – Calcutta, Bombay, Madras, on the pattern of the London university. Teaching of Law and Engineering should be organized these universities. These universities must have Chancellors, Vice-Chancellor, Fellows and Senate.
- *Importance of Graded Education*: School education must be graded in to primary, middle and higher.
- *Expansion of General Education*: Education should be made available to all. Dispatch suggested, universal education this way Chaslewood wisely touched the feelings of the public and criticized the filtration theory.
- *Grant-in-Aid for Education*: Following type of institutions were declared eligible for grants:

  1. Institutions following the rules and regulations enforced by the government and which were prepared to get them inspected by government inspectors.

2. Institutions run very well by private organizations.
3. Institutions free from communal feelings and not observing distinction of caste, community and creed.
4. Institution charging fees from students and not giving free education.

The dispatch advised the Government of India to formulate rules for grant-in-aid on the pattern followed in Great Britain and introduce various types of grants for different types of educational activities. Such as, Student stipend, Teachers salary, Reading room, Building construction and Scientific instruments and furniture. Grant-in-Aid system encouraged private enterprises in educational field and education would expand with a greater speed. It benefitted most missionaries.

- *Teachers Training:* At that time no arrangement for teacher training. Efficient teachers were very few:
  - Dispatch recommended at least one training college in each province for training of teachers.
  - Special training colleges should be established for subject as engineering, medicine, law and other professional subjects.
- *Women's Education*: Despatch encourage women education and suggested women should be given education in all the provinces.
- *Education and Employment*: The aim of education was not only to obtain government services. The purpose of education was to develop human qualities. So education obtained with a wider outlook not only to obtain services.
- *Vocational Education*: Suggested for vocational education through schools and colleges.
- *Publication of Books in Indian Languages*: New books and translation of some great works should be published in Indian languages.

The Government accepted these recommendations, since these reflected desirable modern trends. They made it an educational policy and gave it legal authority. That's why it known 'magna carta' of Indian education.

The revolution of 1857 was responsible far reaching changes in Indian education. Dispatch end the monopoly of missionaries over education. Under the influence of the dispatch British Government established a general council of education of India in England. When Lord Rippon become the Viceroy the institution asked him to carry out a survey of education in India.

On reaching India, Lord Rippon appointed an Indian Education Commission on February 3, 1882. Its Indian members were Anand Mohan Bose, Sayyad Mahmood, Budev Mukerjee, T.K. Tailang, P. Ranganand Mudaliar, Maharaja Jitendra Mohan, Thakur and Haji Gulam. Its member secretary was B.L. Rice (DPI of Mysore).

Merits of Wood's Dispatch

Woods dispatch may be regarded as a revolutionary step taken up by a foreign rule in India. It gone a new direction to education in the country. According education in India become more purposeful, definite and progressive.

- The dispatch started a new era in Indian education.
- It determined an educational policy in India and made it constitutional.
- It made the government fully responsible for education.
- It studied the total problem of education from primary to university level and gave useful suggestions for each stage of education.
- It made education systematic.
- It reorganized the utility of Indian literature, culture and knowledge.
- It prepared an administrative set-up for education in each province and recommended for the appointment of directors, deputy directors and inspectors of schools.
- By giving a universal character to education the dispatch abolished the filtration theory.
- Universities opened at Calcutta, Bombay, Madras and a number of schools and colleges were also started keeping in a view of recommendations of the dispatch. Thus, education got a good stride.
- The dispatch honoured Sanskrit, Arabic, Persian and other Indian languages.
- Recommended stipends for poor and deserving students.
- Advised to raise he salary of teachers and emphasized he necessity of teachers training.
- By grant-in-aid system many schools were benefited and it

also led to opening of new schools. It helped the expansion of education.

- Teachers training were opened in various provisions.
- It revived the necessity of women education.
- It emphasized the necessity of vocational education. So arrangements were made for the same. Thus, the public got an opportunity for becoming self-dependent.
- It proved to be a strong foundation of structure of education in the country.
- It is the basis of all future reforms in education.

Demerits/Defects

- Theoretically the dispatch provided a wide outlook on education. But in practice education remained a means for earning a livelihood. Thus, the dispatch limited the scope of education.
- The dispatch encouraged English, because it had recommended that the newly educated persons into English would be given preference for government services. Thus one had English schools were opened and on the other the development of indigenous schools was hampered.
- Department of educations, educational officers-provinces. As a result education was caught in he net of mechanical government control. So the flexibility was lost in education.
- Religious education discouraged the dispatch. This was great get back to Indian culture and to the development of spiritualism in the country.
- No real vocational education as advocated by dispatch the purpose of vocational education remained to enable Indians to get some services and not to become self-dependent.
- Universities established in British nature and spirit. The Senet were nominated by British East India Company. Government occupied a strict control over the universities. They functioned like some government departments.
- The dispatch had recommended that education should be above communal considerations. But regarding the Christian missionaries the dispatch showed a soft attitude, i.e., free book on Christian religion for school libraries, Christian religious classes after school hours, inspectors should not interfere the working of school engaged in imparting Christian religious education.

Education Under the British Administration, 1857-1947

In 1857, the 1st struggle for Indian independence took place and it put an end to the administration of British East India Company. The British parliament took over the reins of administration in India.

Hunter Commission/Indian Education Commission, 1882

On February 3, 1882 Lord Rippon came to India. He appointed the First Indian Education Commission, with Mr. William Hunter, a member of the Viceroy's Executive council as the chairman.

Aims

- to assess the position of primary education and to give suggestions for its reforms.
- to evaluate the work of the missionaries in the field of education.
- to find out if the government institutions should be allowed to continue.
- to assess the utility of grant–in–aid system.
- the main purpose of the commission was to study the problem of primary education and to suggest measures for its reforms.

But the Commission also choose to look in to the affairs relating to secondary and higher education.

The Commission had 21 members including 7 Indians. It worked for 10 months and produced a report of 700 pages. Commissions made several sitting, the whole country. It obtained more than 300 suggestions from various groups of persons.

Recommendations

Policy for Primary Education

- Primary education should aim not only preparing the students to enter in to higher education. But it should aim at spreading public education all right.
- It should be useful for general life of the people at large.
- Teaching of subjects that will enable the student to stand on his legs and will also be helpful for him in his practical life.
- The medium should be vernaculars/Indian languages.

Curriculum: The organization of the curriculum left to provisional governments with suggestion that they should organize the same in their respective areas according to the needs of the locally concerned. But, subjects useful for life should be incorporated in the curriculum. Agriculture, physics, trigonometry, geography, medicine and accountancy should be included the curriculum.

Financial Administration: The local budget should invest in education and provincial government should give one-third or one half as aid to the local government. Remaining part of the local budget collect through, school fees and other sources.

Establishment of Training Institutions

It recommended the opening an adequate number of *normal schools* for the training of teachers.

Indigenous Education: Indigenous institutions or *pathashalas* that are run by Indians according to Indian traditions of education. Following suggestions regard them:

- The government should encourage such institutions.
- The government shouldn't interfere in their curriculum in any way.
- The government should special financial aid for inclusion of subject of practical value in the curriculum of these institutions.
- Poor students in these institutions should be given stipends and scholarships.

Secondary Education: *Expansion*—Government should entrust the responsibility of secondary education wholly to the Indians and should only give financial grants for removing certain difficulties (grant-in-aid).

Curriculum, should split up into two literary and science:

1. A curriculum—subject that were to be useful for higher study
2. B curriculum—vocational, occupational and practical subjects.

Higher Education

1. The number of the teachers, expenditure of the college, efficiency and local needs must also kept in mind while giving grants-in-aid to colleges.
2. Non-recurring or special grants may be given to the colleges for establishing furnished library and other educational equipments, if needed.
3. Varied and vast curricula should be arranged in these

colleges so that the students must have the subjects of their choice and aptitude.

4. Meritorious and promising students may be sent to foreign countries for higher education on government scholarships.
5. To raise the moral standards of the students such books should be compiled which may contain the principles of human religion at large.
6. The number students receiving free education should be limited.
7. As compared to government colleges, private colleges should be authorized to receive lesser fee.
8. While appointing teachers such Indians should be preferred who have received education in European universities.

System of Grant-in-Aid

- Managers of private institutions must be consulted while reforming the males in regard to grant-in-aid system.
- The rules should be translated in vernacular and their copies must sent to the managers of aided institutions.
- No interference should be made in the internal administration of the aided institutions.
- Institutions situated in the backward areas or such institutions that lack resources must be given grant-in-aid.
- Special educational officers should be appointed to give counsel to the managers of government aided institution.

Education Department

- The number of inspectors in every province should be raised so that every institution may be inspected.
- Indians should be appointed on the post of district inspectors of schools as far as possible.
- The inspectors of the primary school should be local as far as possible.

Education of Women

Commission felt the Pained and pitiable condition of the women education of that time. Based on that Commission recommended:

- Arrangement of public funds.
- Curriculum for girls should be different from that boys.
- Lady inspectresses for girls schools.
- Decent arrangements of the hostels.

- Special arrangement for education of *parda* observing ladies.
- Only lady teachers should be appointed in girls schools.

Muslim Education

The Commission felt that the education of the Muslims was not getting sufficient and proper attention. The indigenous Muslim schools should be encouraged in the localities where Muslims are in majority, the teaching of Hindustani (Urdu) and Persian should be given:

- Muslims should be given a proportionate representation in the government appointment.
- Normal schools should be opened for training of Muslim teachers.
- For Muslim schools, Muslim inspectors should be appointed.

Education of Harijans, Backward Classes, Aboriginals and Hill Tribes

- All schools run by the government, municipalities and local boards, should be directed to admit children of Harijan and backward.
- Special schools should be opened for them places where an objection is raised to the admission of these harijans and backward.
- School teachers and inspectors make judicious efforts to remove caste prejudices.
- Children of these tribes may not be charged any fee.

Religious Education of any sort should not be given in the public schools, religious education may be imparted in the private institutions and government shall have nothing to do with it.

- While giving grant-in-aid to institutions imparting religious education, attention should be paid to their teaching work only.

Criticism

- Encouraged private enterprises, this helped development of education in the country.
- Indian languages were neglected.
- Inspectorate interfere in the working of institutions without any resultant responsibility for their improvement.

Indian University Commission, 1902

In 1899, Lord Curzon was appointed Governor-General of India. He toured Asia from 1882 to February, 1885 prior to the appointment and got amble opportunity to study geographical conditions and the importance of India. Therefore, when he become governor-general, it was natural for him to make certain fundamental reforms in the Indian administrative set-up. The work that he accompanied in his seven years rule, would have taken decades for others to perform. With in the short period Curzon paid attention to each every aspect of administration. At this time the wave of nationalism flowing fast. Social reformers demanding national education.

Curzon convened a conference with himself in the chair with the view to reform Indian education. Education Directors from every province and representations of Christian missionaries were invited in the conference. It continued for 15 days and considered every aspect of Indian education from primary to university. It's is known as *Simla Education Conference* (1901).

In accordance with his education policy declared at Simla Conference, Curzon appointed Indian University Commission headed by Raleigh, one of the members of his executive council. It is also called 'Secret Education Commission' because there was not a single Indian in the Commission.

Terms of Reference

- To survey future prospects and the conditions of the universities in India established by the British Government.
- To suggest ways and means for the organization and working of Indian universities.
- To lay down the procedures by which the standards of higher education may go up at the earliest.

Suggestions

The commission visited various universities:

1. The senate and syndicate should be re-organized. The members of the senate and syndicate should be reduced to 9 and 15 respectively and term should be 5 years.
2. Certain facilities for teaching should be given after amending the constitution of the universities.
3. There should be a suitable representation of the teachers and the scholars of the affiliated colleges in the university senate.
4. The rules for recognition should be strictly observed and enforced.

5. Affiliated colleges should be strictly supervised by the universities.
6. Universities should appoint teachers to impart higher education.
7. Suitable amendments should be made in the curriculum and the exam system of the universities.
8. Hostels should be built for the students.
9. Arrangements for scholarships should be take place according to the position of the students.
10. There should be a managing committee for every college. It should appoint competent teachers, pay attention towards the discipline and construction of buildings and hostels etc.
11. Standard of matric exam should be high. Intermediate course should be stopped. B.A. degree should be of three years.

Commission observed, "The purpose of education in India is not to receive education but to pass exam."

Evaluation

Indians thought that wanted to suppress nationalism. There was no representation of any Indian in the commission though later on Dr. Gurdas Banerjee and Syed Hasan Bilgrami were made members. At this time, the wave of nationalism was flowing fast. Some able and scarifying social reformers demanding 'National Education'.

On the basis of Indian Education Commission (1902) Lord Curzon decided to frame the educational policy of state. An Education Act was put forward on 11th March, 1904. This later became a law.

Calcutta University Commission/Sadler Commission, 1917-1919

Background: Movement of Liberation

Curzon's policy of *divide and rule* and the consequent impetus to the national struggle for independence gave birth to the realization that our country needed a nationalist education. At the Calcutta Conference of Indian National Congress in 1906, Annie Basant declared that, throughout the country a national education should be organized. In 1910, Gopala Krishna Gokhale put forwarded a proposal for free and compulsory education (Gokhale's Bills, 1910) but he withdrew it when the government assured that such a scheme would be implemented.

The appointment of the Commission was proposed in 1914. But due to the outbreak of the First World War it could not be possible. Proposed Chairman Lord Haildon had refused to head it. The government too concentrated its attention and energy over the war. However, the Government had become keen to find out the defects in the educational system and felt necessity to do something for education in order to pacify the public.

The First World War (1914) had a detrimental impact upon education. After its conclusion government appointed the Calcutta University Commission (1917). The Commission was appointed on September 14, 1917 under the chairmanship of Dr. Michail Sadler, The Vice-Chancellor of Leeds University England, it had six members, Dr. Gregory, Prof: Ransay Muir, Sir Hartog, Mr. Horniel, Dr. Zia Uddin Ahmed and Sir Austosh Mukherji.

Aims of the Commission

It was mainly concerned with the problem of Calcutta University, yet in its report it deals with different aspects of education. It made recommendation in regard to university, secondary, women, professional education. It also recommended the establishment of an inter-college council. Whose developed from these the University Grants Commission (UGC) of today.

Recommendations

Secondary Education

- Secondary and higher education are interlinked. Secondary education is the main prop of higher education. It is not possible to bring about revolutionary changes in the field of higher education without making far reaching changes in secondary education.
- Admission to the university should take place after intermediate stage and not after the matriculation as was done at that time.
- Intermediate (higher secondary) should be separated from university education.
- A three years degree course should be instituted.
- Tutorial classes and seminars should be provided in higher education.
- Instructions should be given in medicine, engineering, agriculture, commerce, education, science and arts.

- Adequate provision of finances should be made for efficient running of secondary education.
- There should be diversification of curriculum.
- Vernacular should be the medium of instruction through out the high schools, except the teaching of English and Maths.
- A board of secondary and intermediate education should be established in each province for curriculum construction and exam conducting. It must be autonomous and free from official interference.
- Classes of intermediate stage should be small so that the teacher and the boys may come in close contact with each other.

Higher or University Education

- Government control of the universities should be less and flexible.
- University teachers should be appointed by Selection Committees constituted specially for the purpose.
- In the place of Senate and Syndicate there should be court and executive council for the management of the university.
- An academic council should be set-up.
- Degree course was to be of three years.
- Honors course as distinct from the pass course should be introduced.
- Provisions should be made for imparting instructions in engineering education, medicine, law, agriculture and technological courses.
- Closer co-operation should be maintained between college and universities, two types of colleges may be established – firstly, such affiliated colleges that are situated outside the area of university and secondly, the colleges are situated with in the specified radius of the university.
- The commission recommended that the oriental studies should be cultivated in the university.

Recommendations About Calcutta University

- There had been a tremendous race in the number of students at the Calcutta University and it was not possible for the university to manage this number efficiently.

- Teaching resources of the Calcutta University should be re-organized.
- There was a good deal of rise in the number of colleges in the neighbouring areas of sub-urbans of Calcutta. Therefore, Muffassil colleges should be developed in such a way that there may be gradual rise of new university centres.

Recommendations for Training of Teachers

- The number of trained teachers should be increased without any delay.
- Education should be made subject of study at the intermediate and BA exams.
- Department of Education should be created at the universities of Calcutta and Dacca.

Recommendations for Education for Women

- The government should start *Parda* schools for those girls who parents have desire to educate their daughters upto the age of 15-16.
- Co-education should be encourage at such places where there were no separate institution for the girls.
- Special provisions for the training of women teachers should be made.
- Provision should be made for medical courses for women.

Recommendations for Technological, Professional and Vocational Education

- The Commission felt that education should not only prepare the boys for government post, it should also encourage them to have technological and vocational education.
- Applied sciences and other allied subjects should be included in the university courses and proper arrangement should be also made for their teaching.
- Courses of intermediate colleges should be revised and given a vocational base.
- Professional and vocational course should be introduced in the universities.

Inter-University Board

In order to establish coordination in the working of various Indian universities, Sadler recommended the establishment of inter-university board. On the basis of the report arrangement for constituent colleges, incorporated colleges, professors, readers, court, academic council, etc., were made Indian universities.

Though the report was influenced primarily for the Calcutta University, it came to the influence the structure of universities of Mysore, Patna, Banarus, Aligarh, Dacca, Lucknow and Hydrabad. After the establishment of Allahabad University in 1887, no new universities was opened for next 30 years. But the number of colleges increased. It is beyond the control of these universities. Sadler emphasized the necessity of opening new universities.

Table–5.1
Higher and University Education, 1917

Sl. No.	*University*	*Affiliated Colleges*	*Number of Students*
1.	Calcutta	58	28,618
2.	Madras	53	10,216
3.	Allahabad	33	7,807
4.	Punjab	24	6,558
5.	Bombay	17	8,001
	Total	**185**	**61,200**

Hence, efforts were made to open some new universities during the period, i.e. :

1. Mysore University (1966) it ceased the situation of Madras university.
2. Patna University (1917) for higher education of Orissa and Bihar.
3. Banarus Hindu University (1916) Madan Mohan Malavia did admirable work on the establishment of BHU.
4. Aligarh Muslim University founded by Sir Sayyid Ahmed Khan.
5. Lucknow University (1921) Sir Har Court-Butler and Talukdars of Avanth take initiative.
6. Dacca University (1920) (now in Bangladesh since 1971).
7. Osmania University (1980) (Urdu medium, founded by Hyderabad Nizam).
8. Allahabad University 1921 (purely residential university).
9. Lady Hardinge College, Delhi 1916 (for medical education of women).

10. SNDT school Poona.

Conclusion and Evaluation

It gave out recommendations which were of great value to the higher education in India as a whole.

Changes in Universities: The recommendations of the commission were accepted by the Government. Reforms and changes were introduced in the universities of India. They now become centres of teaching and research, not just exam centres.

Important of Vocational Courses: The recommendations in regard to the instruction of technological, professional, vocational courses did a lot of service to the country.

Historical Value: The Commission accomplished a historical task. It has been the source of great inspiration to higher education in India.

Criticism

The Commissions recommendations were severally criticized by many educationists of the day. The recommendation in regard to the establishment of unitary residential teaching universities was not in consonants with the financial resources of Government of India.

Hartog Committee, 1929

Background

When British Government made India an ally in the Second World War, it promised to give freedom to the nation. But when the War came to an end the British Government didn't give their promise. This made Indians unrest. Inorder to meet the situation, government passed Government of India Act, 1919 creating a diarchy. After Second World War Government of India had to bow down to the popular will. It made serious attempts to convince the people of India that they wanted to the transfer power to India and make it a free country. With this aim in view, Montague—Chemsford report formulated Government of India Act, 1919. It was passed by Parliament in 1921. It introduced diarchy in province. Subjects of administration divided into two. Education was transferred to representatives of people, rights within a limited sphere. Finance was kept back as reserved subjects. Without finance education couldn't proceed. This created problems and a difficult situation for the progress of education. Diarchy didn't prove successful in India. A lot of criticism was levelled against it.

Simon Commission and Hartog Committee

Seeing the dissatisfaction of the Indian people about the Government of India Act, 1999 Simon Commission was appointed on November 8, 1927 to enquire in to the working of administration under Government of India Act, 1919. In order to satisfy the Indian people it was felt necessary to give due importance to education in India. With this aim in view, Simon Commission appointed an auxiliary committee under the chairmanship of one its members, named Sir Philip Hartog to inquire into the condition of education in India.

Sir Philip Hartog, had served as a member of Sadler Commission. He was the Vice-Chancellor of Dacca University. The Committee gave suggestions for reforms of education, at all levels.

Findings and Revelations: Hartog Committee inquired into all the aspects of education in India. It presented report in September 1929. It was valuable in the sense that it tried to feel the pulse of education in India.

Terms of Reference: The Committee was appointed to inquire the organization of various aspects of education in India and gave out its suggestions for its overall improvement and progress.

Recommendations – Primary Education

After pointing out the defects – wastage and stagnation in the field primary education – Hartog Committee put forwarded its recommendations.

Defects of Primary Education

1. Difficulties in the path of progress.
   - Rural problem, i.e., in our population 70 percentage of people living in villages. Therefore, primary education is more a rural problem than a urban one.
   - Poverty, illiteracy and conservatism – villagers do not appreciate the advantages of education. They are unwilling to send their children to schools due to conservation and economic reason.
2. Unfavourable Circumstances
   - For the convenience of the villagers it is necessary to have atleast one primary schools in every village.
3. Ill Health
   - poor hygienic conditions, epidemic, seasonal illness, casteism, religious barriers and communal feelings.

4. Wastage and Stagnation
   - Wastage meant the premature withdrawal of children from schools at any stage before the completion of the primary course. Retention in lower class of a child for a period more than what was needed for that class.

Causes of Wastage and Stagnation are illiteracy, poverty, lack of trained teachers, insufficiency of inspectors, unscientific and stereotype method of teaching, lack of regularity, defects of education act, unsatisfactory distribution of schools and large areas without a school.

Recommendations

- Planning to make primary education compulsory.
- Government inspection and control.
- Qualitative development instead of increasing number of schools.
- At least four years duration for primary education.
- Time-table of this schools should be drawn up in accordance with the environment and circumstances of the schools.
- Elimination of bad school.
- Liberal and scientific and practical curriculum.
- Reduction of wastage of stagnation.
- Centre for rural welfare-primary school should serve as centres for rural uplift works, medical relief, adult education, mass literacy, sanitation and recreation etc.
- Standard of teachers should be improved, refresher courses and attractive salary much offered to them.

Evaluation

The recommendations were welcomed by the officials. The Indian didn't appreciate them. According to Indian leaders expansion was more needed than consolidation. The Government continued the policy of consolidation. The idea of compulsory primary education was side tracked.

Secondary Education

Defects

- Examination oriented.
- A lot failures at matriculation level.

Recommendations

- Remodelling of middle vernacular exams—even after reaching that standard of education boys couldn't do anything of practical value in life.
- Industrial and commercial courses—the student should be encouraged to offer this courses as they would be great help in practical life.
- Alternative courses—it would help the student to choose the courses of their choice and according to their aptitude.
- Middle stage examination—exams should be held at the completion of the middle stage of the Anglo-vernacular course. If boys could be drafted into a line of study, suited to their talents and aptitudes on the basis of the result. Those who not have any aptitude for study could be drafted into life.
- Improvement of training colleges—the Committee recommended the improvements in the quality of training colleges—modern method should be employed-refresher courses should be organized.
- Better working condition for teacher—the salaries and services conditions of the teachers should improved so as to attract really capable persons to the job.
- Security of job—the Committee found that there was no security of service for the teachers. There was no provision for contracts. The service of the teacher's could be dispensed with short notices. The Committee recommended the removal of such evils for the improvement of secondary education.

Evaluation

- Emphasis of industrial/commercial subjects help to making a provision for the students to take up practical occupations.
- Lying a hand on the pitiable condition of the teachers.
- No education can be successful unless the teachers are well paid and enjoy the security of the tenure.

Higher Education

Defects

- *Low Standards:* Number of universities increased, but their standards had go down. Due to the low standards of the exams Calcutta University attracted students from distant parts of India as far as Travancore in South.

- *Defect of Purpose:* Commission observed, "Graduate on leaving the college is only too often a man with wide or living intellectual interest, with no discipline or experience the world of art, with no training in leadership and with little sense of his responsibility to others." The main aim of higher education is inculcate a taste for learning in the students and it prepare right type of men for the society. Higher education had failed to achieve the purpose.
- *Unhealthy Competition:* Commission felt that there is a unhealthy competition between the universities. Hence, they paid more attention to increasing the number of students than raising/improving the standards of education.
- *Overcrowding:* Most of the universities were overcrowded.
- *Lack of Balance:* The activities of universities and colleges were not well-balanced. The atmosphere there in was only partially developed to the able put for the right type of leaders needed by the country. It had failed to develop corporate life amongst the students.
- *Neglect of Honour's Courses:* The university didn't have properly organized Honour's course. This led to an unbalanced growth in the field of education.
- Wastage, in the field of higher education leads to exam results were poor. Therefore, the universities and the affiliated colleges were causing a good deal of wastage of money spent on higher education.
- *Low Standard of English*: Many of the students are unable to follow lectures, owing to their defective knowledge to English, which is used as the medium of instruction and the mischief is not limited to the universities, for universities standards rest upon those of the secondary schools, which feed them.
- *Inadequate Libraries:* There were also not very well-equipped and rich libraries in the universities that are very much needed for higher education.

Recommendations

- *Unitary as Well as Affiliated Universities:* For a country like India unitary university alone cannot meet the requirements of higher education. Therefore, the Committee recommended establishment of affiliated universities along with unitary, residential and teaching universities. The teachers of affiliated colleges should be appointed by the universities. This procedure will raise the standards of education.

- *Libraries:* Each universities should provide and maintain library. There should be a well-equipped central library in order to enable teachers to keep themselves up-to-date the field of education.
- *Raise in the Standards of Secondary Exams:* In order to raise the standard of university education, the standard of secondary education/examination should be raised.
- *Improvement of University Work:* In the interest university education efforts should be concentrated on improving the university work, on confining the universities to the proper function of giving good advanced education to students who are receive it.
- Provision for Honour's course should be make separate from pass course. It should be taught at the few universities selected for the purpose. In the teachers of the colleges and the universities should put in joint efforts in collaboration and coordination with each other for the successful working of these course.
- *Employment:* Graduates shouldn't suffer from unemployment. Technical training should be developed to check this evil. Universities should also open employment bureau to help the students to get suitable job.
- *Mass Dissemination of Knowledge:* It is the prime duty of universities. The universities should aim at spreading social and political consciousness in the masses at large. They should organize extension lectures inorder to educate the pupil at large.
- *Examination for Administrative Services:* Departmental exams should be held to recruit the graduates in the administrative services.
- *Restricted Admission:* Restrictions should be imposed on admission universities. The standard of university education should be raised. The job in universities should become a noble one.
- *Technological and Vocational Education:* Committee suggested for the establishment of technological, occupational

institutions. Provision for technological and industrial education should be made in the universities as well.

- *Education of Harijans:* Harijans should receive education along with other caste Hindu and not in separate schools.

Education of Women

- Equal importance should be given to women education: for boys and girls equal amount should spent on both. No partiality, no discrimination, no neglection based on gender.
- Every province should appoint experienced and educated ladies to draw plans for the expansion of women education.
- Ladies should be given representation in all the local bodies and the educational bodies.
- More primary schools for the girls should be established in rural areas were convenient, girls should also be allowed to study in the schools meant for boys.
- Arrangement for higher education of the girls, should be made even in rural areas and small towns.
- In the secondary classes the curriculum for girls should be different from that of boys.
- The girls should be taught Home Science, Hygiene, Music, etc.
- Efforts should be made towards encouraging women to take up higher occupational and industrial education.
- Greater attention should be paid towards the training of women. This would produce sufficient number of trained ladies who could take up teaching jobs.
- The number of inspecting staff should be raised.
- Education of the girls at primary level should be gradually made compulsory.
- Priority should be given the education of women.

Education of Muslims

- Government should pay greater attention to the education of Muslims as they educationally backward.
- The establishment of separate institutions for Muslims has created segregation. Therefore, Muslims should be given education in schools meant for other people as well.

Evaluation and Conclusion

Hartog Committee threw light on the main problems of education in India. In the words of Noorullah and Naik, "The report of the Hartog

Committee, however came as a triumph of the official view for it attempted to show that the policy of expansion had proved ineffective and wasteful and that a policy of consolidation alone was suited to Indian conditions.....on the other hand, the non-official view, in general, gave a cold and hostile response to the Hartog Committee."

Abbot-Wood Report, 1936

Background

A Central Advisory Board of Education (CABE) in India had been established in 1921. It was disbanded due to financial difficulties. It was revived in 1935 as a result of Hartog Committee report. At its first meeting it recommended that technical and vocational education should be imparted along with the education of liberal arts. In order to have a comprehensive view of the problem, a committee with Wood and Abbot—the two educationists of England was formed. Mr. Messrs Wood (Director of Intelligence, Board of Education, England) and Mr. Abbot (Chief Inspector of Technical Schools, Board of Education, England) are came to India in the winter of 1936 by the invitation of Government of India. They tour only Punjab, Delhi, United Provinces of Agra and Oudh (UP). The committee submit its report in 1936 itself. This report had two parts. First deals with the General Education and second Vocational Education and Its Organization.

Recommendations—General Education

- Primary education should put into the hands of the trained women teachers.
- Secondary and university education, 3+3 years each.
- Curriculum must organize on scientific basis, rural curriculum should be related on the environment of the educand.
- Teaching of English and vernacular—the medium of instruction throughout highschools should be some Hindustani language, however English should be a compulsory language for all the pupils in these schools.
- Creative manual works should be the subject of study in every school.
- Training of teachers should be consist of two stages. First, pre-employment preparation in the normal school/ training

college. Second, systematic/short time training for experienced teachers.

- Teaching of art: greater attention should be paid on teaching of art.
- Physical education is not just end with physical training and games, it must be creative.
- Committee recommended inspection and control over the institutions.

Vocational Education

- Committee found that there was a problem of unemployment in India, which needed solution in a scientific manner. They therefore recommended reconstruction of educational system.
- Purpose of vocational education: industrial needs, employment
- Importance of vocational education: "If general education brings about the development of the non-material culture of a country, Vocational education does the same thing for material culture."
- Separate institutions should be established for vocational education.
- People in cottage industries should be given proper training. So that heavy industries may not harm them.
- An advisory council for vocational education should be established in each province in order to establish a close co-ordination between industry and education.
- Trade school should be established to vocational education. They are two types – First, the junior vocational schools, i.e., three years course after 8th standard. Second, the senior vocation schools, i.e., two years course after 11th standard.
- Part time vocational school for men in service – two and half days per week.
- Arrangement for teaching of agriculture should be made.
- Junior/senior technical schools should be established in industrial zones only.
- Vocational guidance should be given to students, to choose a vocation to fit in with their aptitudes.

Conclusion and Evaluation

- *Hurriedly Written*: Wood and Abbot were educationists of

eminence but they didn't get ample time to make thorough survey on education. They wrote out report hurriedly.

- *Valuable Suggestions:* Inspite of its being hurriedly written the report contains very valuable suggestions.

Sergeant Report, 1944

In the post war period the attention of Government of India was drawn towards the plan for development of Indian life in its various phases. To meet the requirements, the reconstruction committee of the officers of executive council deputed John Sergeant, the Education Advisor of the Government of India to draw up a memorandum for the development of Indian education in the post-war reconstruction period. He submitted his memorandum before Central Advisory Board of Education (CABE) in 1944. The scheme was known as 'Sergeant Scheme of Education'/report by CABE/post-war educational development in India. This was the first report that prescribed a comprehensive picture of education in India. The CABE accepted this report and recommended its implementation through out the country. This report consists 12 chapters. Here we only made hints of some more important areas.

- Compulsory and free and free education should be provided to all the boys and girls within the range 6-14 years of age. Their education sub-divided into two groups:
  - Junior basic—6-10 years.
  - Senior basic—11-14 years.
- Pre-primary basic schools should be opened children between 3-6 years. In these schools good manners and social knowledge should be taught.
- For bright children between 11-17 years of age, high schools should be open with six years curriculum. Which should be sub-divided into two parts:
  - literary high—school: Indian languages, mother tongue, English, social science, mathematics, general science, agriculture and music.
  - Vocational high school—vocational, commercial subjects, wood work, metal work, engineering subjects, shorthand and typewriting.

In these two types of schools mother tongue should be the medium of instruction and English should be compulsorily taught as a second language. 50 percentage of the students of the schools should be given free education and for encouraging bright children, scholarships should be introduced. Home Science for girls in the place of general science.

- Abolition of intermediate programmes/classes—11th should be added to high school and 12th to first undergraduate programme.
- Establishment of University Grants Commission (UGC) for bringing a uniformity in university education in the country.
- Opening part time and full time school for teaching technical and professional subjects. By these schools four types of workers may be produced. i.e.:
  - *High Class*—For this high school passed students should be admitted to technological department of the university.
  - *Low Class*—Under this category students who have passed vocational high school will be trained for the foremanship and chargemanship.
  - *Skilled Artisans*—Students who have passed the senior high school will be admitted in this type of training for acquiring skilled craftsmanship.
  - *Ordinary Craftsmanship*—Students after passing the class 8th will be admitted for this training in ordinary craftsmanship. After acquiring reasonable proficiency, they will be absorbed in the group of skilled artisans.
- General and vocational education for adults for educating them practical affairs for life.
- The report has emphasized the necessity of able well-trained teachers on the ratio of 1:30 for junior basic and 1:20 for senior basic. The report also observed that trained teachers should be given handsome salaries in order to that able persons might be attracted towards teaching profession.
- *Health of Students:* The Sergeant report paid particular attention to the health of students. For this it recommended periodical checkup and giving information about health principles from time-to-time. Free medical treatment for ill students also been suggested.
- *Special Schools:* Report recommended separate special schools for the dull and handicapped children.
- *Establishment of Employment Exchanges:* The report

emphasized the necessity of establishing employment exchanges for providing suitable employment to students coming out after completing their studies.

- *Recreation Facilities:* The report stressed the necessity for organizing healthy recreation facilities to students.
- *Appointment of Educational Specialists:* The report has recommended the appointment of some education specialists in order that education in the country might be well organized and its standard might be quite high.

Evaluation

The Sergeant report has been the outcome of the experience of the British Government that India was behind in education than other advanced countries of the world.

Merits

- First comprehensive scheme.
- Criticism and suggestions—which contained a thorough study of Indian education and suggestions for its reform.
- Importance to teachers—the committee concerned the salary and condition of teachers.
- Equal opportunities to students— it recommended provision of equal opportunities to all students at various stages of education.
- Education of handicapped also considered.

Demerits

- Copy of British system.
- Not original—it was only the patch work of the recommendations of different commissions and committees.
- Ideals not means—it laid down only ideals to be achieved, but not means to achieve those ideals.

A Critique of the Educational System Under British Rule

The Significance/Merits/Advantages/Virtues

- It brought Indians touch with western knowledge and science.
- This system created social and political awareness in the society.
- It led to scientific development—Ramanujan, Jagadish Chandra Bose and C.V. Raman were famous scientists of this period.

- It inspired the development of literary and cultural consciousness.
- Popular political and social institutions were established.
- It developed national feelings.
- More good than harm.

The view of M.R. Paranjape is that, "This education system was a foreign plant which could not take root suitably in Indian soil."

Defects/Demerits

- This education was contrary to the atmosphere of the country.
- It sought to destroy the national character and qualities.
- Its objectives were vague and undefined.
- It lacked a clear plan for education.
- It was based on and guided by colonialism.
- The nations innate talent could not developed because English was the medium of instruction.
- Local educational institutions were neglected.
- The principle of downward filtration was followed.
- It stimulated communal feelings.
- Education became dependent upon the government.
- Christianity should be worshipped instead of Indian language.

It would be clear that English education which was patterned on the British model and was imposed on Indians had no change for success. The system however gave birth to a new class of intellectuals in India which in its feelings and aspirations was much closer to the English. This system, during the 175 years rule of Britishers in India could educate only 15 percentage of the people.

POST-INDEPENDENT DEVELOPMENTS IN EDUCATION/ EDUCATION IN INDEPENDENT INDIA

The movement of education in India took a significant turn from the fateful night of August 15, 1947. Slaves had finally won independence and in the free air of independence, attention turned towards changes in education, formulation of an educational policy, and the needs of the country. In the early days of independence India's educationist felt that it was not possible to find the right path without altering the structure of education. In the world of ours, founded upon science and technology, it is education alone which determine the level of prosperity, well-being and security of individuals. The success we achieve the task of national reconstruction depends directly upon the qualities of our students emerging from our colleges and universities.

Today, education has undergone multi-faceted growth and progress. In consequence also literacy has increased. The history of education in India took significant turn after independence. Education was given an important priority by the government of India. The stress was on *indianization of education* and making it more purposeful and dynamic. We achieve this through various commission and policies. An overview of the recommendations of these commissions and policies is attempted below:

University Education Commission/ Radhakrishnan Commission (1948-49)

Dr. S. Radhakrishnan born in Sarepally, Nelloor district, Andhra Pradesh, brought in Thiruthani, Tamil Nadu. He start his career as a lecturer in philosophy at Madras Residency College in 1909. In 1918, he was the professor of philosophy in Mysore University and then Calcutta University. He is served as a Vice-Chancellor of Andhra University and Banarus Hindu University. In 1952, he was the Ambassador to USSR, and then Vice-President of India and in 1962 the President of India.

This Commission was appointed under the chairmanship of Dr. S Radhakrishnan, experts from USA and UK were invited to serve this commission. A number of educationists of the country were also made its members. This Commission was appointed through a resolution of the Central Ministry of Education on November 4, 1948. In all there were 10 members of the Commission. The Commission was require to study the problem of University education in the country and to suggest measures for its reforms keeping in view the needs and aspirations of the people. Dr. Abdul Kalam Azad, Minister of Education, inaugurated this Commission on December 6, 1948 and gave it the necessary directions. They visited various universities in the country and studied their varying problems deeply. Interviewed a number of university teachers and students. Prepared and sent a questionnaire and at finally commission submitted its report within a year.

Recommendations

The Aims of University Education

- The aim of the university education should be to produce

able citizens who can take up national responsibilities successfully in various fields.

- It is a duty of the university to preserve and develop the culture and civilization of the land.
- The university should generate the new ideas and discard those which are likely to prevent the growth of the nation.
- The university should provide the opportunities to acquire all kinds of knowledge.
- The university has to educate the mind and soul of the student in order that he may grow in wisdom.
- It is the responsibility of the university to create a consciousness in students for protecting the directive principles of the constitution.
- The university has make new discoveries and invention and it has to develop new original ideas in order to make the society strong.
- The university has to instill moral values in students while making them well-disciplined.
- The university has to develop the spirit of universal brotherhood and internationalism in students.

Teaching Standards

The Commission has attached great importance to high teaching standards.

- Only intermediate passed students should be admitted to universities.
- In every state a good number of intermediate colleges should be opened. If intermediate classes are attached to universities at some places, they should be shifted on separate premises.
- Intermediate class students should be given opportunity for obtaining vocational education.
- A degree college affiliated to a university shouldn't have more than 1500 students in it. Similarly a teaching university shouldn't have more than 3000 students.
- The teachers should prepare their lectures more carefully and they should take special interest in tutorial work.
- No book should be regarded as a textbook and in no course textbook should be prescribed.
- A minimum percentage of lectures should be fixed for students. Students falling below this percentage of attendance shouldn't be allowed to sit at the exam concerned.

- For tutorial work, suitable teachers should be appointed.
- Provision should be made for good libraries and well-equipped science lab.

Teacher's Qualification and Emoluments

The Commission has recognize the importance of good teachers for the sake of high standard of education. For the appointment of suitable teachers for universities, commission recommended enhancement of scale of pay for the teachers.

- The financial condition of the university should be improved and they should be made free from debts.
- The university teachers should be given handsome salaries for relieving them of their economic difficulties. For this purpose the commission recommended scale of pay for various categories of university teachers. That is, professor, reader, lecturer and fellows and instructors.
- Commission also made recommendation related to the pay revision of college teachers.

Post-Graduate Teaching and Research

- A close relationship should be maintain between teachers and research scholars. Admission to PG classes should be governed by all India exams.
- Ph.D scholars should be chosen on all India basis.
- Ph.D scholars producing good research work should be given opportunities for further studies.
- The Education Ministry should grant stipends to those D. Litt and D.Sc. degree holders who have convinced capacities of high order of research.
- D.Litt and D.Sc. degrees should be awarded only on original works.
- Universities should be given adequate financial assistance.

The Curriculum

The Commission has given the following recommendation for re-organizing the university curriculum:

- Knowledge should be considered as one whole, that is integrated approach, subjects doesn't consider as water tight compartments. There should be a connecting bond between the general, intellectual and vocational education.

- The course of studies for universities and intermediate colleges should be reorganized on the above principles.

Professional Education

Vocational education, teachers training, engineering, technical and medical education may included under professional education.

- *Education in Trade in Commerce*: Commerce students should be given practical instruction in institutions of trade and commerce for three or four years. Their education shouldn't be only bookish.
- *Teachers Training*: Greater attention should be paid on practical experience, and less on theoretical. Teachers of training colleges should have enough teaching experience in schools. Higher degree in education should be given to those students who have already taught for a number of years. Teachers of training colleges should do original researches the field of education.
- *Engineering and Technical Education*: Institutions imparting education in engineering and technology should be nationalized. They shouldn't be allowed to be a property of some persons/private sector. More colleges of engineering and technology should be opened in the country. The curriculum of these institutions should be diversified according to the needs of the country. Provision should be made for higher researchers in these institutions. Greater importance should be attached to the acquisition of the practical skill and knowledge in those institutions. Provision should be made in these institutions for special researches for high order in the field of technology. These institutions should be free to manage their own affairs. They shouldn't be controlled by the Ministry or Bureaucracy.
- *Education in Medicine*: Researches should be made in the Ayurvedic and Unani system of medicine and they should be developed. Greater importance should be attached to preventive methods and nursing. Not more than 190 students should be admitted to a medical college within a year and not more than 10 patients should be kept under a student. Institutions for PG medical education should be well-equipped with tools, medicines and experienced teachers. Special training should be given to students for treating patients in rural areas.

Education of Women

- Education of women may be similar to that of men in certain aspects. But it should be different also in some others in view of their different nature and duties of life. Greater facilities should be given for promoting women education.
- Women should be well-informed about their rights and duties pertaining to the society and nation.
- In institutions where co-education prevalent, special facilities should be provided for the women.

Religious Education

- Instruction in each institution should be begun with self-meditation.
- Biographies of great religious leaders of various religions should be taught to the first year students of the UG classes.
- Essentials of all religions should be taught to the second year students of the graduate course.
- The third year students should be taught the essentials of philosophies and problems of religions.

Medium of Instruction in Universities

- India is a land of languages, the various states stand for their own regional languages. The commission studied the difficulties involved in this sphere and has given suggestions for solutions of the language problem.
- Excepting Sanskrit, any Indian languages should replace English as the medium of instruction at earliest. Sanskrit cannot be made the medium as it involves many practical difficulties.
- The students of universities and higher secondary schools should be taught the national language along with English and regional languages.
- Regional language should be the medium of university education. Certain subjects at the university stage should be taught through the medium of national language.
- The national language and the regional languages should be developed.
- A committee of the scholars of all the regional languages should be formed for reconstructing technical terms in sciences.
- Teaching of English should be continued in high schools

and universities in order that the students are acquainted with achievement in other countries.

Students Welfare and Character Formation

The university should protect the interest of students and should develop the physical, intellectual and spiritual capacities of students. For this

- admission should be on merits and scholarships should be given on merits to poor and deserving students.
- sports, gymnasium and games should be organized.
- two years compulsory physical training should be introduced except for NCC cadets and physically handicapped.
- students union made free from politics.

University Examination System

- It should be reformed.
- The Government of India should appoint a committee of experts/educationists for the same.
- An exam board of three members should be constituted in each university.
- *De-linking Degree from Job*: For any government service a university degree shouldn't be considered as essential.
- The exam standard should be raised. The standard should be the same for all universities.

Administration

- The university education should be brought under the concurrent list of states.
- The Central Government should have only limited powers on universities.
- Each university should teach, so the idea of an affiliating university should be rejected.
- A visitor, a Chancellor, Vice-Chancellor, syndicate, faculty, academic council, senate, board of studies, selection committee, finance committee should be appointed in each University.

Finance

- Universities should be given maximum financial assistance in the form of grants-recurring and non-recurring.

- The State Government should shoulder the entire cost of the university education.
- Income tax concessions should be given to those persons an firms which give donations to educational institutions.

Universities in Rural Areas/Rural Universities

- The Commission recommended for the opening of rural universities for meeting the requirements of the people in rural areas.
- Most of universities in India in urban areas. They cater to the needs of only urban people. University education is not patterned on the needs and aspirations of the rural people.

Evaluation

- The Commission has realized that the leaders in the various walks of life in the country have impact of university education on them.
- Commission took into account the entire aspects of university education in the country.

Merits/Highlights

- It made recommendations helpful to harmonize the oriental and occidental cultures.
- Many systems prevalent in the west in the sphere of education were freely adopted without spoiling the spirit of Indian culture.
- Recommendation regarding Establishment of rural universities (70-80% of India people residing in villages).
- Since India is a religious country, the Commission has recognized the necessity of introduction of some kind of religious/moral education in universities, in order to control the violent waves of materials of the present day civilization.
- The Commission rightly perceived the various in adequacies of the existing university education and drew the attention and given suggestions.

Demerits/Limitations

- The Commission's view on religions and moral education was vague and ambiguous.
- Though the commission frankly criticized the defects of the existing system of exam, its suggestions for reform of the system was not at all satisfactory.

- Similarly the suggestions of medium of instruction and established of rural universities didn't prove to be effective.

Secondary Education Commission/Mudaliar Commission, 1952-53

In September 23, 1952, the Government of India appointed the Secondary Education Commission under the chairmanship of Dr. A. Lakshmana Swami Mudaliar, Vice-Chancellor of Madras University. Sri A.N. Basu, was appointed as its secretary.

Members of the Commission toured round the country. The various state governments fully co-operated with the efforts of the Commission. The Commission studied the various problems of secondary education in the country and submitted its report on August 29, 1953 in 240 pages consisting of the chapters.

Scope/Terms of References

To understand the problems to secondary education in India and suggest measures for the reforms of its various aspects, such as aims, curriculum exam, system, teaching methodology, teachers training, building, administration and control.

Defects of the Existing Secondary Education

The Commission has pointed out the following defects in the existing pattern of secondary education. The Commission has grouped the defects in to the following five categories:

- Unpracticalness of secondary education which is not useful in future life.
- Inability of secondary education for effecting all-round development of students.
- Unsuitable medium of instruction, i.e., the mother tongue is not the medium of instruction.
- Absence of practicalness in secondary education. As a result, it is not developing the habit of independent thinking and initiative in students.
- Secondary education is not able to promote good character formation in students.

Recommendations

Aims of Secondary Education

- *To produce ideal citizens:* Commission has realized that no nation can process without a national feeling along with social feeling. Therefore, it has laid down that the aim of secondary education should be to produce such ideal citizens who imbued with strong national and social feeling.

- *To develop capacity for earning money:* After having secondary education one should be able to earn enough for maintaining himself.
- *To develop human virtues:* Man is a social animal. So he should have the spirit of co-operation, discipline, humility, love, kindness, and the feelings of brotherhood. The curriculum must have such subjects which may inculcate these virtues in students. Science, literature, fine arts, humanities, music and dance are some of such subjects.
- *Quality of leadership:* Secondary education should develop the quality of leadership in students.

Duration of Secondary Education

The Commission has recommended that the secondary education should be for children between 11-17 years of age. Secondary education should begin after 4-5 years of primary education.

It had divided this 7 years education in to two:

- Junior/middle secondary/senior basic stage education—3 years–6, 7, 8th classes.
- Higher secondary education—4 years—9, 10, 11 classes.
- 12th class should be added to the 1st UG.
- Commission suggested abolition of intermediate colleges.

Curriculum

Multi-purpose Schools—To open multi-purpose schools according to the varying needs/interests of students. Multi-purpose schools means, schools offer courses in agriculture, industry, fisheries, finance, along with traditional subjects.

- The multi-purpose schools should be opened near the industrial zones/institutions. The students of these two types of institutions should learn from each other.
- They should provide terminal courses in Technical, Commerce, Agriculture, Fine Arts and Home Science.
- The aim was to divert the students to different vocations at the end of the secondary course.

According to the Commission, the existing curriculum was narrow, overcrowded, bookish and exam dominated. The curriculum must be flexible, elastic and related to the needs of community.

- Agriculture should be made a compulsory subject for schools in village.
- Home Science should be made compulsory for girls and other subjects should be common for both boys and girls.

Diversification of Courses

- *Middle Secondary*—languages, General Science, Social Science and a Craft are Core subjects.
- *Higher Secondary*—11 groups of optional subjects coming under Humanities, Science, Technical subjects, Agriculture, Fine Arts and Home Science. The university education is based on these optional subjects.

Medium of Instruction—Three Language Formula

The *mother tongue/regional language* (regional language when it is not the mother tongue)/*state language* should be made the medium of instruction, throughout the secondary stage.

English and Hindi (Devanagari script) should be introduced at the end of the junior basic stage. While teaching these languages, it should be kept in view that the teaching of both these languages shouldn't start in the same year.

Thus, Hindi and English are recommended as compulsory subject of study at the secondary stage.

Selection of Textbooks

The Commission has opened that text-books should be selected on the basis of their merits and utility. For this purpose, the commission has recommended the appointment of a high power committee.

1. A High Court Judge.
2. A member of Public Service Commission.
3. A Vice-Chancellor of a University.
4. A Principal of Some Government Educational Institutions.
5. Two eminent educationists and the Director of Education of the State.

Character Formation

Character formation is important aim of secondary education. This is useful not only for the individual but also for the nation.

In fact, the character of the nation is reflected by the character of its citizens.

Teaching Method

For improving the standard of teaching the commission has suggested that the Central Government should appoint a committee of experts which should make research for finding out ways and means for improving the teaching methods.

Health Education

All the students should be medically examined at least twice a year.

- Full medical facilities should be available for students.
- They should be given knowledge or health principles also.

Improvement of Teachers Status

- Trained teachers should be appointed to teach higher classes.
- Teachers should be given Pension, Provident Fund, and Life Insurance benefits in order to give them some economic security.
- The retirement age for teachers should be 60 years.
- The children of teachers should be given free education.
- Teachers and their dependents should be given free medical service.
- The teachers should not be permitted to take up tuition of students.

Training and Qualification of Teachers

The Commission has suggested that for junior classes at least higher secondary and for senior classes at least graduate teachers should be appointed. These teachers should be given two years training.

Management and Administration of Secondary Schools

- A board of teachers training should be established.
- Central and state committees should be organized for giving advice on secondary education.
- The district inspector of schools shouldn't only find faults with teachers but should also assist them in performance of their duties.
- The State Government should organize a committee for management and administration of schools. This should responsible for management and administration but it must not interfere with the work of the principal.

Finance

- The Central Government should give financial aid to states for education.
- The donations to educational institution should be exempted from income tax.
- No Octroi and toll tax should be levied on goods purchased for educational institutions.

Duration of Session and Leave

- The school should be opened at least 200 days per year.
- The schools in rural areas should be closed at least for 7 days at the time of sowing and harvesting, in order that the students may help their family in agricultural pursuits.
- The number of holidays should be reduced.
- The least 35 hours should be devoted for teaching per week.
- The principal should be empowered to decide, about local holidays and school hours.

Arrangement of Buildings

- School building should away from the noise of cities.
- The school building should be adequately ventilated.
- A class shouldn't consist of more than 40 students.
- Each school should be proper desks, chairs.
- There should be a well-equipped reading room.
- Each school should have a big hall where all the students may assemble for some group programme. This should decorated with pictures of national leaders.

Guidance and Counselling

Commission pointed out the need for guidance and counselling in secondary schools. All schools should have trained guidance officers and career masters.

Examination Reforms

Regarding examination, the Commission recommended that more credit (importance/allotment) should be given to internal tests and cumulative records. The final evaluation should be based on both the internal and external assessment and given importance to student profile.

Evaluation – Highlights/Merits/Advantages

- The diversification of courses was a realistic approach to the problems of education.

- The opening of multi-purpose schools was quite in tune with the needs of the times.
- The guidance and counselling programme was an innovative one.
- Suggestion regarding school building and duties of the inspector of schools are also healthy.

Demerits

- Specialization in secondary stage itself is not desirable.
- How can a High Court Judge uses the suitability of a textbook for schools?
- The Commissions suggestion regarding the high power committee for selecting textbooks is ridiculous and unrealistic.
- The Commission not chosen to pay adequate attention, on the various aspects of women education and religions education.
- According to some critics, it lacks originality and it is nothing but "old wine in new bottle."
- The three language formula was a burden on students.
- Multi-purpose schools—good idea but in practical side, schools must turn to be factories/laboratories.
- University education is based on optional in secondary education. Therefore, most of them neglect subjects like Agriculture, Art and Music.

Indian Education Commission/Kothari Commission, 1964-66

The various five-year plans started and helped the growth of the country in many areas. Education appeared to be one of areas, which indicated many problems and needed our efforts for immediate solutions. Our government had been conscious of this situation. So it appointed the University Education Commission in 1948, Secondary Education Commission in 1952, for suggesting reforms in education.

The recommendations of these commissions couldn't be implemented in their entirely. Consequently the defects in the area of education persisted.

For removal of these defects the Government of India appointed an Educational Commission in 1964 under the chairmanship of Dr. Daulat Singh Kothari, Chairman of UGC.

Aims of the Commission

To study the various problems of education in the country and suggest measures for their removal. Mohd Karim. Chhagala (Education Minister, Government of India) emphasized the need of determining an educational policy for the country.

Appointment of the Commission and Functions

The Commission was appointed on July 14, 1964 through a resolution of the government.

The Commission started its work on the birth day of the Father of the Nation, October 2.

Members of the commission, D.S. Kothari (Chairman), J.P. Naik (Member Secretary), L.K. Gopala Swami, A.R. Doud, V.S. Jha, K.G. Saiyidain, P.N. Kripal, B.P. Pal, M.V. Mathur, Trigun Sen, S. Pannadhikar, Rojer Revelle (USA), H.A. Elvin (London), Jean Thomas (France), Shumovsky (Moscow) and Sadatoshi Thara (Tokyo).

The Commission appointed 7 working committees and 12 study teams for studying the various problems of education.

The Commission toured round the whole country and studied the various problems involved deeply and submitted its report to the government after 21 months. The Commission has sub-divided its report into 20 chapters, and it submitted to education minister of India on June 29, 1966.

Recommendations

The Commission has asserted that the progress of the country, development of finance, social security and welfare activities can be ensured only through education. Therefore, education should be given highest priority in any scheme of national development.

Commission put forward a national education scheme for the next 20 years. This Commission has given Indian education in a new direction.

The Commission has reflected upon the entire spectrum of education, from its objectives to its economic aspects.

With reference to the prospectus of this Commission, contemporary minister for education, Sh. Mohd Karim Chagla, Said that the prospectus was a kind of *Magna Carter for Teachers*.

Education and National Aims

National aims can be achieved through education alone. The national goals of education are:

- Increase in production.
- Social and national integration.
- Consolidation of democracy.
- Speeding the process of modernization.
- To build character through the development of social and spiritual values.

Educational Structure and Standard

General Education should last for a period of 10 years. 4 years lower primary, 3 years higher primary and 3 years lower secondary. (4+3+3) 2 years higher secondary and 3 years first undergraduate programmes (10+2+3).

Teacher's Status

- It is necessary to improve the economic, social and professional status of the teachers.
- The scale of pay of teacher of government and non-government schools should be the same.
- A suitable increase should be allowed in the scale of the pay of teachers.
- Proper facilities of residence etc., should be provided to the teachers working in rural areas.
- They should be provided proper facilities of receiving education through distance mode.

Teachers Education

- Isolation of teacher's education should be removed and extension service department should be established in each training institution.
- A state board of teachers education should be established in each state, for make proper provision of teachers education at all stages.
- Curriculum must re-organized and become more practical.

Equalization of Educational Opportunities

In India 2 types of inequalities are found in the field of education, i.e.,

1. In the education of boys and girls.
2. In the education of developed and backward classes.

In order to remove these inequalities lower secondary education should be made free. Higher secondary school and university education should be given free to the poor and meritorious students.

There is a need of reducing the cost of education, sufficient number of textbooks should be kept in the libraries of educational institutions.

Expansion of School Education

- School education needs to be greatly expanded.
- By the year 1975-76 and by the year 1895-86 proper provision should be made for primary education of all the boys and girls upto the age of 5 and 7 respectively.
- 20 per cent and 50 per cent of the student at lower secondary stage and higher secondary stage respectively should be given professional education.The number of students should be regulated at this stage.

School Curriculum

Lower Primary Classes (I-IV)

- One language—mother tongue/regional language.
- Mathematics.
- Study of environmental science should be taught in Classes III and IV.
- Creative activities.
- Work experience and Social Service.
- Health Education.

Higher Primary Classes (V-VII)

- 2 languages—
  1. Mother tongue/Regional language,
  2. Hindi/English.
- Mathematics.
- Science.
- Social Science.
- Art.
- Work Experience and Social Service.
- Physical Education.
- Education in Moral and Spiritual values.

Lower Secondary Classes (VIII-X)

- Three languages—Mother tongue, Hindi and English. (In Hindi speaking areas one modern Indian language besides Hindi)
- Mathematics.
- Science.
- History, Geography, Civics.
- Art.
- Work Experience and Social Service.
- Physical Education.
- Education of moral and spiritual values.

Higher Secondary Classes (XI and XII)

- Any 2 languages (one Indian, one modern foreign language)
- Any 3 subjects to be selected from the following subjects.
  - One additional language.
  - History, Geography, Economics, Logic, Psychology, Sociology, Art, Physics, Chemistry, Maths, Biology, Geology, Home Science.
- Work Experience and Social Service.
- Physical education
- Art and crafts
- Education in moral and spiritual values.

Place of Hindi

English will continue to be used as a language of intellectual exchange in higher education. However, English cannot be a medium of exchange of views for the majority of the Indian people.

In the course of time this language will certainly be Hindi. Hence efforts should be made to spread education of Hindi in all parts of the country.

Place of English

English should be used as the medium of instruction in all India Educational Institutions and Universities. The study of English started from the school stage.

Place of Classical Languages

Sanskrit language occupies a special importance and position in the national education system.

School Administration and Supervision

- Provision should be made for common school system of public education.
- Administration should be kept separate to the supervision and teaching.
- The work of supervision should be conducted by the education department.
- A state board of schools should be established in each state.
- A national board of education should be established in the ministry of education in order to advise the government in regard to school education.

Higher Education

- The UGC should develop 6 universities from among the existing universities into major universities where in best type of graduation/international standard.
- Clusters of advance courses should be started in each major universities.
- Regional language should be the medium of pre-graduate and English for PG courses.
- The examiners should not be given any remuneration for examining the answer books.

Education of Agriculture

- Dr. D.S. Kothari, "It is important to observe that in our system of education that is to be given today."
- Each state should have atleast one agricultural university. New universities should be established.
- Agricultural polytechnics should be established.
- Agriculture should be included in the curriculum at primary, secondary and university level.

Vocational, Technical and Engineering Education

Having completed school education, the students, should be provided facilities of short-courses, correspondence courses, and short extensive courses.

- A special provisions should be made for engineering education to the girls.
- Provision should also be made for imparting education in chemical technology, aeronautics and astronautics.

Education of Science

- Study centres should be established for the higher education of science and mathematics.
- The number of students taking such subjects in the University should be increased.
- Famous Indian scientists working foreign countries should be invited to return India.
- Science and Technology should be made an indivisible part of educational system.

Adult Education

- Illiteracy should be ended in all corners of India within a period of 20 years.
- To achieve this, schools should be converted into the centers of community life.
- Comparatively more efforts should be made in the rural areas to end the illiteracy.
- Correspondence courses should be started for the expansion of adult education.
- A network of libraries should be spread throughout the country.
- A national board of adult education should be established for organization and administration of adult education.

Common School System

For the universalization of education the Commission recommended that common school system should be introduced.

Evaluation

With reference to the prospectus of this commission, the contemporary minister for education, Sh. Mohd Karim Chagala, said that the prospectus was a kind of *Magna Karata for Teachers.*

This preface led to many important turning points in the sphere of education.

Highlights

The commission presented a comprehensive study of educational problems in the context of the national needs and aspirations.

Limitations

Many of the recommendations of the commission same as previous commissions. As a result most of the problems of education remain unsolved.

NATIONAL POLICY OF EDUCATION (1968, 1979, 1986, 1990) AND REVIEW COMMITTEES

National Policy of Education (NPE, 1968)

The necessity of national policy of education cannot be over emphasized, as it related to the essential development of a country.

In our country the problem of education has been discussed at great length from time-to-time. Accordingly, certain committees and commissions have been appointed by our government in the past, as we have already detailed out.

But, it has never been possible for the government to implement the recommendations due to adverse circumstances as experienced by those of the helm of affairs.

However, it was in 1968, for the first time, that a NPE was formulated for preparing suitable hands for shouldering responsibilities in the various fields of our national reconstructions.

In 1967, our Central Government appointed a parliamentary committee for formulation of a National Policy of Education (NPE).

On the basis of the recommendations of this committee a NPE was formulated and formally declared in 1968. In this policy following 17 programmes have been included. They are:

Free and Compulsory Education

The primary education should be made free and compulsory for the girls and boys within 14 years of age according to the Clause 45. Wastage and Stagnation should be prevented at this stage.

Improvement should be Effected in the Standard of Teachers, Scale of Pay and Teaching Methods

Due recognition should be accorded to teachers in society. Their salary should be according to their capability and level of training. Facilities should be provided to teachers for free thinking, further studies and research. In service training should be organized for them.

Development and Protection of All the Indian Languages

Regional languages should be developed. The 3-language formula should be implemented. The gulf between the general masses and intellectuals should be bridged through development of regional languages.

Equality of Educational Opportunities

All the classes of people should be given equal educational opportunities. The common school system should be implemented. The feeling of national integration will be strengthened if all the children study together.

Identification of Gifted Children

It is necessary to identify gifted persons in different walks of life. Special provision should be made for education of gifted children.

The Provision of Work Experience and NSS (National Service Scheme)

Due importance should be given to this provision. Opportunities should be provided for participation in co-curricular activities.

Science Education and Research

For the development of the country, science education and research should be duly encouraged. The study of science and mathematics should be made compulsory in the general education upto Class X.

Education in Agriculture and Industries

Priority should be given to these items. For this, at least one agricultural university should be established in each state. A survey of man power and technological and industrial needs should be made from time-to-time.

Production of Books

Textbooks shouldn't be changed very often. Attention should be paid on production of literature for children.

Reform in Examination System

Reliability and validity of exams should be determined. The method of periodical evaluation should be adopted.

Reform in Secondary Education

Facility of secondary education should be made available to the children of all categories... poor and rich, boy and girls, SC & ST.

Some technical and industrial education should be given even at the secondary stage according to the needs of the country.

Education at University Stage

- Admission to university and degree college should be made according to the available library and laboratory and research facilities.
- New universities should be opened only when the required provision for the same, are duly made in advance.

Part-Time Education and Correspondence Curriculum

This may be made at university stage. This facility may be provided to high school passed students, teachers interested in further studies and to the interested workers in various fields.

Expansion of Literacy and Adult Education

- The expansion is necessary for national development and for speeding up production.
- Library services, TV and Radio programme should be suitably modified for this purpose.

Sports and Games

- Attention on physical education is necessary
- Sports and games should be encouraged.
- Special encouragement should be given to good players.

Education of Minorities

Education is necessary for protection of rights of minorities.

Change in the Educational Structure

The 10+2+3 pattern should be adopted through out the country.

National Policy of Education, 1986

NPE (1986) is the continuation of National Policy of Education (1968) and based on the recommendations of Kothari Commission. In 1985, it was decided to review the implementation of National Policy of Education (1968) and to formulate new educational policy. Accordingly a status paper *challenges of education – a policy perspective* launched by Government of India. In this document a comprehensive appraisal of the existing system of education was made. A country-wide debate took place on educational reform in the country.

Finally, on April 20, 1986 a New National Policy of Education was placed before the Indian parliament for consideration and approval.

A Programme Of Action (POA) was also chalked out for the implementation of National Policy of Education.

Main Features

1. *Based on Constitutional Principles:* It derives its inspiration from the ideals and values of democracy, secularism and socialism enshrined in our constitution.
2. *National Form of Education*: At least 75 per cent of the curriculum should be identical for all the states. 25 per cent may be related to the particular local conditions of the state.
3. *More Emphasis on Learning*: The teacher must not harbour the notion that the child learns through his teaching alone. Teacher try to create an environment in the class that the children may learn many things through their own creativeness.
4. *De-linking Degrees for Any Service.*
5. *Vocationalisation of Education:* As far as possible, education should be given in the natural environment. The child must acquire some skill in some area of his interest. National policy of education advocated for inclusion of scientific and technical subjects in the curriculum. Fifty per cent of students at matriculation level should encouraged to study vocational courses, according to their interests. This kind of vocationalization will minimize the unemployment problem.
6. *Importance of Moral Values:* Education is a tool for bringing in desirable changes in a society. Therefore, importance of moral values in life should be pointed out wherever possible in teaching.
7. *Emphasis on Reforms in Examination System*: 'Grade' should be given in exam in the place of 'division'.
8. *Education for the Weaker Section of the Society*: The education of SC/ST Girls, handicapped has been greatly emphasized.
9. *Ever-Continual Primary School*
   - Each primary school will have at least two-room building with at least two teachers. Of these two teachers, one will be a lady.
   - Each primary school will function throughout the 12 months, a year. Thus, all the young children in an area will be receiving primary education.
10. *Importance of Sports and Games:* National policy of education

recognized the importance of sports and games, because participation in them will maintain the health of children.

11. *All India Educational Service:* In order to tone up educational administration, national policy of education has emphasized the necessity of starting an All India Education Service Cadre.
12. *Open University*: National policy of education emphasized starting of open universities.
13. *Right Persons Alone to be Teachers:* This National policy of education has considered the training of teacher as very important for raising/falling standard of education. Therefore, the policy mentioned about, the salaries, residential facilities and refresher courses of the teachers.
14. *New Educational Institutions*: National policy of education 1986 recommended that DIET and 'District of Education' should be established.
15. *Modernization of Education*: For modernizing education, computerization—correspondence courses use of TV, radio-satellite, video cassets must be needed.
16. *Establishment of Navodaya Schools*: Admission to Class VI on the basis of a Test. For admission there should be a predetermined ratio for boys/girls, urban-rural in Navodaya schools. No financial criterion. Hostel facility, Free boarding, lodging must be provided. Twenty per cent of 8th passing transferred for other states, with a view to promote national integration. Three language formula must follow in Navodaya Schools.
17. *Protection of Environment Necessary*: The students and teachers will be urged to protect rivers, lakes, hills, mountains, forests and pasture lands.
18. *Women Education*
    - Standard of women education should be raised.
    - In vocational and technical education women will be assigned their proper place in order to equate them with men as far as possible.
19. *Adult Education*
    - A literacy programme will be organized for making illiterate persons literate with in the age group of 15-35. For this purpose continuing education centres will be established in rural areas.
    - Distance and vocational education will be given/utilize through mass medias.

20. *Early Childhood Care and Education (ECCE)* will receive high priority and it will be integrated with Integrated Child Development Services (ICDS) programme.
21. *Operation Black-Board (OBB)*
    - Minimum facilities will be provided to a primary school with at least 2 rooms, charts, maps, a black-board, carpet and other essential material equipment.
    - In the Operational Black-Board the co-operation of NGO's, local bodies and voluntary organizations will be enlisted.
22. *Minimum Levels of Learning (MLL)* will be laid down for each stage of education.
23. *Link Language* will be promoted.
24. *Preservation of Own Culture*:
    - There appears to be a wide gulf between the modern formal education and our cultural traditions.
    - NPE (1986) wants to bridge this gulf.
    - Our fine arts, Agriculture, and oriental studies must be promoted.

Evaluation

NPE's made an attempt for a national curriculum for the whole country.

- Attention paid on providing equal educational opportunities.
- Accountability of Government of India to teacher education recognized.

Demerits

NPE's are silent on condition of those schools which are run throughout the country on commercial lines by certain persons/bodies.

Conclusion

Based on NPE (1986), Government of India evaluate education well in each 5 years and put directions for future developments.

The NPE (1986) was evaluated by 2 committees:

1. Rama Murthi Committee, 1990.
2. Janardhan Reddi Committee, 1992.

As a result of the recommendation of the same, modifications were made in the NPE in 1992. In 1994, new curriculum introduced.

Prof. Rama Murthi Committee, 1990

In 1990, National Front Government was formed an education committee under the chairmanship of Sarvodaya Leader Prof: Ram Murthi.

- About 17 members also associated.
- The main purpose of the committee was to critically examine the NPE's and suggest new measures for promoting industrialization and development of rural areas of the country.

Committee presented its report in January 1991. Some of the more important points.

Early Childhood Care and Education

- Necessary help should be provided to each primary and middle school.
- The children of the deprived classes should be given special care on priority base.
- The Anganwadi system should be continued.

Education of Scheduled Caste, Tribal Peoples and Educationally Backward

- In the areas where the population of the SC and Tribal people is dense arrangements should be made for informal education.
- Remedial educational provisions for the same.

Universal Elementary Education

The following points regarding Universal Elementary Education as detailed out NPE (1986) have been emphasized:

- Universal enrolment.
- Qualitative improvement.
- To Promote relationship between school and community.
- To encourage decentralization in educational planning and management.

Adult Education

- The purpose of Adult Education should be development of adults.
- Mass movement should be encouraged for Adult Education.

Vocationalization of Education

For students from 9th-12th standard the following model of courses should be accepted:

(a) Optional group,
(b) General core, and
(c) Vocational core.

The students should be given freedom to choose any one group.

The children who not obtained vocational education through formal should be given vocational courses through informal methods.

Higher Education

- University education should be given only to the chosen few.
- Autonomous colleges should be established according to UGC directives.
- The state should establish agricultural universities for rural development.
- For promoting qualitative improvement of teachers, the universities should organize Faculty Improvement Programmes.

Technical and Management Education

- In technical education special attention should be given on lab work.
- Teachers should be selected on all India basis.
- For qualitative promotion of teachers, provisions should be made for study leave and training.
- Residential accommodations should be given both to teachers and students.
- Learning resource centres should be established.

Teacher Education

Findings

- The current teacher education is theoretical.
- This is separate from schools, college and universities.
- The instructions obtained during course are not relevant to the real situations of the schools.
- The emotional aspects of teacher trainees are entirely ignored in training institutions.

- The assessment system is not criterion oriented.

Suggestions

- The training programme should be based on skills.
- More attention should be paid on emotional aspects of trainees.
- The training duration should be made longer.
- It should be experience oriented and based on real situation.
- The curriculum prepared by NCTE should sent to training institution, and it finalize on that base.
- Educational complexes should be established.

Janardhan Reddy Committee Report, 1992

Janardhan Reddy Committee was appointed in 1992 in order to make a detailed examination of the Rama Murthi report under the Central Advisory Board of Education.

Recommendations

Educational Progress of SC, ST, Tribal: The State Government should appoint committees in order to educate SC/ST/Tribal people.

Common School System: Emphasized common school system in order to provide all needed facilities to the neglected backward classes.

A spirit of social accountability should be developed in order to raise the educational level of the backward class.

About Navodaya School

- Navodaya Vidyalayam should be established in all the districts of each and every state and the expenses in this regard should be made by the State Government, with the help of Central Government.
- Supervision must be made each year of Navodaya in order to assess the effectiveness of their working.
- The validity of the method of admission of students and teachers in the Navodaya schools should be critically examined.
- Students and teachers of the Navodaya School alert and conscious of their progress.

Universal Education

- By the beginning of the 21st century the target universal elementary education must be completed.

- Girls of SC/ST/Tribal people should be compulsorily sent to school.
- With in a radius of 1 km there must be at least one primary school.
- The Operation Black Board should be adopted in each and every area.

Adult Education: The Reddy Committee accepted in total the Total Literacy Campaign programme.

Secondary Education: NPE should be revised for making secondary education job oriented. Towards the fulfillment of this goal more optional subjects should be included in secondary schools.

- Special provision should be made to include computer operational training in all schools.
- Like IGNOU some secondary school may also be organized.

Universities and colleges of sub-standard nature must not be allowed to be opened, because this kind of tendency is clearly visible in certain areas of the country.

- State Council of Higher Education should be established in each state in order to check to the above mentioned tendency.
- NCC in universities and colleges should be encouraged.

Central Council of Rural Institutions

This council in each state should look after the educational needs of the rural people according to the Gandhi philosophy of life.

AICTE: Such a council should be appointed by the Central and State Government in order to look after the needs of technical education is respective areas. The approval of technical education will be compulsory.

Examination

- Central and State Governments should make a joint effort regarding examination conducting.
- The load of school bags of children must be reduced.

Teachers Training

- Must not be through correspondence.
- Organization of an educational tribunal.
- An Indian education service should be started, like IAS, IPS.

Financial Provisions: In National Budget, at least, 6 per cent should be given to the provision for education.

- Educational budget directed towards universal elementary education, and adult education.
- The technical and management education programmes should be self-financing enterprises.

Learning Without Burden—Report of the National Advisory Committee Appointed by MHRD

Yashpal Committee (1992-93)

MHRD of Government of India appointed a National Advisory Committee under the chairmanship of Prof: Yashpal (former UGC Chariman) on March 1, 1992.

Terms of Reference

'To advise on the ways and means to reduce the load on school students at all levels particularly the young students while improving quality of learning including capability for lifelong self-learning and skill formation. To doing this the committee may,

1. Examine all aspects related to curricula, entrance criteria and exit attainments at various levels.
2. Look at the impact of examinations, admissions to higher education, institutions including professional courses.

The Committee

Prof: Yashpal (Chairman, former Chairman, UGC), Prof-Krishna Kumar (Central Institute of Education, Delhi University), Prof. T.S. Saraswathi, (Head, Department of Child Development, M.S. University Baroda) Dina Guha (Psychologist, Bombay), Smt. Vibha Parthasathi (Principal, Sardar Patel Vidhyalaya, New Delhi), Dr. V.G. Kulkarni (Director, Homi Bhabha Science Centre, TIFR, Bombay), Prof: Poromesh Acharya (IIM, Calcutta) are the members. Dr. G.L. Arora (Director, SCERT, Delhi) was the member secretary. K.R.P. Singh is the special associate. Padma. M. Sarangapani and Subhasri Datta Sinha are the Research Associates. The secretarial assistance done by Smt. Meena Taneja (Steno, NCERT).

Committee submitted its report on 15th July, 1993 entitled *Learning without Burden*. In its work a large number of teachers, principals, syllabus and textbook constructors, organizations are associated.

Findings of the Committee

1. *The Problem of Curriculum Load*
   Preamble
   - "A lot is taught, but little is learnt or understand."
   - Size and weight of school bag.
   - Physical load and learning load.
   - Middle class children slog through homework, tuitions, coaching classes of different kinds.
   - Leisure has become a highly scarce commodity.
   - No time to play, to enjoy pleasures, to explore the world.
2. *Joyless Learning*
   - 'Covering' the syllabus seems to have become an end.
   - In several states teachers encourage children to attend after-school tuition.
   - Both the teachers an the child have lost the sense of joy.
   - Education as mainly a process of preparing for examinations.
   - Aims of education like 'development of child's total personality' are the shibboleths of teacher training institutions.
3. *Examination System*

   If (exam) focuses on childrens ability to reproduce information to the exclusion of the ability to apply concepts and information on unfamiliar, new problems or simply to think.
4. *Textbook as the 'Truth'*
   - Our textbooks appear to have been written primarily to convey 'information' or 'facts' rather than to make children think and explore.
   - The distance between the child's everyday life and the content of the textbook further accentuates the transformation of knowledge in to a load.
   - Alienation of subject-matter from children's perspective and life.
5. *Language Textbooks*
   - Textbooks are not written from the child's view point. Neither the mode of communication nor the selection of

objects depicted, nor the language conveys the centrality of the child in the world constructed by the text.

- The textbooks used for the teaching of mother tongues are written in such stylished diction and sentence-structure, that children cannot be expected to see the language used in them as their own.
- Words expressions and nouns used by children and others in their milieu are all absent from textbooks. An critical, sophisticated style dominates textbook lessons, re-inforcing the tradition of distancing knowledge from life.

6. *Observation Discovered*

- Treating pictures as substitutes for experience "we forced textbooks asking children to observe a picture of the object under study rather than asking children and the teacher to go out and observe the object and itself in nature." Example, Vth standard science textbook, "look at the picture of a cactus plant, observe the tick green structure."

7. *Structure of Syllabus*

- Gaps in the syllabi between the lower primary and high school stage.
- Repetition of the some content.
- No interaction between persons involved in the preparation of syllabi and textbooks for secondary classes.
- Repetitions leads to boredom and a sense of load. Example study of nutrition and health repeating in 3rd, 4th, 5th, 7th, 8th and 10th classes even questions at end almost same kind.
- History, 'covering' several decades. Supposed to 'cover' 'all' of India's history in 3 years.

8. *Teaching Everything*

- 'Geography'—all continents being 'covered'.
- Science subjects beyond the capacities of teacher, they encourage private tuition.
- Mathematics in Class I pupils are supposed to go up to 100 (compared to this British child in this class spends the whole years working with numbers upto 20).

- Mathematics – little application in the real life of the child.

9. *Starting Early* [Pre-school sector of the education system]
    - Official stipulations that no textbooks be used at this stage.
    - The sense of compulsion comes from a wide-spread feeling that unless academic training of a child starts early, he/she cannot cope with the fast-paced pedagogy and the competitive ethos of the later school years.
    - Our national commitment to the development of human resource is daily challenged in our nurseries and primary schools.
10. *Not Just Urban Problem*
    - Abysmally poor condition of schools.
    - Absenteeism among teachers.
    - Problem of high drop-out rate.

Roots of the Problem

1. Knowledge v/s Information.
   As a period knowledge, explosion, new topics, concepts, information are added to syllabi. Example: 'Valency' taught in Class VII, whereas in European children do not hear about till standard nine. All new knowledge to be produced by others and our job is simply to learn this knowledge.
2. Isolation of experts from classroom realities.
3. Centralized character in curriculum planning, production of textbooks, etc.
4. Concept of 'Teaching the text'.
5. Competition based social ethos, especially in urban areas, trends like English medium schools, entrance tests, quiz culture, talent search etc.
6. Absence of academic ethods –
    - lack of adequate infrastructural facilities, rigid administrative structures and growing cynicism, (fault finding mentality) are responsible for the absence of academic ethos in majority of schools.
    - Children's educated by us, while they grow older freshness go away, as does romance and curiosity.
    - Libraries, we see with locked doors.

Recommendations

1. A number of organizations and departments organize competitions of various levels/areas. In this, individual achievement must be discouraged and group achievements must be encouraged.
2. The process of curriculum framing and preparation of text-books must be de-centralized and ensure working teachers involvement on the same.
3. NGO's, voluntary organization in pedagogical innovations be provided greater freedom and support.
4. Endorse the idea of setting up education committees at village, block, district level to under take planning and supervision of schools.
5. Sufficient contingency amount be place at the disposal of heads of schools.
6. At least three parallel systems of school education (syllabus, textbooks and examination) are running concurrently in different states.
7. In each state schools are affiliated to state board of education, CBSE and CISCE (Council for the Indian School Certificate Exam). CBSE enjoys the prestige of being elite. Therefore, jurisdiction of CBSE be restricted to Kendriya and Navodaya Vidyalayas and all other schools be affiliated to the respective state boards.
8. The opening and functioning of Nursary/Pre-schools must be regulated. The 'over education' and 'formal teaching' in this level must be discouraged.
9. The weight of school bags/books must be reduced. There is no justification for torturing the young children. We compelling pupils to carry heavy bags. Textbooks should be treated as school property and no need for children to purchase.
10. The nature and character of homework needs a radical change. At primary level shouldn't be given any homework.
11. The teacher-pupils ratio should reduce to 1:30.
12. Greater use of electronic/mass media be made the creation of a child centred social ethos in the country. A regular TV programme addressed to students, teachers and parents possibly called 'Skikha Darshan' should be launched.

13. In-adequate programme of teacher preparation leads to unsatisfactory quality of learning in schools.
    - The B.Ed. programme should offer specialization in secondary, elementary, nursery education.
    - The B.Ed. programme should re-structured and make it more practicum centred. Duration of B.Ed. either be 1 year after UG or 3-4 years after HSC. The trainees should enable to acquire the ability for self-learning and independent thinking.
14. The continuing education/in-service programmes designed systematically and conducted imaginatively.
15. The public exams reviewed with a view to ensure replacement of 'Quiz type' questioning by the concept-based questioning.
16. A project team with a number of sub-groups be set up in each state to examine the syllabi and textbooks.
17. Mathematics curriculum for Primary classes be reviewed with a view to slowing down the pace at which children are required to learn basic mathematical concepts and broadening the scope of maths to include areas other than number work. (space and shape related concepts and problem-solving).
18. Language textbooks should be adequately reflect the spoken idiom. An attempt should be made in future textbooks to give adequate representations to children's life experiences, imaginary stories, poems and stories reflecting the lives of ordinary people in different parts of the country.
19. Science textbooks should provide natural/real experiences and it must be connected and analyzed social life and issues.

Conclusion

The report touches all aspects/spheres of education. It highly affect the curriculum reforms of Kerala in 1997.

Ninth Five Year Plan on Education 1997-2002

The Ninth Five Year Plan Launched in the fiftieth year of our independence covers the period 1997 to 2002. The plan lays special emphasis on primary education and information technology.

- Early Childhood Education.
- Primary/Elementary Education.
- Adult Education.

- Secondary Education reform.
- Technical Education.
- University higher education.
- Structural arrangement of curriculum.
- Use the media and educational technology.
- Womens empowerment.
- Language develop and book promotion.
- Management Education.
- Free education for Girls.

Kerala Self-Financing Act, 2006
(Professional Education Bill)

The Kerala professional colleges or institutions (prohibition of capitation fee, regulation of admission fixation of non-explorative fee and other measures censure equality and excellence in professional education. An act provide for prohibition of capitation fee, regulation of admission, fixation of non-exploitative fee, allotment of seats scheduled caste and scheduled tribes and other socially and economically backward classes and other measures to ensure equality and excellence in professional education and for matters connected there with or incidential thereto.

U.R. Anatha Moorthi Commission, 2006

Recommendation Academic Matter

- There is need to grant autonomy to individual institutions in matters design of curriculum.
- Thought the change in curriculum should be a continuous and ongoing process.
- The present system of selecting research fellows based on a national level of examination.
- No faculty members should suffer in his/her research endeavours for want of funds.
- The universities and colleges should focus equally on academic and job oriented courses while planning for new programmes to make higher education relevant for the world of work.
- All universities and colleges should have the autonomy to start self-financing courses.
- All conventional universities should establish synergic linkages with open and distance education, universities with a view to augmenting the enrolment in the higher education

system but with out compromising on their programmes offered in the conventional face-to-face mode.

- Institutions of higher education should have the autonomy to adopt continuous comprehensive system of students.
- Each higher education institution should set up an internal quality assurance cell with a view to continuously assessing its performance on objective and pre-defined parameters.
- Well-established and high quality institution may be granted seemed to be university status and the procedures for the same should be simplified.
- Participation in national and international seminars and workshops is important for professional development of teachers.
- Strong need for improving the quality of orientation programmes and refresher courses.
- The higher education institution may use suitable combination of the scores obtained both in the entrance test and in the qualifying examination for admissions.
- All higher education institutions need not focus on all areas of study.
- With a view improving the quality of research in the country use of international bench marks such as citation insides, parents should be encouraged and a national repository of doctoral these created.
- Though each of university should draw up its academic calendar providing for dates of admission schedule of vacation, holding of examination and declaring of results.

Education Ancient Kerala

Kerala stands fore most in education among the Indian states. Per capita expenditure on education is greatest in Kerala. Education in Kerala cannot be cut off from the main stream of education in India. Centuries ago, these, existed in Kerala institution such as 'Saalai', 'Sabhai', 'Madom' and 'Kalari', all in the line of the Gurukula system. Thirkanamathilakam, Parthivapuram, Moozhikkulam and Kanthaloor were a few of the higher centres of learning in Kerala. Vedic literature, Grammar, Astronomy and politics were some of the subjects taught in these centres.

Several cottage schools were functioning in all the villages in Kerala. The 3 R's were taught in every school. In selected schools

Amarakosam, Sidharoopam, Ashtanghrudayam and Jyothisham were taught.

With the coming of European missionaries, there was Stir in the educational field of Kerala. Francis Day in his book. *The Land of the Perumals* states that in A.D. 1773, tax exempted gift-lands to build churches and church schools were very liberally given to European missionaries by the kings of Travancore and Cochin.

In those days caste discrimination was at its peak, and a large bulk of the community—the parayas, pulayas, ulladas, kammalars, kaadaas, thodaas, paanaas—were in a state of complete neglect. The missionaries gave them primary education.

Since independence, especially since the formation of Kerala state in 1956 the progress made in Kerala with regard to education has been rapid and appreciable.

Conclusion

Yet in India education is not completely progressed when world has reached in a new era of education and technology India has to go further distance forward.

MODEL QUESTIONS

1. Education in India under the British rule was first ignored then opposed and finally get on provisional autonomy"—Comment on this statement citing relevant reforms introduced by British rulers.
2. What are the main features of Macaulay's Minutes on Indian education and evaluate it?
3. What are the major recommendations of Hunter Commission (1882)?
4. What are the major recommendations of Indian Education Commission (1964-66)?
5. Write a brief note on National Policy of Education (1986) and programme of action (1992).
6. What are the general observations of the Yashpal Committee Report (1993)?
7. What is meant by oriental-occidental controversy?
8. What was the effect of Abbot Wood Reports recommendations?

REFERENCES

1. Annie Amala, et.al. *History of Education*, Discovery Publishing House, New Delhi.
2. Chaube, S.P. *History of Indian Education*, Vinod Pustak Mandir, Agra.
3. *Development of Indian System of Education*. Dr. Ramashakal Pandey.
4. *Land Marks in the History of Modern Indian Education*—J.C. Aggarwal.

5. *Learning without Burdon*—Report of the National Advisory Committee Appointed by MHRD, Govt. of India.
6. Sharma, R.N. *History and Problems of Education in India*, Surjeet Publications, New Delhi.
7. *Teacher and Education in A Developing Society*—J.C. Aggarwal.

Net http://groupsgoogle.co.in/group/bangalore.

6

Structure and Issues of Education in India

There are about 888 thousands educational institutions in the country with an enrolment of about 179 millions. Elementary Education System in India is the second largest in the world with 149.4 millions children of 6-14 years enrolled and 2.9 million teachers. This is about 82 per cent of the children in the age group.

STRUCTURE OF SCHOOL EDUCATION

A uniform structure of school education, the 10+2 system has been adopted by all the states and union territories of India. However, within the states and the UT's, there remains variations in the number of classes constituting the primary, upper primary, high and higher secondary school stages, age for admission to Class I, medium of instruction, public exams, teaching of Hindi and English number of working days in a year, academic session, vacation periods, fee structure, compulsory education etc.

Stages of School Education in India

(a) The primary stage consists of Classes I-V, i.e., of five years duration, in 20 States/UTs namely Andhra Pradesh, Arunachal Pradesh, Bihar, Haryana, Himachal Pradesh, J&K, Madhya Pradesh, Manipur, Orissa, Punjab, Rajasthan, Sikkim, Tamil Nadu, Tripura, U.P., West Bengal, Andaman and Nicobar Islands, Chandigarh, Delhi and Karaikal and Yanam regions of Pondicherry. The primary stage consists of Classes I-IV in remaining stages/UTs.

(b) The middle stage of education comprises Classes VI-VIII in as many as 18 States/UTs. viz., Arunachal Pradesh, Bihar,

Haryana, Himachal Pradesh, J&K, Madhya Pradesh, Manipur, Punjab, Rajasthan, Sikkim, Tamil Nadu, Tripura, U.P., West Bengal, Andaman and Nicobar Islands, Chandrigrah, Delhi and Karaikal region of Pondicherry. Classes V-VII in Assam, Goa, Gujarat, Karnataka, Kerala, Maharashtra, Megahalaya, Mizoram, Dadra and Nagar Haveli, Daman and Diu, Lakshadweep and Mahe region of Pondicherry and Classes VI-VII in Andhra Pradesh, Orissa and Yanam region of Pondicherry. In Nagaland Classes V-VIII constitute the upper primary stage.

(c) The secondary stage consists of Classes IX-X in 19 States/ UTs, viz., Arunachal Pradesh, Bihar, Haryana, Himachal Pradesh, J&K, Madhya Pradesh, Manipur, Nagaland, Punjab, Rajasthan, Sikkim, Tamil Nadu, Tripura, U.P. , West Bengal, Andaman and Nicobar Islands, Chandigrah, Delhi and Karaikal region of Pondicherry. The high school stage comprises Classes VIII-X in 13 States/UTs viz., Andhra Pradesh, Assam, Goa, Gujarat, Karnataka, Kerala, Maharashtra, Meghalaya, Mizoram, Orissa, Dadra and Nagar Haveli, Daman and Diu, Lakshadweep and Mahe and Yanam regions of Pondicherry. However, the higher secondary/senior secondary stage of school comprising Classes XI-XII (10+2 pattern) is available in all the Stages/ UTs through in some States/UTs these classes are attached to universities/colleges.

Age Restriction for Admission

The minimum age for admission to Class I of the primary school stage is generally 5 + or 6+ years. In 22 States/ UTs the minimum age for admission to Class 1 is 5+ years and in 7 states/UTs the minimum age for admission is 6+ years. There is no age restriction in the case of Mizoram. In Gujarat the minimum age for admission is 5+ years (voluntary) and 6+ years (compulsory). In Lakshadweep, the minimum age for admission in 5½ years.

Medium of Instruction

Mother tounge/regional language is the medium of instruction at the primary stage of education in most of the States/ UTs. Facilities for studying in a medium other than regional language vary considerable in different States and Union Territories.

Teaching of Hindi

Apart from Hindi speaking states, teaching of Hindi is compulsory in most of the non-Hindi speaking States/UTs, though the classes from which the teaching of Hindi is compulsory differ from state-to-state. Teaching of Hindi is not compulsory in the states of Tamil Nadu, Tripura and Karaikal region of Pondicherry.

Teaching of English

Teaching of English is compulsory in all the States/UTs, except Bihar. However, the classes in which teaching of English is compulsory differs from State-to-State/UTs.

Public Examinations

In all the States/UTs public examinations are conducted at the end of X and XII classes by the respective state boards of secondary and Higher Secondary Education. The minimum age for the secondary school examination varies from 14+ to 16+ years in Andhra Pradesh, Arunachal Pradesh, Assam, Bihar, Gujarat, J&K, Karnataka, Kerala, Maharashtra, Manipur, Orissa, Punjab, Tamil Nadu, Tripura, West Bengal, Andaman and Nicobar Islands, Delhi, Lakshadweep and Pondicherry. In Mizoram, the minimum age for secondary school examination is 13+ years. Other States/UTs either do not have age restriction or have not prescribed any age restriction. The minimum age for higher secondary school-examination varies from 16+ to 18+ years in Arunachal Pradesh, Bihar, Gujarat, J&K, Kerala, Maharashtra, Punjab, Tamil Nadu, Tripura, Andaman and Nicobar Islands, Delhi, Lakshadweep and Pondicherry. In other States/UTs, either there is no age restriction prescribed or if it exists, it has not been indicated. In some of the States/UTs, the first public exam is also conducted at the middle stage of school education.

Number of Working Days

The number of working days of school education in a year is generally more than 200 days in all the States/UTs.

Academic Session

The academic session begins from different months of the year in the different States and Union Territories. However, in most of the states, the long vacation periods are availed in the summer season while in some of the hilly states, these falls in the winter months.

Compulsory Education

Compulsory education has been enforced in four states and UT's at the primary stage of education while in eight States/UTs there is compulsory education covering the entire elementary stage of education. As many as 20 States/UTs have not introduced any measure of compulsion up to the year 1997-98.

Free Education

A majority of States/UTs have introduced free education in Class I-XII of their schools.

Tution Fees Per Annum Per Child in Government Schools

In the States/UTs where education is not free for Classes IX and above the annual fee varies considerably from the highest level of Rs. 360 for Classes XI and XII in the case of Meghalaya to the lowest at Rs. 48 in the case of Assam.

FINANCING OF EDUCATION

From 1968 onwards, goal has been to get apart 6 per cent of national income on Education. In spite of resource constraints as well as competing priorities, the budgetary expenditure on education by Centre and States as percentage of Gross National Product has steadily increased from 0.8 per cent in 1951-52 to 3.3 per cent in 1994-95.

Para 11.4 of NPE 1986 states that, "the investment on education be gradually increased to reach a level of 6 per cent of the national income as early as possible. Since the actual level of investment has remained for short or that target, it is important that greater determination is shown now to find the funds for the programmes laid down in this policy. While actual requirements will be computed from time-to-time on the basis of monitoring and review, the outlay on education will be stepped up to ensure that during the 8th Five Year Plan and onwards it will uniformly exceeds 6 per cent of the national income."

The total budgetary expenditure on education by the education departments of the Centre and States has increased from Rs. 644.6 millions in 1951-52 to Rs. 3,00,000 millions in 1995-96. In terms of its share in total budgetary expenditure, it has increased from 7.9 per cent in 1951-52 to 11.1 per cent in 1995-96.

There are, at present 130 plan schemes in the department with a total Eighth Plan outlay of Rs. 74430 millions. The total plan out lay of the Department for the year 1996-97 is Rs. 33827 millions. There are 18 centrally sponsored schemes, which account for 65.7 per cent of the total plan outlay. Mid-Day-Meal scheme is the major centrally sponsored-scheme with 1996-97-outlay 14,000 millions. Other major centrally sponsored schemes are Operation Black Board, Non-Formal Education, Teacher Education, Post Literacy and Continuing Education and Vocational Education with 1996-97 outlay of Rs. 2790 millions, Rs. 1582.5 millions, Rs. 1170 millions, Rs. 755 millions and Rs. 820 millions respectively.

Organizational Structure of Education in Kerala

The General Education Department is one of the important departments in Kerala. The Director of Public Instruction (DPI) is the Head of the Department. The Director is also the Commissioner of Government examination in the State. Additional Directors, Joint Directors, Senior Administrative Officer, Senior Finance Officer, Law Officer, Deputy Secretary, Accounts Officers, Deputy Directors, Assistant Directors and other staff in the headquarters assist him. The Joint Commissioner, The Secretary, The Assistant Secretary and other staff , located in the Praeekshabhavan, assist him in various government examinations conducted by the Department.

For administrative convenience and improving the efficiency in school education, district officer are functioning in the 14 revenue districts of the state headed by Deputy-Directors of Education. Each revenue district is divided into Educational Districts and further into Educational sub-districts there are 37 educational districts and 161 educational sub-districts in the State. Deputy-Director of Education (DDE) heads each District Educational Offices and Assistant Educational Officer (AEO) heads each educational sub-district officers. The DEO attends the administration of high school, training schools and other special types of school in the educational district. The AEO is primarily responsible for the administration of all primary schools within the sub-district. The department plays an eminent role in the physical and mental development of all pupils studying in schools. There has been tremendous growth in educational facilities at all levels of education in the State during the last 50 years. The private and public sectors together played significant role in attaining the present level and their contribution to the field are remarkable.

10 + 2 + 3 PATTERN OF EDUCATION

By 1980, this pattern had been introduced in 15 States and 8 Union Territories. The states of Haryana, Himachal Pradesh, Madhya Pradesh, Meghalaya, Punjab, Rajasthan and Uttar Pradesh also accepted the new pattern in principle. Now almost all States and Union Territories have accepted the pattern. According to National Policy of Education 1986, it is a 'great achievement'.

Objectives

The new pattern envisaged that by providing work experience and vocational courses education will be linked with productivity. It will prepare students for entry in gainful employment after completing higher secondary education. It was expected that students will not rush for university degrees. It aimed at making students more mature and knowledgeable. It was intended to avoid specialization at an early stage.

Ten-Years Common Course

The pattern envisages a common course of general education for all students at this stage. There is an undifferentiated course of general education for all without any diversification of courses. The main emphasis has been on providing a wide spectrum of knowledge relevant to life and to develop different aspects of personality especially at the secondary stage comprising Classes IX and X. Courses at this stage include the following subjects: (1) Science, (2) Mathematics, (3) Languages, (4) Social Studies including History, Civics, Geography, Economics and Commerce, (5) Two Languages, (6) Work Experience, (7) Health and Physical Education and (8) Additional Language—Optional.

Higher Secondary Stage (Classes XI and XII)

A broad based general education at the secondary stage to be followed by two years of diversified and vocational education will have 2 types of courses i.e., Academic and Vocational.

It was visualized by the Education Commission (1964-66) that at the end of the ten years of school education a proportion of students would step off the school system and enter working life (about 40%); some more would step off the stream of general education and enter vocational courses whose duration would be one to three years (about 30 %); and the remaining would continue further in the stream of general education whose duration will be one, and ultimately two years.

Main Characteristics of the 10 + 2 + 3 Pattern

1. It envisages 10 years of schooling with common and undifferentiated courses in Classes IX and X.
2. It provides for 12 years of Higher Secondary Education in place of the 11 years, the usual school pattern.
3. The first degree course to be of three years after 12 years of schooling.
4. The first degree to be attainable after 15 years of education.
5. It provides for the compulsory teaching of science, mathematics, social studies, two languages, work experiences.
6. It provides for various vocational courses in Classes XI and XII.
7. It provides for two levels of courses in some subjects.
8. It provides for specialization after 10 years of schooling.
9. It provides for a core course in Classes XI and XII.

NATIONAL AND STATE LEVEL BODIES OF EDUCATION

Central Advisory Board of Education (CABE)

CABE, the highest advisory body to advise the Central and State Governments in the field of education, was first established in 1920 and dissolved in 1923 as a measure of economy. It was revived in 1935 and had continued to be in existence till 1994. Despite the fact that in the past, important decisions had been taken on the advise of CABE and it had provided a forum for widespread consultation and examination of issues relating to educational and cultural development, it was unfortunately not reconstituted after the expiry of its extended tenure in March 1994.

CABE has a particularly important role to play at the present juncture in view of the significant socio-economic and socio-cultural developments taking place in the country and for the review of the NPE which also due. It is a matter of importance therefore, that the Central and State Governments, and educationists and people representing all interests, should increase their interaction and evolve a participative process of decision-making in education, which enhances the federal structure of our polity.

National Open School

The National Institute of Open Schooling (NIOS) formerly known as National Open School (NOS), established as an autonomous institution under MHRD, Government of India in 1989. NIOS mainly caters to the educational needs of the out of school children in general and those belonging to school drop-outs and socially and economical backward section of the learner population. It started with academic courses at secondary and senior secondary levels. However, the concept of open schooling has changed considerably in the last few years. The system is becoming more sensitive to the occupational and life related needs of learners. Today the focus of the NIOS covers right from the elementary education to courses at the pre-degree level, both academic and vocational. NIOS has shown a steady growth in student enrolment, number of courses and study centres. It has developed into the largest open school in the world with 1330 thousand students on its roll. It attempts to reach out physically, mentally, socially and geographically disadvantaged groups through suitable learning material and delivery mechanism.

NIOS is also gearing up for making a significant contribution in India's efforts for UEE by stressing on it foundation courses and linking up with Non-formal education and alternative schooling system operating in the country. It uses new technologies for training and teaching purpose mainly to increase access and ensure quality.

District Institute of Education and Training (DIET)

DIET is an organization conceived in the NPE, 1986 for ensuring the quality of education mostly at the primary level within the district in which it is established. Pursuant to the provisions of NPE on teacher education, a centrally sponsored scheme of restructuring and reorganization of teacher education was approved in October 1987. One of the five components of the scheme was establishment of DIET's. Till 1994 central assistance had been sanctioned under the scheme for setting up a total of 363 DIET's in the country.

DIET-Mission

"To provide academic and resource support (vide para 1.5) at the grassroot level for the success of the various strategies and programmes being undertaken in the areas of elementary and adult education, with special reference to the following objectives:

1. *Elementary Education:* "Universalization of primary/ elementary education.

2. *Adult Education:* NLM targets in regard to functional literacy in the 15-35 age group."

The above is to general mission statement. It will have to be translated into specific goals for the DIET, so as to suit the needs of individual states and districts, and will be ultimately operationalized through specific performance norms set for individual DIET's.

DIETS Pace-Setting Role

Pursuit of excellence would have to inform all activities of the DIET's, in which context, it will have two inter-related aspects:

(i) Excellence in the institute's own work, and

(ii) Helping the elementary adult education system in the district, in achieving excellence.

As far as the first aspect is concerned, efforts will be made to provide to DIET's all necessary physical and man power resources. But it will be for them to harness these and other available resources in the best possible manner, so as to achieve and promote excellence.

In this context, DIETs will also have a very important pace setting role to play. They will be expected to became models for other educational institutions in the district in terms of meticulous, efficient and effective planning and execution of functions, harmonious and creative organizational climate, maintenance of a clean and attractive campus etc.

Functions of DIET

I. Training and orientation of the following target groups:

(i) Elementary school teachers (both pre-service and in-service).

(ii) Headmaster, heads of school complexes and officers of education, department up to block level.

(iii) Instructors and supervisors of non-formal and Adult Education (induction level and continuing education).

(iv) Members of Village Education Committees (VECs), community leaders, youth and other volunteers who wish to work as educational activities.

(v) Resource persons who will conduct suitable programmes for the target groups mentioned at *(i)* and *(iii)* above, at centres other than the DIET.

II. Academic and resource support to the elementary and adult education systems in the district in other ways:

(i) Extension activities and interaction with the field.
(ii) Provision of services of a resource and learning centre for teachers and instructors.
(iii) Development of locally relevant materials teaching aids, evaluation tools etc.
(iv) Serving as an evaluation centre for elementary schools and programmes of Non-Formal Education and Adult Education.

III. Action research and experimentation to deal with specific problems of the district in achieving the objectives the objectives in the areas of elementary and adult education.

State Council of Educational Research and Training (SCERT)

- SCERT, Kerala is an autonomous body entrusted with planning, implementation and evaluation of all academic programmes from pre-school to higher secondary levels.
- SCERT, Kerala was established in 1994.
- The Hon. Minister for Education is the Chairman.
- Secretary General, Education department as Vice-Chairman.
- Director, SCERT is the convener of the governing body.

Departments and Activities Under SCERT

1. *Department of Curriculum, Textbooks and Evaluation (DCTE):* DCTE is responsible for preparation and revision of curriculum and textbooks, preparation of handbooks, refresher courses, orientation and training programmes for teachers, headmasters, DEO's and DDEs on curriculum-related topics.
2. *Department of Teacher Education (Pre-Service and in-Service) and Extension:* DTE's areas of action are organizing teacher training programmes (both in-service and pre-service) for the TTI's and DIET's, orientation courses for teacher educators in TTI's.
3. *Department of Educational Technology (DET):* Develops the curriculum, syllabus, textbooks, and handbook for teachers. Evaluation tools and other teaching learning materials for IT education in High School level. It also provides technological support to all other departments of SCERT.
4. *Department of Art, Physical, Health and Vocational Education:* DHPVE is established with a view to cater to academic quality in non-scholastic areas like art, health and physical

education. Training to music teachers, work experience teachers, drawing teachers etc.

5. *Department of Non-Formal, Continuing and Special Education:* NEE is envisaged for organizing educational programmes for marginalized and out-of-school populations to draw them into mainstream education.
6. *Department of Research Documentation and Dissemination:* This unit conducts sponsors and co-ordinates inter-disciplinary research with focus on theory, policy relevance, methods and processes of the educational, curricular and training programmes carried out by SCERT. It is also responsible for the evaluation of the massive teacher training programmes.
7. *Department of State Institute of Educational Management and Training (SIEMAT):* SIEMAT is in its initial stage and plans to organize managerial and training programmes of Educational Administrators and to carry out major research programmes.
8. *Kerala State Open School:* KSOS was established in the year 2000 under SCERT, with the mission of universali-zation of education, by providing greater access and equal opportunities. The inherent flexibilities and options in this system, aim to cover a large population of learners.
9. *Population Education (POPED):* The activities of POPED are two-fold: population education programmes supported by the Government of Kerala and those funded by UNFPA. It conducts several programmes for teachers, students, opinion makers, administrators of school education about adolescent education , help education, AIDS education etc.
10. *National Talent Search Examination (NTSE):* SCERT plays a major role in preparing students for the NTSE (conducted by NCERT by administering the screening test at state level)
11. *Publications:* The Kerala Journal of Education, Research and Extension-Half Yearly.

National Institute of Educational Planning and Administration (NIEPA)

Is an autonomous organization financed by the Department of Secondary and Higher Education, Ministry of Human Resource Development.

Objectives

- To undertake, promote and co-ordinate research in educational planning and administration.
- To provide training and consultancy services in this educational field.
- To train an orient key level functionaries as well as senior level administrators from the Centre and States.
- To collaborate with other agencies, institutions and organizations in issues related to education.
- To provide facilities for training and research to other countries particularly of the Asian region in the field of educational planning and administration.
- To prepare, print and publish papers, periodicals and books.
- To share experience and expertise in the area of educational planning and administration with other countries.

National Council of Educational Research and Training (NCERT)

Is an apex resource organization set up by the Government of India, with headquarters at New Delhi. They assist and advise the Central and State Governments on academic matters related to school education.

NCERT undertakes the following programmes and activities:

- Research
- Development
- Training
- Extension
- Publication
- Exchange Programmes

University Grants Commission (UGC)

UGC established in November 1956 as a statutory body of the Government of India through an Act of Parliament for the co-ordination, determination and maintenance of standards of university education in India. UGC has six regional centres at Pune, Hyderabad, Kolkata, Bhopal, Guwahati and Bangalore. The head office of the UGC is located at Bahadur Shah Zafar Marg in New Delhi.

Objectives

- Promoting and co-ordinating university education.
- Determining and maintaining standards of teaching, examination and research in universities.

- Framing regulations on minimum standards of education.
- Monitoring developments in the field of collegiate and university education.
- Disbursing grants to the universities and colleges.
- Serving as a vital link between the Union and State Governments and institutions of higher learning.
- Advising the Central and State Governments on the measures necessary for improvement of university education.

National Assessment and Accreditation Council (NAAC)

Is an autonomous body established by the University Grants Commission of India to assess and accredit institutions of higher education in the country. It is an outcome of the recommendations of the National Policy in Education (1986). Established by the UGC in September 1994 at Bangalore.

Objectives

- To arrange for periodic assessment and accreditation of institutions of higher education or units thereof, or specific academic programme or projects.
- To stimulate the academic environment for promotion of quality of teaching-learning and research in higher education institutions.
- To encourage self-evaluation and innovations in higher education.
- To undertake quality—related research studies, consultancy and training progamme.
- To collaborate with other stakeholders of higher education for quality evaluation, promotion and sustenance.

National Council for Teacher Education (NCTE)

The National Council for Teacher Education as a statutory body came into existence in pursuance of the National Council for Teacher Education Act, 1993 on the 17th August, 1995. NPE (1986) recommended the council for improving the teacher education. NCTE has its headquarters at New Delhi and four Regional centers at Bangalore, Bhopal, Bhubaneshwar and Jaipur.

Objectives

- The main objectives of the NCTE is to achieve planned and co-ordinated development of the teacher education system throughout the country.

- The regulation and proper maintenance of norms and standards in the teacher education system.
- The NCTE is very broad and covers the whole grant of teacher education programmes including research and training of persons for equipping them to teach at pre-primary, primary, secondary and senior secondary stages in schools, non-formal education, adult education and distance (correspondence) education courses.

SPECIAL ISSUES OF EDUCATION IN INDIAN SOCIETY

Equalization of Educational Opportunities

Significance of Equalization of Educational Opportunities

The Indian Education Commission has observed. "One of the important social objectives of education is to equalize opportunities, enabling the backward or underprivileged classes and individual to use education as a lever for the improvement of their condition. Every society that values social justice and is anxious to improve the lot of the common man and cultivate all available talent, must ensure progressive equality of opportunity to all sections of the population. This is the only guarantee for the building up of an agalitarian human society in which the exploitation of the weak will be minimized."

Education as an Equalizing Factor

Prem Kripal observed, "The quest for the quality of life which is the essence of modern education offers new hope and opportunity to poor and materially deprived societies. With the right type of education a developing society can attain the satisfaction harmony and comprehension that may elude a more prosperous community. Education could, indeed, be the most potent factor in eventually reducing the gap between affluence and poverty which is widening so alarmingly in terms of per capita income. Though education cannot do much in equalizing money incomes in the short run, it can certainly do far more in enriching the quality of life for the poor as well as the rich.

Equality of Educational Opportunity as Seen by the International Commission on Development of Education (1972)

The Commission felt, "Foreseeing the advent of democracy to the world of education is not an illusion. It may not be a perfect democracy, but when has this ever existed? Yet it will at least be a real, concrete practical democracy, not inspired and built by bureaucrats or technocrats, or granted by some ruling caste. It will be living, creative and envolving." For this to be achieved the commission suggested the following steps:

1. Educational structures must be remodeled to extend widely the field of choice and enable people to follow lifelong education patterns.
2. Subject-matter must be individualized.
3. Pupils and students must be aware of their status, their rights and their own wishes.
4. Authoritarian forms of teaching must give way to relationship marked by independence mutual responsibility and dialogue.
5. Pedagogical training must be geared to knowing and respecting the multiple aspects of human personality.
6. Guidance must replace selection.
7. Those making use of educational institutions must participate in their management and policy making.
8. The bureaucratic aspects of educational activity must be broken down and its administration decentralized.

Equal Opportunity does not Mean Identical Education

There is no doubt that no two individuals are alike. They differ in tastes manners, attitudes and aptitudes, beliefs etc. Any attempt to provide precisely the same educational programmes and opportunities is likely to be met with failure. Equal opportunity implie that the rich and the poor alike should have equal access to these educational system and programme without any hindrance. All material barriers should be removed caste, colour or creed should not put any check on an individual to pursue course of education in accordance with his ability and aptitude.

How Does Inequality of Educational Opportunity Arise?

The Education Commission 1964-66 has mentioned the following causes:

(a) *Lack of Educational Facilities*: There are many places and areas in the country where primary, secondary or collegiate institutions do not exist and children residing therein do not have the same opportunity as those who have these facilities in the nighbourhood. There are at present glaring imbalances of educational development in different parts of the country. The educational developments in the states show wide differences and even wide differences are found among the districts.

(b) *Poverty of a Large Section of Population*: Children coming from the poor sections of the community do not have the same chance to study in the neighbourhood of an educational institution as those who come from richer ones.

(c) *Differences in the Standards of Educational Institutions*: Differences in the standards of schools and colleges lead to educational inequality. Students coming from rural educational institutions do not compare well when admissions to professional courses are made on the basis of selection tests.

(d) *Differences in Home Environments*: A child from a rural household or an urban slum having illiterate parents does not have the same opportunity which a child from an upper class home with highly educated parents has.

(e) *Disparity in Education of Boys and Girls*: Due to the conservative nature of the Indian society there is a wide disparity between the education of boys an girls at all stages an in all sections of education.

(f) *Disparity Due to Advanced Classes and Backward Classes*: Another factor that has led to inequality of opportunity in education is the existence of different types of classes i.e., advanced classes and backward ones.

(g) *High Private Cost of Education*: The private costs of education required for textbooks supplies, co-curricular activities etc., have increased very substantially in recent years and these amount to several time the tuition fees. The parents are required to incur very heavy expenditure for this purpose.

Ways and Means of Reducing Inequality of Opportunity in Education

(a) *Tuition Free Education*: School education is completely free in advance countries and our country should also gradually work towards a stage when all education should be tuition free.

(b) *Reduction in Other Costs*: It is felt that parents are required to incur heavy indirect costs on the education of their children. These indirect costs include costs incurred by parents on textbooks, supplies, uniforms, co-curricular activities etc. It may reduce through.

   (i) free textbooks at the primary stage,
   (ii) book banks, and
   (iii) grants for purchase of books.

(c) *Scholarship*: There should be an adequate programme of scholarships so that the best use in made of the available talent.

(d) *Transport Facilities*: Adequate transport facilities may be provided in the rural areas so that students are encouraged to attend educational institutions.

(e) *Day-Study Centres and Lodging Houses*: A large number of day-study centres at the secondary and university stages should be provided for students who do not have adequate facilities for study at home. Lodging houses i.e., places where students can stay throughout the day, and even at night, but go home for food, may also be provided.

(f) *'Earn and Learn' Facilities*: As a supplement to the programme of scholarships, facilities for students to earn and pay a part of their expenses should be provided as large a scale as possible.

(g) *Special Facilities for Girls*: Special incentives may be provided to the girls.

(h) *Education to the Backward Sections of the Society*: Special investigations regarding important aspects of spread of education amongst the tribals and their effects may be carried out.

(i) *Admission Policy*: There is a great need to introduce an egalitarian element in admissions to institutions so that students coming from rural areas are not handicapped due to language or some factors.

(j) *Special Assistance to Backward Areas or States*: Necessary programmes for the upliftment of the backward areas should be there in government policies regarding education.

Universalization of Elementary Education (UEE)

Universal Elementary Education continues to be a constitutional provision and national commitment in India. In the initial stages, the strategy was to achieve this goal by relying entirely on the formal system of education. From seventies onwards India moved towards a more realistic approach, beginnings of Non-formal education in India. In the late seventies the government launched National Adult Education Programme (NAEP). By the eightees, an integrated approach to universalize education emerged which later got incorporated in the broader objective of Education For All (EFA). This change in perspective from UEE to EFA is in line with the changes taking place in the international scene.

From Access to Achievement

India has made tremendous progress in expanding schooling facilities and in improving enrolments in the primary classes. Then the attention is increasingly shifted from enrolment drives to strategies to improve retention and learner achievement. The NPE and Programme of Action (POA) has underlined these very dimensions of educational development in India. Therefore, the focus seems to be shifting from equity in access to equity in achievement.

Shift in Targeting

India started with the overall objective of expanding the primary education system. With the emergence of disparities in the process of development, the effort was to target the efforts. In the subsequent periods, our efforts were focused on the ward regions, disadvantaged groups and girls in general.

Social Implication of UEE

- Education is a right and not a privilage.
- Attain universal literacy and there by persuading for further education, elimination of social discrimination and for achieving social justice.
- Reduction of in equalities.

Wastage and Stagnation

Wastage means pre-mature withdrawal of children from school. Stagnation means retention of children in the same class for more than one year(s) on account of unsatisfactory progress or poor achievement.

Two forms of wastage in education are withdrawals from schools and failures in exams. By wastage it is meant the premature withdrawals of children from schools. The major objective of primary stage is attainment of literacy; a child who is withdrawn from school before reaching standard V is considered a cause of wastage. The extent wastage may be assessed roughly by computing the diminution in enrolment from standard to standard over a series of year. Large number of pupils drops off or pushes off, causing wastage.

Stagnation is meant the retention of pupils in a standard for more than one year on account of unsatisfactory progress or poor achievement. It is measured with the number of attempts made by pupils to pass any standard.

Causes of Wastage and Stagnation

General Causes

- poverty and illness of pupils.
- un-educated parents.
- distance from home to school.

Academic Causes

- over crowded classes.
- over crowded curriculum.
- dogmatic and stereo-typed methods of teaching.
- poor quality of teachers.
- admission of under-aged children.
- ill equipped school plant.
- treat of examinations.

Solutions

Providing free textbooks, notebooks, uniform mid-day meals

- 'Shift system' of schooling.
- Starting of new school in 'no-school areas.'
- Arranging special classes for the backward.
- Giving the medical aid to the needy.
- Adopting upgraded teaching in primary section (i.e., taking standard I to IV as one unit, abolishing, detention in those classes).

Population Education

This is the age of progress and development. In every walk of life, human achievements are well-acknowledged. Scientific progress has made man the master of this universe but he could not control the self. The problem of population is alarming almost everywhere in the world. Population explosions have made the sociologist worried about the future existence of man. It is one of the most fundamental of human problems. It affects every aspect of man's life- individual, national and international. It affects health, wealth and happiness of individual families. It affects prosperity and progress of nations, it affects international security and peace. Most countries of the world are confronted with the problem of food supply, living standards, social, economical and educational concerns.

The idea of population education is based on the following major assumptions:

1. The unprecedented population growth is responsible for retarding economic progress of the country.
2. It prejudices the health and well-being of the younger generation.
3. The country is pledged to raise the standard of living of the people since chronic poverty provides a constant stimulus to unrestrained population growth.
4. Population education is not to be mixed with sex education or the methods of family planning. It is a motivational force for clearing the right attitudes to family size.
5. Population is not only to be considered quantitatively but also qualitatively.
6. The education of birth rate is not a "once for all affair", rather is should be on a continuous basis.

Meaning of Population Education

It is quite different from sex education or education for family living. The national seminar on 'Population Education' held in Bombay in August 1969 made the following recommendation to define the concept:

The objective of population education should be to enable the students to understand the family size is controllable, that population limitations can facilitate the development of a higher quality of life in the nation an that a small family size can contribute materially to the quality of living for the individual family. Students at all levels have a right to accurate information about the effect of changes in family size and in national population, on the individual, the family and the nation so that this body of knowledge is utilized to control family size and national population.

Population should not be treated merely as a quantitative phenomenon or just an essay in numbers. It is the quantity of the population that is most relevant both as factor of growth and an end product of growth and numbers have to be treated in terms of the effect they have on quality either by way of deterioration or of improvement.

In terms of broad objectives, we may now say that 'population education' as in integral part of general education seeks:

1. To develop an understanding of some demographic concepts and processes.
2. To develop an understanding of the influence of population trends as the various aspects of human life.
3. To develop an understanding of evil effects of ever population on the environment and concomitant dangers from pollution.
4. To develop an understanding of biological factors and phenomenon of reproduction which are responsible for continuation of the species.
5. To develop an awareness of the population policies and programmes of the country.
6. To develop an attitude of responsibility and mutual help and co-operation in all aspects of personal and family living.

Specific Objectives of Population Education

It is quite essential to develop the curriculum of population education for different stages, differently keeping in view that mental development of the children. In the following lines, we are giving the objectives of the population education for primary and secondary stages separately.

Primary Stage

Here we mean the education for 7 years as recommended by Education Commission for the children up to 14 years of age.

(a) *Information and Knowledge*

1. To develop in children an awareness of the growing population in their locality, neighbourhood, state and country.
2. To develop in children an understanding of visible impact of growth of population in some locality and neighbourhood etc.
3. To enable the children to appreciate the advantages of a small family in relation to food, clothing, shelter and education.
4. To enable the children to acquire an elementary knowledge of plants and animals life-process, growth and decay.

(b) *Skills, Abilities and Attitudes*

1. To help children develop good hygienic habits so that they keep both their person and environment clean.
2. To help children develop the skill of locating information about population of villages, districts, states etc.
3. To help children keep the record of personal expenses.
4. To help children to compare and contrast the life in rural and urban area.
5. To help children collect data about population of their state and country.

Secondary Stage

It should include 3 or 4 years of education after 7 or 8 years of schooling, for the children between the age of 14 and 18 years.

(a) *Knowledge an Understanding*

1. To develop an understanding of the density of population in various parts of the world.
2. To develop an understanding of the growth rate of population in India and various parts of the world and its cause.
3. To develop an understanding of the need to maintain a balance in population.

(b) *Skills, Abilities and Attitudes*

1. To develop an ability to collect data about population, growth rates, density of population, natural resources.
2. To develop an appreciation for the difficulties faced in large families with small-income.
3. To develop an appreciation for the difficulties—social, and sanitary-arousing out of overcrowding.
4. To develop the appreciation for the fact that superstitions are detrimental to a better living and checking of population growth.

Adult Education

Education begins at birth and continues throughout life. It is constant and ongoing. It develops man power for different levels of economy and empowers the poor masses to become self-reliant enough to participate, in the process of national development.

Adults have to play various 'in evitable roles' in their life and they must learn to cope with them as they arise. About one-third of world's non-Literates reside in India.

Definition

In 1952, UNESCO's International Directory of Adult Education Stated, "In essence, Adult Education is so closely related to the social, political and cultural conditions of each country that no uniform or precise definition can be arrived at."

In 1967, Jesup, F.W. and Townsend Coles observed, "... There is no internationally accepted definition of Adult Education."

Aser, Deleon, "... All kinds of education for adults – in school and out of school, formal, informal, full time and part time for persons who no longer attend schools as well as for those who never attended a school and so on."

Paulo Freire, "Adult Education is a cultural action for freedom."

The regional seminar on Adult Education and Development in Asia and Oceania, held at Bangkok from November 24- December 1980 observed; "Although different countries use different terms, 'Adult Education' has been recognized as an acceptable term for many. The terms of, Non-Formal Education, Continuing Education, Complementary Education explain different forms and approaches of Adult Education."

Definition of Concepts Used for Adult Education

- *(a)* *Continuing Education:* Derek Rowntree (1981), "The availability of structured education experience throughout a persons life."
- *(b)* *Further Education:* Blond's Encyclopaedia of Education (1969); "Further Education is a general term used (in UK) to describe full or part-time education for those who have completed their secondary education. Further education includes, technical, commercial and art education and adult education."
- *(c)* *Lifelong Education:* Brian Groom Bridge; ".... Its rationale is in part the same as that for adult education, except that it intricically involves a radical reform of organization, form and content of all other phases of education, and also implies a greater recognition of the educational functions of non-educational agencies...."

John Dewey, "*Education is life,
Education is growth,
Education is social process.*"

(d) *Literacy* : Carlo. M. Cipolla, Literacy and Development in the West (1969); "In an advanced industrial society a person with less than 10 or 12 years of schooling is functionally illiterate."

(e) *Functional Literacy:* UNESCO (1951),."A person is literate who can, with understanding both read and write a short-simple statement on his everyday life."

(f) *Non-Formal Education:* Coombs (1973); "Any organized, systematic educational activity outside the framework of the formal system (designed) to provide selective types of learning to particular sub-groups in the population, adults as well as children."

(g) *Recurrent Education:* Organization for Economic Co-operation and Development (OECD) 1968; "Recurrent Education is formal and preferably full time education for adults who want to resume their education, interrupted earlier for a variety of reasons."

(h) *Social Education:* Maulana Abdul Kalám Azad, first Education Minister, Government of India, "This is where the need for adult education in our country we have given it the name of social education, become imperative. By social education we mean education for the complete man."

A Committee was setup under the chairmanship of Mohan Lal Sexena to report on adult education, the report called, " *A Scheme for Social Education*. They defined Social Education. As course directed towards the production of consciousness of citizenship among the people and promotion of social solidarity among them."

Explanation of Synonymous Concepts

Adult Education, Adult literacy, Continuing Education, Further Education... and all these terms cannot same meaning.

Need for Adult Education in India

- Mahatma Gandhi, "Mass Illiteracy is India's sin and shame."
- For economic development, i.e., there is a high correlation between literacy and percapita income.
- Agricultural development, i.e., education/training help the farmers for better use of the modes/factors of production.

- Industrial development.
- Population control.
- Cultural development, i.e., educated easily welcomes changes.
- Political development.
- Social development, i.e., better us of his/her leisure.
- Education for a changing world.
- Vocational efficiency.
- Awakening the people.
- Reaping benefits of new knowledge, i.e., made a connection between centres of research and excellence with homes.
- Knowledge of Basic skills, i.e., healthy life, civic education.
- Improvement in the quality of leadership followership especially in rural areas.
- Awakening the backward classes.
- Women empowerment.
- Awakening nomadic rural population, i.e., the end to isolation.
- Awakening of diverse groups like lawyers, doctors, teachers, they also the beneficiaries of adult education, they take a course for joy sometimes. Example: a foreign language, music etc.

Workers Education v/s Adult Education

Workers education is not adult education. In adult education every adult, may get the benefit of learning whether he is a worker in an industry or not. Workers education is not open to all but limited to workers.

National Level Agencies of Adult Education

(a) *Central Board of Workers Education (CBWE):* The Government of India constituted a central board to took after the affairs of workers education. It was entrusted with the

- function of administering workers education.
- planning, programmes.
- allocating funds.
- advancing the cause of workers education.

CBWE has opened regional and sub-regional centres for workers education in all states. CBWE's headquarters at Nagpur.

(b) *Indian Adult Education Association (IAEA)*: IAEA formed in 1939, one of the apex body of Adult Education. IAEA's two organs are *Indian Journal of Adult Education* and *IAEA News Letter*. IAEA conducting annual conferences, Dr. Sakir Husain memorial lecture, presentation of Nehru Literacy award and Tagore literacy award etc.

(c) *Nehru Yuva Kendra Sanghatan (NYK)*: Through NYK's network of youth clubs all over the country is working for the development of non-student youths groups of 15-35 years. NYK organizing various awareness programmes, vocational training etc.

(d) *Shramik Vidya Peeth (SVP):* SVP, in earlier known as Polyvalent Adult Education Centre. Now SVP called Jana Shikshan Sanghatan (JSS). JSS dealing with the working classes in and around cities. Nearly 100 JSS's are working all over India.

Agencies of Adult Education in Kerala

(a) *Kerala Grandha Sala Sangham (KGS)*: KGS established in 1945 with 47 libraries. Now 5000 and above rural libraries are affiliated with KGS. KGS organizing experimental functional literacy programmes, publishing of books, literacy programmes, etc. KGS's libraries function as a community centres.

(b) *Kerala Shastra Sahithya Parishath (KSSP):* KSSP is a cultural organization which tries to popularize science among ordinary people. KSSP, organizing classes, lectures, book publishing, club activities, fairs, quiz programmes etc. KSSP played a major role in the Total Literacy Programme. KSSP received UNESCO's Literacy Award in 1999.

(c) *Kerala Association for Non-Formal Education and Development (KANFED):* KANFED, aim to linking non-formal education with development. KANFED published books, guides, workbooks for neo-literates. KANFED, conducting mass awareness programmes and helping common man who desire for lifelong education.

Women Education

Importance of Women Education

"Truly no argument is required in defense of women's education. For my part, I have always been strongly of the opinion that while it may be possible to neglect men's education it is not possible to neglect women's education. The reasons are obvious. If you educate the women, probably men will be affected thereby, and in any event children will be affected."

—*Jawaharlal Nehru* (1889-1964)

Significance of Women Education

Gandhiji observed in 'True Education', "The question of the education of children cannot be solved unless effort are made simultaneously to solve the women's education. And I have no hesitation in saying that as long as we do not have real mother teachers who can successfully impart true education to our children they will remain un educated even though they may going to schools."

Dr. S. Radhakrishnan has very emphatically stated, "Women are human beings and have as much right to full development as men have. The position of women in any society is a true index of its cultural and spiritual level."

NPE (1968), "The education of girls should receive emphasis not only on grounds of social justice but also because it accelerates social transformation."

Table–6.1
Sex-wise Literacy Rate 1951-91

Year	*Persons*	*Males*	*Females*
1951	18.33	27.16	8.86
1961	28.31	40.40	15.34
1971	34.45	45.95	21.97
1981	43.56	56.37	29.75
	(41.42)	(53.45)	(28.46)
1991	52.11	63.86	39.42

Notes

1. Literacy rate for 1951, 1961 and 1971 related to population aged five years and above. The rates for the years 1981 and 1991 relate to the population aged seven years and above. The literacy rates for the population aged five years and above in 1981 have been shown in brackets.
2. The 1981 rates exclude Assam where the 1981 Census could not be conducted. The 1991 Census rates exclude Jammu and Kashmir.

Phenomenal Progress Since Independence

Importance of education of women has been recognized since the achievement of independence. Accordingly strenuous efforts have been made in this area. The following figures reveal that literacy among women has proportionately as compared with men. Yet much more is needed to bring it at par with men.

Table–6.2
Number of Women per Men in Higher Education Since 1950-51

Year	Number of Women per Hundred Men
1950-51	14
1960-61	17
1965-66	24
1981-82	38
1982-83	39
1983-84	40
1985-86	42
1987-88	46
1988-89	46
1989-90	47
1990-91	47

Table–6.3
Enrolment and Percentage of Girls Since Independence

Item	1950-51	1960-61	1970-71	1980-81	1986-87
1. Number of Girls in Primary Classes	54,00,000	1,14,00,000	213,00,000	283,00,000	3,61,00,000
2. % to total enrolment (Boys & Girls)	28.17	32.6	37.4	38.6	40.1
3. Number of Girls in Middle Calsses-VI-VIII	5,00,000	16,03,390	3,90000	88,00,000	1,02,00,000
4. % to total enrolment	16.1	23.9	29.3	32.97	35.4
5. Number of Girls in Secondary Schools 10+2 Intermediate (IX + alone)	2,00,000	6,00,000	19,00,000	35,00,000	54,00,000
6. % to total enrolment	14.36	18.2	25.0	29.4	30.7

Table-6.4
Percentage of Girls 1989-90 and 1990-91 in the Respective Age Group Population

Classes	1989-90			1990-91		
	Boys	Girls	Total	Boys	Girls	Total
I-V (6-11 years)	111.5	83.6	99.9	115.9	85.97	101.03
VI-VIII (11-14 years)	73.0	44.6	59.1	73.38	46.13	60.11

Disparities

- The illiteracy rate is high in rural areas among ST women.
- While illiteracy among women in Kerala is 13.07 per cent (1991), this is as high as 79.16 per cent in Rajasthan and 76 per cent in Bihar.
- Percentage of women enrolled in arts (Higher Education) is 55 per cent compared with 20 per cent in science courses.

Women Universities

Out of about 190 universities (including equivalent institutions), there are 5 women universities.

Problems of Women Education and Methods of Popularization

From the time many committees and commissions have expressed concern regarding slow progress of girls and women education in India. Reference may be made to the following in this regard:

1. The University Education Commission (1948-49).
2. Smt. Durgabai Deshmukh Committee (1959).
3. Smt. Hansa Mehta Committee (1962).
4. M. Bhakta Valsalam Committee to look into the causes of public support particularly in rural areas for girls education and to enlist public co-operation.
5. Education Commission (1964-66).
6. Resolution on the NPE (1968).
7. Report of the Committee on the Status of Women in India (1974).
8. Challenge of Education 1985.
9. NPE (1986).
10. Programme of Action (POA), 1986.

Causes of Slow Progress

- Economic backwardness of the rural community.

- Lack of proper social attitudes in the rural areas for the education of the girls.
- Lack of educational facilities in rural areas.
- Lack of women teachers.
- Lack of proper supervision and guidance due to adequate women personnel in the inspectorate.
- Lack of proper incentives to parents and children.
- Lack of suitable curriculum.
- Co-educational aspects.

Education of the Women and Rural Population

"Women all over the world have a great role to play in bringing peace in the tension-ridden world", (*Speech of Late Prime Minister Rajiv Gandhi, Hindustan Times, March 25, 1986*). That is, women use holding important positions in all walks of life; no high office is barred to them, not even the prime ministership of the country.

No development programme can be successful in India unless it is seen from grassroots development perspectives. This is due to the fact that the soul of India lies in villages, as Mahatma Gandhi said during the national movement and this is also true today, when more than two-thirds of the people live in rural areas. Therefore, rural development constitutes an inseparable and necessary component of the national development process. However, no rural development can be conceived of ignoring the development of the women who constitute half of the rural population but enjoy an unequal, differentiated and lower socio-economic status.

Problems of Rural Women

The problems of rural women are different from those of male persons. The women's issues, issues in rural areas can be categorized into three main groups, namely, socio-cultural, economic and political. They are as follows:

(a) Socio-Cultural Issues

Socio-culturally, women in rural areas are treated as inferior and subordinate to their male counterparts. The main causes are as follows:

- *Established Tradition*: Super situation, worn-out customs, social beliefs, norms and unwritten taboos that have pervaded the Indian rural society for ages.
- *Female Illiteracy*: The inferior status of rural women is mostly due to the lack of female literacy in rural areas. In most cases,

the school site is far away from the habitats for which the female children are not able to go to school. The female child in rural areas is preferred to remain at home to help her mother in household chores rather than going to schools. Female drop-out in schools is still a marked feature and female literacy in large number is yet to be achieved.

- *Health Condition is very Poor*: The health condition of rural women is very poor. It has been admitted that, age-old tradition, social taboos, superstition, ignorance and poverty prevent the rural women to avail the medical facilities. They do not come to the hospital in time and only when their conditions becomes serious, they come for treatment and their death becomes inevitable, even if proper treatment is given to them at their last stage.
- *Lack of Adequate Hospital Facilities*: Lack of medicine, absence of lady doctors in remote areas, and no provision of mobile dispensaries, which are responsible for bad health plight of rural woman.
- *Imparting health education to the rural women is completely absent.*
- In the *economic point of view*, rural women are in a state of poverty. Rural people in general, are poor.
- *Severe Malnutritious*: In social status, the position of women was very low and they were neglected of having nutritional food by the man.
- *High Mortality Rate*: In the early stages, status of women was very low in the society. So they were neglected from health care measures and they were considered as liability rather than asset.
- *Low Social Status*: The status of women was very low as compared to man in rural areas. The soul power to control any family matters are jealously guarded and control by men in the household. In spite of the fact that women are engaged in both productive and reproductive work.
- *Early Marriages*: In the earlier period the marriage age of women was 12 or 13 years. So the girls faced by so many psychological and physical problems.

b) Economic Issues

In the economic point of view, rural women are in a state of poverty. Rural people, in general, are poor. But rural women are poorer than the rural men. Women have little property rights. For, land and whatever savings the family possess, that belong to the male persons. Even if rural female participation in the economic process is always higher than the total male participation and the urban female participation, their work always remain unpaid or underpaid. They do not earn cach money as they are not engaged in gainful employment in formal sectors.

Lack of Economic Power: Women's are not equal to men in society. In the case of wage, women's average wage was very low as compared to men. So focuses on improving women's control over material resources and strengthening women's economic security. Its strategies are built around strengthening women's positions as workers and income earners by mobilizing, organizing or unionizing and providing access to support services SEWA, Proshika etc.

(c) Political Issues

In a developing society like ours, the traditional social taboos, societal ideologies and myths associated with a patriarchal heritage prevent women from developing strong links with the wider network of social contacts. Women's environment tends to act as a barrier to political stimuli, so restricting the likelihood that they will participate in politics.

In short, political status of women can be defined as the degree of equality and freedom enjoyed by women in the shaping and sharing of power and in the value given by society to this role of women. The Indian constitution guarantees political equality through the institution of adult franchise and Article 15, which prohibits discrimination interaction on grounds of sex. It is stated that neither the governmental officers nor this NGO's have tried to encourage the women villagers to speak out their needs on which a new line of planning for development can be made. Further, the participatory institution in the village area is the Panchayats. Realizing the low participation of rural women in these local institutions, provision are made for reservation of seats for women in local bodies by 73 Amendment of the Constitution, 1992. This is certainly a significant step in political empowerment of women and consequently, their participation in decision-making bodies of rural areas.

Need for Upliftment of Women in Rural Areas

According to Gandhiji, the spirit of India lies in the villages. The development of the country such as India is predominately dealt with the progress of the villages. Substantial part of the village population consists women class. So the all round development of the village can only possible.

- *Mother, is the Backbone of the Family:* An ignorant mother of family can't lead the family successfully. An educated mother would not like their children to be less educated than themselves.
- *To Eradicate Health Problems*: Careful look at the research priorities reveals that low priority to women's health issues as the establishments predominately manned by the males. In order to remady this, it is important that women get a chance to functional all levels of health care establishments. If the mother is educated, she will be aware of their childrens health. This leads to the improvement of society.
- *To Check Population Explosion:* The enormous population growth leads to increase in shortage of water, environmental pollution and decline in resources. Women should be aware of population problems. A literate mother will be aware of the population problems.
- *To Eradicate Social Evils:* There is urgent need to create awareness among the women to eradicate social evils. No amount of government help can achieve the desired results, unless the women themselves realize the need of such a change. This requires proper education to women about their rights and duties. Social evils such as child labour, child marriage, forced marriage by parents, harassment by husbands/in laws, traffic in women etc., can be removed through awareness class.
- *Upliftment of Society*: Nearly 50 per cent of our population is women. So for the all round development, it is necessary to activate woman in the process of nation making.
- *Progress of Nation*: For the progress of the country the women participation is necessary in each and every development process of the nation.
- *To Provide Economic and Social Security*: One of the biggest problem facing rural women is a sense of insecurity. As longer women feels insecure she can't come up in life. The

economic independence creates confidence and provides social security. The voluntary organization should take up concrete step if necessary in collaboration with government agencies to provide more and more employment opportunities to women.

- *Evil of Dowery System:* Dowery is one of the major social evil which is responsible for the misery in many families of the rural areas. The voluntary organizations have a very significant role to play both in prevention an cure of this social evil as the judiciary could not do much without clear evidence.

  Voluntary organizations have a significant role in uplifting the status of women in the society. Unless voluntary organizations take an active part in the movement of liberation of rural women, nearly governmental agencies can't achieve the desired results.

Status and Power of Rural Women

In primitive time women would appears to have been fully equal, both mentally and physically to man. At that time, there was no permanent union between man and woman. Afterwards, the custom of marriage arose out of which developed in turn the home, the family, the tribe, the nation. Then, it was the women who reared the children, performed general domestic labour. Then the condition was improved, there was a fixed home and the women remained the property of her husband who had absolute right over her. Gradually, the man overpowered the women through establishments and laws which were controlled the whole society of the nation. As far as rural woman concerned the status of them are very low than the urban woman.

Now-a-days the states of rural women in the society is far better than that of before. It is the result of the progressive works of various voluntary organizations, women bodies, political parties and governmental bodies. Voluntary organizations can contribute much than government agencies to promote the status of rural woman and the woman themselves should be aware of their rights and duties in the society.

The collective strength of rural women can promote much progressive works in the process of development in the sates. For example, in Kerala the Panchayat level the Kudumbasree, i.e., the small organized unites of women in village, ward level are contributing their collective man power in the developmental process of Kerala. They started many small scale industries such as soap working, hand weaving, cattle farming and vegetable cultivation etc. Now-a-days Kudumbasree is one of the important organization which contributes various factors which leads to the development of villages. In fact, still now there is not any organization of man which contributes development work in the states.

Women's Education in Rural Areas

The women's education is now considered to be a desirable among higher income group in rural areas. The female literacy as well as the proportion of school goers or educands among women is indeed very low than men. The two main occupation in rural areas are cultivation of land and labour including agriculture labour. It is formed that female literacy among the labour is very low. Among the cultivators a useful classification is that of the size landholding. The female literacy as well as the proportion of school govers or educants among women indeed very low among households having less than two ackers of land.

The education of rural women may be summed up as follows: the pace of education is much slower among women than among men. The advanced communities forming a minor fraction of village population have now realized the importance of educating their daughters and this process is gradually persuading the other weaker sections of the rural population.

The first step in the education of rural women ion dealt with literacy and enrolment in primary schools in the villages. But even in the big villages the schools have just been started. The percentage of school going girls are very low in rural areas.

Causes of the Backwardness of Women Education

There are two factors into operate against the girls of secondary stages:

1. There is a strong tendency to withdrawn the girls from education when they grow up.
2. At the secondary stage, the parents like to separate the girls from schools. As the schools were none in these villages. But the boys were sent to secondary schools in the neighbouring

villages and many of them may stay therefore their study. But very few rural parents are willing to do this.

With the advance of women's education in rural areas the number of girls reaching higher stages of education is little increased. The progress of education in rural areas is inevitably changing the patterns of social and cultural life. This not only influence the backward classes of rural communities but also the women folk of these communities. An important influence of parents especially that on the progress of education is the influence of the mother in the case of girls. Educated mothers would not like their daughters to be less educated than what they themselves are. It is in this that lies the best guarantee of the progress of women's education in future, in the rural areas.

Women Empowerment

The year 2001 has been declared as the year of women's empowerment for enhancing the states and sustainable achievement in women's empowerment. According to Dr. Amertya Sen, there are mainly 3 problems faced by the women, i.e., illiteracy, lack of health and malnutrition. Education is the most significant factor of development and the only tool for realizing empowerment.

Women Empowerment—Rural Areas

There is a great number of girl students who dropout from school at secondary level and higher secondary level. Specially in the rural areas the preference is given to home related works and not to education. For the empowerment of these rural women, open and distance education can play very important role.

Potentialities of Rural Women

Women's potentialities as mothers, as household managers, as income-earners and as protectors of the environment are always under-valued and this has become major factor for male dominance in society. Women not only give birth to children, but they raise them to full citizens who will have an active role in building the nation and the society. Women can perform these functions, only when they are properly educated and they themselves can maintain good health. A woman's education and good health are assets for the society as she is the builders of the future citizens.

Women are household managers as they have to manage the domestic activities in an efficient manner. Particularly in rural areas, in many families the male persons migrate to the near by urban area to earn cash money and they come home occasionally. The burden of household management falls upon the shoulders of women. Therefore, women need education to manage the household affairs. Rural women, in most cases, are income-earners. It is estimated that rural women earn more than the rural male folk.

Suggestions for Removal of Backwardness of Rural Women

In case of the backwardness of rural women, many plans and programmes had already been implemented by the Government, but the response of the rural women to these measures very negligible.

Hence, following suggestions can be made for development of women from grassroots development perspective:

(a) The potentialities of rural women should be properly identified and encouraged and not to be ignored. All development programmes should be made in consonance with the development of potentialities of rural women of a particular area. No common development programmes for women will work out, as the rural women pose a different picture from the urban women as well as the problems of tribal women are not the same as the women of the general caste. Hence, the chalking out any development programme for women, emphasis should be on indigenous problems and priorities. Therefore, planning should be decentralized upto the grassroots level.

(b) Education of rural women should be undertaken on war-footing measures, as immediate and urgent need by opening primary schools in every village and providing sufficient cost-free study materials.

(c) Monetary incentives should be given to the teachers of the rural primary schools as well as to the parents of girl child for sending their children to school. Without proper education women cannot enjoy the benefits of development nor they can participate in the process of decision-making in family, in community and in rural local bodies.

(d) Adequate health facilities including free medicines, vitamins pills, medical education, nurses, midwifes and lady doctors should be provided for women in rural areas. If women would be physically weak, they would be a liability not only for the family, but also for the nation as a whole.

(e) Periodic appraisal of the progress of rural women by the governmental agencies as well as by the non-governmental agencies is necessary. The responsibility of development of the rural women not only on governmental bodies, but the home agencies like parents, husband, family members and relative; community agencies like voluntary associations, community centres, women organizations, co-operatives, schools, teachers etc. Governmental agencies like Panchayats, legislature, bureaucracy and planning bodies; and media agencies like newspaper, T.V., radio and films should hold the responsibility or development of rural women. All these agencies should be active and dynamic and should work in co-operation and harmony particularly, on three counts, namely to check corruption, to implement the policies vigorously and to motivate women to participate in decision-making.

Backwardness of rural women is not a natural but a social phenomenon having its root on social customs, traditions and beliefs. But it is a liability for the nation as a whole. Hence, it is to be uprooted by providing equality, dignity, freedom and opportunity to empower rural women in order to be not only as efficient mother and housewives, but as the active citizens having positive roles in the nation building process. In the past, development programmes for the rural woman have often failed, because their potentialities were not known, their needs were ignored, they were not listened to and policies were made for them by keeping them aside in the formulation stage as well as in the implementation of the programmes. But, if a "sustainable social process is to be built from below," there is the need to ensure genuine empowerment at the grassroots.

Vocation Education

Since the beginning of time occupational knowledge and manual skill gave, in one form man to man and from generation. This transmitting process, whatever, its form of organization, has developed into the educational process that has now given rise to expansion and developments of what may be formed as vocational education. The term vocational education is meant to cover both unorganized and organized methods of transmitting knowledge, skills and competence. Vocational education refers to activities designed to contribute to occupational proficiency.

Vocational Education—Criteria

Any curriculum which embraces vocational considerations will include these elements:

1. Work experience.
2. Industrial visits.
3. Careful vocational guidance before admission to and through out the course.
4. Problem-solving and the practical application of skills and knowledge.
5. A relationship between the courses and employment opportunities, locally or nationally.

Terms Defined—Vocational Education

The basic word here is vocation. It means any calling/ occupation or business. It may not be of technical nature-vocation is a very broad term. Vocational education is that education which trains you for vocation.

UNESCO (1974), "Vocational education as a comprehensive term embracing those aspects of educational process involving in addition to general education, the study of technologies and related sciences and acquisition of practical skill, attitudes and understandings and knowledge relating to occupations in the known sectors of economic and social life.... Such an education would be an integral part of general education and a means of preparing for an occupational field and an aspect of continuing education."

Vocationalisation of Education

Vocationalization of education means to provide a strong vocational bias to secondary education. Vocational courses should be introduced high schools along with general subjects. It implies that general and vocational education should be segregated, rather than two should be galvanized.

Need of Vocationalisation of Education

1. For achieving economic development of the country. Our country a land or plenty natural resources, even though, the lack of trained man power results a poor economy.
2. For making secondary education a self-sufficient course.
3. For solving the problem of un employment among uneducated.

4. For meeting varying aptitudes, interests and talents of students. Well-planned practical subjects only can meet the different aptitudes, interests and talents.

Way and Mean of Vocationalization of Education

- Vocational Surveys.
- Establishing new schools in rural areas.
- Counselling and placement.
- Close connection with employment agencies.
- Apprenticeship and recruitment programmes.

District Primary Education Programme (DPEP)

District Primary Education Programme is a programme conceptualized and evolved on the basis of varied experiences the country possesses and supplemented by the experiences of various international agencies directly involved in the funding of primary education projects in the developing countries. DPEP considers that what is to be done at the district level need to be decided by those at the district level itself. It is envisaged as a centrally sponsored scheme with flexible parameters. These parameters are meant to ensure that the plan is within the framework of national concerns and priorities.

Objectives of DPEP

1. To provide access all children to primary education through formal primary schools or its equivalent through alternatives.
2. To reduce overall dropouts at the primary level less than 10 per cent.
3. To increase achievement levels by 25 per cent points over and above the measured baseline levels.
4. To reduce disparities of all types to less than 5 per cent.

The focus of each plan may vary depending upon the levels of development of primary education in the selected district. In some districts, the priority may be more on access; in certain cases the focus may be on retention; and in still other cases focus may be on achievement. The criteria to identify districts under the programme are:

1. Educationally ward districts with female literacy below the national average.
2. Districts where Total Literary Campaigns (TLC) have been successful leading to enhanced demand for primary education.

The DPEP is an attempt to initiate a process of planning from below. The framework of the programme envisages initiating and completing the process of planning first at the district level. The state level intervention strategies and plans are meant to facilitate the successful implementation of the district plans. It can be seen that looking at linkages between state district plans in this framework changes the relative roles to be played by agencies at different levels.

Planning Competencies

DPEP envisages planning responsibility to be undertaken entirely by the people at the district level. This necessitates developing planning competencies at the district level. The national and state resource organizations help in developing planning competencies. This help was of two kinds:

1. In developing basic framework for planning education at the district level.
2. Organizing programmes to train the local level people.

While the broad parameters are decided through a consultative process, the districts have the full freedom to put targets, to evolve strategies and to schedule activities. In short the planning exercise takes into account local requirements and priorities them and thus it becomes an exercise in developing local level competencies in planning. Moreover, financial outlays are ensured to achieve the thus set targets.

The district plans under the DPEP envisage first to achieve the horizontal integration of the district level programmes and to vertically integrate them with the state level and national level initiatives. This helps in ensuring local autonomy, competency and administrative capability. The process of capacity building is a part and parcel of the planning exercise. The district plans are drawn for a period of 6-7 years with detailed schedules and activities for each year. The allocations are made each year based on the performance in the previous year and evaluation of the proposals for the coming year.

Sarva Shiksha Abhiyan (SSA)

SSA, a programme with a clear time frame for universal elementary education. A response to the demand for quality basic education all over the country. An opportunity for promoting social justice through basic education. It's an effort at effectively involving the Panchayati

Raj Institutions, school management committees, village and urban slum level education committees, PTA's, MPTA's, Tribal Autonomous councils and other grassroot level structures in the management of elementary schools. An expression of political will for universal elementary education across the country. A partnership between the Central, State and the Local Government. It's an opportunity for states to develop their own vision of elementary education.

Basic Features of SSA

SSA is an effort to universalize elementary education by community-ownership of the school system. It is a response to the demand for quality basic education all over the country. The SSA programme is also an attempt to provide an opportunity for improving human capabilities to all children, through provision of community-owned quality education in a mission mode.

Aims of SSA

The SSA is to provide useful and relevant elementary education for all children in 6-14 age group by 2010. There is also another goal to bridge social, regional and gender gaps, with the active participation of the community in the management of schools.

Useful and relevant education signifies a quest for an education system that is not alienating and that draws on community solidarity. Its aim is to allow children to learn about and master their natural environment in a manner that allows the fullest harnessing of their human potential both spiritually and materially. This quest must also be a process of value based learning that allows children on opportunity to work for each other's well-being rather than to permit mere selfish pursuits.

SSA realizes the importance of Early Childhood Care and Education and looks at the 0-14 age as a continuum. All efforts to support pre-school learning in ICDS centres or special pre-school centres in non ICDS areas will be made to supplement the efforts being made by the department of women and child development.

Objectives of SSA

1. All children in school, education guarantee centre, alternate school, 'Back-to-School' camp by 2003.
2. All children complete five years of primary schooling by 2007.

3. All children complete eight years of elementary schooling by 2010.
4. Focus on elementary education of satisfactory quality with emphasis on education for life.
5. Bridge all gender and social category gaps at primary stage by 2007 and at elementary education level by 2010.
6. Universal retention by 2010.

Education For All (EFA)

Education has continued to evolve, diversify and extend its reach and coverage since the dawn of human history. Every country develops its system of education to express and promote its unique socio-cultural identity and also to meet the challenges of the times. There are moments in history when a new direction has to be give to be an age-old process. That moment is today. The Government of India announced in January 1985 that a New Education Policy would be formulated for the country. A comprehensive appraisal of the existing educational scene was made followed by a country wide debate. The views and suggestions received from different quarters were carefully studied.

It is relatively a new concept. This is our academic dream for universalizing education in the country, which is enthusiastically supported by the Government also. As per scholars view, education is the foundation, on the basis of which the future of a country is largely determined. The direction of a country is directed according to the education, people receive there. Elementary education is the basic foundation of education on which the future of a student largely depends. Needless to say that education has a crucial contribution to make towards promoting national integration, understanding and a sense of togetherness and harmony. There is, therefore, great need for an integrated and value-oriented education with a national perspective. The task of covering all the illiterates in the age group of 15-35 years, is a formidable programme, also to be linked effectively with various development programmes. The expansion and effectiveness of adult education provides a further impetus to this growth.

At the core of the education for all partnershiop is the belief that education is the key to sustainable development and peace and stability within and among countries, and accordingly that is indispensable for people to participate fully in the societies and globalized economies of the 21st century.

While it may be assumed in many countries that all children can go to school, that was not the case for 14 years old Vijaya Lakshmi in Andhra Pradesh, India. She and almost 2,50,000 other young children in this region are employed in the cotton seed industry as bonded labourers-forced to work long hours in difficult conditions to return loans given to their families. Vijaya Lakshmi has been lucky enough to benefit from a world education programme that provides relevant, practical life skills for child girl labourers, but many girls in similar circumstances never go to school at all. Working to help a family takes priority, even though education has the most potential to help break these long-term cycles of poverty.

Those committed to universal education generally assert that much more is at stake than just getting kids into school. Rather, they claim, education is a major part of the solution for many of the world's development problems. Education and literacy, they note, are pre-requisites for economic growth and poverty alleviation; the knowledge and decision-making skills gained in school improve family health and well-being; an educated electorate usually makes better political decisions; education protects children from situations of abusive child labour and trafficking; and education helps to stop the spread of HIV and AIDS.

Despite all these benefits, governments are hot pouring resources into improving access to quality education. While some countries are making notable commitments to education, progress is often uneven with in countries and others are making little progress at all. About 100 million children of primary school age in the developing world do not attend school and, in about one-third of countries, one out of every three children that begins primary school will not finish it. Getting kinds in school is one thing; keeping them there is another.

None of the above is to say that the international community has not come a long way in providing at least a primary school education for many of the world's children. It has advancements, since the 1950s, for example, have been substantial, with primary school enrolments increasing more than three-fold in the past 50 years. But there is still much to be done. In many cases, for example, the quality of education, which is fundamental to keeping kinds in school, has received less attention than expanding access. About one fifth of the world's adult population still cannot read or write. And in many countries, the reality is that an individual will have greater educational opportunities if they are not poor, female, or residing in a rural area.

Education for All: Meeting International Goals

There has been no shortage of consultations on how to better educate the world's children. These include major international meetings held in Thailand in 1990 and Senegal in 2000, both sponsored by several UN agencies. At the latter, over 160 countries adopted six goals aimed at providing a good quality basic education to all children, youth and adults by 2015. The "Education For All" movement gained particular prominence the same year when world leaders on behalf of nearly every country, unanimously adopted the Millennium Development Goals in 2000. Two of the eight goals include the achievement of universal primary education and the elimination of gender disparities in all levels of education by 2015.

There is a chart included in this topic which shows countries stand on progress toward the education for all development index, which includes universal primary education, adult literacy, gender access, and quality of education.

Table—6.5

The World Countries Progress Towards the Education

	Far from EFA	*Inter-mediate Position*	*Close to EFA*	*EFA Achieved*
Sub-Saharan Africa	16	7	1	-
Arab States	5	19	1	-
Central Asia	-	2	1	2
East Asia and Pacific	3	7	2	3
South and West Asia	3	1	-	-
N. America/W. Europe	1	20	4	8
Central and Eastern Europe	-	1	12	4

(As on Global Monitoring Report 2006, p. 68)

There is growing awareness among governments of the powerful ties between education and development, and, as a result, a greater willingness to invest in this sector. Some countries have, in fact, made remarkable progress. Of 155 countries, 47 have achieved universal primary education and another 20 are on track to do so by

2015, notes the UN Educational, Scientific and Cultural Organization (UNESCO).

Adds a UNESCO brochure on this topic, "Many countries—not only in the richest parts of the world but also in Latin America, the Caribbean, East Asia, and even in Africa—are now approaching universal primary education for the first time. Countries such as Botswana, Brazil, China, Mexico, Sri Lanka and Tunisia are showing the way."

Bangladesh doubled primary school enrolment, especially for the rural poor, over a period of about 15 years. Strong government commitment, incentives for poor families, parental involvement in school management, curricula focused or real life skills, and the leadership of Non-Governmental Organizations (NGOs) all played a role.

Despite increasing primary school enrolment in some countries and the achievement—or near achievement—of full enrolment in North America, Europe, Latin America and East Asia, many countries in Sub-Saharan Africa, South Asia, and in the Arab and North Africa region continue to fall behind. Tens of millions of children remain out of school in these regions, including some 40 million in Sub-Saharan Africa alone. In total, UNESCO officials claims that 67 countries are at risk of missing of the goal of universal primary education by 2015.

Where gender parity in education is concerned another millennium development goal- girls' enrolment. Still lags behind that of boys in about 40 countries at the primary level, but in nearly twice as many countries at the secondary level.

When families must choose which children go to school, usually the girls lose out. Girls are more likely to have household tasks that keep them from going to—or staying in-school. Furthermore, the mere lack of safe transportation and separate toilet facilities for girls can keep them out of school. And in some areas, religious fundamentalism puts girls at a serious disadvantage—like in Afghanistan where attacks by a resurgent Taliban are forcing the closure of some girls schools.

While a lack of resources can diminish the quality of education in significant ways, it's also a widely accepted fact that more schooling generally leads to both higher individual earnings and a country's overall economic growth. The international commission on education for the 21st century, a UNESCO task force, recommended in the late 1990s that governments invest at least 6 percent of their Gross National Product (GNP) on education, covering all grade levels.

Simply reducing the barriers to attending school can have an impact too, especially in developing countries. "Evidence shows that scholarships, lower fees, and subsidies in the form of food and cash transfers conditional on school attendance increase girls' and boys' enrolment rates.

In spite of this putting a well-trained teacher in every classroom is vital to ensuring that every child has access to a quality education, but many areas lack either enough teachers or teachers with adequate training.

MODEL QUESTIONS

1. What is functional literacy?
2. Write of short note on Sarva Siksha Abhiyan.
3. What is meant by wastage and stagnation in primary education? What are its causes? Suggest ways to reduce them.
4. "Expansion of vocational education would help to meet the man power need of India." Do you agree? Give reasons for your answer.
5. Explain the meaning of 'Education For All'. Suggest measures to be taken to make EFA a reality.
6. Explain the role of DIETs.
7. Give the full forms of:
   (a) NCTE
   (b) NIEPA
8. Discuss the slogan 'EFA' in the light of "Education as a fundamental right."
9. Critically examine the role played by NAAC in the improving the quality of education at university level.

REFERENCES

1. Aggarwal, J.C. (2003). *Development and Planning of Modern Education*. Vikas Publishing House (P.) Ltd., New Delhi.
2. Chandra, S.S. (2003). *Adult and Non-Formal Education*, Surjeet Publishers, New Delhi.
3. Nanda, S.K. (2000). *Indian Education and its Problems Today*, Kalyani Publishers, New Delhi.
4. Pathak, C.K. (2003). *Adult Education – Millennium Challenges*, Rajat Publishers, New Delhi.
5. Rao, V.K. (1999). *Vocational Education*, Rajat Publishers, New Delhi.
6. Ruhela, S.P. *India's Struggle to Universalize Elementary Education*.

7. Singh, U.K. and Sudharshan, K.N. (2004) *Adult Education*, Discovery Publishing House, New Delhi.
8. Singh, U.K. and Sudarshan, K.N. (2004) *Vocational Education*, Discovery Publishing house, New Delhi.
9. Taneja, R.P. *Dictionary of Education*, Anmol Publishers (P) Ltd., New Delhi.
10. Venkataiah, S. (2002). *Vocational Education*, Anmol Publishers (P) Ltd., New Delhi.

URL's

1. www.edu.gov.
2. www.cde.ca.gov.
3. www.oneworld.net

7
Education in Ancient and Medieval India

EDUCATION DURING VEDIC PERIOD

An Introduction to Educational Heritage of India

Vedas occupy a very important place in the Indian life. The basis of Indian culture lies in the Vedas, which are four in number:

- Rigveda,
- Samveda,
- Yajurveda, and
- Atharvaveda.

Scholars differ as regards the causes and time of the rise of Vedas. This remains still in mystery.

The Vedas are the original source of the philosophy of life and system of education in ancient India. The knowledge derived from the Vedas alone can give real happiness to an individual. Only he can acquire this knowledge who has lined a life according to the four Ashramas:

- *Brahmacharya,*
- *Grihastha,*
- *Vanaprastha, and*
- *Samnyas.*

Generally, the word *veda* means *to know*, but it is the veda which inspires man to get the knowledge of *Brahma* (God).

The ancient *seers* of India regarded *redemption* as the primary goal of knowledge and for this they advocated both material and spiritual education of the individual.

F.E. Keay says, "Modern Education supplies to the young separate keys for opening every separate lock, whereas the ancient vedic system of education provided one master key which fails not anywhere."

Vedic System of Education

System of Admission was not like today. Student life in vedic society began with *Upanayana,* when the student goes to his chosen teacher called *Acharya.* The centre of learning called *Gurukula,* which was considered as the *second womb* for the child. The ceremony was performed for three days. During the three days period, the Guru holds within him the 'Sishya' as in a womb, impregnates him with his spirit and delivers him a new birth. The student emerges as *dwija* (twice born). The ceremony was performed at the ages 8, 11, 12 for the Brahmins, Kshatriyas and Vaishyas respectively. His parents given him only his body, or physical birth. But his Guru gives him his second birth, which is spiritual.

The *Upanayana* unfolds his mind and soul. After this ceremony, the student emerges as a *Brahmachari,* a new and changed individual both externally and internally. With the passage of time the ceremony came to be confined to Brahmin class only.

The Seats of Learning/School

The home of the Guru/Acharya was the seat of learning. It was situated in natural surroundings, not artificially consisted. It was a hermitage, amid sylvan surroundings, beyond the distractions of urban life, functioning in solitude and silence. Thus, in ancient period, we believed in domestic system of education.

The student lived with teacher as a member of his family and was treated by him in every respect as his son.

Man making was the basic aim of education. The personal touch of the teacher and the living relationship between student and teacher humanized the learning process.

The student belongs to the teachers, but not to the school. In the modern system, the teacher teaches the class, not the individual students. But in vedic period, the education was imparted to each individual with their differences.

The *guru* acted as the super ego or conscience and inculcated in the minds of the students the high ideals of morality and spirituality.

The environment or setting of *gurukula* contributed a lot towards the personality development of the students.

Duties of *Sishya's*/Studentship

(a) *Begging alms:* It was the usual rule for the brahmachari to go about begging for his teacher and the *gurukula*. Begging has certain educative value. That is,

- It produce in the students a spirit of humility and renunciation.
- It makes him ego less and less assertive.
- It helps him in the complete organization of personality and a deeper loyalty to the gurukula system.
- It was a sort of ritual for the cultivation of impersonal relations in life.
- It taught the students to feel how unattached he is to any ties.
- A sence of independence.
- Contributing to a sense of self-hood.

(b) *Tending the Sacred Fires*: Go to the forest, cut and collect fuel and fetch it to the *gurukula* for tending the scared fire. Worship of 'agni' by offering of choice objects had much spiritual and cultural significance. The *Agnihotra* ceremony was performed in the *gurukula* to enable the students to understand the reality of religion in the form of sacrifice.

Regulations Governing Student Life

Early Rising

The *guru* helped the students to lead a life of discipline and orderly routine. One such discipline was early rising. A student had to quit his bed before sun rise and before his teacher. If the sun rises, and he sleeps out of willful laziness, he had to mutter 'Gayatri Mantra' and fast for the whole day.

Prayer

A student had to offer his prayer thrice a day,

- Morning,
- Mid-day, and
- Evening.

Bath

To obtain physical purity, which was intimately connected with mental purity.

A student had to take regular bath everyday. At the time of both he had to mutter the hyms to waters.

Dress

Brahmacharis were using hempen, silken and woolen cloths. The dress was white and spotless.

Food

A student should support himself by begging. He should take his food with due permission of the *guru*. On seeing food, he should be delighted. He should not speak ill of it. He should mutter prayer at his meal. He should take his meal abstaining from speach.

Sleep

A student lie on the bare ground. He should sleep on a lower bed than that of his *guru* and should rise before and sleep after his *guru*.

Celibacy

The student had to observe celibacy. They had to control sexual impulses and should retrain from sexual inter-course.

- They should always avoid women.
- They shouldn't cast lustful eyes on females.
- Killing of human seen (*Viryathya*) was considered as a heinous sin like slaughter of brahmana.
- Unconscious discharge of seed was followed by muttering of certain hymns.

Such a observation of celibacy helps the student in their physical, intellectual and spiritual power.

Age of Studentship

The age at which a student begins his education varied from time-to-time. The duration was about 12 years. Many students who stayed in the *Ashrma* for more than 30 years.

Duration of Education

In the house of the teacher, the students was required to obtain education upto age of 24, after which he was expected to enter domestic life. Students were divided into three categories.

1. Those who obtaining education upto the age of 24 called *Vasu.*
2. Those who obtaining education upto the age of 36 called *Rudra.*

3. Those who obtaining education upto the age of 48 called *Aditya*.

The Students Uniform

Ajina is the upper garment used by the student, made out of skin of certain animals, that different to various castes.

Brahmana – Krishna Era black buck.

Kshatriya – Rurtu or spotted deer.

Vaisya – Vasta goat.

All other castes – Cow.

Vasa is the lower garment made of fibre of *alasi* plant or *kusa* grass or *karpas* (cotton). This dress should be woven or manufactured in the home of the student. Different castes had to use *vasa* of different colours.

Danda: A student was also required handle a *danda* or staff of wood of lengths which are different castes. *Danda* is the symbol of long life and holiness.

Mekhala

The uniform of a student also comprises a mekhala or gridle made of different materials for different castes.

Dressing of hair of a *brahmechari* arranged according to rules. A student cannot have hair style according to his sweet will. He should cover the head, except the tuft of the hair on the crown.

Characteristics of Vedic Education

Universal Education

The concept of universal education is never a new idea in India. The ancient Indian educationists advocated that education should not only cater to the needs of a 'few', but for the society as a whole.

The course of study and training were not, of course uniform for all the castes.

Education of Castes Other Than Brahmin

The *Brahmin* represented the intellectual and spiritual interest of the society. The administration and war was the normal duty of *Kshatriya*. The *Vaishya* received the required training for the economic upliftment of the society – commerce was his chief pursuit. There is little evidence regarding the education of the *Sudras*.

Education of Women

Education was not denied to women. She received education with men. They enjoy equal right with men.

Aims of Education

What were the aims of education in ancient Bharat? Difficulty in answering such a question. It is because, there is no book written by any *rishi* on this. Does this mean that all education of the Hindu's was aimless? The question put us faulty, for education is but one of the many aspects of life. Life has an aim. Education doesn't have any aim. Aim of life determines the aim of education. The aim of life, in Ancient India was the observation of 'dharma'. Hence, the observation of *dharma* was the aim of education in Ancient Bharat. *Dharma* means observation of duty.

Moksha

Moksha is the final stage in to which *dharma, artha* and *kama* automatically culminate.

The aim of education is to enable an individual to understand truth by education for chittivirtti-Nirodha or Yoga. (The science of science and the art of arts in Hindu system). Other aims of education are,

- Emphasis upon knowledge and experience.
- Sublimation of instincts.
- Spirituality.
- Development of character and personality.
- Fulfillment of duty, discipline, obedience, performance of hostly duties, rendering help to others.
- Preservation of culture.

Curriculum

Grammar, Rhetoric, Astrology, Logic (Hetuvidya), Nirukti, (etymological interpretation of words) and Kalp (rituals as given in vedas), Vedas, vedic literature, spiritual and moral lessons, shabda vidya (Learning of words/phonology), silpa vidya (science of arts and crafts), physical education like, archery, riding, wrestling, hunting, fist-fighting, hurling of animals, swimming, running, jumping, digging, dancing and race courses.

For developing physical and mental strength, early marriage was not in practice in vedic age. Professional and technical subjects like Ayurved/chikitsavidya (medicine and surgery), astrology, astronomy, mathematics, artha sastras etc., were given due importance.

Monito System

Credit goes to the ancient educators for inventing the monitoral system. If the member students growing, a most advanced/senior student selected as a 'pitthiachariya' (Assistant Master).

Methods of Teaching

- Debates and discussions for training in logic.
- Logical discussions organized between two scholars/ groups.
- *Muakhik*—oral.
- *Chintan*—thinking.
- *Manan*—reflection.
- *Question*—answer system.

No new word was taught unless it was ascertained that the previously taught word was correctly learnt with correct pronunciation. The oral method meant for students of average intelligence and thinking (*Chinthan-Manan*) for those who were highly endowed.

Guru

Guru enjoyed predominant place not only in his *gurukul* but in the entire society. He was regarded as a great guide for all. To his pupils he showered all love and affection and used to teach them whatever he knew, but before doing this he always tested the deservingness of a particular pupil. The pupils were free to discuss points freely with the *guru*.

He was more respected than the king in society. The *Guru* was regarded as a *Rishi* (sage) or *Acharya* (one who practices what he professes). The *guru* was given this significant place, because without him it was impossible to attain knowledge.

He used to bring light wherever there was darkness. Thus, the people always felt his necessity whenever, there was a difficulty in solving any issue or problem. It is believed that the attainment of salvation was not possible without the help of *Guru*.

Restrictions on Teachers

The *Guru* was expected to lead a life a penance free of worldly things. He, too, was required to follow all the rules of strict discipline, thinking and meditation, which were prescribed for the students.

Supreme Knowledge

It was compulsory for the students to have full faith in the teacher. Only students were considered as deserving of attaining real knowledge of supreme truth who had full faith in the teacher. So the student was always in search of a real *Guru* for attaining real knowledge and the *guru* wanted to find out a really deserving student who he could give all that he knew.

***Samavartan*—The Convocation Address**

After 12 years education students assemble near their *acharya* for blessings before going home. The *guru* used to give some pieces of advice for happy and smooth running of their future life. The *guru* used to tell them how to lead a life of a householder (*Grihastha*) how to take care of the society/nation and how to serve humanity as a whole. The teacher used to tell all these in a ceremony which was known as *Samavartan Samaroha* like the modern convocation address.

Analysis of Vedic Education

An analysis of the achievements of education in this ancient period indicates that the aim of education was to make the individual a useful and productive member of society.

The educational achievements of this age were as follows:

1. Education emphasized the development of spirituality.
2. Great attention was paid to the development of the child's character. Teachers laid stress on the integral development of the individual personality.
3. Social skills was evolved through training in the fulfillment of duties.
4. Efforts were made for the preservation and propagation of the national culture.
5. Education was free. Its expenses were borne by the society and the king.
6. Self-study (*Swaadhyaya*) was considered more important.
7. The examination was oral one.
8. During this period, vocational education was also vogue like Military Science, Agriculture, Animal Husbandry, Veterinary Science, Medicine, Chemistry, Arts, Handicrafts and Education in Commerce.

The Concepts of Purusharthas

The ancient sages, who were the founders of Indian culture, laid down the concept of purushartha. There are four purusharthas.

Dharma (Virtue)

Dharma is a moral value to be achieved by human beings only. It is superior to *artha* and *kama*. Truth, kindness, purity, etc., come under *dharma*.

Artha/Wealth

Artha or wealth helps in the satisfaction of material, biological and economic desires.

Lack of wealth weakens human resolve and often leads to adopting illegal and immoral ways of obtaining satisfaction.

Therefore, under Indian system of ethics it is permissible to acquire wealth by the right means/ways. *Artha* and *Kama* were the guiding principle of Grihstashrama.

Kama

Kama (enjoyment of pleasure).

Moksha has Two Shades of Meaning

1. Absence of all pain and suffering.
2. A state of bliss.

Attaining 'Moksh' is the highest goal of life. It is fourth and final *purushartha*.

Besides the above four values, the Indian philosophical system also holds other values like truth goodness and beauty. *Dharma* and *moksha* were the guiding principle in *vanaprastha* and *sanyasashrama*.

Traditional Indian Values

Spirituality

Realization or self.

Opposed to materialism and worldliness.

Simplicity

The ancient Indian seers were the embodiment of simplicity.

Tolerance

It is the essence of vedic culture.

Non-violence (Ahimsa)

It is an integral part of our culture. Hinduism, Jainism, Budhism and Gandhism propagated the concept non-violence.

Truth

- Chief goal of life.
- 'Truth alone triumphs', the main slogan of our culture.
- Gandhi's *sathyagraha* is based on truth.

Self-Realization

- *Moksha*: It is the ultimate identification of the individual self with the absolute.

What is the significance/importance of these values in contemporary education? You just think about our great cultural heritage of India and todays materialistic outlook of life.

EDUCATION DURING BUDDHIST PERIOD

Introduction

Vedic education in its later stages, controlled by Brahmanas and that caused to:

- dominance of Religion and
- deprivation of the Shudras right to education.

Education of the Brahman period came to be allied with the national and social life. Ritualism had increased and the people were profoundly troubled.

A sense of aimlessness prevailed in society. In such circumstances, Buddhism emerged as a reaction to vedic ritualism. Buddhists began to establish educational monasteries in competition to the vedic system of education. Initially, these Buddhist monasteries provided education only to Budhists, but gradually they came to impart education to all classes.

Budhist education came in to existence in the 5th century B.C. Brahmanas deprived the common people of their right to education, and hence the emergence of Buddhism granted the people the freedom to obtain education and to practice their religion themselves.

The Buddhists imparted education in Sanghas/Collective groups/congregations. In Buddhism there was no opportunity for the individual to obtain education independently, away from his 'sugham'.

Buddhism and Its Educational Implications

The Life of Lord Buddha

Lord Buddha has been the founder of Buddhism. He was born in 563 B.C. at Lumbini of Kapilvastu Nagar of the Kingdom of Nepal. Shuddhodan, the king of Shakya dynasty in the south of Nepal was his father. Maya Devi was his mother. At the time of birth Lord Buddha's name was Siddhartha. A week after his birth, his mother, Maya Devi died and his step-mother Majaprajapati brought him up. During the first sixteen years of his life Siddhartha received an education in policy of state administration and also in military science. He was married to a girl named Yasodhara. After marriage, for three years he looked after the state affairs. During this period Siddhartha became a father to a son born from Yasodhara. The son was named Rahul. Even during his infancy Siddhartha was of peaceful nature and he evinced a tendency towards Sanyas, i.e., (renouncing the world). Consequently, he became interested in Yoga an turned indifferent to worldly pleasures in the "Shunya." Thus, all religions are depend upon others and all are changeable. All these are indescribeable also. Their indescribability (Anivarchyata) in relation to Shunya is known as "Modhyam Marg" or middle course. According to this middle course a thing signifies completely neither "feeling form" (*Bhava Roop*) nor does it indicate "Dearth form" (*Abhava Roop*). The element which cannot be described the words may be appropriately regarded as "Shunya." Thus, the philosophical purpose of "Shunyavad" is infinitiveness, i.e., Bhavatmak and not *Abhavatmak* (dearthness). From the practical viewpoint "Shunyavad" refers to the cycle of birth and death and from the spiritual view point Shunyavadis Nirvana or salvation.

The Impact of Buddhism

Buddhism spread in India and in many other countries of the Asian continent. Today, there are very few Buddhists in India scattered here and there. But this religion particularly spread in Sri Lanka, Burma, Tibet, Russia, Mangolia, Indonesia, Vietnam, Cambodia, Thailand (Shyam), China, Japan and Korea. In Japan, China and Tibet various branches of this religion have been developed. These branches do not exist in India. Buddhism and its philosophy have immensely influenced Indian philosophical systems. Consequently, in many contexts, Buddhism has been vehementally criticized also. There are many common points between Buddhism and

Brahmanism, but their basic stands are different from each other. In Indian sculpture, architecture, literature, painting and drama the impact of the character of Lord Buddha can never be forgotten. Ashok, Kanishka and Harshvardhan embraced Buddhism as immensely contributed to its growth and expansion. Due to these kings Buddhism remained as a state religion in India for long. It will not be an exaggeration to say that it is from Buddhism that the ideals of service to the people, compassionate view point to all and *Moksha* (salvation) have come into the Vaishnav religion (Brahmanism). Impact of Buddhism may be clearly seen on the sophists. In the Christian religion the concept of Joseph of the Greek and Roman Church appears to be compatible with Buddhism. The countries where Islam was spread were originally centres of Buddhism. Therefore, the impact of Buddhism was but natural on the followers of Islam. In fact, it is a truism to remark that even today Buddhism is found as a world religion, because even now its followers are in crorers. The place of Buddhism is certain in the future world, no matter whatever other religion is propounded.

Educational Implications of Buddhism

Arya Satya (Four Truths)

'This world is full of miseries' is the first truth as viewed by Lord Buddha. He has regarded the various miseries of the world as a nature of man. If one realizes this truth from the very beginning he will do nothing which may cause may trouble to him. Then he will so conduct his life as to ensure his physical, mental, moral and spiritual development. Thus, he will become a good citizen. If the parents and teachers are motivated by this first truth of Lord Buddha, children will be developed in a desirable manner and our educational system will be transformed.

In the second *Arya Satya* (truth) Lord Buddha says that one's ignorance is the cause of misery. Due to ignorance one gets involved into various intricacies of the world. In the third truth, he says that if the drives generated due to ignorance are destroyed, then a person will rise above all attachments (Rag), rivalry, lust and anger. In fact, to obtain this victory is to achieve salvation. Through the fourth truth, Lord Buddha has indicated the parth towards destruction of worldly miseries. In this indication he has spoken of eight devices (Ashiangik Marg) which may help one in getting himself free from worldly miseries.

Lord Buddha has prescribed a middle course to be followed. He had opposed to torture the body through hard penance. The middle course consists of eight devices. By following these eight devices the ultimate aim of education may be achieved. To obtain salvation (*Niryan*) is the ultimate end of life. Salvation is the freedom from the cycle of birth and death. In fact, this may also be accepted as the ultimate purpose of education.

The Ashtangik Marg

The first step of the Ashtangik Marg is *Samyak Drishti*, i.e., the appropriate insight. This insight will help one to be away from worldly complexities. For being away, *Samyak Sankalp* or appropriate will-power is necessary. This will-power will help one to proceed towards the path of salvation. After having thus proceeded, *Samayak vach* or appropriate speech is necessary. This may be possible through control over oneself. This control will assist one towards proper behaviour with other. After achieving this control, one should exercise the restriction over his physical and mental aspirations. This type of restriction has been termed as *Samyak Marmant* which means to shun all types of violence through thought, word and deed (*Mansa, Vacha* and *Karmana*). After Samayak Marmant comes *Samyak Ajeev*, means to earn his bare living through justice. *Samayak* Ajeev is to be followed by *Samyak Vyayam* which purports that one should entertain only auspicious thoughts in his mind and should shun evil ones. The seventh *Marg* (device) as enjoined by Lord Buddha is *Samyak Smriti* which means that one should always remember the basic elements of the acquired knowledge. The eighth marg (device) is *Samyak Samadhi* which amounts to perfect concentration of attention after purifying one's inner self. *Antakkaran Kshuddhi*, for salvation this concentration is very necessary. Needless to add that the above *Ashtangik Marg* (eight devices) are full of very powerful education meanings.

The Theory of Karma

According to Lord Buddha 'sin' and piety (rightcousness) are the outcomes of one's own deeds. The sinner reaps miseries both in this world and in the other beyond, and the *pious* (Punyatma) man harvests happiness. Due to one's own efforts someone is rich and the idel one is poor. It is the outcome of one's own deed that one is ill and the other is healthy. One is learned and the other is ignorant. Thus, the various peculiarities in the world are not God's creations but the outcomes of some deeds. Thus, Lord Buddha has given the message to the mankind that one gets miseries due to his own deeds. Therefore, he is quite capable of removing them. Thus the theory of Karma has been propounded very strongly. Lord Buddha firmly believes that God is not the giver of the result of any deed. In fact, the deed, itself, gives its outcome to the doer. Needless to remark that Lord Buddha's theory of Karma is pregnant with noble educational meanings. If our educational centres become imbued with the ideals of Karmavad and the parents, teachers and students begin to behave acccrodingly, all will be " up and doing" and everyone will be the maker of his own destiny. Then no one will curse his fate and sit idele, doing nothing. In some other contexts, we have already referred to this ideal.

The Concept of Boddhisatva

To attain *Boddhisatva* is the ultimate objective of Buddhism. This position may be accepted as the highest ideal for any person. A person enriches with this position is embedded with spiritual excellencies. The objective of Boddhisatva is to sacrifice one's life for the welfare of others. Thus long with spirituality he is equipped with the cravings for the welfare of all. He is an embodiment of compassion and benevolence. In short, it will not be too much to say that the ultimate purpose of education also should be to make each student a Boddhisatva. If this becomes possible there will be no one miserable in this world. Then one's miseries will be taken up by others as their own and they will try to remove the same. If our education succeeds in achieving this objective this very earth will become a heaven.

Since the Mahayan school has given great importance to the ideal of Boddhisatva, the above educational implications are applicable to the Mahayan schools as well.

The four great truths of Lord Buddha's teachings are, world is full of miseries, there is a cause for misery, miseries may be wiped off and device for removing misery. Soul is not eternal. Man is himself responsible for his own miseries. Education to make the students depend upon their own efforts. The ultimate purpose of education is to sacrifice one's life for the welfare of others. Freedom from worldly fabrications provides salvations, good education should guide one to their salvations.

Buddhist System of Admission – Pabbajja

The *vinaya pitaka,* a famous Buddhist scripture states the nature of admission. Let him who desires to receive ordination first cut off his upper robe so as to cover one shoulder, salute the face of the *bhikshu* with his head; and sit down squatting; then let him raise his joined hands and tell them to say "I take my refuge in the Buddha, I take my refuge in the Dharma, I take my refuge in Sangh."

This act of admission was called '*Pabbajja*' (going out of home). After pabbajja, the student was called as *Shramana/Samner.* The 'Samner' had to renounce all his worldly and family relationships. That 'Shraman' was given ten suggestions to follow, i.e.

1. Practice non-violence
2. Speak truth
3. Do not steal
4. Do not collect
5. Observe celibacy
6. Give up luxury
7. Renounce wealth and do not touch women
8. Do not use fragrant things.
9. Do not eat anything untimely
10. Do not use soft and very comfortable bed.

Any caste could be admitted and after being he didn't belong to any caste. After admission he had change his old clothes/ old ways/ manners of living. For the *Pabajja.* The minimum age was eight years. When *Samner* attained twenty i.e., when he received 12 years education he had to under go the *Upasampada.* The *Upasampada* ceremony entitled a student for full-fledged membership of the monastery. *Upasanpada,* was democratic in nature. The 'Shraman' had to present himself before all other monks. One could be admitted for *Upasampada* only when the majority of the monks voted in the favour of the same. After *Upasambada* the male monks were called *Bhikshu* and female monks *Bhikshuni.* After *Upasambada,* Shraman was regarded as a full-fledged member of the monastery, and his/ her all worldly and family relationships ended.

Contrary to vedic education, student never came back to householder life, he cut off his worldly relationships for ever.

NATURE OF BUDDHIST EDUCATION

The Buddhist education system was residential by nature. A group of young 'Bhikshus' or monks living in a vihar under the guardianship of a common teacher, the Upadhaya or acharya who was the individual responsible for,

- Their health,
- Studies,
- Manners,
- Morals, and
- Spiritual upliftment.

Student-Teacher Relationship

Students were required to serve their teachers, beg for alms, eat food thrice a day, bath themselves with pure water and live in discipline. Dr. Altekar, "a teachers relation with his new students was akin to the father-son or parental relationship."

Feminine Education

Women occupied a position inferior to men. Initially, they were prohibited from joining 'Sangha'. Later on they were granted admission. Separate monastries were established for women. Lord Buddha had regarded ladies are the source of all evils. So he had advised during his life time not to admit women in monasteries. But after some time due to the insistance of his dear pupil Ananad, Buddha had permitted women for admission with many restrictions and reservations.

Strict rules were enforced for women monks. The first-two years was their probotion period. The women monks were not allowed to meet any male monk in lonliness and their residence arranged separately. They were regarded as lower in status than the male monks.

Vocational Education

The monks of a Vihar were taught spinning, weaving and sewing in order that they meet their clothing requirements. They were taught architecture that enable them to build-up a maintain vihars.

Aims of Education

Buddha preached his followers the four 'Noble truths', i.e.

- There is sufferings in life.
- This suffering has a cause.
- This suffering could be removed by destroying its cause.
- The cause of suffering is 'Thrishna'/desire.

The most important aim of education is to show the path by which an individual can assimilate this craving or remove his desire and ultimately obtain 'Nirvan'. The desire can only be removed by following the eight noble fold path or the *Arya Asthang Marga*. The aim of education is to make familiar with these paths and practise in life i.e., Right views or faith, Right aspiration, Right speech, Right action, Right livelihood, Right effort, Right mindfulness and Right contemplation.

Another aim of Buddhist—education was to teach the monks the law of varna, its working and transmission of souls. The doctrine states, "A man reaps what he sows. A man acts, so shall be. Every individual is the maker of his own destiny."

Another prominent aim of education was the teaching of Ahimsa. Non-violence towards life is recognized as an integral principle of life. Other important aims of education are:

- Development of human qualities.
- Purity of behaviour.
- Obedience to religion.
- Building up of character.
- Development of power of reasoning.
- All-round development of the individual.

Curriculum

Curriculum chiefly spiritual in nature, because the chief of education was to attain Salvation/Nirvan. Suttanta, Vinaya and Dhamma were the main subjects. Besides these spinning, weaving, printing of cloth, tailoring, sketching, accountancy, medicine, etc., were the other subjects.

Methodology

Oral method, Lecturing and Memorise themselves are well-practicing methods. Special emphasis was laid on the purity of conduct, because it was thought that if one was not good in behaviour, he couldn't learn anything for his development.

At first the teacher gave a lecture on a certain topic and the students were required to listen to him with rapt attention. Afterwards students were expected to memorize the same. The students used to react before other fellow students what ever they had committed to memory. During this period the art of writing had developed but it couldn't touch the field of education, the writing materials were not in abundance for all.

Assembly

On the beginning (*pratipada*) and close (*purnima*) of each month learned people used to assemble together, for maintain the moral standards of the Bhikshuks. In the assembly each monk used to confess and describe his immoral behaviour frankly. The assembly used to deliberate upon such confessed immoral behaviours of various monks and impose punishments.

The Nature of Mass Education

The Vihars/monasteries support from the people in general to whom they would go for alms. So the time of begging the monks used to remove the religious doubts of people through conversations/short and apt lectures. In this way monks tried to educate the masses.

Centres of Learning

Dr. Altekar opines that the Buddhists raised India's international stature by the high level of education in their monasteries, since students from as far as Korea, Tibet, Java and other distant centuries were attached to them.

During this period some prominent centres of education sprang up. There was no discrimination between students on any basis. Some of these centres possessed on international reputation.

Wherever Vihars/Monsteries established, educational centres too emerged. Among the most notable universities to develop during this period were the universities at, Taxila, Nalanda, Ballabhi, Vikrama Shila, Odantpuri, Nadia, Jagdalla and Mithila.

Taxila, was an important centre of education during the Buddhist period. It was the capital of Gandhar. It had been founded by King Bharata after of his son Taxa. In Taxila:

- Students started their education at the age of 16.
- The university provided education in numerous subjects, such as vedas, vedanta, grammar, ayurveda, military science, astrology agriculture, commerce, treatment of snake bite (Sarpa-damsha chikitsa), magical charms (tantra vidya), etc.

Nalanda University was situated in Bihar. It was an internationally famed Buddhist centre of education. It became famous because it was the birth place of Sariputra the discipline of Lord Buddha. Kings of the Gupta dynasty took interest in the growth of the university. Thirteen of its many monastries served as hostels for the students. Students received free education and university fulfilled all their needs of food, clothing, medical treatment, education, etc. Vedas, philosophy, Puranas, medicine etc., taught here. The method of teaching was discussion and question-answering.

Students of this university earned great respect in many foreign countries. Students came from Java, Sumatra, Japan, China, Ceylon and other countries. Nalanda continued to serve, preserve and propagate Indian culture for 800 years.

Bullabhi from 475 AD – 775 AD, Ballabhi, in Kathiawar was a famous centre of Buddhist education. Heun Tsang visited Ballabhi in his travels. 'Ballabi' imparted education in politics, diplomacy, medicine and various other disciplines.

Vikramashila was located on the banks of the Ganga in Magadha, Bihar. Many important religious texts were translated into the Tibetan, language at this university. 'Vikramashila' provided education in grammar, logic, philosophy, tantra, etc.

Table – 7.1

Comparison between Vedic and Buddhist Education

Sl. No.	*Vedic*	*Buddhist*
1.	Education was conducted in the *gurukul* or teacher's house	Education was imparted in schools/ vihars/universities.
2.	Students lived as members of a family	Education was institutionalized
3.	The emphasis was upon the study of the Vedas and allied subjects.	Emphasis was upon propagation of religion and study of general
4.	Sanskrit was the medium of education	Praakrit was the medium
5.	Brahmanas were the teachers	Teachers were chosen from among the monks.
6.	Education was not available to every class	Education was universal
7.	The students life was rigorous	It was convenient, lacking in rigour
8.	Education was free	A fee was payable in some form or the other
9.	Sanskrit was taught	Pali and other languages were taught

Conclusion

In the sphere of education, the Buddhist period has its own contribution. Dr. F.E. Kaey, "The Buddhism played a significant role by putting and end to the monopoly of Brahmanic schools and it thus grave a rise to a general desire for education among all people, as a result public schools evolved."

MEDIEVAL INDIAN ISLAMIC EDUCATION

Introduction to Islam

"*Read:* *In the name of the Lord who Createth*
Creath man from a Clot.
Read: *Any thy Lord is the most bounteous*
who teacheth by the pen
Teacheth man that which he knew not"

—(Sura- Alakh, 96)

These are the very first words of Holy Quran, which were revealed to prophet Mohamed (570-632 AD) by Allah.

Educational Implications

The significance of reading, writing and teaching in Islam is obvious. Reading, writing and attainment of knowledge are the basic ingredients and means of education, and Quran gives first priority to education.

According to Quran, Allah is the creator, sustainer, and teacher of man. It is Allah who educated the first man Adam. Holy Quran says: *And He taught Adam all the names*—(Sura Al-Bakara Chapter 2, Ayath 31)

In Islam, next in importance to the Quran is *Sunnah* which is the collection of the saying and actions of the prophet Mohamed. The Sunnah is also called *Hadith* or traditions of prophet Mohamed.

Prophet Mohamed declared, " To seek knowledge is a religious duty of every Muslim, man and women."

"Seek knowledge from cradle to grave."

(Ibn-e-Maja)

While different educationists have emphasized different aspects of man to be attempted through education. It is Islam which has taken its very broad meaning. Islam doesn't confine education to four walls of the school. It included all the aspects of life of man. Islam is not mearly a ritualistic religion nor it is confined to some beliefs and personal prayers only. It presents a complete way of life, a system of values, a code of conduct, a unique ideology, a socio-economic order, a manual of politics, and above all the doctrines of faith in one ness of Allah (God). The teachings of Islam provided guidelines to entire humanity to all aspects of life such as economics, education, commerce, jurisprudence, and culture etc.

The entire world and especially the scientifically advanced and materially prosperous nations are facing a grave moral crisis. The teaching of Islam provide a solution to the problems of an individual as well as those of humanity. The significant characteristic of Islam are the concept of oneness of God and Equalty of man kind.

Indian Islamic Education (1192-1757 AD)

Mohamed Ghori laid the foundation of Muslim Rule in India in 1192 AD. He was succeeded by several Muslim dynasties like, slave, Khilji, Thughlak, Sayyid, Lodi and Mughal. The Muslim education took shape under these dynasties. Education depended for its progress mostly on the attitude and enthusiasm of Individual rulers.

Main Features

The Muslim rulers helped in the spread of education in India. They patronized scholars by giving them jobs in their courts and opened many schools and colleges.

Types of Educational Institutions

The *Maktab* is a primary school often attached with a mosque. Instruction in Quran to the common feature of Maktabs. Sometimes instruction in 3R's was also included. Primary education was also carried on in private houses. The teacher called 'Maulavis'. Education began with the ritual known as *Bismillah* (in the name of God) which was performed at the age of 4 years 4 months and 4 days. On this day the child adorned with a new crown and he sent to his teacher, the Maulavi, and the education inaugurated with a recitation from the Quran. This ceremony called *Zarfishani* (sprinking of gold) in the case of girls.

Madrassa's were school for higher learning; these too were generally attached to mosques. Some of them rose to the status of universities. The course in Madrassa's included Grammar, rhetoric, logic, theology, meta physics, literature, jurisprudence and science. Madrassas were aided by Government. There were arrangement for hostels in madrassas. They were owned privately as well as by the State.

Role of the Teacher

Medieval Islamic education emphasized personal relationship between the teacher and the student. It was individual education rather than mass education. A teacher had a small group of students and he imparted instruction according to the level of intelligence of students, talking and listening to them, observing them and being observed by them, encouraging and praising, scolding and punishing them. Teachers were held in high esteem and their students considered it a privilege to follow their example.

Methodology

Emphasis was placed on memorization in addition to reading, writing and arithmetic. The most prevalent method was the oral. Individual attention was paid to students. The monitor system had been used in maktabs and madrassas.

Student-Teacher Relationship

Student-teacher relationship were not marked by intimacy. The relationship is based on sincerity and purity. Though teachers received a low salary they had an important place in society. People respected them and bestowed faith on them. The teacher had a paternal attitude towards his wards. It was believed that the students who served their teachers made god happy.

Reward and Punishment

There was a system of severe punishment to maintain order and discipline, but brilliant scholars were also rewarded.

Medium of Education

During the Muslim period, Arabic and Persian were the median of education. However, after the growth of Urdu, education began to be imparted through this language.

Vocational Education

Prof: Weber observed, "The skill of the Indians in the production of delicate woven fabrics, in the mixing of colours, the working of metals and precious stones and all manners of technical arts..... enjoyed a worldwide celebrity."

During the Muslim period, there was provision for vocational, technical and professional education. Feroze Shah Tughlaq maintained a regular department of industries. The institutions provided technical education/training in handicrafts known as

Kamkhanas. No Regular Fees would be paid to the 'Kamkhanas. Apprenticeship' system is functioning here.

Curriculum

Medieval—Indian education stressed the co-ordination of religious and non-religious (general education). While general education was born out of practical needs, religious education stemmed from religious belief.

Elementary curriculum includes, reading, writing, arithmetic and religious education. Curriculum at the higher stage consisting Study of Ethics, Divinity, Astronomy, Algebra, Geometry, Physics, Medicine, Natural Philosophy, Retoric, Law, Rituals, Accounts, Agriculture, Economics and History.

For Hindu's, their religious books were prescribed. They were also allowed to study in madrassas and many of them studied Persian and acquired mastery in it.

Science started receiving importance over philosophy during the medieval period. Theological curriculum (Dars-E-Nizami) followed all over India. The Arabic university at Deoband maintained the high tradition of theological studies.

Women's Education

Women education was almost neglected in the Muslim period. However, the evidence sometimes young girls were taught in schools. In the harems of king and nobles, sometimes some attempt was made to educate the ladies who lived within and some of them attained distinction, like Sultana Razia, Chand Sulthana, Gul Badan, Began Satina Sulthana.... Royale noble ladies get education but great mass Muslim women who received no education at all, except domestic training in the performance of the duties of the household.

Examination System

No annual exam of the modern type. Evaluation was a built-in, continuous process. Promotions were based on assessment by the teachers themselves. Degrees came to be awarded for specialized and in-depth study in various branches, like,

Fazil—specialist in logic.
Atim—specialist in theology.
Qubil—specialist in literature.

Town Centred Education

Muslim education in India was mainly centred in the towns and cities. It was in contrast to the Brahmanical education. It is because,

1. Muslim population in the early years of Muslim rule was in many places largely an urban population.
2. The Muslim education developed on the patronage and encouragement of the ruling sovereigns, the nobility and the gentry who lived in capital towns and cities.

These towns included places like Delhi, Agra, Fetehpur Sikri, Jaunpur, Lahore, Ajmer, Bihar, Lucknow, Hyderabad, Ahemedabad, Jullundar, Bijapur, Multan etc.

State Centred Education

Muslim education during this period was not only patronized but also guided and controlled by the State. The state schools employed, salaried teachers and education was free for poor and promising students. The office of the sardar/sheikul-Islam (Minister for ecclesiasiastical and judicial affairs) had the responsibility of co-ordinating state and private educational institutions.

The Significance of Medical Islamic Education

- Encouragement by the State.
- Special stress on teaching of Arabic and Persian.
- Emergence of Urdu.

The evolution of a new language 'Urdu' which emerged from the inter-mixing of Arabic and Persian.

- Religious Influence.

The education of this period was profoundly influence by Islam.

- Materialism.

Muslim education sought the spread of education from the practical and materialistic view points.

- Developing of Historiography/History-writing.

Example: Babar nama, Akbar nama etc.

Aims of Education

- Propagation of knowledge.
- Propagation of religion.
- Propagation of religious laws.

- Worldy progress.
- Strengthening the administration.
- A Critique of Muslim Education.

Merits

- The compulsory nature of education. The pursuit of knowledge treat as a sacred duty.
- Personal contact between teacher and students.
- The practical aspect of education.
- The combination of religious and secular education.
- The development of Ardent literature and history.
- Free education.
- The students encouraged in their study by stipend and reward.

Demerits

- Pre-dominance of Arabic and Persian.
- Pre-dominance of worldly view point.
- Impermanence of institutions – i.e., short life of institutions.
- Education not extensive/ no mass education.
- Partial neglect of female education.
- Disproportionateness between reading and writing.

Conclusion

The history of Muslim education has been the history of a system of government and a social system extending over 700 years.

It must be remembered that Muslim education was primarily confined to that minority of the population. In spite of this however, the extent and influence of Muslim education in India was by no means inconsiderable.

MODEL QUESTIONS

1. What are the characteristics of the vedic system of education? How does it differ from the Buddhist system? What are the common features found in the two systems?
2. State the traditional values of life according to the Indian tradition.
3. Write a note on 'Maktabs'.
4. State the merits and demerits of education during Buddhist period.
5. Name the Purusharthas.
6. What are the special features of Muslim education?

REFERENCES

1. Amala, Annie, *et al.* (2006). *History of Education*, Discovery Publishing House, New Delhi.
2. Chaube, S.P. *History and Problems of Indian Education*, Vinod Pustakmandir, Agra.
3. Ghanta, Ramesh & Dash, B.N. (2006). *Foundations of Education*, Neelkamal Pub (P) Ltd., Hyderabad.
4. Pandey, Ramshakal. *Teacher in Developing Indian Society*, Vinod Pustakmandir, Agra.

8

Thoughts on Education

A GENERAL INTRODUCTION TO PHILOSOPHY

Some people think of philosophy as a subject to be studied—an abstruse, difficult or even useless subject. 'Thought' (noun), for them, is only a record of what great men thought (verb). Reproducing these ideas is, in the words of the French philosopher Marcel, 'thought thought' (*la pensee pensee*). But if one wants to philosophise one should reconstruct the *thinking* (now), or practise 'thought thinking' (*la penseee pensante*). The Greek words *philia* (love) and Sophia (wisdom) together make the compound word jílosóíá or love of wisdom. Hence, the study of philosophy is not one of gathering more and more information or knowledge. It is a deep quest, it is a never-ending process. It is comparable to science, not as product, but as a process, set on a higher plane.

Everyone has a philosophy in the sense of a stable outlook on life, which guides their every thought, word and action. It is the philosophy of commonsense. But it is possible to critically look at it, analyze it, deepen it, synthesize it. Such a systematic philosophy will be more consistent and reveal less self-contradiction. But even such systematic philosophy is continuous with the philosophy of commonsense. The philosophic enterprise is triggered by curiosity, the need to solve problems (of a practical or intellectual nature), the need to fill in the gaps in experience, the search for meaning of awareness, the interest in symbolic expression, inspiration or *darsana* or the pleasures of philosophy.

The major functions of philosophy include the following:

1. *Synoptic Function*: The philosopher attempts to get a total view of things, "to see life steadily and see it whole," to combine the fragments of knowledge given by daily experience into a totality.
2. *Normative Function*: Philosophy, and more particularly the normative sciences of logic, aesthetics and ethics, is expected to provide guidance about aims, norms, standards and values.
3. *Practical Effects*: Sometimes jokes appear setting out philosophy as useless and impractical theorization. This may really happen in the transactions of inferior philosophers, or due to the absent-mindedness of even the great thinkers. But some schools make practicality the acid test of philosophy. Dewey says that "Theory is in the end the most practical of all things" and argues this thesis out. Even distant ideals set out by philosophers are often realized in course of time. Napoleon said that without Rousseau, the French Revolution could not have happened. Explosive ideas have revolutionized education, politics and other aspects of life more than is commonly realized. It is because philosophy is a way of life and note mere theory that it contributes to wisdom.
4. *Critical Function*: Philosophy criticizes our basic assumptions; it questions commonsense; it criticizes its own method and that of science; it criticizes the way we use basic terms and concepts. Socratic questioning of statements which everyone seemed to take for granted is one of the earliest examples. Kant's *Critique of Pure Reason* has raised the critical function to new heights. Dewey has pointed out that the criticism of philosophy is not transcendental, but arises from ordinary experience. It criticizes just the familiar things like our ordinary beliefs, knowledge, action, enjoyment and suffering. "It differs from other criticism only in trying to carry it farther and in pursing it methodically."
5. *Limiting Function*: The limiting is an offshoot of the critical function. It arises when the territory of knowledge and possibility of knowledge is stretched to its utmost through critical questioning. Kant's drawing of the limits of perception is a major landmark in the theory of knowledge. Wittgenstein's *Tractatus* is an attempt to draw a limit to

> thinking, or rather to the expression of our thoughts. "In order to draw a limit to thinking we should have to be able to think both sides of the limit (we should therefore have to be able to think what cannot be thought). The limit can, therefore only be drawn in language, and what lies on the other side of the limit will simply be nonsense (that which can be neither proved nor disproved)."

There are three basic dimension of philosophy (1) Ontology or theory of existence (it is also explored as meta-physics which transcends physics). Assuming the reality of physical objects, the properties and regularities regarding physical bodies is studied in physics. Even till about four centuries ago, the precursors of what we call the sciences were studied under the term 'natural philosophy'. But when the sciences began to be investigated by objective methods, what lies beyond the knowledge yielded by such methods became the domain of the philosopher under metaphysics. (2) Epistemology is the theory of knowledge; Greek episteme means knowledge. (3) Axiology is the theory of values.

SCHOOLS OF PHILOSOPHY

Depending on the point where one draws the limits of thinking, and what one takes as one's basic premises, different schools of philosophy take shape. The concepts of education and its different sub-components also differ according to different schools. Some systematic schools would assume that to develop an adequate philosophy of education, one must thoroughly understand general philosophy and then develop its applications in education. There are others like Dewey who think that education and philosophy are two sides of the same coin—the more theoretical side is called philosophy and the more practical side is called education.

Schools of philosophy are specific perspectives or standpoints from which various issues are viewed and evaluated. Four Major schools are studied in the B.Ed. Course. Strictly speaking, it is not possible to sort out philosophers into neatly divided groups as idealists, realists, naturalists and pragmatists. A philosopher may take an idealistic point of view in the theory of existence (metaphysics/ontology), but take a realist position in theory of knowledge (epistemology), and a pragmatic standpoint in applications. Furthermore each major school has sub-schools which may fall in the intersecting set between schools. Recent developments in the sciences, particularly in physics and psychology, have tended to bring the opposing schools nearer. Still, a systematic study of the schools would help a student of education to analyze various components of thinking about existence/ reality, knowledge, values and how they get applied in society and in education. It would also help the student to sharpen his own thinking and find new classifications and applications.

Idealism

General Statement and Tenets

Idealism can be discerned in the debates of thinkers from the earliest periods when philosophy emerged as a field of knowledge. The term is derived from idea + ism, with 'l' inserted to separate the vowels and effect euphony (good sound effect). Idealism is "the philosophy which holds that reality is of the nature of mind" (Hocking). Philosophers like Hegel and Croce maintain that all genuine philosophy is idealism because the principle in every case is an idea. But the commonsense view of idealism as ideal + ism also finds many supporters, especially when discussing absolute values. Absolute Truth, Beauty and Goodness can be approached closer and closer, but never fully grasped, at least in finite human experience. Socrates held that absolute knowledge cannot be attained by man, but *love of wisdom* (*philosphia*) is possible for the person with this deep quest. Besides these two view there is also the 'holistic' view of idealism. In Calderwood's view, idealism is "a unifying of reality; a representation of the totality of being as explained under a single conception, or according to an ideal scheme."

Hocking defines idealism as "the philosophy which holds that reality is of the nature of mind." Whereas the sophists claimed to teach particular knowledge, Plato's teacher, Socrates pursued the quest after universal knowledge; this knowledge cannot be 'taught' through external sources; the learner must be helped to 'recollect' the knowledge hidden in his mind, which can be drawn out (through the Socratic dialogue). The teacher is only a 'midwife' in the birth of knowledge. This knowledge deepens into self-knowledge and broden's out to universal knowledge. There are other views too to idealism.

Idealism is one of the oldest schools of thought in the world of philosophy, originating human nature itself, continuing from the primitive man to his present counterpart in some modified form or the other. From the metaphysical standpoint it has overtones of spirituality since it believes that ultimate existing element is spiritual in nature. The entire universe is an extension of the mind or soul. From the epistemological standpoint it is better called idealism, implying there by that thought or idea has greater validity than the physical object. The term idealism cannot different concept when placed in various contexts.

Importance of Idealism

Adams; "Idealism is one form of other permeates the whole of the history philosophy." GTW Patrick, "Idealists refuse to believe that the world is a great machine. They deny the supreme importance of matter, mechanism and the conservation of energy, as explaining our world. They feel the some how certain sciences, such as psychology, logic, ethics, aesthetics, have to do with things basal and intrinsic, that they are quite as much a key to nature's secretes as are physics and chemistry. They believe that the world has a meaning, a purpose, perhaps a goal, and that there is a kind of inner harmony between the heart of the universe and the soul of man, such that human intelligence can pierce through the outer crust of nature and penetrate to its being, at least in some measure." This explanation of idealism highlights its distinction from materialism.

Idealism v/s Realism

Idealism has been also compared to realism. Brubackar; "Some realists take the view that mental functions can be reduced to bodily ones, while certain idealists make matter a function of the mind. The idealists arrive at their monism by pointing out that it is central in understanding the world."

Idealism as the Oldest Philosophy

It is perhaps the oldest philosophy in the world. Many of the world's leading philosophers and educators are idealists. This philosophy continues to extert great influence on education. In the western world idealism began with Socrates and Plato and in the east, it originated from the Upanishads.

Chief Exponents of Idealism

1. The Vedic Rishis.
2. Plato—A Greek philosopher (427-347 BC).
3. Kant—A German philosopher (1724-1804 AD).
4. Hegal—A German philosopher (1770-1831 AD).

5. Froebal – A German philosopher (1772-1852 AD).
6. William. T. Haris – American Philosopher (1835-1909 AD).
7. Swami Dayananda (1825-1883 AD).
8. Rabindra Nath Tagore (1861-1941 AD).
9. Aurobindo Ghosh (1872-1950 AD).

Upanishads and Idealism

Asatoma Sad Gamaya,
Tamaso Ma Jyoti Gamaya,
Mrtyor Ma Amartam Gamaya,

Lead me from unreal to the real
Lead me from darkness to light
Lead me from death to immortaility

—Brihadaranyk Upanishad

Yastu Vijnananan Bhanati
Tasyendriyani Vasyani

Sadasvaisya Saratheh (He who is possessed of supreme knowledge by concentration of mind must have his senses under control, like spirited steeds controlled by a charioteer)

— Kathopanishad

Idealism in Education

The idealistic school in education is represented by Plato, Comenius, Kapila, Kant, Pestalozzi, Schopenhaver, Hegel, Froebal, Dayananda, Tagore and Gandhi. All these educational idealists believe that man is born with a spiritual-self. He can realize his spirituality and understand its true nature only through the agency of education. Rusk; "Education is expected to enlarge the boundaries of the spiritual realm." Idealists also believe that it is through the agency of education that the ideals of race and its cultural pattern are preserved, transmitted and modified subsequently, in the light of new situations.

Forms of Idealism

Idealistic philosophy of education takes various forms. One form of idealism is due to Hegal. The other form is due to Lubnitz and the third form is associated with the name of Bishop Berkely. These three forms assume:

1. Universe is a great thought process. The physical universe is thought made visible. We come into contact with great absolute thought through art, philosophy and religion.

2. Matter is essentially mental or spiritual. Every atom is a psychic entity and has life, mind and energy.
3. Things exist and have reality only when they are perceived by our mind.

Fundamental Principles of Idealism

1. Spirit and mind constitute reality.
2. Man being spiritual is a supreme creation.
3. God is the source of all knowledge.
4. Values are absolute and unchanging.
5. What is ultimately real is not the object itself but the idea behind it.
6. Man is not the creator of values.

Philosophical Principles of Idealism in Education

1. Stress on spiritual environment.
2. Self-realization as the aim of education.
3. Relatively unimportant place for the child in the educative process.
4. Development of the child in accordance with adult standards.
5. Stress on disciplining the child.
6. Emphasis on book-knowledge.
7. Positive education.
8. Education as the dynamic side of philosophy.

Chief Characteristics of Idealism

1. The universe exists in spirit.
2. Mechanical explanation of the universe is inadequate.
3. Teleological explanation of the universe.
4. Man is central in creation.
5. Emphasis upon normative and social sciences.
6. Normative description of the universe.
7. Conceptualism in epistemology.
8. Universe is knowledge.
9. Greater emphasis upon the mental or spiritual aspect of the universe.

Idealistic Aims of Education

1. *Self-Realization,* making actual or real the highest potentialities of the self. The aim is to enable each one to become his highest and truest self. The goal of educative effort-self realization is

meant for all. It is not the prerogative of the few education. The hierarchy of values which help in the process of self-realization may be as *(i)* an appetite for learning, *(ii)* clear speech, *(iii)* effective use of health, knowledge and health habits, *(iv)* recreation, *(v)* aesthetic interests and *(vi)* character.

2. *Realization of Spiritual Values:* Truth, Beauty, Goddness are the eternal values. One of the main purposes of life is apprehension and appreciation of these values. Each spiritual value is unique and has no equal or parallel.
3. *Enrichment of Cultural Heritage:* "Religion, morality, art, literature, maths and science" says Ross "are the products of man's moral, intellectual and aesthetic activity through out the ages."
4. *Unfolding of the Divine in Man:* Froebal, "The object of education is the realization of a faithful, pure inviolable and hence holy life. Education should lead man to clearness concerning himself, and in himself, and to unity with god."
5. *Development of Personality:* The most important aim of education according to idealism is the development of personality. This has been called man making Vivekananda.
6. *Development of Will Power:* Self-realization requires development of will power. H.H. Horne has given eight points for the realization of this ideal.
7. *Synthesis of Man and Nature:* Aim at achieving an understanding of nature in human beings and educating the educand with the permanent laws which guide and control natural phenomena.
8. *Character Development.*
9. *Rational Enlightenment.*
10. *Intellectual enlightenment.*

Concept of Idealistic Curriculum

1. It lays stress on the nature of the child.
2. Curriculum should emphasize the higher values, like truth.
3. Curriculum provides humanities a place of prominence, rather than positive science.
4. Ethics, religion and arts find an important place in the curriculum.
5. Importance to physical education, hygiene, physiology, physical skills, gymnastic and athletics.

The following arrangements of curricular studied is recommended by idealism.

Table – 8.1
Idealistic Curriculum

Objective	Study
1. Training of Body	Health and Hygiene
2. Intellectual Development	Languages, Literature, Sciences, Maths, History
3. Development of Aesthetic values/taste	Poetry/music
4. Moral development	Metaphysics

Idealistic scheme of education can be shown in the following way:

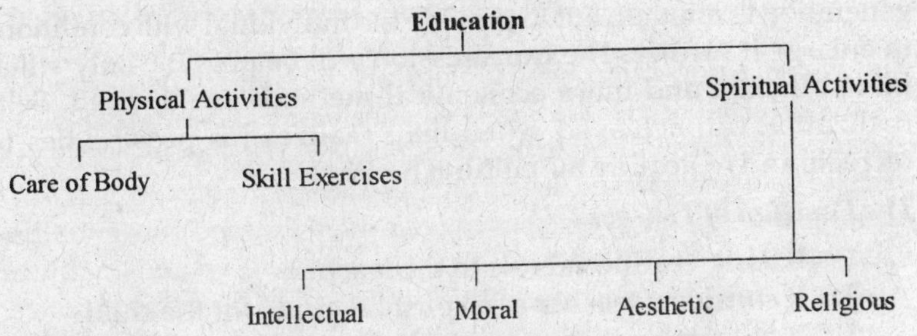

Idealism and Method of Teaching

1. Learning through reading
2. Lecturing
3. Learning through memorization and discussion
4. Learning through imitation
5. Questioning/Cross Questioning
6. Single and Group projects
7. Socratic method
8. Dialectical method – Plato
9. Method of induction/method of invention
10. Inductive and deductive method – Aristotle
11. Logical method – Hegal
12. Instruction method – Herbart
13. Play way-in-education – Froebal
14. Practice and Repetition – Pestalozzi

Idealism and Discipline

1. Idealism not in favour of free discipline.
2. Strict discipline for self-realization.
3. Higher values of life through self-discipline.
4. Self-imposed regulation and discipline.
5. Idealism believes inner discipline.
6. Idealism advocates cultivation of higher values of life through moral and religious instruction.
7. Idealism accepts restraint on freedom.
8. It requires the teacher to present good examples because the child considers teacher to be an ideal person to be emulated by his pupils-impressionism.

Function of School

The function of school is not only to transmit the culture from one generation to another, but to provide the individual with conditions to enlarge it further. The transmission will be possible only when more efficient and more economical methods are devised. Self-realization can achieved when man realizes his possibilities to recreate and re-acquire the cultural heritage.

The Position of Teacher

1. It assigns a special role to the teacher.
2. It considers teacher as a spiritual guide for the child.
3. It accepts teacher as an ideal person.
4. It regards the teacher as the priest of man's spiritual heritage.
5. It holds the teacher as friend, philosopher and guide.
6. 'He works like a gardener'.
7. Idealist teacher is one who has attained self-realization.
8. The teacher is only a 'midwife' in the birth of knowledge.

Idealism and Textbooks

1. More emphasis to humanities subjects
2. Preference to vedic, epic, moral, art textbooks.

Influence of Idealism in Contemporary Education

1. Wider and Higher Aims.
2. The Ideal Teacher.
3. Integration and multisided curriculum.
4. Moral Education.
5. Self-discipline.
6. Psychological methods.

Contribution to Education

1. Idealism has given higher place to mental and spiritual than to physical world.
2. Idealism aims at providing the means of acquainting the student with great achievement in literature, art, mathes and science.
3. Universal education.
4. Moral/religious education.
5. Emphasis on personality development.
6. Provide direct guidelines for aims, curricula, teachers role and methodology in education.
7. Education is ideal centred.
8. Idealistic philosophy restore values.
9. Many educational schemes and plans have had their beginning in idealism.

Weaknesses and Limitations of Idealism in Education

1. Spiritualism not considered scientific research.
2. Idealistic concepts like 'Spirit', 'mind', 'soul' and 'The cosmos' have little relevance in classroom.
3. Idealism stresses imitation; younger generation prefers invention and originality.
4. Too much emphasis an manners, modesty.
5. Curriculum payless attention to technology.

Criticism

1. Utopian Aims.
2. Theoretical Methods.
3. Lack of Specialization.
4. Neglect Science, technology, vocational subjects.
5. Teacher centred.
6. Well and good but not practical.

Conclusion

In conclusion, we may say that idealistic philosophy of education stresses the exaltation of human personality through self-realization. It emphasis his higher values of life but at the same time, it does not disregard the present life of man. It only advocates that present life is only a means to achieve higher ends. Then it stresses self-discipline and the creation of a school environment in which the pupils may willingly behave in a disciplined manner. This philosophy also recommends an ideal teacher who is well-equipped.

Realish

General Statement and Tenets

Realism in its elementary form is the simple philosophy of commonsense. But it tends to be asserted as a school in reaction to (1) extreme subjective idealism which asserts that the objects that we see and touch everyday do not exist except as perceptions in individual minds: (2) the degeneration of idealism to memorization of mere words instead of live wrestling with thought; and (3) the inefficient forms of child-centred, activity-centred pedagogy.

The main tenets of commonsense realism are:

1. There is a realm of nature which exists beyond or outside our minds.
2. Nature existed before we knew it, exists whether or not we know it, and will continue it exist after we pass away.
3. The attributes of physical objects exist just as we know them, except for errors of perception which are verifiable as errors. The true nature of a thing is not altered by the mere circumstance of its being known.
4. Experience is the touchstone of what is real. 'Seeing is believing.'
5. Physical nature follows or manifests a network of laws.

While realism is so simple for practical purposes, complications arise when we probe into the nature of the reality. Commonsense realism is accepted and tested by physics, and when physics goes deep enough it goes far away from commonsense. Among Indian schools, *Vaiseshika* realism started with commonsense, but in its elaborations reached far beyond commonsense, but revealing a high level of analytical acumen relevant even for modern scientific thought. Before analyzing some typical forms of western and Indian realism, it would be useful to summarize the forms it as taken in its development.

1. *Materialism:* This view seems so obvious, but when probed as to 'What is matter?' the materialist is forced say 'Never mind' even as the idealist responded to the question 'What is mind?' with 'Never mind'. – Apart from the arguments of the idealist, modern physics itself poses questions and

reveals data which make crude materialism untenable. During the 19th century, Dalton's atomic theory and Darwin's theory of evolution were used as planks to support materialism. When matter was thought to be composed of indivisible particles called atoms, materialism seems to have a stable support. But when the atom was split, and shown to be decomposable into energy packets and even waves, this soilid support of materialism vanished.

2. *Energism:* Spencer was inclined to treat energy as the ultimate components of reality. But since that too seemed to be 'non-stable' as the ultimate unit, it did not have a stable foundation.
3. *Law-abidingness:* Even before scientists could probe deep into the nature of electricity, they were able to formulate the laws governing electricity, which have been more or less stable. So rather than probe into the ultimate nature of reality, where the frontier seems to be continually altered, most realists accept that nature is a cosmos, subject to regularities that can be stated as scientific laws, with which predictions can be made. This could provide a base for extension into philosophical investigations too.
4. *Independence (of Subjective Perception):* Against the view of schools which would reduce reality to perceptions in individual minds, the position that reality (whatever is nature may be) is external to the perceiver seems to be a ground on which almost all realists can meet.

Some Landmarks in Western Realism

Just as Plato as held to be fatheı of idealism since even Socrates is known through Plato's dialogues, Plato's disciple, Aristotle, is recognized as the father of realists. Aristotle defined nature as a principle of motion and change. It is a cause that operates for purpose. Matter is potentiality and form is actually. An event is determined by several causes of which matter is just one (material cause), the others being: efficient cause (that which initiates the change), formal cause (the kind, type) and final cause (purpose). The formal and final causes introduce an idealistic element also into Aristotle's philosophy. But Aristotle insisted that the form or universals existed only in things [whereas, Plato held universal ideas alone got be real, and the actual phenomena to be shadows]. Aristotle made empirical studies in fields such as physics, biology, psychology. But apart from his contributions to literary criticism, it is his deductive logic which has come to stay. Another stream in early Greek/Roman philosophy is the naturalistic philosophy of Lucretius, and the atomic theory of Democritus, both with a typical realistic stance.

In Medieval Catholicism., St. Thomas Aquinas adapted Aristotle's ideas into Christianity and developed a realism which is both ideal and material. Universal principles (Aristotelian forms) are necessary constituents of existing things, but the presence of matter is needed to account for the existence of particular objects and for the multiplicity of things. He insisted upon the substantial unity of spirit and flesh in the continuum of human experience, yielding a philosophy which is not only speculative but also practical, not only rational but also capable of a certain intuitive grasp of reality. According to St. Thomas, senses help man to know individual objects of a material nature, while immaterial mind grasps universal aspects.

Francis Bacon's *Novum Organum* insisting upon patient compilation of factual data from external reality and derivation of general truths by the method of induction was turning point in the history of philosophy, considering the excessive use of deduction as the main or only source of arriving at conclusions, starting from artificial propositions. The Lutheran reformists emphasized learning about nature by actual observation, just as spiritual insights should be obtained by direct reading of the Bible. As a result of work by Ratke and others, real schools (*Reallschulen*) were started in Germany.

This trend could be traced not only to Lutheran Reformation, but also to *sense realism*, founded by Moravian Bishop Komensky (Comenius) and developed by the English philosopher John Locke. John Locke is a typical empiricist holding that all knowledge rests entirely on experience. He refutes the old belief that we are born with certain innate ideas. The mind is like blank sheet of paper upon which lessons are inscribed, primarily through sense experience. That is why ideas are not uniformly distributed among men. Education is a powerful instrument for furnishing one with ideas. The mind is passive and receptive at the stage of receiving the impressions; but it is also capable of active, rational reflections. The sense data are organized and generalized with the help of reason.

Locke held that we are not immediately aware of the physical objects themselves, but of our ideas about them. Ideas are the residuals which sense perception leaves in the mind. Reflection helps to add new ideas by association. Primary qualities such as extension, solidity, shape, motion and number are completely objective in the sense that they reside in the object. They can be felt by more than one sense. Secondary qualities such as colour, taste, smell and sound are not objective; they are effects made in our minds by the objects. But they are not less real because they are mental. (Berkeley rejected the objectivity of primary qualities too and made them all mental).

Locke is also an exponent of social realism. Montaigne was still more famous as a social realist. This became a model of liberal education for the upper classes of society in Europe. Social living was given more importance than cramming of the classics.

Humanistic realism was emphasized by other thinkers like Erasumus, Rabelais and Milton. It came as a reaction to the narrow humanism which leaned too strongly on early Greek and Roman traditions. Humanistic realism did emphasize classical studies, but it attempted to give it meaning and interpretation in the context of the immediate environmental setting.

Herbart, like Locke, rejected the doctrine of innate ideas; but his theory of mental activity and organization was much better developed. He posits the existence of plurality of reals to explain the contradictions observed in experience. All objects are complexes or patterns of these reals. Though the reals themselves do not change, the patterns of these reals continually change, resulting in changes in objects (e.g., growth of a tree).

Herbart's contributions, especially the theory of apperception, has been influential in psychology and education till very recently.

Realism claims a number of important philosophers of the 20th century. Moore and Russell are exponents of analytical philosophy. Moore defends commonsense realism. Russell covers a wide field, and uses a variety of approaches, ranging from simple exposition to mathematical analysis. He is particularly forthright when he expounds his objectivistic point of view. According to him, mind is physical, and experimental psychology is a physical science.

Whitehead has postulated a realistic theory of organisms. He holds that the terms materialism would apply to abstract entities, which are the product of logical discernment. All concrete entities, even an atom is an organism. "Biology is the study of larger organism, whereas physics is the study of smaller organisms." This view may be seen as the realistic correlate of Leibiz's monadism.

Some Landmarks in Indian Realism

Only Yogacara Buddhism and some dimensions of upanisadic speculations among the idealistic schools come close to pure monism of the mind or spirit. The other idealistic schools are dualistic and concede the reality of the physical world too. Even the advaita schools, while denying absolute reality to the physical world, concedes its practical existence. Even in epistemology, in which idealism generally excels, the foundations of knowledge (*pramanas*) formulated by the realistic school of *Nyaya* is the framework which all *astick* schools use to counter Buddhistic logic. Out of the several realistic schools, a brief mention is made of three typical ones.

Lokayata or *Caarvaka* is a typical *nastik* school. It asserts that matter is the only reality and that perception (*pratyksha*) is the only form of valid knowledge. It denies the so-called higher categories of mental existence, which can be explained in physical terms. Belief in soul, life after death, heaven and hell are all falsehoods perpetrated by the priestly class.

Jainism and *Buddhism* are also *nastik* schools because they refuse to accept the authority of the Vedas to establish entities or statements that cannot be established by perception or inference. Of the two, the contribution of Buddhism to epistemology has been cited under idealism. The Jain schools have contributed enormously to ontological realism. The Jain metaphysics with focus on their atomic theory is presented here in some detail.

Jain realism is plurastic. It admits two co-existing but independent categories—*jivas* and *ajivas*. They are both eternal and uncreated. *Ajivas* are sub-divided into two categories—formless (*arupa*) and those with form (*rupa*). Formless *ajivas* include *dharma* (principle of motion, *adharma* (rest), space and time. Matter (*pudgala*) is *ajiva* with form. Material things do change as particular things, but as matter they continue to exist eternally. Matter exit in six different forms of different degrees of fineness and visibility. We perceive only gross matter. Subtle matter is beyond the reach of our senses, but it is transformed into different degrees of *karma*.

Jains believe in the atomic structure of the universe. Atoms are infinitesimal, eternal and ultimate. They have no beginning, middle or end. They are neither created nor destroyed. They are formless, but constitute the basis of all form. Like Leuipus and Democritus, Jains believe that atoms are homogenous and produce different elements by varying combinations. *Karma* is matter in subtle form. The soul, in its transaction with the outer world, is literally penetrated with the particles of subtle matter. Thus, a special body called *karmanasanra* is built up, which does not leave the soul till its liberation.

Among the *astik* (orthodox—'believing' in the Vedas) schools *Nyaya-Vaiseshika* system is distinctly realistic. *Nyaya* is concerned with logic and is used in debates about knowledge, while *Vaiseshika* is concerned with ontology. The *Vaiseshika* analysis sets forth in detail the doctrines of the *padarthas*. A *padartha* is an object that can be thought (*artha*) as well as named (*pada*). The term is not limited to the objects of the physical world. It covers all aspects of experience. The *Vaiseshikas* break up *padarthas* into six categories, viz., substance (*dravya*), quality (*guna*), activity (*karma*), generality (*samanya*), particularity (*visesa*) and inherence (*samavaya*). Of these, the first three have real objective existence. Generality, particularity and inherence are products of intellectual discrimination. They are logical categories only.

The objects in the external world present themselves to use as real, as entities with a self-subsistence. Substance (*dravya*) exists over and above the qualities. Quality and action *inhere* in substance. There are nine substances in all, which account for all things, corporeal and incorporeal. They are: earth, water, light, air, ether (*askasa*), time (*kala*), space (*dik*), soul (*atman*) and manas. *Vaiseshika* admits non-material substances too, like souls. In fact, the real is not the material substances, but their minima. Kanada, the most famous exponent of this school has elaborated an atomic theory which differs in some detail from those of the Jains and the Greek thinkers.

There have been endless disputes between the Buddhist schools and the *Vaisesika* realists about the validity of categories like universals. The Buddhists and the other nominalists claim that generalities are only names. Only individual horses are real. There is no 'horseness' apart from actual horses. Platonic (idealistic) realists will attribute more reality to the generalities. *Vaisesika* realism gives equal importance to the material and non-material reals. They make a distinction between sats (existents) and *bhavas* (presences). Though originally only six categories were listed, a seventh, *abhava* (absence) was also added. It may be questioned how 'absence' can be a real or a 'presence'. Here the argument is made that when we say 'My purse is empty', what does the word 'empty' correspond to is raised, and the perception of the absence of the keys is claimed to be a real situation. Further analysis lead to destructional absence, absolute absence and mutual absence- all these make *Vaisesika* a brilliant and refined model of realism, giving reality to even many mental entities. The Buddhist counter arguments about 'emptiness' (*sunyata*)- extending to seen as well as unseen entities, their doctrine of momentariness, flow etc is equally brilliant. Irrespective of the conclusions, the philosophizing process in the Indian debates is a highly intellectual exercise with significance for the modern philosophical as well as scientific discourse.

Educational Applications

Concepts of Education

Realists define education as the conditioning of the nervous system by physical means so as to make it more amenable to physical direction, to make the individual more of a piece with the environment (lodge). The realist ideal of education is therefore to open wide the doors of the senses, and to welcome physical reality. Bertrand Russell pleads that the individual should mirror the world, as within a camera, to sense the diversified spectacle of nature and the history of humanity. But this mirroring should, be tinged with emotion and with the consciousness of power to change.

Metaphysics

The metaphysics of commonsense realism accepting the world as real makes it simple and easy to approach educational problems directly. It also helps to correct the escape mechanisms which would follow from some extreme mentalist schools. The Hindu realistic schools are dualistic; they include mind as a sixth sense, besides being and organizing principles. This makes it easy for them to study psychology on same plane with physics. Since Samkhya-Yoga schools are also dualistic, their educational and general tenets discussed under realism apply here. Sankhya philosophy has *prakrti* as the twin initial principle along with *purusa*. The yogi starts with the reality of the physical body and other external factors while on his jouney to the final state of 'enstasy' – the state of peace an calm. The realists believe that reality is a cosmos and is finished.

Epistemology

All Indian schools discuss the way of approaching knowledge (*pramanas*) using the framework developed by the realist Nyaya school: *pratyaksa* (perception), *anumana* (inference), *sabda* (verbal testimony) and *upamana* (analogy). The *Nyaya* school accepts all the four. All the other *astik* schools accept the first three *pramanas* to establish the validity of their arguments, and all of them accept vedic testimony as valid *sabda*. The Buddhists accept perception and inference only. The *lokayata* materialists accept only perception.

The realists' theory of knowledge follows from their concept of mind. Drake says, "In physical terms knowledge consists in our afferent and efferent relations to things known, that is, in events in the sense-organs, the neural arcs, and the muscular system." But realists generally believe that explanations and theorization beyond a point can lead us to forget the real fact. The fact is "we know, we know that we know and we know what we know." Retention of knowledge is explained by realists in terms of intensity, recency and frequency. Learning is explained in terms of links or bonds of external association forged through mere repetition. The system of meaning and insight which idealists make much about is explained in terms of familiarity born out of frequent repetition. Realists believe in the correspondence theory of truth. Since the world is a cosmos, it is possible to formulate dependable scientific laws. There is a correspondence between the facts of the outer world and the knowledge, the final court of appeal is the senses, which open the door to the outer world. Hence realistic curriculum is systematic and representative of the world. Ratke, one of the earliest to develop realist curricula, emphasized the principle of 'First the thing itself, and then the explanation' and 'All things through experience and investigation.' All the arts and sciences should be taught and the vernacular should be used in teaching.

Aims and Values

The realists' statements of aims of education are closely related to the demands of external order to which the pupils have to adjust. Locke starts with the dictum of 'a sound mind in a sound body' and gives primacy to the vigour and health of the body. The next aim which he stresses is virtue, which is obtained by the formation of good habits and a long discipline of desires. Various moral traits such as justice, liberality, fortitude, truthfulness, industry and sound breeding are emphasized. Locke also places knowledge as an aim, but with an idealistic tint, emphasizing formal discipline of the mind. The social realists considered education in frankly utilitarian way, as the preparation for the life of 'the man of the world.' The humanistic realist aimed at mastery of life in one's own surroundings natural and social, through a knowledge of the broader life of the ancients. Latin classics are studied, not to make young Romans, but to attain a knowledge of human motives, of human life in institutions, of life in contact with nature, through a knowledge of the broader life of the ancients.

Herbart makes moral development the chief aim of education. He also states development of many-sided interest as a related aim.

Herbart Spencer also regards moral education as the chief goal of education. His five subsidiary aims of education are drawn from the concept of preparation for complete living, i.e., preparation for: 1. direct self-preservation; 2. indirect self-preservation; 3. rearing children; 4. citizenship; and 5. ways of spending leisure. This is a typical realistic analysis of the aims, since realists hold existing adult life as the norm for pupils to prepare for. The five-fold preparation analysis also makes out a case for the introduction of science, which was neglected in British schools in Spencer's time. Physiology, hygiene, physics and chemistry are necessary for direct self-preservation. Science and arts leading to securing of food, clothing and shelter help indirect self-preservation end so on (the human sciences are arts come into satisfy the last two aims).

Whitehead advocates education for disinterested intellectual curiosity and aesthetic appreciation as educational aims. Bertrand Russell forecasts that science gives increasing evidence that one day man on earth will go to utter destruction. While it lasts, man can have the pleasure of experiencing the splendour of the universe and the enhancing beauty of nature. He can enjoy culture and knowledge, strive to obtain peace through the renunciation of futile personal desires. Russell advocates the inculcation of physical health and energy, friendly feeling, appreciation of beauty, enjoying the intrinsic delights of ideas, and independence of thought. Realism, except very modern varieties of the school-pre-supposes a stable order outside the individual and it tries to reproduce the order of this cosmos in the individual. Hence realists believe in deriving educational objectives through carefully made job analysis and activity analysis of the social and natural environment, word them as behavioural objectives, and organize them systematically in a hierarchy. Statement of objectives in terms of clearly specified terminal behaviours has helped to give concrete shape to the realistic curricula, and facilitated objective evaluation.

Curriculum and Methods

The concept of finished cosmos makes the curriculum and methods systematic and stable. Their inductive approach invokes them to learn from the external world – either directly through observation, or through the medium of the textbook, models and the teacher.

Comenius coined the motto, 'Things before words'. Examples should precede rules. He organized object lessons and prepared illustrated textbooks. He attempted to completely reorganize human knowledge along Baconian lines. The aim of this movement was to give "an accurate anatomy of the universe dissecting the veins and limbs of all things in such a way that there shall be nothing that is not seen, an that each part shall appear in its proper place and without confusion. It is not merely a matter of collecting facts, but one of arranging facts relating to all the arts and sciences around universal principels."

The realists have on the whole presented the learner as a passive recipient. But they have also contributed to correct backwardness through the effective use of external influences. They have also helped to fight the battle against excessive verbalism in schools. Locke's sense realism was universal, but his social realism was class-bound. It was set in the context of a class-conscious achieving society. The 'gentleman' created by the English Bourgeois Revolution of 1688 was not 'born'; he had to be 'made' through education – through travel and study of different cultures and manners. A job analysis of the social skills that the newly created 'gentleman' needs to acquire seems to underlie Locke's prescriptions in social realistic education.

Humanistic realists like Rabelais and Milton Emphasize the study of nature and immediate social surroundings as well as the classics in Greek, Latin and Hebrew. There is a combination of the dominant religious motive of the time, the broad humanistic conceptions of the poets of the past and present, and a typically realistic slant in the way of approach and use of content.

Huxley, the scientific humanist of the 19th century, seems to bring out the spirit of humanistic realism in a way much different from, and perhaps better than what was attempted by exponents who are credited with the movement on account of their bringing classical humanistic studies under the realistic orbit. Unlike Locke, whose social realism is class-bound, Huxley had a passionate concern for the common man. He also believed that the emerging education in science and technology, which was despised by the upper classes, would find better reception from the lower classes. He says, "The English nation will not take science from above, so it must take it from below." He believed that there is no difference between aristocracy and the lower classes in intellectual capacity and that a good education is that which helps to discover this capability and tap this vast reservoir of untapped ability.

The realistic methods of presentation are also objective and systematic. Wherever, possible it will be done through presentation of the objects of the natural and social environment—either directly or through simulated forms, models, pictures etc. The realist will not hesitate to use the systematic lecture. He believes in the correspondence theory of truth. The facts corresponding to reality are presented, when the real thing is not available for pedagogic use'—through models, pictures and words which correspond exactly with the reality.

Locke has developed a method of systematic presentation of sensations from the different objects of the environment and impress the idea in the mind, which was originally 'blank'. An idea, to Locke, is that which is 'the object of understanding when a man thinks'. The two sources of ideas are sensations and reflections upon these sensations in thinking. Thinking is a function of the mind operating on ideas. Hence, all ideas arise either directly or indirectly from external material objects that impinge on the senses. Complex ideas (beauty, courage, nation, etc.) are made in the mind by combining and relating simple ideas or by abstracting ideas from their essential components. Association of ideas another major concept in Locke's epistemology as well as his pedagogy. This has been developed on scientific lines by modern behaviourist psychologists.

Montaigne, the social realist would send the pupil early in to the world to get the education obtainable from immediate contact with men. Whereas Rousseau emphasis one's own experience with minimum contact with other men, Montague lays stress on learning through the experience of others. Hence, a study of history gets a prominent place in his system of education. Travel abroad is a means of education of the young gentleman. "Many strange humours, many sects, many judgements, opinions, laws, and customs, teach us to judge rightly of our own actions, to correct our faults and to inform our understanding, which is no trivial lesson."

Bacon advocates presentation of particular facts discoverable through observation and inductively proceed to general laws. The phenomena of nature would be primary, and that of mind only secondary.

Herbart has developed a systematic method to prepare the mind of the learner to receive new ideas. Then the teacher presents the new ideas in a systematic way. The student is helped to compare and abstract the ideas. Then he is helped to form the generalizations and apply them. This analysis has ruled pedagogy for more than a century. Recently this is being substituted by certain models of teaching, particularly those of a receptive or behavioural stance.

As a result of the realistic movement, the real schools (*Realschulen*) were started in Germany, emphasizing the vernacular language and practical studies. [Earlier the classical Gymnasium was the only education offered above the purely elementary level]. In America, the practically oriented 'academy' was opened in 1751 on the suggestion of Benjamin Franklin. In the exploration-oriented, achieving society of the USA, the practical academies had far more supportive climate than in Europe where the verbal study of the classics dominated till recently. The American situation also stimulated the development of systematic curriculum planning based on scientific techniques of job analysis and life analysis. But the curricula thus developed tended to spill over quickly into the pragmatic mood, though in the manner of collecting and analyzing them, the realistic base was strong.

The realists' systematic approach to the division and deeper probe into knowledge give rise to specialization. The essentialists take a realistic stand, but discourage excessive specialization. They say that such specialization neglects the needs of common humanity. Many realists defend specialization, but seek to correct it by some kind of re-integration. Herbart suggested correlation and concentration (taking one subject as the base and weaving the others round it) as remedies for extreme compartmentalization. He conceived of knowledge as an integrated system of ideas which provides the basis for apperceptive assimilation of new ideas. Ideas which are learnt without being utilized are called 'inert'. Inertness can be avoided by forming new combination of ideas and following them out in to their consequences (e.g., algebra can be saved from inertness by showing that quantity pervades every sphere of interest). Whitehead also suggests a rhythm in presentation of ideas in cycles relevant in the conquest of knowledge: romance, precision and generalization. In the first stage new subject is presented in its glamour of novelty. It is systmatised and deepened at the stage of precision. The general, laws and principles come in the third stage.

The realistic values have already been indicated along with the aims. Objectivity, impersonality, a humility and self-effacement born out of the vastness, majesty and inexorable law-abidingness of the universe is the core around which it is built. Yet Russell and other top realists have managed to build in positive emotional values in realist investigation and living.

The Realist Teacher

Strives to be clear, systematic and objective and experts his pupils too be or become so. He is impartial. He holds facts and truth in great regard, and attempts to extend the frontiers of knowledge through exploration of the real environment. As a teacher, however, he suppresses his discoverer personality and seeks to let the facts speak for themselves. He expects students to deal with the subject themselves in course of time and make their own discoveries. Individual differences among students are studied in a dispassionate way and dealt with on scientific lines. The pupil personalities are studied from this point of view without getting romantic attachment to pupil personalities.

More recent realistic analysis has yielded elaborate models. Oliver Martin gives a phenomenological analysis of teaching and learning. He descirbes teaching as a triadic relation involving the teacher, the student and the kind of knowledge. The teacher-student relation is asymmetric. The teacher can be said to have taught only if the student has learnt. But the teacher himself has learnt it prior to the teaching act. Several teaching models have been developed with reference to the teacher-student interaction.

Pragmatism

Prologue

Pragmatism is a typical modern philosophy that found its natural expression in the USA. Kill Patrick holds that pragmatism is "not so much a new philosophy as a new attitude, a new method of approach to philosophic problem." More than two thousand years ago Aristotle took the position that speculative activity, pursued for its own sake is superior to practical activity' in contrast to this view, pragmatism puts emphasis on what is practical, efficient, useful and satisfying. Many philosophers expect to find absolute standards for truth, beauty goodness. The programatists make these relative to human conditions. Absolute 'mansions of philosophy' may look perfect in paper. But they may not be fit for human habitation.

Two antecedents of typical pragmatic elements from antiquity may be cited. One is from ancient Greece. Among the wandering teachers called sophists, who claimed to teach New Athenian youth new things needed to deal with the conditions met with in their time, Protogoras has been identified as the greatest. His dictum was 'Man is the measure of all things,' thus questioning absolute, unchanging values. In ancient India Jains are thought to have developed an awareness of multiple standpoints, as seen in the story of the six blind men who touched different parts of an elephant and described the elephant differently. Even in talking about the ultimate issues, they developed the *syad vada* or probability discourse. When questions about whether the soul exists, whether even the earth is real are asked and disputed among different points of view ranging from absolutists and sonyavadins, the Jains preferred to prefix everyone of their seven ways of stating propositions with a *syad* (maybe): *syad asti* (may be, it exists), *syad nasti* (maybe, it does not exist), *syad asti-nasti* (maybe, it is existent and non-existent), syad *anirvacaniya* (maybe, it is inexpressible), *syad asti anirvacantya, syad nasti anirvacatya, syad asti-nasti anirvacaniya.* This is healthy reaction against absolutist assertions. The *syad vada* comes close to the scientists' stand that repeated experimentation increases the probability rather than assure certainly.

The objection of critics as to how an entity can be existent and non-existent at the same time is answered by the case of paper burning. It ceases to exist as paper, but the elements of paper (cellulose), namely carbon, hydrogen and oxygen continue to exist as CO_2 and as H_2O. The concept of *anirvacaniya* about ultimate things also seems to be a healthy standpoint scientifically and philosophically—though religion may need to be moved by faith. When Buddha was asked whether God exists, Buddha replied with silence. When asked "Is God non-existent?" was also replied with silence. Some have understood the silence as 'No'; but some understand it as *anirvacaniya*. The great linguistic analytical philosopher Wittgenstein took a realistic picture theory of language in his book *Tractatus*. But he closed with a significant statement: *Woveon man nicht sprechen kann, daruber muss man schweigen* (Whereof one cannot speak, thereof one must be silent). In his philosophical investigations, Wittgenstein takes a pragmatic stand about language, presenting it as a series of games, serving different purposes. It will be seen that the greatest of idealists are often found to 'descend' into a pragmatic mood when they wanted to be sure that their lofty ideas worked. Vivekananda's football as pre-requisite to effective leading of the *Gita*. Mahatma Gandhi's craft-centred education as a solution to the nation's problems, Christ's admonition that 'You shall be judged by your works' are pragmatic modes. Gandhiji's basic education was proved to work at Sewgram, Wardha and in institutions run by his disciples. It failed only when it was converted into governmental schemes and words, instead of problem-oriented purposive action.

Landmarks and Tenets

Charles Peirce (1839-1914) was the first to use the term pragmatism. It is derived from the Greek root, means, 'active' or 'efficient' (*prayogigam*). Pierce derived his conception of pragmatism from his theory of meaning. Meaning of an entity is to be derived and tested from its objective and observable consequences from our experience of from controlled experiment. William James (1802-1910) was the populariser of pragmatism, though not always in the sense in which Peirce intended it. The following anecdote would however explain the essence of the pragmatic approach.

William James was once walking through the meadows of Canada when he came across a group of campers disputing about a problem which they had set themselves. The problem was this: A squirrel was clinging to one side of a tree and a man was standing on the opposite side. The man tried to go round the tree to catch the squirrel. The squirrel also went round to avoid the man, always keeping on the opposite side of the tree. Thus, the man had completed one circle round the tree, and the squirrel also had gone round the tree once. Has the man gone round the squirrel? Our of the twelve members of the group six said 'Yes' and six said 'No'. They wanted James to settle the issue. Instead of giving a ruling based on his own opinion, James asked them to examine what they meant by 'going round'. It may mean 'being to the north of, east of, south of, west of, and again to the north of'; or it may mean, 'being to the front of, to the left of, to the back of, to the right of, and again to the north of'; or it may mean, 'being to the front of, to the left of, to the back of, to the right of, and again to the front of'. They could now see that by the first criterion, the man had gone round; and by the latter, he has not, because he has always kept in front of the squirrel.

The pragmatist thus helps to develop operational definitions, which help to solve or even dissolve the problem. Without such practical thinking people can go on arguing endlessly each one having a different idea about the point at issue. F.C.S. Schiller (1846-1937) was another popularise of pragmatism. His views go by the term 'humanism' because of his man-measure theory. The greatest contributor to educational pragmatism was John Dewey (1859-1952). He not only contributed to building up his philosophy in several educational contexts, but also helped to test them in his laboratory school. His approach is sometimes called experimentalism because he insisted on experimental or experiential testing. It is also called operationalism, because hypotheses and action plans are developed through mental operation, and testing is often conducted through physical operations. It also called instrumentalism, not only because philosophy became an instrument in helping to solve problems, but also because man is a tool (instrument)—using animal. Mind, which was given priority in idealism, and denied by many schools of realism, was seen as instrument in biological adaptation—the superior adaptation of the human being to his environment.

When the tree finds that its supply of water is short, all that it can do is to shed its leaf and prevent further loss of water. Plants in arid zones already have the adaptation to conserve water. The animal can walk to the place where it finds water. Man alone can arrange to bring water to where he is using his physical and mental capabilities, and the tools devised by him.

Pragmatism is a protest against both mechanistic naturalism/realism on the one hand and absolute idealism on the other. It is against a ready-made cosmos. The universe is still in the making and human beings help in its making. The world is characterized throughout by process and change. Everything changes, grows, develops. Pragmatism is thus close to the Indian heterodox schools of Becoming rather the orthodox schools of Being. The world is not only constantly changing; it is precarious. There is always an element of unpredictability and hazard. There can be unseen dangers as well as unexpected achievements and joys. Progress is not inevitable. Regressive mutations are also possible. In spite of the hazards, pragmatism is not pessimistic. Man must face life and make the most of it by his own diligent effort.

Pragmatism is frankly pluralistic. The ultimate cannot be reduced to one substance, either mind or matter. As Butler says, "The following world in which pragmatists believe is a world of many different things, a world of multiplicities, strictly speaking, a 'multiverse' rather than a universe."

Pragmatism tries to get away from the catch-words or categories set by realism as well as idealism. Matter and mind, body and soul, subject and object—are all too abstract, too far away, too unreal. Pre-occupation with these categories leads only to unprofitable discussions. "The only things", says James, "that shall be debatable among philosophers shall be the things definable in terms drawn from experience." Most pragmatists, like Dewey and James speak as if experience were the only reality. Hence, they are referred to as empiricist. James goes so far as to earn the name of radical empiricist.

The idealist tends to believe in certain absolute or at least a relatively stable scheme of values Pragmatism questions this stand. Kilpatrick attempts to explain musical values with man's experiments with various sounds, and of experience with the pleasant sounds and sound combinations. The theory of art compatible with Dewey's instrumentalism is that of functional fulfillment. But then it has also been pointed out that many objects preserve their artistic value after they have lost their utility, as exemplified by articles in the museum. Progressive phases of approbation by the hearers and spectators also seem to have had an important part to play in the evolution of art forms. The danger of deciding artist merit by playing to the gallery has also been raised.

The pragmatic theory of goodness is also similar to their theory of beauty. Since absolute value are denied, there can be no objective and universal criterion of goodness. The moral quality is identified in the last analysis with the social. Anthropological studies seem to show that a sense of moral obligation arises naturally out of normal human relationship. The role of culture in shaping moral values is emphasized by pragmatists.

In the matter of religious values Dewey and James differ. If we eliminate the differences among religions nothing seems to be left expect "the bare reference to something unseen and powerful." Dewey proposes to reject all beliefs in supernatural powers and a substitute a way of life, freed from superstitions which he considers religious. "Faith is rather the conviction that certain conditions and thing could exist, should exist, and includes our willingness to devote all our intelligence and power to bring about their realization." Dewey's religion is nothing other than idealized social morality. William James is more favourable to religion, but his proofs of God's existence are heterodox. He shows by the pragmatic method that God is what we live by. He says, "Our passionate need for taking the world religiously justifies the venture. It is better to yield to the hope that religion may be true than to yield to the fear that it may be false." Thus religion works in practice.

The pragmatic view of truth is the most unconventional part of the philosophy. The realists hold the correspondence theory: "Truth is that which conforms to fact, which agrees with reality, which corresponds to the actual situation." The consistency theory, as in mathematical proofs is preferred by idealists. The pragmatist does not believe in absolute turth; nor would he like to drop the term. He would redefine the term from his standpoint. The truth of an idea or proposition is determined by its successful, useful consequences. An idea is true if it 'works'. Three criteria are given for usefulness: (1) usefulness in promoting understanding (e.g., all laws of science); (2) utility in dealing with nature and the external world (e.g. most laws of science); (3) usefulness in being emotionally agreeable or comforting, and enabling one to live more effectively. James accepts all the three criteria; Dewey accepts only the first two.

Though pragmatism is close to commonsense, its concept of truth seems to deviate from it. James rejects the view that truth is an eternal, unchanging whole. Truths are many constantly changing. We make truth. Truth is a functional relation between our ideas and the sphere of our thinking, feeling and action. Truth is a normal and healthy relation between our ideas and our behaviour. A true idea is one which 'works in practise', just as a healthy heart is one that performs its functions effectively. According to James radical Empiricism, truth is not pre-existent. Propositions become true or false only after verification. "The truth of an idea is not a stagnant property inherent in it. Truth happens to an idea. It becomes true, is made true by events. Its verity is in fact an event, a process....its verification.

Dewey's instrumentalism or operationalism also presents truth in a similar vein. According to Dewey modern science is not interested in mirroring what exists or in discovering antecedent reality; its chief interest is in knowing how things change. In all experiments the scientist initiates changes. Even in astronomy where he cannot change the course of the stars, he alters the instruments. [The launching of artificial satellites and space travel during the last five decades has brought even astronomy clearly within the experimental scheme]. Operationalism asserts that ideas are empirical, that they are statements, not of what is, or what has been, but of acts to be performed. Lodge says that according to pragmatism, H_2O is not water, but is a method of producing water. [It might be even more pragmatic to consider H_2O as a means of using water].

Dewey extends his operationalism even into mathematics and logic. He holds that the new logic should be "a unified theory of inquiry," which will help to conduct "experimental and operational inquiry." The pattern of enquiry which he proposes includes: activity, problem, observation of data, formulation of hypotheses, and testing of hypotheses.

The pragmatist is against the idea of an absolute mind or even of substantive individual mind. But he is not adverse to speak of mental functions. Psychologists influenced by pragmatism avoid nouns such as mind, memory, attention etc. But they freely use verbs, adverbs and adjectives such as remembering, forgetting, attending, mental, slowly, quickly etc. The pragmatist's 'mind' is biological and social rather than physical.

Educational Implications

Pragmatism differs from the other schools which first attempt to develop the philosophical principles and then seek applications. Here the principles and applications come together. In fact, Dewey holds that education and philosophy are two sides of the same coin. He defines philosophy as 'the general theory of education.' Because of his close relation, inbuilt educational application.

Concept of Education

The pragmatist avoids a priori definitions of education. Education starts with experience, is part and parcel of experience, and becomes an attempt at reconstructing experience along widening circles. He finds it easier to say what education does than to say what education is. Dewey says that "The only true education comes through the stimulation of the child's powers by the demands of the social situations in which he finds himself."

Dewey attacks the concept of education as preparation for the future. It does not use children's motive power. Since the work has no relation to the present, children tend to postpone it indefinitely. The right preparation for the future is to make the best of the present. Concepts such as unfolding, drawing out and pumping out, according to Dewey, are not based on the child's initiative. On the positive side, growing is emphasized as the essence of education. Growing is actually 'a continuous leading into the future.' "Life is a self-renewing process through action upon the environment. Continuity of life means continued readaptation of the environment to the needs of the living organism." Education is the means of this social continuity of life. Education is also considered as direction. Direction implies that energies are led in a certain continuous course, instead of dispersing aimlessly. In a general sense every stimulus directs activity. Effective direction involves a focusing and fixation of action in order that it may be truly a response, and this requires an elimination of unnecessary and confusing movements." But coercive methods of direction are unproductive. It must be self-direction. If a definition is required education may be defined as a reconstruction of experience.

Epistemology and Metaphysics

Pragmatists avoid discussing about the nature of ultimate reality. They start with experience as the basis of reality. As one works with it the experiences becomes riches and deeper. For them reality is an unfinished house, and the learner should help in building it further. They don't make assertions about final reality with certainty. Their approach is similar to the *syad vada* of the Jains, with their probability and unspeakability discourse. In their researches they ask questions about what a thing does rather than what it is.

The pragmatic theory of truth and knowledge appears to fit well with the experimental temper of modern science, and makes philosophy continuous with science. It provides a framework for fitting in the increasing mass of 'truths' which continue to expand into indeterminacy. It makes the researcher not a mere onlooker, but an active participant in the process, a maker of truth.

Pragmatism differs from traditional empiricism in two ways. First, it does not think of the senses as mere gateways of knowledge and of sense perception as a passive process. Experience is not primarily an affair of knowing; it is first of all a process of acting, doing, living. Secondly, pragmatism does not regard compilation of facts as constituting knowledge. Data which are not put to work yield desirable ends are no value. The method of science is more important than its content. Even pupils learning science work in the stance of the scientist.

Aims and Values of Education

Pragmatism is against absolute ideals and predetermined fixed goals in education. It is futile to seek and end outside of educative process and make education sub-ordinate to it. Dewey distinguishes aims from ends.

When the wind blows about the sands of the desert, there is an effect or result, but not an end. The sands may soon be shifted in another direction. When bees gather pollen, make cells and make honey, each step paves the way for the next. The results of such action can be called ends. But the activities of the bees are carried on mechanically. If the consequences of the action can be anticipated in imaginative foresight, it will become an aim. An aim is a foreseen end...

The aims should be those of the pupils, not of someone else. It should be dynamic, operational. The aim is not the target, but hitting the target.

The pragmatic teacher does not believe in absolute values. Such values are far removed from the child's experience and the pupil may not even try to reach out to it. If the teacher sermonizes on the values, they will just verbalize it. On the other hand, if values grow out of real situations and activities they will be real and growing. Through problematic activities involving choice, trial and effect, pupils will be trained to value. Truth values will develop out of sensing problems, hypothesizing, experimenting and verifying. Moral values develop in real social situations. Even beauty values can be developed through functional fulfillment.

Curriculum and Methods

The pragmatic theory of curriculum steers clear of the formal training of the mind which gives too little importance to the content, and of the essentialist schools which give too much to it. Dewey seeks to reconcile what others consider contradictory into a dialectic. The child and the subject are simply two poles in the education process. They are not opposed to each other. The curriculum is a dialectical interaction between the two. If the curriculum is translated in terms of the child's experience and maturity level most of the problems would vanish. The pragmatists are against premature verbalization and formalization of the curriculum, against a wordy knowledge rather than a working knowledge, with young children. With grown up pupils formal statements of the stored knowledge of the race may be appropriate. The pragmatists prefer a situational of a pre-structured or systematic curriculum. The systematic organization of content in the book need not imply that pupils will carry this system in their mind. The classifications and system that pupils themselves make will be most fruitful. It is wrong to divide the subjects as liberal and vocational studies. Work done with intelligence, with relevance can be produce both intellectually and economically. Study can be vocational and liberal at the same time.

Educational methods are not antithetical to matter. According to Dewey, "method is the effective direction of subject-matter to desired results. It is antithetical to random and ill-considered (ill-adapted) action." Method is based on a reflection upon experience. The demarcation of matter from method results in an isolation, which leads to (1) neglect of concrete situations of experience; (2) false concept of discipline and interest; (3) learning becomes a direct and conscious end in itself; (4) methods are reduced to cut and dry routine, following mechanically prescribed steps.

Inquiry approach and environmental approaches comes naturally to the pragmatist. The typical pragmatic methods include project method and Dewey's activity programme. The project has four steps; purposing, planning, executing and judging; these steps should of the pupil and not that of the teacher. Activity programmes has the following steps: problem, collection and analysis of data, projection and elaboration of suggestions or ideas (hypothesis), experimental action and testing. Here again care should be taken to see that the steps do not become mechanized routine. In each stage the responsibility of the pupil is important.

Discipline, Interest and Effort

The schools which pitch their target far from the level and interest of pupils have to resort to artificial motivation, and exhortation to put in 'effort'. When this also proves ineffective external disciplining procedures are attempted. In pragmatism, interest, effort and discipline are naturally related. Dewey connects 'interst' etymologically with 'between'. Interest connects things that are otherwise distant. It creates an attitude of concern, of participation. Once the pupil takes interest in the activity, he will be able to put forth more effort in order 'to endure in an intelligently chosen course in the face of distraction.' Thus interest helps to develop genuine discipline in the class. Externally imposed negative discipline will be minimal or totally absent in the pragmatic school.

The Teacher

The pragmatic teacher does not start with a *pirori* theories or fixed goals. He takes life as he finds it. He helps pupils to develop their own goals. He steps in only when the children cannot do the work by themselves. Even these interventions will be brief and of a catalytic nature. He will not consider his work as successful till the pupil is 'liberated from teaching' at least with reference to the specific tasks taken. Gradually the pupils' sense of independence will become general. The pragmatic teacher takes the pupil into confidence in setting up educational goals, in planning, executing and judging. He understands the needs, interests and capacities of each pupils, but not as fixed quantities. His pupils continually develop new interests and display new capacities. He respects the freedom of the pupils. He is a leader of group activities, but takes care to develop pupil leadership too. His plans are flexible. He is sensitive to the curricular and self-building potentialities in various environmental situations.

Limitations

Ignores spiritualism, problems selected by the students quite often are found to have no relation with real life situations. Puts heavy demands on the teachers only a few teachers can cope with the demands.

Naturalism

General Introduction

At least three varieties of naturalism are current in discussions in educational philosophy. One is designated variously as physical or mechanical naturalism. This coincides mostly with realism discussed above (except social realism, humanistic realism and some sophisticated aspects of India realism). Aspects like sense realism and even some more refined forms may overlap with this variety of naturalism. The tenets and educational applications may be carried over here from the previous section. Some extremely refined forms of realism (bordering on objective idealism) may not carry over thus. The second variety of naturalism is biological naturalism. This focuses child nature, the child as a growing developing organism, displaying different characteristics according to the level of development. The third variety of naturalism is 'romantic naturalism' associated with Jean-Jacques Rousseau. Since the first one is presumed to be carried over, and the second is condensed, much of the present analysis will be loaded with Rousseau's naturalism.

Basic Tenets

Many schools of naturalism are a protest against the artificially and complexity of modern society, against the fetters imposed in institutional life, against the aberrations created in 'civilized' life and against the repressions in forced external discipline. They decry the verbalism of the school which substitutes words for things. They demand a going back to the natural way of life, to primal nature itself. Rousseau pictures the 'natural' state of man in glamorous terms as full of joy, freedom and opportunity for healthy natural growth; as an 'integral' as compared with the 'fractioned' social life; as containing all the worth-while values of life and education, robbed by the so-called civilized life. Nature represents external natural setting, contrasted with the busy city life; it also means child nature, which has its own ways, different from that of adult ways and competencies. These should be respected for the sake of ensuring healthy growth and a sound education. The understanding of child nature and growth patterns have now been taken over by developmental psychologists (vide Hurlock and others). This aspect may be called biological naturalism. But it was Rousseau who fist called attention to education according the stages of child growth.

Naturalism does not have the absolute epistemology of idealistic schools. But it questions what goes on in the name of nurturing knowledge in the school. It is sheer verbalism. In fact, knowledge unfolds naturally in the child. When it is related to child growth, as done by Rousseau and biological naturalists, it may be treated as an anticipation of the genetic epistemology (intellectual structures or schemas being constructed according to stages of development) of

Piaget. Nature itself is a value and the matrix in which other values emerge, according to naturalism.

Educational Applications

Concept of Education

The forceful attack on what by the name of education was first exposed in the modern period by Rousseau. The pathology of the school is fully exposed. He attacks the slavishness, conformity, suppression of individuality, cruelty imposed on children by imposing a meaningless curriculum induced by the school claiming to prepare for a future—which is uncertain. [This negative critique of the school as later taken up by Ivan Illich (*Deschooling Society*), Pal Goodman (*Compulsory Miseducation*), Paulo Freire (*Pedagogy of the Oppressed*), Reimer (*The school is dead*) and others. The concept of direct pedagogy emphasizing impression and instruction is being substituted in naturalistic schools by an indirect pedagogy extolling expression from within.

The concept of education is natural unfolding. Rosseau calls this 'negative education'. In this context 'negative' has a very positive meaning. It simply means that the child has all the potentialities to grow from within and reveal the various competencies in due course. Premature imposition will only spoil the realization of the objectives and yield only half-baked products. The educator's function is to just protect the child from harm and allow him to grow at his own pace.

Values and Aims

As against the idealist who claims to have lofty ideals in some mental realm, or the realist who claims to imprint specific objects externally in a on ordered way, Rousseau insists on nature's way in getting the educational outcomes emerging from inside. If at all values are to be seen they have to be sought in nature or in the child. He opens *Emile* with the statement: "Everything is good as it comes from the hands of the author of nature; everything degenerates in the hands of man." He also holds child nature to be intrinsically good. "The first movements of nature are always right. There is no original perversity in the human heart." The concept of preparation for a distant future emphasized by idealists and realists is questioned. There is nothing more absurd than fixing an objective which is far above the level of child or far distant in terms of time and offering negative external motives to cajole him or to force him to achieve it. The age of gaiety should not be spent in the midst of tears, punishments, threats and slavery. Independence and freedom are natural values. All that the school should do is to remove the fetters and constraints. Rousseau says, "Civilized man is born, lives and dies in slavery: at his birth he is wrapped in swathing bands; at his death he is nailed in a coffin; throughout the time he wears the image of man he is bound hand and foot by our institution."

Some people see natural values as 'epicurean values' of "Eat, drink and be merry; for tomorrow we die." This is based on a misunderstanding. Epicurus himself led a frugal saintly life, reducing his consumption and wants. Satisfaction of all one's wishes and greed may bring immediate joy but bring suffering as a consequence. Lasting joy is got by controlled natural living. This was the life which Epicurus led and which many 'idealistically' oriented naturalists advocate. Hence natural life is a simple and disciplined life, which helps one to overcome sorrows. Many idealists too share this view.

Curriculum and Methods

The naturalist is against an overloaded curriculum imposed externally. For very young children it will take the form of play and other activities suited to the age and environment. It is all the better if chosen by the children themselves. Premature education of the mind is discouraged. Healthy growth of the body will help the growth of the mind and spirit. Externally imposed bookish curriculum is condemned. "I hate books. They only help one to talk about what one does not know." The only book which Rousseau will allow Emile to use is *Robinson Crusoe* – which is a symbol of learning through discovery in natural conditions away from civilized society. The whole design of Emile's education is by self-education in such settings.

Learning should come from things and not from words. When Rousseau said, "Childhood has its own ways of seeing, feeling and thinking, different from adult ways" and when he said that the educator must 'lose time' rather than 'save time' by keeping the child engaged in doing something in the school [which is beyond his capacity], he was anticipating the modern ideas of Piaget and Montessori. Montessori's didactic apparatus were designed to allow the child to learn arithmetic and reading as his capacity grows without forcing him prematurely. When the time comes the child 'explodes into' arithmetic or reading. In 'losing time' with the apparatus designed by Piaget's disciples instead of doing formal addition, subtraction and multiplication in the lock-step style, the child may be developing schemas far ahead of the child who is doing mechanical arithmetic, and when the schemata are fully formed, he may work very fast and overtake the plodding child who was working mechanically, falsely assimilating higher mental tasks in lower mental schemata.

Curriculum different to two stages. In earlier stage nothing to be taught except what the child asks for. Physical activities and health training, play, stories and songs are the early lessons. In this stage importance is given to training of the senses.

In later stage, Physiology, Physical Science, Natural Science, Mathematics, Language, Psychology, Social Studies, Anatomy and Study of Nature through manipulation/exploration of the environment are suggested. Experiment/practicals are the methods.

The Teacher

The Teacher must must learn the methods not from books, but by observing nature's ways and following her methods. The teacher should not use a level or type of discourse which the child will not understand. The teacher must be a companion, a friendly observer, creating the right conditions for learning in the natural setting.

Discipline

External discipline, especially, punishments and threats, are to be avoided. Rousseau advocates the discipline of natural consequences. If the child breaks the window-pane, the mentor will not punish the child; nor will he replace the glass. The child will catch cold, and Rousseau expects the young child to form the connection between breaking the glass and catching cold.

Another concept of natural discipline is called emancipation (from repressive discipline). Some experiments is Summerhill and other centres allow boys and girls to mix freely and grow naturally without threats, punishments and unnecessary restrictions. Some of the fears expressed by orthodox people did not come about, at least to the extent anticipated by them. Even Gandhiji attempted such approaches to some extent at one stage in South Africa. Children growing up naturally under healthy conditions free from threats and unnecessary constraints do not develop repressions or display defense reactions to the extent to which excessive external discipline.

A Brief Criticism

Rousseau's powerful critique of educational aberrations in his time [some which exist even today] was instrumental in making education child-friendly, natural, more joyful, and when done in the optimal way even more achieving in the long run. But Rousseau himself did not put his ideas into practice. His own children were admitted in orphanages. It was his disciples, and those influenced by him directly—such as Pestalozzi, Froebel and Montessori who gave a positive form to 'negative education', education through free joyous activity, education in natural conditions, Children's garden (Kindergarten) etc.

While attaching societal aberrations Rousseau overlooked the positive contributions of society. The cases of children brought up by wolves and away from human interaction shows that the natural man is a fraction, while the social man is a whole. Nature is to be complemented by social and sensible educational action. Rousseau was right in condemning social aberrations which denatured the child. But the outright attack on all social and institutional action was unjustified.

The doctrine of natural consequence may not work with young children who cannot see the connection between their action and the dangerous consequence which will come much later. Even when the connection is made, the child can learn from an experience only if he is alive. The presence of the parents and other adults around the child is also endowed by nature. The natural help which they would render on certain occasions should not be artificially withheld. The free play of natural education, supplemented by judicious social and educational 'intervention', preferably in 'invisible pedagogy' seems to produce optimum results.

The Eclectic Tendency in Education

Meaning of 'Eclectic'

The dictionary meaning of the word 'eclectic' means 'selecting or borrowing', 'choosing the best out of everything', 'broad', the opposite of exclusive. An eclectic is one who selects opinions from different systems especially in philosophy.

The doctrine of the eclectics is the name applied to certain Greek Thinkers in the second and first centuries, B.C.

According to eclectic tendency in education, modern education wants to synthesize the brief forms of all the past movements into a new structure. It aims at establishing relationships among all principles. Psychology, science and social sciences have mainly influenced the methods of teaching, teaching-material, educational aims and school management. In fact, every movement has influenced not only every field of education but also every field of life. This tendency is carrying us to a good age where we would be able to establish new ideals, values and standards over narrow feelings and ideas.

Key Elements

Following are the key elements:

1. The modern tendency in education is to do away with the existing differences present in the conflicting ideologies.
2. Eclecticism accepts common principles in the theory and practice of education.
3. There are some common points regarding the development of the individuality of the child, his physical environment and social ends which are quite eclectic in nature.
4. Eclecticism does not consider the need of following a particular theory, idea or philosophy dogmatically or supporting an idea perennially in the field of education as everything is subject to change and change forms the true essence of life.
5. All the philosophies are complimentary.
6. The modern eclectic tendency in education reflects its aims, objectives, methods and techniques of teaching through the cumulative experience of the human race.
7. The harmonious blend of diverse philosophies is called eclectic tendency.
8. No educational thinker is exclusively an idealist, or a naturalist or a pragmatist.

The fusion of the following psychological, scientific and socialist tendencies during the 18th and 19th centuries in the aims of education, methods of teaching, contents of education, school organization, supervision and management etc., is clearly visible.

1. Rousseau, Pestalozzi, Herbart and Froebel psychologized education, Rousseau advocated child centred education.

He pointed out different methods of teaching at different stages.

For the success of teaching work, Pestalozzi expressed that education must develop the innate powers of the child by providing experiences. He, therefore, laid a great stress for the introduction things in place of abstract ones.

Herbart advocated the scientific method of teaching. He gave the five famous steps of teaching.

Froebel emphasized, "The true method of education consists in considering the mind of the child as a living whole in which all the/ parts work together to produce harmonious unity."

2. The scientific tendency improved and developed the idea of liberal education and suggested the building of perfect citizens by imparting professional, technical and higher education according to ability, interest and age at every stage of education.
3. The socialistic tendency advocates that education is social process.

Eclecticism and Aims of Education

Schools of philosophy differ from each other as regards the ultimate aims of education but in the proximate aims they do not have variance. None of the schools of educational philosophy denies the child an education that will make him to 'be good man' as well as 'good citizen'.

Eclecticism and Aims of Curriculum

All the philosophies of education support life-centred education. According to them, if there can be one subject for education, that subject is 'life'. They take a broad view of curriculum as 'total experience.'

Eclecticism and Methodolism

'Method according to circumstances' is the kernel of all philosophies. Importance of direct experience is recognized by lending their support to 'play-way' and 'learning by doing.'

Eclecticism and Discipline

All the philosophies of education advocate that example of the teacher to regulate the conduct of children is better than precept of the teacher. Discipline through knowledge and knowledge through experience is the under-current of all educational philosophies.

Eclecticism and the Role of Teacher

Eclectic tendency is clearly visible in the job of the present-day teacher. Earlier he was primarily concerned with imparting information. Now his work has become very challenging, delicate and complicated. He is expected to have some knowledge of various disciplines i.e., philosophy, psychology, sociology, etc. Present-day situation puts heavy demands on the teachers. Hence, teachers have to be careful in their approach to quote M.V.C. Jeffreys, "School life makes very heavy demands on the teachers whose services as guides, philosophers and friends is much more important than their work as academic instructors. There can be no more demanding job, mentally and morally than teaching; and anyone who suggests that teachers have a clean and cushy job, with short hours and fantastically long holidays, is culpably misinformed. Teachers are responsible not only (in the manner of employers) for their pupils as whole persons. They are the chief agents in creating ethos which is admittedly the least definable, though perhaps the most important quality of a school. It has been well said that a teacher should be an authority, and in authority, but should not be authoritarian. In other words, the good teacher's authority derives from his knowledge, experience and wisdom, and not from his status.

According to eclecticism, an ideal educational system should be idealistic in its objectives, naturalistic in its setting and pragmatic in its methods and programmes of work. One philosophy should not be emphasized at the cost of other. All the philosophies should be fused into a unity. In education the 'Modus Operandi' should be to receive inspiration from the cumulative experiences of whole race and not from one generation preaching one particular ideology. This is called eclecticism.

EDUCATIONAL IDEAS AND CONTRIBUTIONS OF GREAT EDUCATORS

Plato (428-347 BC)

Introduction

Greece has been famous for its civilization, culture and contribution to the field of knowledge since olden days. Western educationalists have off and on pointed towards this importance of Greece. Rusk in his Doctrine of Great Educators' has very rightly said, "It is to Greek thought that we turn when we wish to consider any of the problems of ethics, education or politics. Greek thought has, in addition to its originality, a surprising university."

Plato was the foremost of the Greek philosophers and educationists. He has influenced not only his countrymen but also educationists of other countries. He influenced Rousseau so much that he said, "If you wish to know what is meant by public education, read Plato's 'Republic'. It is the finest treatise on education ever written."

Life of Plato

Plato was born in 428 B.C. in Athens. He belonged to a very respectable family of Athens and naturally, was an aristocrat not only by birth, but by tendencies as well. He got an opportunity to study the works of Homer and other literatures of Greece. He was also a sportsman of the first order. He had won many wresting belts and was also a great warrior. On the other hand, he had great love for literature and politics. He wrote many poems and took part in politics. He wrote many poems and took part in politics as well. Although he did not succeed as a politician, he did contribute towards the progress of Greek civilization.

At the age of 20, he came in contact with Socrates, and their relationships was simply strange. They belonged to two extremes of society. Plato hailed from an aristocratic family while Socrates was a poor sculptor. Plato was very much influenced by Socrates. The death of Socrates in the year 399 B.C. had a deep and lasting effect upon Plato. He thought it was against humanity. After this incident, Plato travelled in several different countries and came back to his motherland at the age of 40. He had now grown quite mature and wanted to put his ideas into actual practice. With this end in view, he opened a school in 386 BC, known as 'Academy', where he taught until his death in 347 B.C. The main objective of this Academy or the 'University' was to train politicians, who would become the sort of philosopher ruler described in 'The Republic'. He aimed at making an individual an ideal citizen.

Works of Plato

Views of Plato in regard to education and other aspects of life are contained in his works. He lived upto the age of 60 year and wrote about 400 books but only 9 of them are available to us. The important ones among them are following:

(a) *Republic*: This book contains Plato's conception of an ideal state and discourse on nature of justice.
(b) *Laws*: It seems that this book was written to clarify certain national portions of republic.
(c) *Protragoras*: This book deals with the virtues, principles and ideas of Socrates.
(d) *Symposium*: This book contains his views on the ideals of 'the truth', 'the good' and 'the beautiful'.

Plato's Philosophy

Plato thought that the ills of society could not be eliminated until philosophers ruled the state. Therefore, the education of each philosophers became most important for him. 'The Republic' is a statement of that aim i.e., to train philosophers-statesman. The philosophy contained in the 'Republic' expresses Plato's belief in two worlds. They are:

(a) the world of ideas; and
(b) the world of objects and senses.

(a) The World of Ideas

According to Plato, this is the real world because the idea are eternal, unbounded and unchangeable. This is the worldly of mind and abstraction. Since that is true/real, it is away from the world objects. He has also said that these ideas are related to each other in an heavenly order. Ideas are celestial and eternal thoughts. They are heavenly because worldly objects are created according to them. They are complete in themselves.

(b) The World of Object and Senses

The world is unreal and transitory. Anything that is beautiful today fades away tomorrow. Only the ideas about those beautiful things linger on. That is why Plato said that it is the world of ideas that is real. Inspired by this principle, he regarded that, 'the truth', 'the good' and 'the beautiful' are the eternal qualities of the world.

In the VIIth volume of the 'Republic' (Plato, 1964. *The Republic*, Penguin Books; Pelican, Vol. VIII, p.514), he provides a more vivid picture of the platonic metaphysics. There is a low wall built along the way, just like a screen over which players might show their puppets. There are moving figures, who hold various objects made of wood and stone. The prisoners can seen only their own shadows or the shadows of one another created on the wall by the fire,

Likewise, they see the shadows of the objects which are being carried by the moving figures.

Thus, the metaphor describes the conditions under which we lead our lives like prisoners—the only knowledge we can have of the events outside us is that of the shadows cast by these events. The sounds we hear are vague and confused. This is the illusionary perception of the world from which only a few can ascend to pure thought or the highest realm of knowledge. Only a true philosopher can have such a true vision.

Thus, Plato's doctrine of 'Forms' or 'Ideas' has traditionally been known as 'idealism', some try to seek 'realism' in his philosophy as they think that his ideas are real because they have an absolute existence outside the mind of man. The fact is that Plato in his outlook and philosophical reflections such as the simile of the cave (from 'Republic'), seeks the idealistic doctrine which is further confirmed by his concept of forms.

Plato on Education

It is in Plato's 'Republic' that his chief treatment of education can be discovered. Rousseau reflected: If you wish to know what is meant by public education, read Plato's 'Republic'. Those who merely judge books by their titles take this for a treatise on politics, but it is the finest treatise on education ever written."

Both in the 'Republic' and the 'Laws', Plato reflects that the pupils shall be regarded as belonging to the state rather than to the parents. This law applies to females as well as males. This communistic ideal, which he projected in the 'Republic' that children are the property of the state, is re-emphasized in the 'laws'. In the 'republic' as well as in the 'Laws' the state is made responsible for the education of the children. Plato, therefore, is blamed for forerunning the communistic ideal long before the spread of communism.

Aims of Education

According to Plato, the following shall be the aims of education:

Inculcating the Idea of Good Citizenship and Virtues

Plato has suggested that children should be given virtues and the qualities of citizenship should be developed in them, so that the unity and the integrity of the state may be maintained.

Development of the Body as Well as Soul

Education must aim at providing perfection to the body, as well as the soul. In the absence of a sound body, a person cannot have a sound mind and that is something not good for education. Along with the body and the mind, the nature, reason, intelligence and behaviour should also be trained. The child should also be taught to be able to co-ordinate his personal interest with that of the state.

Vision of Truth

Plato believed that God is truth. The 'truth', the 'beauty' and goodness are the internal qualities of God. Education should aim at the achievement of these aims.

Appreciation of Beauty

'Beauty', according to Plato, is one of the external aims of life and therefore, it is quite natural for education to be able to equip children to appreciate beauty in whatever form and whenever it is available and seen.

Plato and Curriculum

Every man who thinks about education has to give out his views in regard to the content material of education, Plato had done the same. The main subjects proposed, in the curriculum in the 'Laws' and in the 'Republic' are the same. They are:

Music and Physical Training

During infancy or early years of childhood, Plato has suggested that music and physical training must be taught. This will lead to harmonious development of the body as well as the soul.

Teaching of Mathematics and Geometry

Plato has also prescribed the teaching of mathematics and geometry for early education. He believes that the teaching of these subjects leads to exactness in the children. He also suggested teaching of these subjects which leads to the formation of the background of philosophy. He also suggested timely examination in order to test the knowledge acquired by the children.

Curriculum for Higher Education

For the education at higher classes, Plato has prescribed higher mathematics, geometry, mathematical music, astronomy, philosophy, etc. After philosophy, Plato praised mathematics.

Philosophy

Plato gave supreme importance to the study of philosophy. He believed that it is the philosophy that brings to mind the truth in all its forms. He was also of the view that only a person who knows other sciences well can acquire knowledge of the philosophy.

Plato and Methodology

Plato has suggested only one method of teaching and that is presentation of the subject material in the most interesting manner. While prescribing this, he suggested that the natural faculties and interest of the children must be taken into consideration. Without this consideration, education cannot prove to be very effective. 'Play' which is given so much importance today in the field of education was also recommended as a method of teaching by Plato as well. In his book entitled 'laws', he has emphasized the importance of play. He feels that the pleasure that play inculcates in children has great importance in education. If education could be imparted through his pleasure, its effect is sure to be lasting and useful.

Plato's Influence

Plato's influence on late educational thought and practice can be seen at different times. His curriculum considered music, arithmetic, geometry and astronomy important for study at school.

According to whitehead, platonic views have encouraged the study of art and brought in the importance and dignity of mind against the matter. Plato's Academy was really the first University in Europe. His 'Schemes of Education' were so appealing that not only in the medieval but the post-medieval times as well they were accepted, through with slight changes.

There is no doubt that Plato is blamed for creating for his ideal state a society of classes and a totalitarian scheme, which could have influenced the communists or the Nazis and would lead to the ideal of 'indoctrination', but he presented a formal scheme of education which is being practical even today.

Above all, Plato in his 'Republic', except in the study of technical education, presented that, education, should aim at the ideal of 'citizenship' and 'leadership'. It should lead to intellectual growth and enlighten pupils to find the actual truth or 'The Good', it should also lead to perfect self, development and help reaching the stage of self-realization, which is the ideal of idealistic philosophy.

Plato is also known as the fore runner of the idea of equal opportunities for both sexes and to bring into the realm of education the growth of moral and religions aspects, which could fit into the schemes of education of all the developing countries of the world at all times.

Conclusion

Plato was the follower of Socrates, Aristotle was a disciple of Plato. Plato was one of the greatest philosophers of democracy and he has propounded democracy in its best form. He also believed that the government of the people, for the people, and by the people is the best government. This government can be successful only when the citizens are well-equipped to live upto the standards of democracy. Even today 'Republic' attracts the attention of educationists, politicians as well as social reformers. Plato understood the importance of education as well as philosophy and presented it before the world in a very skilful and nice manner.

Maria Montessori

Introduction

Maria Montessori, the originator of the Montessori method, was born in 1870 in Italy. She was an Italian lady doctor who later on become one of the prominent educationists of the world. Here first desire was to become one actress and for this purpose she actually joined a dramatic school. However, she realized that her mission in life was a different one and she left this to become a doctor. But the doors of the medical colleges were practically closed for women in those days. She tried a trick and was successful in getting an admission. She signed herself M. Montessori when she applied for admission. The authorities could never think that a lady would apply. Thinking her a man, she admitted and became the first Italian lady to get the degree of Doctor of Medicine. For seven year from 1900 to 1907, she worked as a professor of anthropology in the university of Rome. There she got the opportunity to come into contact with children. There was a ward of mentally deficient children in the hospital attached to medical college. She was asked to superwise these unfortunate children. She took a keen interest in the study of such children and in their education. She discovered,

(i) Mental Deficiency results from the 'dullness of senses'.

(ii) 'Sense training' was the best method to achieve marvelous results in their education.

(iii) If the same method of sense training is employed to education normal children, far better results could be achieved.

Supervisor of Schools

In 1907, she get an offer to supervise some schools in tenement. Children between age 3 and 7 whose parents were mostly out at work and who were neglected and made all sorts of imitation nuisance in their absence attended such schools. The first of these schools opened in 1907 by her and was named 'children's house.' Here she developed a novel method of educating children through the process of 'sense training'.

Inspectress of Infant Schools

She was appointed as inspectress of infant schools by Government of Italy in 1922. She began to impart training to teachers in the new method discovered by her, side-by-side with her job.

Run Away from Italy

Mussolini came into power in Italy and he was a fascist dictator. He wanted to educate children for war. Montessori who was an ardent supporter of child freedom could not work under such regime. So she was obliged to run away from there and proceed to Holland where she founded a school.

The Idea that Inspired Montessori

Child is a body within grows and a soul which develops—"these two forms, the physical and psychic, have one eternal front, life itself." It follows then that "we must neither more nor stifle the mysterious powers which lie within those forms of growth, but we must await from them the manifestations which we know will succeed one another."

Educational Principles

1. *Development from Within*: Like Froebel, she believed that education of a child is from within. "If any educational act is to be efficacious, it will be only that which grows and a soul which develops." She is of opinion that education must help in the complete unfolding of the child's individuality. Suitable environment should be provided so that the child may grow and develop the potentialities that he has within him.
2. *The Doctrine of Freedom of Liberty*: She believes that freedom is

the birthright of every individual and she advocates the spontaneous development of the child through full liberty. She does not believe in putting restraints as she thinks that these may mar or stifle the innate powers of the child."

3. *No Material Rewards and Punishments*: According to her, the development that result from unnatural incentives will also be unnatural. She writes "the jockey offers piece of sugar to his horse that he may respond to the signs given by the reins, and yet neither of these runs so superbly as the free horse of the plains."
4. *Principles of Individual Development*: In the words of John Adams, Dr. Montessori "has rung the knell of class teaching." She believes that every child is peculiar to himself and he progresses at his own speed and rate and collective methods of teaching crush individuality. She treats each child as a separate individuality. She treats each child as a separate individual and recommends that he should be helped and guided in a manner, that helps him in his proper growth and development. The teacher is concerned with his mental as well as his physiological developments.
5. *Principles of Self-education or Auto Education*: Montessori has shifted the emphasis from teaching to learning. She believes that self-education or auto education is the only true education. She advocates that the child should remain undisturbed by adult interference. She has devised the didactic apparatus which attracts the attention of the children, keeps them busy spontaneously, leads them to learn the powers of movements, reading, writing and arithmetic, etc.
6. *Principle of Motor Efficiency or Muscular Training*: She has also attached importance to muscular training as a part of the early education of children. She believed that muscular training facilitates other activities like writing, drawing, speaking, etc. She considers muscular activity as purely physiological in character. She stresses that running, walking, etc all depend on muscular training.
7. *The Teacher as a Directress*: She replaces the word 'teacher' by the word 'directress' as she thinks that the function of the teacher is to direct and not to teach. Her motto should be "I must diminish to let us grow."

8. *No Place for Fairy Tales*: She would like to banish fairy stories from the curriculum of young children since these tends to confuse children and to hinder them in the process of adjusting themselves to the real world.

Thus Montessori revolutionarised education.

Functions of a Teacher

Montessori says, "The educator must be as one inspired by a deep worship of life."

1. *The Teacher as a Gardner:* She thinks that a teacher should care for the child like a gardner who cares for the plant so that natural growth of the child is properly guided and aided in the process of unfolding itself.
2. *The Directress and Not the Teacher:* Dr. Montessori has replaced the word 'teacher' by the word directress and thinks that the primary duty of the person in authority is to direct and not to teach. She considers that the directress should have an extensive knowledge of psychology and laboratory techniques.
3. *Doctor-cum-Scientists-cum-Missionary:* In the words of Montessori, the directress should be partly doctor, party scientist and completely religious. Like a doctor, she should avoid scolding or suppressing the patient in order to avoid worst situations. Like a scientists she should wait patiently for the results and should conduct experiments with her material. Like a religious lady, she should be there, to serve the child.
4. *Faith in Personality of the Child:* She should allow the child to act according to his own inner law. Her business is to provide for suitable environments. She should provide children with suitable opportunities to think for themselves.
5. *Moral Qualities:* "Virtues, and not words are the main qualifications of the Directress." She must acquire moral alertness, patience, love and humility. She must banish anger which is a great sin and which prevents her from understanding the child. The soul of the child, which is pure and very sensitive, requires her most delicate care. Her motto should be "I must diminish to let you grow."
6. *Children's House:* Children's house is the name given to a school by Dr. Montessori. This house provides all the

requirements of a good 'Family House.' As a matter of fact, it has all the qualities of a school, a workshop and a home. There are many rooms in the children's house. Smaller rooms—common room, lunch room, rest rooms, room for mutual work, a gymnasium, a lavatory or a children's bath room—are attached to this main room. The rooms are well equipped according to the needs of the children and to the spirit of the Montessori method. The tables, chains, etc., are specially made for children. They facilitate movement from one place to another. Different shapes and long row-cupboards are also provided. The children keep their dedactic apparatus in the cupboard and than things in a little drawer. The black-boards are fixed on the walls and children draw or past pictures of different kinds on them according to their own interest. The students are provided with flowers, toys, pictures, in-door games, etc. The lunch room contains low tables, chairs, spoons, knives, tumblers, etc.

The children are provided with their own little shelves in the drawing room where they keep their soap and towel for washing. There is a small garden also which is looked after by students themselves. Shelters are provided in the garden so that they can enjoy the open air, can play and work there, may take rest or sleep. They may have their lunch there if they please.

Paedometer to measure height and also the weighing machine are also there in the children's house to keep a record of the heights and weights of the students.

There are three types of exercises that are provided in the children's school:

1. Exercise in practical life.
2. Sense training exercise.
3. Didactic exercise for teaching language and arithmetic.

Exercise in Practical Life

According to Dr. Montessori these exercises are called 'exercise in practical life' because in the children's house real everyday life is carried on in which all house work is entrusted to little ones, who execute with devotion and accuracy their domestic duties, becoming singularly calm and dignified. The students are required to sweep their rooms, dust and clean their furniture and arrange it as they like. They learn dressing and undressing and washing themselves.

They are expected to hang up their clothes tidily. They lay their tables. The children take turns in their various household duties, and learn by imitation to conquer their difficulties in the process. "Enthusiasm and delight, fellow feeling mutual aid are characteristics and of children learning the jobs." The students learn how to wash their hands. They learn how to use wash stands with small pitchers and basins. Children learn how to use their own soap and towels. They learn how to comb their hair, cut their nails and brush their teeth.

The main purpose is to give children training in self-reliance and liberty and also to be independent.

Motor Education

These practical life exercises are considered to be very helpful for motor education. Muscular education is imparted in connection with movements of walking, sitting, and holding objects. The care of the child's own body, managing the household affairs, gardening and manual work and rhythmic movements provide motor education. Children also learn how to walk in straight lines and to balance themselves properly.

Sensory Education

Madam Montessori, like Rousseau, Pestalozzi and Froebel, stresses that the senses are the gateways to knowledge. She attaches more importance to sensory training than even to reasoning and thinking. Various Materials are employed to develop sensory training. The following will explain the method of sensory training:

Table–8.2
Maria Montessori—Method of Sensory Training

Sl. No.	*Purpose*	*Apparatus*
1.	For perception of size	Series of wooden cylinders varying in height only, in diameter only or in both dimensions: Blocks varying regularly in size and rods of regularly varying lengths.
2.	For perception of colour	Pink cakes, brown prism, green and alternately red and blue rods, coloured tablets, etc.
3.	For perception of form	Geometrical insets in mental wood, a chest of drawers contain in plain itself, etc.
4.	For discrimination in weight	Tablets of wood similar in size but different in weight.

(Contd.)

Sl. No.	Purpose	Apparatus
5.	For discrimination in touch surfaces, etc...	Rectangular tables with rough and smooth
6.	For discrimination in sound substances.	Cylindrical boxes containing different

The Methods to be Employed

It has three stages:

(i) Association of the sensory percept with the name—"This is red."

(ii) Recognition of the object—"Give Me Red."

(iii) Recalling the name of the object—"What is this?"

Didactic Apparatus for Teaching Language and Arithmetic

Madam Montessori is of the opinion that muscular skill in children is very easily developed and therefore, the teaching of writing should precede the teaching of reading. According to her, writing is a purely mechanical activity and reading is partially intellectual.

(a) *Teaching of Writing:* There are three factors involved in writing, *(i)* Movements which help in reproducing the forms of letters, *(ii)* Manipulation of the pen and *(iii)* Phonetic analysis of words in writing to dictation.
The letters of the alphabet are cut in sand paper and pasted an cardboards. The students are asked to pass the fingers on them. The students learn to establish the visual muscular images of letters. At the same time, phonetic sounds are also taught in three stages-association, recognition and recall. There are certain exercises through which the students are taught the handling of pen.

(b) *Teaching of Reading:* Montessori was not infavour of reading the sentence aloud. The child is handed over a card on which the names of familiar objects are written and pasted. The child is asked translate the writing slowly into sounds and then he is asked to read faster. After some practice, the child learns the correct pronunciation of the word. Then the child is asked to attach the card with objects lying there.

(c) *Teaching of Number:* A long stain is used for the teaching of numbers. It consists of a set of rods varying in length from 1 to 10 diameters. It is divided into parts painted red and blue alternately. The child learns first to arrange the rods of size and then he counts the red and blue divisions and names the rods as one, two, three, etc. The sings of the numbers are cut in sandpaper and the same procedure of three stages – association, recognition and recall is followed.

Discipline in Children's House

Discipline comes by an indirect route, by developing activity in spontaneous work. Every individual is expected to learn how to control himself by his own efforts and through calm silent activity which is directed towards no external aim but it means to keep alive that inner female on which our life depends. Montessori writes, "in truth, the good are those who move forward towards the goodness which has been built-up their own efforts." Such discipline can never be attained by way of commands by any of the disciplinary methods universally known.

'Directress' of the Children's House: She moves about slowly and silently. She supervises in such a way is any one who needs her is aware of her presence at once, while those who do not need her do not notice her existence.

Merits and Limitations of Montessori Method

Madam Montessori's profound love and affection, keen sensitiveness, artistic imagination and exceptional sympathy for children have given a new touch to the theory and principles of education. In fact, she has ushered in a new era in child education, especially for small children at Nursery stage. The chief merits of the Montessori method are:

1. *Reverence for Small Children*: To madom Montessori, "the child is God." Her school was a temple and duty of the temple was the essence of childhood. She further writes, "Today there stands forth one urgent need – the reform do methods in education and instruction, and he wrote struggles towards this end is struggling for regeneration of man." The method suggested by Montessori gives an important place to the child.
2. *Scientific Basis of the Method*: The method is based upon scientific grounds. Madom Montessori was a scientist and she applied scientific principles based on experiences and observation and not upon prejudice.
3. *Individual Teaching*: Individualism is a key note of Montessori method. Her method is a reaction against collective teaching.

4. *Freedom for Children*: She ranks among the forefront educators who want to give education in an atmosphere of complete freedom. In her method, discipline is self-control and self-directed activity.
5. *Sense Training*: The Montessori method aims at educating the children through sense training. It is based the maxim 'proceed from concrete to abstract'.
6. *Unique Method of Reading and Writing*: Special importance to the learning of writing has been provided in her method. She take into consideration the muscular movement in the process or writing.
7. *Learning through Living*: She has provided practical exercise in her school which enables children to learn good habits of cleanliness and orderliness. Students learn the lessons of dignity, labour and self-help by attending to their needs themselves.

Social Value of the Method

She has provided practical exercise in her school which enables children to learn good habits of cleanliness and orderliness the students learn the lessons of dignity of labour and sociability.

Through her method is individualistic in nature, yet it is full of social values. The social value of serving at the table, launching together and cleaning plates, etc., is beyond doubt. The students perform many other activities co-operatively.

Limitations of Montessori Method

1. *Mechanical and Artificial Nature do Didactic Apparatus:* Too much importance has been given to the didactic apparatus. The critics argue that the apparatus handcuffs both the teacher and the pupil. The pupil is expected to do different types of exercises with the help of the apparatus and the teacher also has to teach using the didactic apparatus with the result that the free expression of the children is limited and so also the work of the teacher. The apparatus is unreal and unnatural.
2. *More Emphasis on Biological Aspects and Less in Psychological:* The teacher in this system takes special care in keeping records of the height, skull, and limbs of teach individual child. She badly observe the temperament and other emotional traits.

3. *Belief in Transfer of Training:* The idea of sense training in Montessori method is based on the old theory of training of senses. She feels that by training particular faculties through particular senses, it will be possible to get advantage of that training in other life situations through transfer of training to the desired field. Modern psychology disapproves this idea.
4. *Neglect of Training of Imagination*: There is no place for fairy tales in the Montessori system. Fairy tales used in a proper way form part of the literary training of children and help in development of imagination.
5. *Lack of Suitable Teachers:* The successful working of Montessori method depends upon teachers who possess the extensive knowledge of child psychology and acquisition of laboratory procedures. It is a failure if we do not get such capable teachers.
6. *Little Scope for Projects and Correlation:* The present tendency is to teach all subjects together in the form of projects. Learning by doing is the key note of present methods of teaching. In the Montessori method the children have to depend upon the mechanical apparatus.
7. *Very Expensive:* The method is expensive and doubtful to bear to us.

Points of Contrast: Montessori and Froebel

1. *Recognition of the Importance of Nursery Education:* Froebel as well as Montessori have given us a method of educating the infant. They have brought about a revolutionary change in the concept of education at the pre-school level.
2. *Education as Development Within:* Both educators regard education as the development of the inner nature of the child. They point out that the function of the educator is to draw the inner nature outwords.
3. *Congenial Environment:* Both the educators stress the importance of providing a congenial environment in which growth of inner nature of the child should take place in suitable manner.
4. *Reverence and Affection for the Child:* Froebel as well as Montessori have greatly stressed that there should be an environment of love and affection for the child; his personality should be recognized and even worshipped.

5. *Stress on Sense Training*: Froebel as well as Madom Montessori have devised apparatus for the training of sense of the child.

Table-8.3
Froebel's Kindergarten v/s Montessori Method

Froebel's Kindergarten	*Montessori Method*
1. Based on philosophical background. The education principles of kindergarten are based on philosophy of Froebel who was a philosopher and who became interested in education afterwards. To understand the method one has to understand his philosophy.	1. Based on scientific background. The Montessori method is the outcome of the efforts of a doctor and scientist. Therefore, it has a scientific foundation. Its principles are clear cut.
2. Scope for development of imagination. For the development of imagination Froebel recommended story telling.	2. No scope for fairy tales. Here realities of life are given more importance.
3. More scope for social development. The children are engaged to work in groups. Same things and same subjects are taught to them together.	3. Comparatively less scope for social development. There is too much stress on the development of the individual child and less on social development.
4. Classroom teaching: Classroom instruction forms an important part of instruction. A fixed time-table is followed.	4. Individual Learning: Montessori is an individualistic out and out. There is no set-time table. Students are free to learn according to their taste.
5. Sense training through gifts: In the kindergarten, there is a set of gifts to be presented to the child in a set order and each child is provided with a gift.	5. Sense training through the didactic apparatus; there is the sensory apparatus for the development of the senses which is entirely different from that of the kindergrarten.
6. Play-way method: The Froebelains put more stress on play activities. All lessons are accompanied by songs, gestures and movements.	6. Self-corrective apparatus is provided to the child this apparatus is to be use in a specific way and it affords little apparatus for play.
7. Importance of manual activities. There is much sense for activities like gardening, nature study, class modeling, etc., in this system.	7. Stress on daily like activities. Besides manual activities like dusting, cleaning, washing, sweeping, etc., the students learn how to take care of themselves.
8. The teacher as a leader.	8. Teacher as a directress.
9. Easily applicable.	9. Apparatus is indispensable.
10. Not a detailed system.	10. A Detailed System.

Principles of Montessori Method

- Development from within
- Children's house
- Self-education
- True education
- Didactic approach
- Training for 3R's – Reading , Writing, Arithmetic.
- Freedom is the birth right of the individual.
- 3-7 years of age, senses are very active.
- Sense training by factor.
- Muscular training.
- Teacher directs no to teach.

Table–8.4
Educational Ideas of Froebal v/s Montessori

Froebal	*Montessori*
– Based on philosophical	– Scientific background
– Scope for development of imagination	– No scope for fairy tales
– More score for social development	– Less cope for social development
– Classroom teaching	– Individual learning
– Sense training through gifts	– Through didactic apparatus
– Play-way method	– Self-corrective apparatus
– Importance on manual activities	– Stress on daily life activities
– Teacher as a leader	– Teacher as a directress
– Easily applicable	– Apparatus is indispensable
– Not a detailed system	– A detailed system.

John Dewey 1859-1952

Introduction

Of all the educational thinkers and philosophers of the twentieth century. Dewey ranks the most prominent position. He is the forerunner of progressive education. He never accepts any principle of education without having any relevance to life and society, without reasoning or scientific basis. As a celebrated educator, his influence is undeniably profound as he believes everything in terms of education and life. In the reform for relevance, his contribution to the area of education is always a guiding force to all educational thinkers and philosophers in modern times.

Life Sketch

He was born on October 20th, 1859 at Burlington, U.S.A. His father was an ordinary businessman and so he had to pass his childhood in a village school. In 1879, he graduated from Warmount university and took up the work of teaching. Thereafter he joined John Hopkins University and received his Ph.D. in 1884. He has taught at the Universities of Michigan, Minnesota, Chicago and Columbia, where he is honoured as professor Emeritus after ten years of distinguished service as an educator. As a prolific thinker, philosopher, educationist and humanist he has amply contributed to the different disciplines—ethics, aesthetics, politics, history, philosophy and psychology upto the age of 92 till the end came on June 1st, 1952.

He was the father of six children, and it is said that the philosophy and the grounding of education that the acquired was more due to his experiments with his children than his usual study. He used to experiment on educational problems with the children and got the various principles of education.

Philosophy of Life

Dewey's views in regard to life can be summed up as follows:

(a) He believes in the fact that truth lies in the human soul. He also believes that those who say that the real power lies in God are actually mistaken and do not realize the real potentialities of the human soul. To believe in some supernatural power, according to Dewey, is foolishness and superstition. It is the man, who is the master of the real power and we need not go out of him to find it out.

(b) He believes that the development of the human soul is constant. It takes according to the requirements of the society.

(c) He also does not believe that a pre-determined truth or value is correct. Truth and values are influenced by time, place and change.

(d) He believed that human thoughts are not static; they are dynamic, changeable, developing and grow according to circumstances.

(e) According to him, actions are the basic of knowledge. He believed that it is the actions that give birth to the experiences which ultimately lead to knowledge.

(f) Social good was the main aim of John Dewey.

(g) Society and nature help to from the personality of a man. A

man divorced from any of the two loses himself. According to Dewey, a man without social set-up is beyond imagination.

Philosophy of Education

In the modern set-up, Dewey has a special importance in the field of education pragmatism has gone around and influenced all facets/ fields of life, but it has special importance in the field of education. According to Dewey, education aims at the "Development of all those capacities in the individual, which will enable him to control his environment and fulfill his faculties."

While explaining and eliciting the meaning of education, Dewey deals with the following ideas:

(a) Education, a social process, allows the individual to be in close relationship with social consciousness.

(b) The process of education is always from the unconscious to the conscious levels of human relationship where freedom is exercised by every individual learner.

(c) With the actions and reactions of the individual learner, education stimulates social relationships. The learner explains his every action from the social point of view.

(d) Education, to be meaningful and effective, should have a psychological basis. It is educator, who should carefully deal with the individual's psychological structure in insight. This will ensure discipline and relevance in work.

(e) The education of the child should ensure translation of all his instincts, tendencies and capacities into social equivalents. All his endeavours in education should have a sound link with the social tradition of the past, which will broadly outline future social actions and contemplations.

(f) There should be a sound basis of education of the individual in concrete terms. It should not be a mere preparation for life, which bears almost no meaning at all, since it is rather theoretical, but should be a way of self-understanding and self-control for every individual learner.

(g) Education as a democratic understanding of the society should contribute to the growth of pupil—experience in relationship with the society.

In view of these ideas, Dewey opened a progressive school in Chicago to experiment his new ideas about education over there. The knowledge that he acquired with the experiment over there, formed the basis of his concept of education. This is known as *progressive education*. The school was officially called the University Elementary School. Its main purpose was to carry on research and experiment in new ideas and methods of education.

For Dewey, education is a problem-solving process, and we learn by doing, by having an opportunity to react in real life situation. In education, not indoctrination, but inquiry is focal. Not simply amassing facts but learning to apply intelligence to problem-solving has top priority.

His philosophy of education stresses the social nature of education, its intimate and multiple relations to democracy and its cultural significance.

Dewey's Concept of an Ideal School

Dewey's concept of ideal school was formed as a result of his philosophy and it manifested itself in the shape of his experimental school at Chicago in 1896. It was known as the laboratory school where no school subject in the conventional sense were taught. Instead, manual occupations related to life such as shop-work with woods and tools cooking and sewing were encouraged. Its programme was in the form of activities such as play, construction, contact with nature, self-expression, use of tools and others.

Dewey regards the school as a psychological necessity in as much as it secures continuity in the child's growth and gives a background of past experience to the new ideas imparted therein. Dewey's conception is different from the conventional one. According to him it is the place, where the child learns through his experience, "Where experiments in life will be carried on and where other experiments in life will be read about and told about because of their results." Dewey's school seeks to train children in co-operation and mutually useful living. Dewey would like his school to be a genuine community like the home, where the pupils are engaged in common pursuits and educative experiences.

Dewey's school will be place where moral education is provided not in the form of separate lessons but through its social and conjoint activities. While examining the needs of a progressive community, Dewey finds that there is no unity and no definiteness in the consciousness of its own needs. The ideal school has to help the community or the society to which it belongs, to attain this consciousness. It has to help the people to have a clear and most systematic idea of what the main needs of modern life are and how these needs can be supplied.

Dewey has his own ideas about an ideal teacher. A teacher is a social servant whose duty is to maintain a proper social order and to see that the children grow in a social atmosphere. He is a "prophet of the true God." The teacher is not to impose his personality or his ideology on the child; his business is to select the influences which should affect the child and to help him in properly reacting and responding to such influences. Even in the matters of discipline he is to simply guide on account of his experience and riper wisdom.

Curriculum

Like the school and education, Dewey has no rigid views about curriculum. He believed that curriculum should reflect the social life of the child and his activities in society. Basing his ideas on these things, Dewey has laid down the following principles in regard to the curriculum.

(i) *Flexibility:* The curriculum should be flexible. It should not be pre-determined. It should be determined on the basis of the interest and experiences of the child and should be in accordance with the social requirements. Curriculum at the elementary school should be based on the four-fold interest of the child. They are:
   (a) interest in conversation and communication.
   (b) interest in inquiry.
   (c) interest in making things or construction.
   (d) interest in artistic expression.

   Hence, curriculum will include such subjects as reading, writing, counting, handwork and drawing.

(ii) *Experimental:* The curriculum must follow the "progressive organization of knowledge consisting of educative experiences and problems." The curriculum should be so organized that it should enrich the experiences already acquired and the problems should be so set that they serve as a stimulus to the learner to add new experiences and ideas to the already existing ones.

(iii) *Utility:* Subjects in the curriculum should be organized according to their utility. The curriculum should be based on the child's interests and inclinations during various stages of his development. The curriculum should include the teaching of reading and writing, counting, manual skill, science, music and other arts. It is not desirable to introduce the child to all these subjects at once, but to teach a subject only when it is desired at a particular stage of mental development.

(iv) *Close to Life:* As far as possible, the curriculum should include only those subjects which can be related to the child's pattern of life at that particular stage. This proximity to life can help in creating a distinctive unity in the knowledge imparted to him, and thereby some harmony can be created in the teaching of history, geography, mathematics and language, etc.

Dewey believed that the educational process has two aspects – psychological and social:

(a) *Psychological:* The curriculum and the method of education should be determined by the child's instincts and abilities. The child should be educated according to his interests and inclinations.

(b) *Social:* According to Dewey, it is necessary to create an atmosphere in the school which will allow the child to take an active part in the social awakening of his group. This improves his conduct and develops his personality and abilities.

Educational Method

1. *Learning by Doing:* The most well-known principle advocated by Dewey is learning by doing, in which the child learns best when he himself performs actions related to particular subjects. The child should be acquainted with facts while he is engaged in activity re lating to those facts. Besides, the child should be confronted with practical difficulties and problems which he should try to solve. Problem solving is a good technique, because it adds to the child's experience.
2. *Integration:* Dewey is of the opinion that there should be integration between the child's life, his activities and the subjects he studies.
3. *Child Centred:* Dewey considers interests and efforts to be of supreme importance in the process of education. The educator must understand the child's interest before organizing the activities which are useful for the child.

4. *Project Method:* Dewey's ideas on educational methods later on led to the evolution of the project method in which the child was made to indulge in those activities which helped in the development of enthusiasm, self-confidence, self-reliance and originality.
5. *Participation in Collective Activities:* In democratic educational pattern, the child should be made to participate in collective activity which can help in evolving a cooperative and social spirit.

Contributions

Impact on Modern Education

Many of Dewey's ideas have had great impact on modern education. Some important facts are:

1. *Impact on the Aims of Education:* Now-a-days one of the important aims of education is the teaching of democratic values. Dewey insisted on developing social qualities in the child. In modern schools, these aims of education have been accepted as valid.
2. *Impact on Educational Methods:* The greatest impact of Dewey's ideas is seen in the methods of education. Dewey suggested that education should be based on the child's own experience, and also the method of teaching should vary according to the interests and inclinations of each individual child. These ideas influenced modern teaching techniques and led to active teaching in schools. One such school is the activity school. The project method is also a result of Dewey's ideas.
3. *Impact on Curriculum:* The impact of Dewey's ideas on the subject of curriculum led to the introduction of manual skill subjects into modern curricula. In selecting the subjects to be taught, attention is now paid to the individual interests and abilities of the child.
4. *Impact on Discipline:* As a result of Dewey's theorizing on the subject of discipline, the educand is trained in self-control and democratic citizenship.
5. *Universal Education:* Dewey's thinking and ideal also led to faith in universal and compulsory education. The current stress on the scientific and social tendency over much to Dewey's influence.

Pragmatism in education is the contribution of John Dewey. It was he, who gave us the idea to move according to reason and acquire scientific attitude in all our actions and advocated universal education. Freedom, self-direction and self-administration are his contributions to the field of education. It was John Dewey who led the activity movement in the field of education. It was on account of Dewey that society and school came in close contact and the experiences of the child were given importance.

Dewey was not only a great teacher, but he was also a great thinker and he had written various books on philosophy, psychology, ethics, political science, education etc. Following are the books that give him fame and place:

1. The school and the society.
2. The school and child.
3. The school of tomorrow.
4. Democracy and Education.
5. How we think.
6. Moral Principles of Education.
7. Education Today.
8. Freedom and Culture.
9. Reconstruction in Philosophy.
10. Interest and Effort in Education.

Mahatma Gandhi (1869-1948)

Brief Life Sketch

Mohandas Karamchand Gandhi, the magic man of Asia, an apostle of non-violence and preacher of truth was born on 2nd October, 1869 at Porbandhar in Kathiaward. His father was a Dewan of a petty state, who was incorrupt and highly practical. He inherited mothers life of criticism, religion and devotion. As a student at school, he was slow shy and hesitant. He passed entrance examination at the age of 17. After completing high school education, he studied Law in England and established himself as a lawyer in Porbandhar. He left to South Africa and stayed there upto 1914. This was the formative period of his political life. In 1919, he started a non-violent and peaceful movement. Hindu-Muslim unity, removal of untouchability and use of Swadeshi goods were his life long missions.

Gandhiji introduced 'Satyagraha' and a metamorphism occurred in his personality as a result of experience in South Africa.

He guided congress policy, launched 'Quit India Movement' and was imprisoned. His entire life was a life of service and sacrifice of devotion and dedication. Gandhiji continued educational experiments at Shantiniketan an Sewagram. Gandhiji not only conceived only conceived the idea of new educational system but also taught his battle for freedom. He actively led the freedom movement and was assassinated in January 30, 1948, at one of his prayer meetings by Nathu Ram Godse.

Factors Which Inspired Gandhiji's Views

Gandhiji was influenced by the teaching of Lord Buddha. Lord Mahavir, Upanishads, Mahabharata. From Upanishads, Buddhism and Jainism, he learnt the concept of Ahimsa. Self-realization and disinterested performance of ones duty were the principles which he learnt from Gita. Gandhiji was influenced by the teachings of Christianity and Islam as well. Jesus Christ's adherence to non-violence deeply influenced him. He learnt the value of Satyagraha from Christian teachings. Tolstoy's "The Kingdom of God is within you" was another source of inspiration to Gandhiji. He learnt from Ruskin the principle of dignity of Labour. From Henry David Thoreau, an American philosopher, anarchist, Gandhiji learnt the "concept of civil disobedience."

To sum up, from several sources – religious and philosophical-Gandhiji learnt many concepts, which were developed and accepted to Indian conditions.

Philosophy of Life

Mahatma Gandhi was a practical philosopher, an eternal seeker after truth and an apostle of peace and non-violence. He believed in 'One God' and his absolute control. Truth and non-violence are the spirit of his life. He is also an incarnation of universal love and compassion. God is life, light and truth. According to Gandhiji, both Ahimsa and Truth are two sides of same coin. Fearlessness is essential for truth and non-violence.

Gandhiji believed in simple living and high thinking and has faith in close relation between spirit and matter. He advised for improving the economic conditions of people with the help of science and technology.

Though, his idea of serving God was by serving humanity, he devoted his entire life to serve people. Gandhiji's philosophy can be summarized as:

- His absolute faith in God
- His personal surrender to his will
- His belief in brotherhood
- His spirit of renunciation
- His idea of continual service to fellow creatures.

Gandhiji was not merely a visionary and a philosopher. His philosophy is dynamic as well as pragmatic. He wished and worked for setting up a new social order based on truth and non-violence and free from exploitation and injustice. This is his dream of *Rama Rajya.*

Philosophy of Education

Gandhiji's thoughts on education constituted the dynamic aspects of his philosophy. The educational thoughts were relevant to the life, needs and aspirations of the emerging society. His philosophy of education is naturalistic in its setting, idealistic in its aim, pragmatic in its method, and humanistic in its outlook.

Gandhiji has self-supporting aspect in his educational philosophy. Education is a kind of insurance against unemployment. His entire scheme of education is rooted in non-violence. 'Basic education' paves the way for creating a new social order, that reflects philosophy of education and life.

Meaning of Education

Gandhiji believed in the total development of personality through education. "By education I mean an all-round drawing out of the best in child and man-body, mind and spirit." He believed in the 'literacy of the personality' and viewed education as a quest for truth and non-violence.

Aims of Education

Gandhiji prescribed aims of education which brings about a harmonious development of an individual. His aims of education are correlative to his ideals of life.

1. *Self-Supporting Aim*

Education should help an individual to earn his living independently.

2. *Cultural Aim*

According to Gandhiji culture is not the product of intellectual work, but the quality of soul permeating all aspects of human behaviour. It is responsibility of teacher to train children to have winsome conduct and career.

3. Character Building

Gandhiji viewed character as a direction, dynamic force proceeding towards a definite direction. The end of all knowledge should be the building up of character.

4. Harmonious Development of Ones Personality

True education according to him was the education which stimulate the intellectual, spiritual and physical facilities of the children.

5. Cultivation of Higher Values of Life

Gandhiji considered cultivation of moral, social, ethical and aesthetic values in an individual as an important aim of education. He emphasized self-resistant, self-insight and self-analysis as an idealist.

6. Preparation for Complete Living

Education should be useful to the child in his later life. It should prepare the child to face problems of life.

7. Sociological Aim for Citizenship Training

Gandhiji insisted on this aim because the future citizens should understand their rights, duties, responsibilities and problems of the country.

He advocates a synthesis of individual and social aims in his scheme of education. Education is a discipline directed to a certain end—Shikshana.

Curriculum

In order to achieve the objectives of education Gandiji prescribed productive craft in the curriculum based on the concept of learning by doing and learning while earning. Integrated curriculum was recommended which was braod-based and covered varied fields of life.

Wardha scheme was against the sterile book centred, examination oriented system of education. His basic education is an education for life and through life and throughout life. It was based on 4 educational principles viz.,

- Free and compulsory education for all children from 7 to 14 years.
- Craft-centred education.

- Mother-tongue as the medium of instruction.
- Education as self-supporting units.

Gandhiji suggested following studies in basic scheme in order to develop whole man—intellectual, physical and spiritual powers.

1. Basic Crafts

Curriculum should include basic crafts such as agriculture, spinning, and weaving , gardening and leather work, wood work and metal work, etc... suited to local conditions. Stress should be laid on principles of co-operative activity planning, accuracy, initiative and individual responsibility. It enables each individual to contribute his share to social growth.

2. The Mother-Tongue

Mother-tongue should be the medium of instruction. This alone can acquaint the child with social heritage, aspirations, ideals, ethics and moral values of his country.

3. Mathematics

The aim of teaching mathematics is to enable students to easily solve numerical and geometrical problems. It is required to measure quantities and values and thereby their reasoning capacities would be developed.

4. Social Studies

This includes history, geography, economics and civics. It inculcates in the students right attitudes and values which develop civic efficiency. It develops a sense of national patriotism and love for international understanding. It develops mutual respect for world religions.

5. General Science

This includes botany, zoology, chemistry, astronomy, physiology and hygiene. It develops the habit of accurate observation and testing experience by experiment.

6. Drawing

The aim of teaching drawing is to train eyes to distinguish colours, to develop the faculty of appreciating and create an ability in the students to earn a living by drawing pictorial graphs.

7. Music

The modulation of voice is as necessary as the training of hand, physical drill, handicrafts and music should go hand in hand to draw the best out of children and create in them a real interest in their tuition.

8. Hindustani

Gandhiji believed that Hindustani was the resultant of 'Hindi and Urdu'. He desired that Hindustani should be written both in Hindu and Urdu scripts.

9. English

English should be taught as a compulsory language after learning seven years in mother-tongue.

Method of Teaching

In Gandhian education system, craft was the centre of teaching-learning process and tried to train the whole man—his body, mind and spirit. This method lay stress on activity, correlation and planning in a co-operative manner. This method designed a time table for five and half hours for study for day. The various methods are:

- Child centred education.
- Activity oriented education.
- Craft centred education.
- Integrated study.
- Life-centred education.

Methods include principle of experience, learning by doing and scope for self-experience also. Discussion method along with lecture and question answer was recommended. The methods should promote co-operative activity, planning, accuracy, initiative and individual responsibility in learning.

Discipline

Gandhiji thought that highest form of discipline came through self-control and not by being free to follow stray impulses. Real freedom came through self-discipline and social control.

Teacher

Gandhiji said that, teachers should be dedicated to their profession. Teacher who possess knowledge skill, enthusiasm, patriotism are inspired by social attitudes and can help in achieving the objectives of education.

Based on all these philosophical ideals Gandhiji envisaged Wardha Scheme or basic education scheme.

Contributions

Mahatma Gandhi is the founder of modern India. He was the apostle of peace, truth and non-violence. He is more known as the emancipator and prophet in the arena of politics, social service, spiritual dynamics and he is one of the teachers of the mankind. The main contributions were:

1. Literary Works

Gandhiji is known more by his life than books. *My Experiments with Truth, Commentary on the Bhagavat Gita* are his famous works.

2. Basic Education/Wardha Scheme

It is an unique, practical system of education built on philosophical basis and on Indian culture.

3. Lifelong Education

According to Gandhiji, 'Education is for life, through life and throughout life. It aims at creating a social order free from exploitation. Everything learnt is related to the present and future of the child. The educational system teaches dignity of labour.

4. Experimental Schools

Gandhiji continued educational experiments at Shantiniketan Sabarmati and Sewagram. Activity and experience were given great importance.

5. Nai Talim

The social philosophy of Gandhiji is termed as 'Sarvodaya'. Sarvodaya aims at all round development of all without distinction of caste, colour, creed, sex and nationality. To achieve the aims of Sarvodaya in India, Gandhiji presented a new educational system called 'Nai Talim' (New Eduation).

Gandhiji conceived a concrete educational programme for 4 stages viz.:

1. Pre-basic education – Children below 7 years.
2. Basic education – children between 7 and 14 years.
3. Post-basic education – Adolescents who have completed basic education it is self-supporting.
4. University education.

Gandhiji's contribution to the world of education was significant. He was the first man to have realized the conditions and circumstances of the Indian way of life and presented comprehensive scheme of education.

Conclusion

Gandhiji's educational philosophy is found to be sound and scientific philosophically and sociologically. He was visualizing a non-violent and democratic social order. To sum up, Gandhiji's educational philosophy is based on high ideals on the one hand and stark realities on the other and reflect essential democratic and socialistic values so familiar and congenial to Indian culture and heritage.

Ravindra Nath Tagore (1861-1941)

"Tagore's idealism is a true child of India's own past and his philosophy is Indian both in origin and development."

—Dr. S. Radhakrishnan

Life Sketch

Rabindra Nath Tagore was born on 6th May, 1861 in Bangal in a educated, rich, respected and talented family. In 1877, Tagore was sent to England for receiving education in law. But in England and in India his formal education got fed up. Tagore got his education mostly at home by self-study.

He was an idealist philosopher. He blended western and eastern cultures. What Jean Jacqus Rousseau tried in Europe in 18th century, Tagore achieved in India on the beginning of 20th century.

Philosophy of Life

He was a follower of *Monim.* As such he writes, "we should try to search for God and thus realize that truth which will liberate us from material bonds of existence and which is capable to illuminate the whole world with its divine light."

Philosophy of Education

1. *Freedom and Joy for the Child:* According to Tagore children should be brought up in a atmosphere of freedom, too many restrictions shouldn't exposed on them lesel they have. "To sit like dead specimens of some museum whilsed lesson where felled at them from on high like hail stones on flowers with out this freedom the schools become education factories,

life less, colourless, dissociated from the context of the universe, within the bare while walls string like eye-balls of the dead."

2. *Creative Self-Expression:* His philosophy is the philosophy of artist and the poet.
3. *Active Communion with Man and Nature:* "The child's mind is sensitive, alert eager and restless to receive first hand knowledge."

Aims of Education

General Aim was to help the individual child realize in and through education the essential unity of man and his relationship with the universe – *the education for fullness.*

Specific Aims

1. Physical development: *Keen senses, play activities* and dancing are promoting for education of body. He considered there is a inseparable bond between body and mind.
2. Intellectual development: 'Education should development thinking and imagination rather than mere memory or storing information about facts which are unrelated.'
3. Social development: 'Service to man is service to god.'
4. Moral, spiritual and mental development.
   - simple living and high thinking.
   - love for truth, goodness and beauty.
   - one should know ones own countries culture.
5. Education aims the individual personality as well as social characteristics –
   - He was against mere science education.
   - Purposeful and meaningful education.
   - Development of international attitude among child.

Curriculum

- Education of the emotions – Art, music, dance.
- Science subjects are not in the expense of spiritualism.
- History of the world.
- Indian culture.
- Excursions and tours.
- Craft for education of mind and senses.
- Physical education – not for just playing, to apply the body for useful work.
- Scout.

Methodology

- 'teaching while walking.'
- nature was the first and best teacher.
- mother tongue should follow on the school.
- only English in higher education sector.
- self-discipline, against punishment.
- learning side by side with travelling.
- work by themselves.
- training of the senses through manual work.
- discussion method.
- question-answer methods.
- activity method—experience centred.
- heuristic method.

Educational Contributions

- His education philosophy and philosophy of life.
- Importance given to religious and moral education.
- Father of child centred education in India.
- Recommended physical education and games.
- Naturalistic tendencies in his philosophy develop intimacy with nature and environment.
- Environmental education.
- Educational tours.

Contributions in the Form of Establishments

- Institute of rural reconstruction—*Sriniketan.*
- Ashram type of schools.
- Brahmacharya Ashram of Shantiniketan.
- Vishwa Bharathi University.

Contribution in Teaching

- Spirit of his teaching.
- Love of nature.
- Joy and freedom for the child.
- Communion between man and man.

Any way, R.N. Tagore was a great philosopher of 20th century. His greatness lies in the fact that while condemning a dead, rigid and lifeless education organized by the alien British rule for Indians, he formulated and planned a system of education on ancient philosophical and spiritual foundations for good of Indian people.

In this sense we can say in the words of H.B. Mukerji—"Tagore was the greatest prophet of educational renaissance in modern India. He waged a ceaseless battle to uphold the highest educational ideal before the country, and conducted educational experiments at his own institution, which made them living symbols of what an ideal should be."

Jiddu Krishnamurthi, 1895-1986

Few thinkers of modern times have made such a diverse and significant impact on the 20th century whereas Jiddu Krishnamurthi. 'To stand-aone' was a major theme for Jiddu Krishnamurthi. 'To stand-alone' was a major theme for Jiddu Krishnamurthi. Throughout the days and years of his teaching he questioned all assumptions even his own, especially his own. Alone and unblinking Jiddu Krishnamurthi looked at the question of life.

Brief-Sketch of His Life

Born in Madanapalli, Madras in 1895, Jiddu Krishnamurthi was placed by his father in the care of, and educated by Dr. Annie Besant. He travelled with her to many parts of the word, and had some of his higher education in England. From time-to-time he had unusual spiritual experiences and transformations. He was deeply interested in education and in schools. He emphasizes 'Integral Education.'

A Peep Into Krishnamurthi's Philosophy of Life

Krishnamurthi refused to be committed to any set of philosophy. Life was the only god of salvation. His teaching is not mystic. Ignorance is a sin. "Life is a movement in relationship." He interested in the direct experience of the living reality.

Highlights of Krishnamurthi's Teaching

The central core of Jiddu Krishnamurthi's teaching is that man has to be a light and himself. Truth is a process of felt discovery. Therefore, the approach to the teaching and to the 'how' of it is not by emulation or approximation, but through self-enquiry. Out of which arises an action that will transform non and his environment.

Religion

True religion was always new voyage of discovery which knows nothing of maps or a destination. A religion mind is a creative mind. Thus spiritual freedom is the hall-mark of his teachings.

Truth

Truth was a chief word for him and is coupled closely to beauty, freedom and love. Truth revealed to us a clear and unprejudiced observation of the outer and inner life. Mind is to be freed from fragmentation. When we accept any ideology we are caught by a fragmentation of authority.

Society

Society is an organism having individuals as its part and parcel. Society is the sum total of human relationships. Self-knowledge will help individuals to solve problems. Each individual should identify his/her relationship with others and with the world.

Freedom

Idea of freedom was the essence of nature of humanity. The greatness of freedom exists when these is complete order. Freedom comes with self-knowledge. It is not only a unique value, but also a unique virtue. Love and freedom complemented one another and are even in separable in their true meaning. The real beauty of life rests in the concepts of freedom. Freedom enlarges our vision of life and actions.

Love

Krishnamurthi's approach to love is simple and direct. He said; "you are asking me why I am not speaking of love and compassion? Does a flower talk of its perfume? It is there, we do not discuss the light of the sun. It is there, we feel its warmth, we see its beauty. We talk of the sun only when its is hidden. The same is with love and compassion. We talk of it when we have not got it."

Education and the Significance of Life

Krishnamurthi, "To understand life is to understand ourselves and that is both the beginning and the end of education." Education is not merely a matter of training the mind, training makes for efficiency. But it doesn't bring about completeness.

The purpose of education is not to produce mere scholars, technicians and job hunters, but integrated men and women who are free of fear for only between such human beings can there be enduring peace.

Education should awaken the capacity to be set aware and not merely indulge in gratify self-expression.

Conventional education makes independent thinking extremely difficult. Conformity leads to mediocrity. We may be highly educated, but if we are without deep integration of thought and feeling, our lives are incomplete.

Education, in the real sense, is the understanding of oneself, for it is within each one of us that the whole of existence is gathered.

Education should not encourage the individual to conform to society but help him to discover the true values which comes with unbiased investigation and self-awareness.

Educational Aims and Functions

- Create human beings who are integrated and therefore, intelligent.
- Create new values.
- Transformation of the human mind and creation of a new culture.
- Create a new generation which enjoys total freedom.
- To help each pupil to discover his own inner psychological resources and to develop his own individual strengths.
- Enable the child to develop masterly in such a way that he should know himself.
- Create right relationships not only between individuals but between the individual and society.

Educational Principles

Krishnamurthi points out the inculation four qualification by the teacher. That is

1. love and compassion.
2. sense of discrimination.
3. self-control.
4. desirelessness:
    - Teaching is not only a wholly and imperative duty but also the greatest pleasures.
    - Krishnamurthi considered self-control as to the mind is most important qualification for a teacher.
    - A true teacher's 'dharma' is teaching and teaching well.
    - Krishnamurthi insists on the fact this sort of immutable interplay between teacher and his students will bring them nearer to each other.

Integral Education

Krishnamurthi propagated integral system of education. He confirms that is only when there is integration of the mind and the heart in everyday action that these can be intelligence and inward transformation.

Education should encourage an integrated outlook on life. If we are without deep integration of thought and feeling, our lives are incomplete, contradictory and torn with many fears. In imparting integral education there can be no functional in reasonable emphasis by the teacher or anyone phase of life. The teacher must him self be a properly integrated human being. Human beings must be integrated if they are to survive after any crisis.

Krishnamurthi proved himself to be a propagator of integral education.

The School

Krishnamurthi opines that school is a place where are learns about totality of life, here, the teacher and taught investigate academic subjects on their own thinking and their own activities.

Those who love their own children will see to it that a right school is started somewhere around the corner, or in their own home.

- The institution should not be more important than the child.
- The principal of a school should work through his enthusiasm and energy and not through domination and authority.
- The school should promote student councils and student representation on committees.

Discipline

- Self-discipline based on understanding and co-operation among teachers and pupils.
- Rewards and incentives should find no place.
- Small size classes and attention to the individual pupil.

The Educators Role

- Teaching should not become a specialists profession.
- Love is essential to the process of investigation.
- People who are experiencing and therefore teaching, are not only real teacher, and they too will create their own technique.

- The educator should enable the child to deal intelligently with human problems.
- The teacher will not depend upon a method, but will study each individual pupil.
- Teacher should try to shape the pupils ways of thinking and feeling and mould them in accordance with their own cravings and intentions.
- The right teacher helps each individual pupil to become aware of himself and the influences around him.
- Dedication and vitality are needed in all teachers.
- The best teachers are those who become teachers by their own choice and not by pervasion.
- The teacher should encourage student to be considerate and to understand the moods and peculiarities of their classmates. Teacher should have some good conducts, Self-control-tolerance-cheefulness-confidence, etc.

Curriculum

To Krishnamurthi, learning is the function of the mind. In the total programme of education stress is to be laid on the development of the mind which had a capacity to think clearly without any illusion. It is to be an inquiry mind.

Above all, Krishnamurthi suggests that the process of teaching and learning is one. Krishnamurthi seems to be opposed to include such subjects in the curriculum which do not enable the child to develop understanding. The past is to be rejected if its does not enable the child to live actively in the present. Religion, history have got then limited value for the learner.

Instructional Methods

- Education system should interactive.
- Observation.
- Physical activities.
- Research and field work.
- Discussion.
- Debate.
- Laboratory and library methods.
- Interactive methodologies.
- Learning by doing.
- Innovative style of teaching.

- Activities like art and craft, dance and music, dramatics, and debates, sports, yoga, swimming, gardening, athletics, work experience in rural centers, dairy farms and agricultural farm.
- 'Whole method' instead of 'part method' – Gestalt view.

Sometimes the teacher thinks that learning means repeating. Krishnamurthi, "but to learn, not to repeat, not to go on with explorations and dialectical arguments and opinions, but to actually learn, requires a great deal of humanity."

J. Krishnamurthi himself adopted several methods to propagate his teaching. He sometimes lectured, gave talks, adopted question and answer techniques, dialogues. All these techniques of teaching may be fruitfully adopted by the teachers even in the classroom.

Guidance

The teacher will not guide the student any particular vocational goal, because that impairs creativity. He can help the student to discover what he is most interested in, so that he may be able ultimately to find his own vocation. An educator is not merely a giver of information, he is the one who points the way for his students to attain wisdom and truth, because he does not teach pupils what to think, but how to think. The true educator is inwardly rich and should be given the highest place in an enlightened society.

Jiddu Krishnamurthi's Schools

Krishnamurthi founded seven schools in India:

1. Rishiwalley School – Andhra Pradesh
2. Rajghat Basant School – Varanasi
3. The Valley School – Bangalore
4. Sahyadri School – Pune
5. The School KFI – Chennai
6. Bageerathi Valley School – Uttar Kashi
7. Balanandhi School – Bombay

Other being located in England, USA and Latin America.

Krishnamurthi Foundation India (KFI)

KFI recognized as a religious, charitable, and educational institutions was set-up in 1928. KFI is engaged in educational and humanitarian works in the light of the teaching of Krishnamurthi.

The Principle Works of Jiddu Krishnamurthi

Krishnamurthi was a voluminous writer. The immense popularity of Jiddu Krishnamurthi as a man, has totality eclipsed his greatness as a writer. The major works are:

1. Education and the significant of life (1955).
2. Commentaries on living (1956).
3. The awakening of intelligence (1973).
4. The begging of learning (1975).
5. The matter of culture (1964).

Conclusion

The story of Krishnamurthi's life is one of the strongest that one can imagine. Krishnamurthi set aside deliberately the allegiance, the devotion of a well-organized bond of a thousand followers for the sake of coming down the steps of the spiritual throne erected for him by Annie Besant and Leadbeater.

It is India's great fortune that men like Krishnamurthi are born on its soil to speak to the world and offer it a set of alternative value.

Swami Vivekananda (1863-1902)

Swami Vivekananda was the greatest luminary of modern India. He was a genious of outstanding merit that modern India has produced. He analysed the cultural heritage of ancient Indian philosophy—the Vedas etc. and elevated the present Indian systems, including the system of education and presented his views on various aspects of human life, including education for the good of people and nation.

Philosophy of Life

Educational philosophy of Swami Vivekananda has been derived from his philosophy of life. So it is in fitness of things that first of all we consider his philosophy which has been derived from the Vedanta.

'Help and not fight' he remembered Indians. 'Assimilation not destruction', 'harmony and peace that dissension' we want, 'it is man making religion we want, it is man making education all-round that we want.' 'Religion means service of the Daridra Narayan'. He believed 'Universality of God' and 'the Divinity of Man'. He argue for 'respect and understanding of all religions' and the equality and brotherhood of men. He declares, 'the supreme virtue of compassion', 'work without attachment, and devotion without nenuciation of the personal ego. Swami Vivekananda believes that perfection is one's heritage.

Main Features of his Philosophy

- Vedanta constitutes the essence of highest spiritual and ethical values of mankind.
- The teaching of Upanishads have strength enough to provide solution to our social problems.
- Man is the incarnation of god.
- The essential parts of all religions are same.
- 'Atma' is the true reality.
- 'Karmayoga' as a system of ethics, and religion is needed for the attainment of self-control and self-realization.
- Service to mankind is the highest goal of all religions.
- The best image of worshipping god is man who resides in every human heart.

Educational Philosophy

According to him, "education is the manifestation of the perfection already in man." Man manifests knowledge, discovers within himself, which is pre-existing through eternity.

Aims of Education

1. Self-Development

"By education I do not mean the present system, but something in the line of positive teaching. Mere book learning wont do. We want that education by which character is formed, strength of mind is increased, the intellect is expanded and by which one can stand on one's own feet. What we want are western science coupled with Vedanta, 'Brahmacharya' as the guiding motto, and also 'sradha' and faith in one's own self."

2. Fulfillment of Swadharma

Vivekananda supported the idea of Swadharma in education. Everyone has to grow like himself. No one has to copy others. It is hence that he condemned the imposition of foreign education. He asked, getting by heart the thoughts of others in a foreign language and stuffing your brain with them and taking some university degree, you can pride yourself as educated. Is this education?" True improvement is self-inspired.

3. Freedom of Growth

Vivekananda is against any type of external pressure upon child. He is a staunch champion of freedom in education. Freedom is the first requirement for self-development. The child should given freedom to grow according to his own nature.

4. Character Formation

"If education is identical with information, the libraries are the greatest sages of the world and encyclopaedias are the rishis."

The aim of education is character building. This depends upon the ideals cherished by the individual. Following things are required for character formation:

- Hard work.
- Moral and spiritual values.
- Gurukula system.
- Formation of good habits.
- Learning through mistakes.

5. To Create Faith in One's Own Self

Education must give one of the *mantram* (the faith) "Arise, awake and stop not till the goal is reached" (Kathopanishad, I, III, 4).

6. To Create Self-Confidence and Self-Reliance

Swami Vivekananda regrets that the existing education in India produces a broker-down young man who lacks in *Sradha* or faith.

7. Emphasis on Practical Side of Life

Swami Vivekananda deplores the wretched poverty of his countrymen, and says that the Vedanta, today in India, should mean to feed the starving millions in the country. Education which doesn't prepare man to attend to this primary want of the people is worthless. Hence education must not over look the practical side of life.

8. To Promote Universal Brotherhood

Education must promote the spirit of self-reliance and universal brotherhood. Swami Vivekananda asserts that "from the highest god to the meanest grass the same power is present in all-whether manifested or not." Education has to call forth this power in every man.

9. To Develop will to Realize the Divinity Within

Education must aim at the development of infinite energy, infinite zeal, infinite courage and infinite patience in man.

10. To Make Conscious to Achieve Perfection

According to the Vedanta, the greatest error is to say that you are weak, that you are a sinner, a miserable creature, and that you do not posses power and you cannot do this or that. Evidently, according to Swami Vivekananda, the teacher must not dishearten the pupil, he must not sold him for his errors, he must make him conscious of his inner powers.

11. To Develop Spirit of Renunciation

Education must generate the spirit of renunciation in man. Without renunciation none can work for others.

Characteristics of a Teacher

1. Purity.
2. Knowledge of the spirit of scriptures (sacred writings).
3. Spiritual force.
4. Teacher as a guide.

Methodology

- Education from within.
- Concrete to abstract.
- Teaching/learning must be consider individual differences.
- Concentration (*Sradha*).

Qualities for the Pupil

- Knowledge resides within the individual.
- The child does his own growing.
- The teacher to serve children.
- Concentration of the essence of education.
- Brahmacharya for concentration.

Medium of Education

- Mother tongue.
- Common language.
- Sanskrit.

Education of the Masses/Social Education

"The great national sin is the neglect of masses." "If the poor cannot come to education, education must go to him."

Means of Education

- Love,
- Help,

- Guidance,
- Concentration,
- Brahmacharya, and
- Discussion and Contemplation.

Types of Education

- Religious education,
- Physical education, and
- Moral education.

Women Education

"Women have many and grave problems but, none that cannot be solved by that magic word: Education? He further says; "There is no hope of rise for that family or country where there is not estimation of women, where they live in sadness. For this reason, they have to be raised first...."

Physical and Health Education

"You will be nearer to heaven through football than through the Gita." This statement itself clear the importance he given to health and physical education.

National System of Education

- 'Learning from other but keeping our own.'
- 'What we want a western sciences coupled with Vedanta.'
- The soil of India is my highest heaven.
- The good of India is my good.

His Contributions

- He revived the spirit of humanism in education.
- He advocated character building and man-making education.
- Empahasis on the inclusion of the subjects on the cultural heritage of India in school curriculum.
- He argue for free and compulsory education.
- Insisted the learning of western technology.
- It is idea of 'equal opportunity to the poor'.
- His organization Rama Krishna Mission (1989).
- Vedanta society (Sanfransisco).

Evaluation

Jawaharlal Nehru; "Rooted in the past and full of pride in India's prestige Vivekananda was yet modern in his approach of life problem and was a kind of bridge between the past of India and her present. His mission was the service of mankind and social awakening through education."

Jean Jacques Rousseau (1712-1778)

Life Sketch

Rousseau was born in Geneva. He lost his mother on the 5th day of his birth. His father didn't care for him. Hence, he became careless and indisciplined. At school he was punished quiet, often and this hurt him very much. For a few months Rousseau worked in the office of the registrar of the city. He soon left the job and began to roam about till he was thirty, when he came back to Paris and got married. But he left his family of five children and started leading a new life for the pursuit of truth. His teachings were found revolutionary and he was watched by the French authorities. So he left for Switzerland and later died while he was in England.

Major Works

- The origin of inequality among men (1753).
- 'The progress of Arts and Sciences' (1750).
- The new Heloise (1759).
- The social contract (1762).
- Emile (1762).

Rousseau's main discourse on education is summarized in Emile. It is full of revolutionary ideas. Lord Merley says, "It is the charter of emancipation of the children."

It is an attempt to teach children the proper methods of education. It has five parts, out of which four are devoted to various stages of education of an imaginary child Emile and the 5th one deals with the education of an imaginery wife for Emile 'Sophy'. Emile aroused reactions everywhere, favourable as well as unfavourable. France and Switzerland banned this book. It was burnt at so many places.

General Philosophy of Rousseau

- Chief exponent naturalistic school of philosophy.
- Pleaded for liberty, fraternity and equality.
- In 'Emile' we can see a detailed description of his education ideas.
- Educational is a process of development in to an enjoyable, rational, harmoniously blended, useful and natural life.

- To live is not merely to breathe; it is to act, to make use of our organs, our faculties and of all those parts of ourselves, which give us the feeling of an existence.
- Discipline is acquired only by natural consequences.

Educational Philosophy

Education is life itself, not a preparation for a future state. Education should result in real development, i.e., development of the nature and virtues of the learner to the highest level.

Positive Education

Positive education is the education that was prevalent in his time. It believed in improving and correcting the nature of the child because it assumed that the child born with vices to be corrected by education. It tried to impose civilization upon him. It didn't recognize the child's individuality. The emphasis was on bookish knowledge and verbal instruction. Too much stress was laid on duty, morality and religion and strict discipline was imposed upon children. It also believed in the formation of nature of the child as desired by the adult and laid stress on future.

The present was sacrificed for the indefinite future and to the tender child was loaded with various bondages and restraints which curtailed his freedom and happiness.

Rousseau has described this education as unnatural and in human and advised the educationists to ACT against it. Since he advised people to act against positive education, the education envisaged by him is called *negative education.*

Negative Education

Negative education is the education that is imparted according to the tendencies and faculties of the child. It develops the sense organs. It doesn't teach the child the qualities of an adult, but safeguards against evils.

Rousseau introduced negative education to fight these false notions (positive education) and to establish the fact that the child is essentially good, as what ever he has is natural and therefore, pure and beautiful.

Vices creep in with the contact of the society and therefore any intervention with his activities will lead to undesirable results. The child upto the age of 12 should not be given verbal/bookish education.

The child should be given opportunity to play jump, roam and live in the open air. Moral education/instruction should be kept away from him and he will achieve moral aims by his own actions.

Negative education is self-education of the sense organs and body. This may be more possible in the playground rather than in the classroom.

The characteristics of Rousseau's natural/negative education are:

- No place for book learning.
- No formal lessons.
- No habit formation.
- No moral education.
- Back to nature.

Aims of Education

- Preparation for the struggle for existence.
- Self-expression.
- Autonomous development of individuality.
- Imprisonment of racial gain.

Contributions of Rousseau

- His stress on the 'concrete' led to 'learning by doing.'
- Rousseau anticipated the modern heuristic method when he declare the child as a 'discover.'
- Showed the way to the teacher what he must study the child thoroughly.

Limitations/Weaknesses

- Neglect or books and other media.
- Faculty conception of discipline.
- Out dated views about women's education.
- Limited scope for learning from nature.

Freedrich Withelm August Froebel (1782-1852)

Life Sketch

Froebel was born in Germany on 21st April, 1782. He lost his mother when he was an infant. His father remarried. The early childhood of Froebel was quiet unhappy because of the indifferent attitude of his father and step mother. Dr. Grooner, the highly influenced person of Froebal. Dr. Grooner was the Director of Model School of John Henrich Pestalozzi. Froebal studied his pre-school education through his perusal of Pestalozzi's 'mothers book'. He founded his school at Reihan, known as 'Universal German Institute', after 14 years at teaching in school. His friends Midden Dort and Langenthal assist him. During this period he develops the ideas of 'play', 'gifts' and 'play songs'. He established his 'Kinter Garton' (children's garden) at Blanken Burg. He married his Kinter Gardner. Froebal believed, children's are tender plants' and teachers are gardners. He recommended women teachers at nursery stage. Because, they can only able to love the children.

Educational Ideas/Philosophy

Child was the sole source, teacher simply followed. Child develop himself with creative activities. He recommended self-activity for the education of children. Play gives joy, freedom and contentment inner/outer rest, peace with world, it is not aimless. Play unifies inner life and peace. It holds the sources of all that is good (Cole, 1950). In Kinter Garton, motivation, unique in its approach. according to him, the whole education is inter-related, therefore all subjects must be inter-related.

Kinter Garton—Features

- Self activities.
- Play—'Hide and Seak.'
- Songs with a motto.
- Playing various educational games in the play circle.
- Importance to gifts and play songs.
- Not teaching/learning aids but 'gifts.'
- Child is lead by his own imagination.
- In classroom chairs are arranged in circle form.
- Songs with gestures.
- Constructive works.
- Gifts and occupation.

I. Six colours balls, through this children get the idea of colour, motion, direction.

II. Sphere, cylinders, cube shaped wooden gifts, through this child understand idea about shape, stability and mobility.

III. Big wooden cubes in small to big sizes, child get from this the elementary ideas about addition and substation.

Curriculum

- Manual work,

- Language,
- Arts, and
- Natural Science.

Main Educational Principles of Froebel's Philosophy

1. The Law of Unity

In his book, 'The Education of Man' (1826), he says; "The true method of education consists in considering the mind of the child as a living whole in which all the parts work together to produce harmonious unity."

2. Creativeness of Childhood

He stressed that childhood is not merely a preparation for adulthood. Childhood is a value in itself and possesses its own creation. The adult must understand the child and guide him accordingly, not interfere with the nature of children and no right to feel superior.

3. Inner Relatedness of all Education

This means that the educator ought to lead the child through such situations as will help to relate his experiences organically one with another. Only thus can the child realize his own personal unity and the unity inherent in the diversity of life.

4. Totality of Educational Endeavour

In order to realize the driving character of the universe and his part on it, man needs his senses and emotions as well as reasons. They all are windows of the soul.

5. Concept of Play and Activity

Froebal, "play is the purest, most important activity of man at this stage... it given these therefore, joy, freedom, contentment, inner rest and peace with the world. It holds the source of all that is good." He suggested the following kinds of play at the kinten garten stage.

1. Play leading to recreation.
2. Play leading to constructive activities.
3. Play for imaginative and intellectual activities.
4. For developing co-operation.
5. Play songs.

Advantages

- Sense training.
- Activity oriented education.

- Learning by doing.

Limitation

Expensive.

Paulo Freire (1921-97)

Life Sketch

He was born on September 19, 1921 in Recife, a port city of northeastern Brazil. He has said of his parents that it was they who taught him at an early age to prize dialogue and to respect the choices of others—key elements in his understanding of adult education. His parents were middle class but suffered financial reverses so severe during the Great Depression that Freire learned what it is to go hungry. It was in childhood that he determined to dedicate his life to the struggle against hunger.

After his family situation improved a bit, he was able to enter the University of Recife where he enrolled in the Faculty of Law and also studied philosophy and the psychology of language while working part—time as an instructor of Portuguese in a secondary school. During this same period he was reading the works of Marx and also Catholic intellectuals—Maritain, Bernanos and Mounier—all of whom strongly influenced his educational philosophy.

In 1944, Freire married Elza maia Costa Oliveira of Recife, a grade school teacher who eventually bore three daughters and two sons. As a parent, Paulo's interest in theories of education began to grow, leading him to do more extensive reading in education, philosophy, and the sociology of education than in law. In fact, after passing the bar he quickly abandoned law as a means of earning a living in order to go to work as a welfare official and later as director of the Department of Education and Culture of the Social Service in the State of Pernambuco.

His experiences during those years of public service brought him into direct contact with the urban poor. The educational and organizational assignments he undertook there led him to begin to formulate a means of communicating with the dispossessed that would later develop into his dialogical method for adult education. His involvement in adult education also included directing seminars and teaching courses in the history and philosophy of education at the University of Recife, where he was awarded a doctoral degree in 1959.

In the early 1960's Brazil was a restless nation. Numerous reform movements flourished simultaneously as socialists, communists, students, labour leaders, populists, and Christian militants all sought their own socio-political goals. It was in the midst of this ferment and heightened expectations that Freire became the first director of the University of Receife's Cultural Extension Service which brought literacy programmes to thousands of peasants in the north east. Later, from June 1963 up to March 1964, Freire's literacy teams worked throughout the entire nation. They claimed success in interesting adult illiterates to read and write in as short a time as thirty hours!

The secret of this success is found in the resistance of Freire and his co-workers to merely teaching the instrumental and decontextualized skills of reading and writing, but rather by presenting participation in the political process through knowledge of reading and writing, as a desirable and attainable goal for all Brazilians. Freire won the attention of the poor and awakened their hope that they could start to have a say in the day-to-day decisions that affected their lives in the Brazilian countryside. Peasant passivity and fatalism waned as literacy became attainable and valued. Freire's methods were incontestably politicizing and, in the eyes of the Brazilian military and land- owners anxious to stave off land reform, outrageously radical.

Eventually, the military overthrew the reform-minded Goulart regime in Brazil in April of 1964. All progressive movements were suppressed and Freire was thrown into jail for his "subversive" activities. He spent a total of seventy days there where he was repeatedly questioned and accused. In prison he began his first major educational work, *Education as the Practice of Freedom*. This book, an analysis of Paulo's failure to effect change in Brazil, had to be completed in Chile, because Freire was sent into exile.

After his expulsion from Brazil, Freire worked in Chile for five years with the adult education programmes of the Eduardo Frei Government headed by Waldemar Cortes who attracted international attention and UNESCO acknowledgement that Chile was one of the five nations of the world which had best succeeded in overcoming illiteracy.

Toward the end of the 1960's, Freire's work brought him into contact with a new culture that changed his thought significantly. At the invitation of Harvard University he left Latin America to come to the United States where he taught as Visiting Professor at Harvard's Center for Studies in Education and Development and was also Fellow at the Center for the Study of Development and Social Change.

Those years were, of course, a period of violent unrest in the United States when opposition to the country's involvement in Southeast Asia brought police and militias onto university campuses. Racial unrest had, since 1965, flared into violence on the streets of American cities. Minority spokes persons and war protesters were publishing and teaching, and they influenced Freire profoundly. His reading of the American scene was an awakening to him because he found that repression and exclusion of the powerless from economic and political life was not limited to third world countries and cultures of dependence. He extended his definition of the third world from a geographical concern to a political concept, and the theme of violence became a greater pre-occupation in his writings from that time on.

It is during this period that Freire wrote his more famous work, *Pedagogy of the Oppressed*. Education is to be the path to permanent liberation an admits of two stages. The first stage is that by which people become aware (conscientized) of their oppression and through praxis transform that state. The second stage builds upon the first and is a permanent process of liberating cultural action.

After leaving Harvard in the early 1970's, Freire served as consultant and eventually as Assistant Secretary of Education for the World Council of Churches in Switzerland and travelled all over the world lecturing and devoting his efforts to assisting educational programmes of newly independent countries in Asia and Africa, such as Tanzania and Guinea Bissau. He also served as chair of the executive committee of the Institute for Cultural Action (IAC) which is headquartered in Geneva.

In 1979, Paulo was invited by the Brazilian Government to return from exile where he assumed a faculty position at the University of Sao Paulo. In 1988, he was also appointed Minister of Education for the City of Sao Paulo—a position which made him responsible for guiding school reform within two-thirds of the nation's schools.

In 1992, Paulo Freire celebrated his 70th birthday in New York with over two hundred friends—adult educators, educational reformers, scholars and "grassroots" activists. Three days of festivity and workshops, sponsored by the New School for Social Research, marked the ongoing, vital impact of the life and work of Paulo Freire.

Paulo Freire died in Rio de Janeiro on May 2, 1997, at the age of 75. He leaves behind a legacy of commitment, love, and hope for oppressed peoples throughout the world.

Publications of Paulo Freire

1. Cultural action of freedom.
2. Education—The Practice of Freedom.
3. A pedagogy of liberation.
4. Critical Literacy.
5. Education from critical consciousness.
6. Pedagogy of home.
7. Pedagogy of the heart.
8. Pedagogy in process.
9. The letters to Guinea-Bissau.
10. Learning to question.
11. Pedagogy of the city.
12. Education as the exercise of freedom.
13. Extension or communication.
14. Theory and practice of liberation.
15. The importance of the reading Act.
16. Pedagogy of the oppressed.
17. Teachers as cultural workers.
18. Letters to Cristina.
19. Pedagogy of the freedom.
20. A revealing of the pedagogy of the oppressed.

Some of Freire's books have been translated into over eighteen lanuages. One of his books 'Pedagogy of the oppressed', written in 1970 became so popular that within three decades of its publication, over 5,00,000 copies have been sold world wide.

Freire's Philosophy

Those who attempt to redress the ills of the suffering of humanity are not leaders who work for the people, but who work with the people as their servants. This is Freire's philosophy which he prefers to title as 'Scientific Revolutionary Humanism'. This is essentially a philosophy involving techniques of adult and non-formal education, though the message is applicable to any form of education.

Educational Philosophy

Freire offers in his book Pedagogy of the Oppressed a detailed analysis of the shortcomings of the prescriptive style of teaching. In prescriptive teaching, the teacher assumes an authoritarian role. Freire refers this as the *Banking System*. In the banking system of education the man's transaction is the act of transferring information from teacher's heads and depositing in the student's heads. Here the students are the depositories and the teacher the depositor. In opposition to this domesticating system, Freire suggests a *problem-posing education* which will break the vertical pattern characteristic of the traditional teacher-student relations, by establishing a horizontal dialogue. According to Freire, "No one can teach anyone else; no one learns alone; people lean together, acting in and on their world." His concept of *Praxis* is man's real function.

Men and women are active subjects with the capacity to examine critically, interact with their environment effectively and transform it appropriately.

Freire feels that previously the role of education was to maintain the *Culture of Science*. But education should aim at bringing about a new awareness of self, a new sense of dignity. According to Freire, education should promote the *Culture of Freedom* by means of which men and women can deal with their environment critically and creatively and can participate in the transformation of their life and society effectively.

Conventional pedagogy emphasizes the development of the person not as a free and self-responsible individual, but as a repository of knowledge and information. This is not conductive to the growth of democratic citizenship thus Freire advocates a pedagogy of the oppressed which promotes democratic values in the individual.

Major Contributions

Freire's ideas are specially relevant to the teachers and educators in developing countries. This is especially true in case of adult, non-formal and extension education programmes, though the values of his philosophy and techniques cannot be ruled out for the education of the younger age groups as well. He betrays no ill-will, malice, hatred or violence against the oppressors while showing his concern, commitment and constructive action for the oppressed. Rather he advocates that the hearts of persons should be won through love, non-violence and peaceful resistance and radical action. Perhaps, nobody has made the world so actuely aware of the subversive potential of education as Paulo Freire. He made the classroom an arena of empowerment for the poor and the oppressed.

MODEL QUESTIONS

1. Mention the educational contributions of Paulo Freire.
2. How far pragmatic philosophy is workable in Indian school? Substantiate your answer with regard to the aim, content and method of this educational philosophy.
3. Write a note on the influence of pragmatism in madom education.
4. What are the main philosophical ideas of idealism? Explain.
5. Describe the contributions of Rousseau to educational thought and practice and asses the relevance of the ideas to the education system of the present.
6. Show how Tagore's philosophy of education is intimately connected with his philosophy of life.
7. What is meant by Eclectic tendency in education?

REFERENCES

1. Aggarwal, J.C. (2002). *Theory and Principles of Education*, Vikas Publishing House (P) Ltd., New Delhi.
2. Ahuja, M.C. (1997). *Glimpses of Some Indians*, Vikas Publishing House (P) Ltd., New Delhi.
3. Belock and Green, J.L. *Philosophy and Education*, Any Prakashan, Meerut.
4. Bhattacharya, S. (1996). *Foundations of Education*, Atlantic Publishers and Distributors, New Delhi.
5. Botia, B. and Bhatia, K. (1992). *The Philosophical and Sociological Foundations of Education*, Doaba House, New Delhi.
6. Butler, J.D. (1966). *Idealism in Education*, Harper and Row, New York.
7. Das, P.N. (2004, May). *Mathrubhumi Thozhil Wartha*, p. 36.
8. Jayakar, P. (1986). *J. Krishnamurti A Biography*, Penguin Books India (P) Ltd., New Delhi.
9. Kneller, G.F. (1971). *Introduction to the Philosophy of Education*, John Willy and Sons, New York.
10. Krishnamurti Foundation India (1991). *Krishnamurti to Himself His Last Journal*, Auther, Madras.
11. Manuel, N.V. *Reading and Challenges in Philosophy of Education*, Unpublished Material.
12. Pandey, R.S. (1991). *A Survey of Educational Thought*, Horizon Publishers, Allahabad.
13. Reeba, K.R. (2002). *Educational Contributions of Jiddu Krishnamurthi*, Unpublished P.G. Dissertation, Mahatma Gandhi University, Kottayam.

14. Saxena, S.N.R. (2006). *Foundation of Educational Thought and Practice*, R. Lallbook Depot, Meerut.
15. Sharma, R.K. and Chandra, S.S. (1996). *Principles of Education*, Atlantic Publishers and Distributors, New Delhi.
16. Sharma, R.N. (2000). *Text Book of Educational Philosophy*, Kanishka Publications, New Delhi.
17. Sharma, S.R. (1997). *Practice of Philosophy of Education*, Mohit Publications, New Delhi.
18. Sharma, Y.K. (2003). *The Doctrines of the Great Indian Educators*, Kanishka Publishers, New Delhi.
19. Shivarajan, K. (2006). *Education in the Emerging Indian Society*, University Central Co-operative Stores, Calicut.
20. Sloss, R.R. (1991). *Lines in the Shadow with J. Krishnamurthi*, Bloomsburg Publishing Ltd., London.
21. Taneja, V.R. (1987). *Educational Thought and Practices*, Sterling Publishers (P) Ltd., New Delhi.

9

Society, Culture and Education

CULTURE AND EDUCATION

The word culture is derived from the Latin word 'cultural' means good manners and good taste. The term culture has diverse dimensions and definitions. Culture is the sum total of human creations and expressions and experiences. It includes everything material and non-material created by man in the process of living. It is a kind of polished behaviour.

Definitions

"Culture is the foundations of the primary thing. It should shows itself in the smallest detail of your contact and personal behaviour, how you sit, how you walk, how you drink etc."

—Mahatma Gandhi

"Culture is widening of the mind and the spirit."

—Jawaharlal Nehru

"Culture is that complex whole which includes knowledge, belief, arts, morals, law, custom and any other capabilities acquired by man as a member of society."

—Edward B. Taylor

'Culture is the handiwork of man and the medium through which he achieves his ends."

— Malinowski

Characteristics of Culture

Culture is Cumulative

All the elements of culture grows as a result of accumulation. Each generation preserve the old culture and we add something new in it.

So the culture, we have today is the total of all the additions made by our prodecessors. Example: our literature, oral prayers, prayer songs, etc leads to writing knowledge and the printing and ultimately that generate the present literature.

Culture is Preservative and Transmitive

Culture should preserve and transmit to the next generation. The transmission is necessary for the programme of mankind. If culture was concerned and transmitted, all the human knowledge and experiences would have been last. Culture is acquired social heritage and this is necessary for the progress of mankind.

Culture is Diffusive

Diffusion means acceptance of cultural pattern. Culture is transmitted not only from generation to generation, but also from one generation to another. Diffusion is determined by social contacts.

Culture is an Acquired Quality

Culture is not innate traits learned through socialization, habits and thoughts are that is called culture. Culture is learned. Any behaviour which is socially acquired is called learned behaviour.

Culture is Social not Individual Heritage of Man

It is inclusive of the expectations of the members of a group. It is a social product which is shared by most members of the group.

Culture Fulfils Some Needs

Culture fulfils those ethical and social needs of the groups which are ends in themselves.

Language is the Chief Vehicle of Culture

Man lives not only in the present but also in the past and future. He is enabled to do because he posses language which transmits to him what was learnt in the past and enables him to transmit the accumulated wisdom.

Forms of Culture

Material Culture

It consists of the tangible forms, any object that man has created for his own use. Example: dress the development of art, new amenities and gadgets indicate the cultural progress of people. Thus, the material aspect of culture includes cultural instruments.

Non-Material Culture

This is another form which is intangible but has a greater impact. Spiritual civilization such as language, literature, art, religion, beliefs, morality, law, and government are the elements this culture. Thus, culture tends to be pervasive teaching every aspect of life.

Structure of Culture

The parts of components or culture are the following:

Cultural Trait

Cultural traits are the single elements of smallest units of culture. According to Hoebal "Cultural trait is a repeatedly irreducible unit of learned behaviour pattern or material product here of." Any culture can be seen as to include thousands of such units. Thus shaking hands, teaching the feet, dipping hats, the kiss on the cheeks as gesture of affection, giving seats to ladies first, saluting the flag, etc., are cultural traits. Thus, traits are the elemental units of culture. It is these traits which distinguish one culture from another. A trait found in one culture may have no significance in other culture.

Culture Complex

According to Hoebal, "Cultural complexes are nothing but larger clusters of traits, organized about some nuclear point of reference." Cultural traits as we know, do not usually appear singly or independently. They are customarily associated with other related traits to form culture complex. The importance of a single trait is advocated who it fits in to a cluster of traits, each one of which performs a significant role in the total complex. Thus, kneeling before the idol, sprinkling scared water over it, putting some food in its mouth, folding hands, taking prasad from priest form a religious complex.

Culture Pattern

A culture pattern is formed when traits and complex become related to each other functional roles. The patterns of culture vary from area to area. The culture pattern of a society consists of a number of culture complex. Thus, the Indian cultural pattern consist of Gandhism, spiritualism, joint family, caste system and ruralism. Each of these is a culture complex consisting of numerous culture traits.

Universals, Alternatives and Specialities

The traits which are followed by all members are called *universals*. As a matter of fact, these traits are so widely shared that, without them, one obviously 'different' or an out cast. Example: 'Saluting the Nations' flag.

The traits in which individuals are allowed a choice, such traits are *alternatives*. Example: shaking the hand and 'Namasthe'.

Specialities are elements of the culture which are shared by some but not all groups within a society. Nearly every group in society-each age group, sex group, occupational group religious group has contain traits not shared by other groups.

Sub-cultures

Sub-cultures are the cultural traits of a particular group or category. They are of course, related to the general culture of the society, yet are distinguishable forms it. The culture of the occupational groups, religious groups, caste, social class, age group, sex group and many others are sub-cultures. The Hindu culture is a sub-culture of Indian culture. Teenage culture, college culture etc are sub-cultures.

Contra Cultures

The term contra culture is applied to designate these groups which not only differ from the prevailing pattern but sharply challenge them. The people trained in those norms are influenced against the dominant cultural norms, hence the name contra culture. The 'hippie' culture is a contra culture.

Cultural Area

The societies having similar cultural traits and complex constitute culture area. Such societies are generally those which live in similar natural environment. *Example:* Malabar Culture in Kerala. However, it is difficult to draw strict dividing lines between different cultural areas, due to over lapping of cultural traits of one with another.

Factors of Culture Variability

- Historical accidents.
- Geographical environment.
- Mobility of human organism.
- Inventions and discoveries.
- Individual peculiarities.
- Change in modes of production.

Functions of Culture for Individual

- Culture makes man a human being
- Culture provides solution for complicated situations.

- Provides traditional interpretations to certain situations.

For the Group

- Culture keeps social relationships intacts.
- Culture broadens the vision of the individual.
- Culture creates new needs.

Cultural Diffusion

Diffusion means the acceptance of cultural patterns from other groups. Ordinarily diffusion is thought of as a movement of traits through space. It is different from transmission of culture which is movement of traits through time that is, from generation to generation. Diffusion take place with and without deliberate attempts. It becomes purposeful when diffusion is organized.

Diffusion can be either direct of indirect. Direct diffusion occurs when persons or groups have actual physical contact. Example: wide acceptance of Arabian food items in Kerala because of Gulf connections. Indirect diffusions is the spread of traits without personal contact. Example: Through radio, printed materials and transport of goods in commerce.

Culture and Education

Culture is the behaviour pattern of the individual or group. Education is the process by which the individual modifies his behaviour. So the relation between education and culture is intense and intimate. They supplement and complement each other. Education as a part of culture has twin functions of conservation and modifications of culture. In its technical sense, education is the process by which society through schools, colleges, universities and other institutions deliberately transmits its cultural heritage from one generation to other. Education is an instrument of cultural change. Education has to preserve the cultural tradition of the race, improve it and hand it over to the next generation. Thus, the preservation, transformation, and transmission of culture are the cardinal functions of education.

Preservation of Culture

Culture is an important aspect of the heritage of any nation. It reflects the level of civilization attained by the society. Hence, the preservation of cultural heritage of the country is one of the aims of education. In the absence of cultural education every individual has to make his progress from the level of savages. Society is keen that its young members shouldn't laps to barbarity and ignorance. Hence, the conservation of culture is given great importance in education.

Transmission of Culture

No society can function effectively without a sound foundation of culture. The aim of the education is to mould the individual in the matrix of the society. That is the function of education is the transmission of culture. Family is the significant institution contributing the transmission of culture, because the child learns his mother tongue initially and essentially from his home. The function of education is to build-up a personality according to the culture of the society. Education should transmit the culture to the new generation and transform the outlook of the young towards life in the light of the past, in the context of the cross-cultural influences of the present and the light of the future demands of the society. The main task of education is to make children adopt themselves to the contemporary culture and familiarize them with the past.

One of the chief task of education is *Acculturation*. Acculturation, the process where by new culture traits are adopted and incorporated in to an existing culture. It is the process of mutual modification of two or more different cultures which are in contact with each other with out much sign of their fusing in to a single homogenous culture. Education act as an instrument for developing culture in the following way:

- Acquiring the students with past cultural wealth.
- Programming cultural studies in different areas.
- Developing critical intelligence to be able to weigh the existing cultural heritage.
- Bringing newly innovated or developed cultural practices into effective use to get wider acceptance.

Transformation of Culture

All living being are subject to change. Today we living in the world of rapid changes and knowledge explosion. Each and every moment, the knowledge multiplying infinitely. It is education that should guide the cultural change towards progress and prosperity. The main task of education is to make the pupils to adopt themselves to the contemporary culture and familiarizes with the past. Education must also create a favourable attitude for cultural change. Old and outdated things are to be discarded. The education assure them to take positive and negative attitudes towards changes.

Impact of Culture on Education

Education is the main source of personality development and hence school is the educative agency. Education serves as an instrument for the transmission of cultural heritage. The curriculum is based on the aims of education which has its solid foundations on culture. If the cultural aspect is not taken in curriculum designing, then there will be no relation between education and society.

Education is a function of total culture. The individual is educated by the entire culture of his group with which he interacts. Culture gives content and directions to the individuals learning, attitude, values, habits, patterns of co-operation and conflict and other international process which is largely on culture. Even the subject-matter of education is dependent on culture.

Thus, the relation between education and culture is found constant and this outcome is the result of the inter-relations among society, school and other agencies of education.

The human progress is directed by the culture of the society and man creates ideals and values, through the culture of society. Society owes to culture its all round development. Through the path of culture the society acquires all the inherent qualities from generation to generation. This work is carried out by education.

As far as a child is concerned he acquired social inheritance since his birth. The social inheritance has an important role to play in the development of child. In the school, it becomes the duty of the teacher to infuse culture in child personality. Thus culture is an innate process which the human beings acquire throughout his life through various dimensions.

Education and Culture are inter-related. Education as a part of culture has the twin functions of conservation and modification of renewal of the culture. Education is conceived as a systematic effort to maintain a culture. "In its technical sense education is the process by which society, through schools, colleges, universities and other institutions, deliberately transmits cultural heritage, its accumulated knowledge, values and skills from one generation to another.

The role of culture is considered in the sense that it should make man able to adjust themselves in his social environment of life. In other words, education and culture outlines its programme according to the needs of the society which in itself for its progress takes active interest regarding education, personality is determined partly by the culture in which it grows. Education is the main source of personality development and hence school is the educative agency.

Impact of Culture on Curriculum

The curriculum is based on the aims of education which turn its base on culture. Thus, culture has come effect on curriculum of education. By curriculum we do not only mean the academic studies but also the extracurricular activities in which students take part. These activities cannot by any means be outside the culture of students.

One of the most persistent problems in education, and one in which there is the least formulated consensus of opinion, is the extent to which the various elements of the programme of studies lend themselves to cultural stimulus. The specialist in the languages, mathematics, the natural sciences, the social sciences, the fine arts, the manual arts, and domestic economy each claims for his own particular field a superiority in basic cultural significance, and the strange thing is that each seems to be able to make out a satisfactory case. The advocates for the "humanities" are particularly insistent that the classics, mathematics, and philosophy are more 'liberalizing' than other features of the curriculum, and are able to bring to bear upon their contention the actual results of the practice of the centuries. The newer studies in the curriculum, such as the sciences and the practical arts, have the advantages of youth. They are adaptable, appealing on account of the freshness of their point of view, and are closely associated with the activities of present-day life.

Impact on Methodology

There are two fundamental elements in classroom method which have decidely cultural influence—that of teacher-pupil relations, and that of the type of workmanship demanded of the pupils. The give and take of question and answer and other phases of teacher-pupil relations cannot be without its effect on similar relationships outside the school room. In addition there should always be an insistence upon cultivated from in the pupil's work. The student's English in the classroom discussions should be as correct and effective as it can be made. Written work should be prepared is as good form in regard to writing, composition and punctuation as the maturity of the pupil will permit. Slovenliness of study and of thinking, bluffing and reckless statement should not be tolerated, at least, should not be encouraged, much of the crudity of form shown in business, society and institutional contact could be avoided by proper insistence upon finished workmanship in our schools.

Impact of Culture on Discipline

The cultural elements in school discipline are numerous and more specific than those in general administration. First among these is the general bearing and cultural attitude of the teachers. A proper appreciation of the needs and requirements of routine will tend to inspire obedience to the necessary mechanical features of discipline, while a sympathetic understanding of the nature and desires and standards of children will lay the foundations of personal leadership and influence.

Wherever discipline can be made *positive and constructive*—that is, wherever adequate interest can be aroused in daily work to forestall trouble, or supervised organizations be used to satisfy the various demands of youthful nature- cultural training is provided in a very natural and powerful way. *Social discipline* requires that the school be made a microcosm of the best standards and usage of society outside the school room, and that these ideals and practices be enforced by all the personal influence the teacher can bring to bear upon the situation, added to the authority of the state which the public schools represent.

The third element in *cultural discipline* is that it must secure self-control and social responsiveness in the pupil. The old idea of discipline as repression has given way to the newer idea of discipline as expression. True culture is inseparable from morality, and no phase of education is more conducive to moral conduct than wholesomely administered discipline.

Impact of Culture on Textbooks

In the hands of a master teacher all ordinary studies are cultural and in the hands of a tiro all are perfunctory. Latin and Greek may be taught with out reference to their cultural backgrounds, while German or French of Italian or Russian or Sanskrit may be taught with special cultural emphasis. Mathematics may be pure drill, while manual training may be pure cultural. Music and painting may be made mechanical, while domestic economy may be made artistic. Dress making and cabinet-making may inspire art no less than architecture, botany no less than aesthetics, book keeping no less than geometry, economics no less than ethics, debating no less than literature, and sociology no less than the classics. The skill and ideals on the teacher, the place of the stress, and the cultural inspiration of the general subject-matter provide the cultural basis, while the cultural values are equally distributed between the aim of the course, the selection of materials, and the methods of handling, the particular subject-matter chosen and textbooks used.

Impact of Culture on Teacher

A teacher is the observatory of culture, a democratic mediator of culture who is determined the best in the culture and to retain the same. He also the architect of the future culture. He draws upon the old culture, accumulates past experiences, and also he constructs new experiences and produces innovations. A teacher is supposed to be discontented with though as they are and to introduce new cultural designs.

Our teachers are merely elementary or even high school graduates, cultivated leadership will be wanting. But the employment of cultivated men in leading position in our organized systems is in excusable. The amount of necessary preparation for all teachers is rising, but a little "speeding-up" in the process would greatly enhance cultural progress.

Teachers should not only be gentlemen or ladies themselves, but they should assume that pupils possess the same qualities. They should show reasonable cultivation in dress, speech and manners and insist upon a like attitude on the part of pupils. It is to be regretted that frowziness of dress, flippancy of speech, and crudity of manners are not confined to children, even in the school room. Personal hygiene, correct speech, respect for the venerable, and polite address are gained more by imitation than by the literation of precepts.

Impact of Culture on School

The first element in the cultural influence of the schools on the community is the teacher's attitude toward community affairs. The second element of community influence is specific help in advancing community standards. Frank discussions about local organizations/ institutions are part of the function of every leaders of youth. The third element of cultural community influence lies in the supervisory functions teachers are frequently called upon to assume in local affairs. The teacher shouldn't only be an active force in the community but he should insist upon the community becoming an active force in the school. Mutuality is the price of all permanent and effective aid. School influence upon the community should be dynamic, should make itself felt at present as well as in the future, and should represent the highest intellectual and cultural standards in every neighbourhood enterprise. The school has to give up its ivory tower isolation. It must be closely linked with the society. "The starting point of educational reform must be the relinking of the school to life and restoring the initimate relationship between them which has broken down with the development of the formal of tradition of education" —Secondary Education Commission.

Cultural Lag

The word lag connotes crippled movement. Hence, cultural lag means the fluttering of one aspect of culture behind the other were concerned with the perpetuation of society and its improvement. The school is not and image of society where virtues and bias of society are reflected. It should serve as a laboratory for testing the traditions, values, beliefs, and attitudes, prevailing in a particular society and taking upon it self the task of making society a better one.

The term 'cultural lag' first coined by W.F. Ogburn in his work "Social Change." Cultural lag defined as the degree which certain aspects of culture lag behind the changes in its other related aspects. All the parts of our modern culture are not changing at the same ratio and since there is correlations or inter-dependence of parts, a rapid change in one part requires readjustment through other changes in various correlated parts. A cultural lag occurs when the different aspect of society fail to adjust themselves to changes effected in some of its parts. The discrepancy between two related parts of a culture because of different rates of change in the parts of a particular culture which changes more slowly than the parts which are related to it.

The change in ideas, belief and value systems, will be slower than the changes in material conditions. In our society the economic system is changing first, industrial economy is replacing the rural economy. A lot of work being done by machines, instead at human labour, but the religious and social structure are not keeping pace with the changes in the economic structure.

Material and non-material parts of culture are closely related. But the state of change which occurs in material and non-material culture is not equal. The material culture change more rapidly than non-material culture. Consequently a lag is created between the two parts of culture.

According to W.F. Ogburn, culture has two aspects, materials and non-material. The material aspect as compared to the non-material is want to progress rapidly. Thus, the non-material aspect lags behind. This action is termed as *cultural lag*.

Culture is changing very rapidly in the sphere of fashion, dress, artificial beautification, art, recreation etc., but the change in the sphere of religions notions is comparatively very slow. The present age is called the age of science and rationalism and the west is considered the most advanced in this respect and now scientific and national is the outlook, concerning beliefs etc.

Conclusion

Education is a function of total culture. All elements of a culture educate. The individual educated by the entire culture of his group with which he interacts. Culture gives content and direction to the individual's learning, attitude, values habits, patterns of cooperation and conflict and other inter-actional process which are largely on culture. Even the subject-matter of education is dependent on culture. The relation between education and culture is constant and through we may not see if we certainly see the outcome of this relationship in school and other agencies of education. Child acquires social inheritance since his birth. In school, it becomes the duty of the teacher to infuse cultural in child's personality.

SOCIALISATION AND EDUCATION

Man is born in the society and continues to live in the society till his death. In the society, he is exposed to different types of influences and he also influences the society. Simply saying socialization is the process of the human being become social being.

Social interaction is the two way process whereby each individual or group stimulates the other and in varying degrees modifies the behaviour of the participants. There an individual is socialized out of this interaction.

"Socialization is the process of developing a personality; it refers to the way that people learn the habits, attitudes, social roles of self-conceptions, group norms and universes of discourse that enable them to interact with the people in the society." How a new born baby moulded into an social being? Without this process of moulding which we call socialization, society couldn't perpetuate itself beyond a single generation and culture couldn't exist, nor could the individual become a person. This process of an individual become a person is also called *cultural conditioning*. Contrary with a individual a person have some duties and responsibilities to the society.

Socialization refers to a problem, which is old and pervasive in human life—the problem of how to rear children, so that they will become adequate adult members of the society to which they belong.

Socialization essentially a matter of social learning and not of biologic inheritance. According to Fitcher, "Socialization is a process of mutual influence between a person and his fellowmen, a process that results in an acceptance of an adaption to, the pattern of social behaviour." Socialization is opposite to individualization.

Elements of Socialization

1. Physical and psychological heritage of the individual.
2. The environment in which he/she lives.
3. Culture of his/her group.

A child is born with some physical and mental capacities in the environment of his family. So socialization is process whereby the individual develops from a babe, responding to the stimuli about it in ways determined by the tendencies it has inherited. This has been described as the dialectic of personal growth. In the course of his experience he observes that others are also like himself, hence he develops not only a consciousness of his own individuality but also of his likeness to others.

Bogardus is right in saying that it is a process of working together, of developing group responsibility of being guided by the welfare needs of others.

Process of Socialization in Different Phases of Life

The process of socialization can be ultimately reduced to the fact that the individual, learns by contact with society. In the home socialization starts with parents, through the love, affection, suggestions, authority, power, security, norms and ideals that child experience.

In out of home, the peer group is the important socializing agency. Here a problem of dominance emerging. From the peer group he/she understand the ways of adjusting himself to another.

The developing individual gradually comes into contact with an increasing number of adults. The neighbours store keepers, etc., and also he/she starts to reading books/periodicals etc.

Adolescence brings the youth a crisis which makes necessary new adjustments to life. Here he/she feels fears, hopes, impulses etc., and he/she compels to re-adjust himself to opposite sex, and forming new attitudes towards other age groups.

When adult marries again he/she faced with a new series of accommodation in his personal conduct. If the spouses successed in adapting themselves each other, further socialization of both results. Failure of socialization here results in marital unhappiness/ emotional divorce or divorce. In due course of events, children may be born and the individual is faced with a new situation – new role i.e., father/mother and the necessity of new adjustments i.e., those of parents.

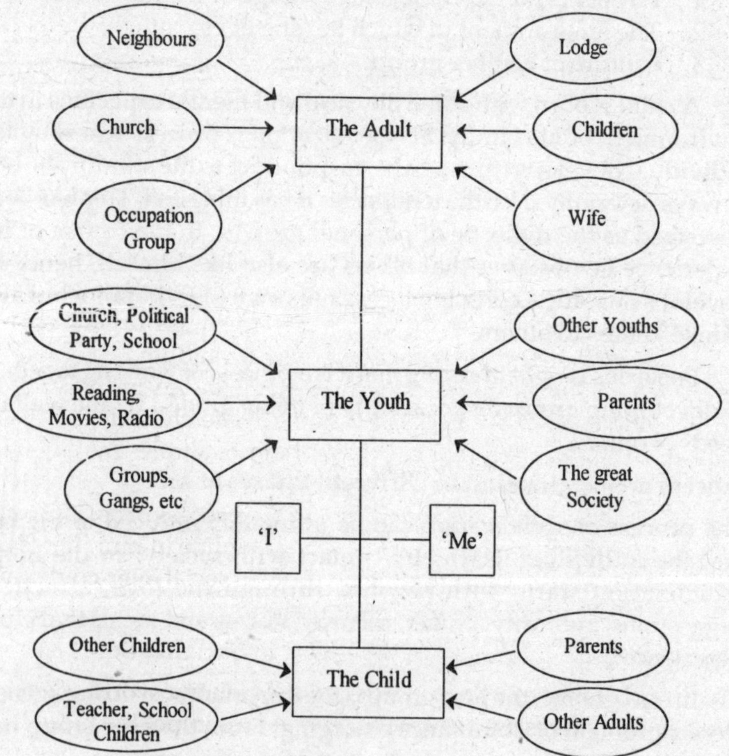

Figure 9.1. Socialization of the Individual.

With advancing age, the mind as well as the body seems to lose its supplements. Here the process of socialization ends. But some exemption are there. Example: some old mens are re-adjust their life style like new generation, men.

Froeid's Stages of Socialization

- Oral,
- Anal,
- Oedipel, and
- Adolescent.

Mechanism of Socialization

1. *Stimulus-Response Mechanism:* As a social being the individuals life story is a story of social interaction. He has come into the world with a physical constitution, a measure of intelligence, ability etc. His/her first cry clamours for help from others or a demand for attention. He/she stimulus others and they respond in the same way. Others stimulated and he/she responds.
2. *Praise-Blame Mechanism:* That is when an individual's behaviour is appreciated or blamed, he/she understands about his behaviour pattern.
3. *Sympathy:* Toleration Mechanism can be cultivated in this.
4. *Suggestibility:* It's an unthinking act. Example: The behaviour/action of a crowd. The suggestibility of the child is greater than that of the adult.
5. *Identification:* By identifying himself with others he/she accepts the opinions of others. In his early age the child cannot make any distinction between his organism and environment. Most of his actions are random.
6. *Imitation:* Imitation means copying by an individual, or imitation of the action of another. The child develops his sense, he/she rejects or accepts them. Example: The language pronunciation.
7. Social Control has a vital part in the process of socialization an individual can develop self-discipline in him/herself.
8. *Language:* Language is the medium of social inter-course and the means of cultural transmission.

Role of Wishes, Interests and Attitudes in Socialization

The world of wishes brings in to being a correlative world of values. Wishes and values are reciprocal. The values impel the individual to wishes and wishes create values. Anything capable of being appreciated is a value. The state of mind of the individual towards a value is an attitude.

W.I. Thomas stated four wishes as the basic motives for social life. They are,

1. response,
2. recognition,
3. aecurity, and
4. new experience.

Human behaviour includes wishes is culturally co-ordinated. Example: wealth, health, knowledge. The whole life process, it at last the process of developing, adjusting and satisfying interests. In the realization of an interests the individual becomes definitely related to a group and achieves a new status which is the same as to say he is being socialized. In short, socialization is the process whereby the original culture is transformed in to human nature and the individual into the person.

Role of Heredity and Environment in Socialization/Factors Affecting Socialization

Every social group whether racially or nationally or culturally defined, differs in manifests respects from other groups. Here the question is whether these differences are determined mainly by heredity or environment?

The relation of life and environment is extremely intimate. The capacities and attributes of an organization are related to the whole environment in which it manifests itself. Also every difference in our habits and our way of living.

Heredity

Every act of generation in nature is the transmission by parents to their off spring of certain characteristics. The complex of the characteristics thus transmitted called heredity.

Environment

Environment, as the term indicates is anything immediately surrounding an object and exerting a direct influence on it.

Agencies of Socialization

The process of socialization is operative not only in childhood but through out life. There are two sources of child's socialization. The first includes those who have authority over him, includes:

- Parents
- Teachers
- Elderly persons.

State

These group of socializing agencies are called *Authoritarian Agencies*. The second are those who are equal in authority to him, includes.

- Play-mates
- Friends and
- Fellow club members.

These group called *equalitarian agencies* of socialization. His/her training varies in content and significance according to the source, the qualities like love, obedience, etc., child adopt from authoritarian agencies and the habits like smoking, drinking etc. child adopt from *equalitarian* agencies. Excemptions are there. The important agencies are:

1. *The Family*

- Parents, physically they are nearer.
- He/he learn his speech and language.
- He is taught societal morality and civic virtues.
- Family, "the cradle of social values."
- The child gets the first lesson of co-operation, tolerance, self sacrifice, love and affection.

2. *The School*

- Second important agency of socialization.
- Education moulds his/her ideas and attitudes.

3. *Play-Mates*

- The relation between the child and his play-mates is one of equality.
- The relationship among play-mates based on co-operation and mutual understanding.
- Mostly similar age.
- The child acquires 'something' from his friends and play-mates which he cannot acquire from parents.

4. The Religion

Religion provide a band of unity in the early societies. In modern society the importance of religion has diminished, yet it continues to mould our beliefs and ways of life.

Religious oriented activities—visiting temple, religious ceremonies, influence and determines his/her course of life and shape of his ideas.

5. The State

State, the authoritarian agency of socialization. State makes laws for the people and lays down the modes of conduct expected of them. The people have compulsorily to obey these laws. If they fail to adjust he/she get punishment. Thus, the state also moulds our behaviour.

Importance of Socialization

It Converts Man, the Biological being into Social Being

Man is not born social. He/she become social by virtue of the process of socialization.

It Contributes to the Development of Personality

Personality is a product of society through socialization which the personality of a new born child is shaped and moulded. It prepares the child to lead an approved way of social life. It also provide enough space for the individual to develop his individuality.

It Helps Become Disciplined

Socialization is social learning. Social learning is essentially the learning of rules of social behaviour. It is through socialization that the child learns not only the rules but also the values, ideas, aims and objectives of life and the means of attaining them. Socialization disciplines individual and helps him to live according to the social expectations.

It Helps to Enact Different Roles

Every role is woven around norms and is associated with different attitudes. The process of socialization assists an individual not only to learn the norms associated with roles but also to develop appropriate attitudes to enact those roles.

It Provides the Knowledge of Skills

Socialization is a way of training the new born individual in certain skills which are required to lead a normal social life. These skills help the individual to play economic, professional, educational, religious and political roles in his later stage.

It Helps to Develop Right Aspiration in Life

Every individual may have his own aspirations, ambitions and desires in life. All these aspirations may not always be in consonance with the social interests. Through the process of socialization an individual learns to develop those aspirations which are complementary to the interests of society. Socialization help him to direct/chanalize his whole energy for the realization of these aspirations.

Contributes to the Stability of the Social Order

It is through the process of socialization that every new generation is trained according to the cultural goals, ideals and expectations of a society. It assures what? It assures the *cultural continuity* of the society. In this regard socialization contributes to the solidarity of the social order.

It Helps to Reduce Social Distance

Socialization reduces social distance and brings people together.

Provides Scope for Building the Bright Future

It is through socialization that a society can produce a generation of the expectations. By giving appropriate training to the new born children the coming generation can be altered significantly.

Helps the Transmission of Culture

By transmitting the contents of culture, ideas, beliefs, languages, skills.... From one generation to the other, socialization contributes to the continuity of culture also.

Socialization of Adults

Socialization is a continues process. It doesn't stop at a certain stage/ age, but instead continues throughout life. The socialization of adults easier than the socialization of a child. Why?

1. The adult ordinarily is motivated to work towards a goal that he already envisions.
2. The new role that he is trying to internalize has many similarities to roles already existing in his personality.
3. The socializing agent can communicate with him easily through speech.

However, the socialization of adults can be a prolonged and difficult process. This is especially so when the roles to be learnt are difficult and the responsibilities of the role are heavy. Further, the norms and attitudes have all ready become deeply internalized in adults and so when the norms and attitudes to be learnt run counter to norms already established in the personality, socialization or adults becomes a difficult process.

Education is synonymous with socialization. Sociologically education is the process of socializing the child. Education has to perpetuate the social and cultural heritage which the present generation has inherited from other generations. This social and cultural heritage consist of experiences, customs, and the values of people. Education aims the socialization of individual. Education brings about the desired behavioural and attitude changes.

Social Change and Education

"Social changes are variations from the accepted modes of life, whether due to alteration in geographical conditions in cultural equipment, composition, of the population, or ideologies and whether brought about by diffusion or inventions within the group" —Gillin and Gillin.

Here the role of education, is the channelization of social change. Society is the network of individuals. The change in the network/relationship is called social change. According to McIver, socialization means a change in the human relationships. The nature of society is dynamic. If in a particular society, there is no change to a long period that leads to explosion e.g., USSR, Nepal. Change is universal. Industrialization, urbanization, progress in science and technology, invention of new machines and tools, innovations on communication and transportation sector are the factors caused for social change.

Social Change—Types

1. Progressive/Positive Social Change, i.e., the change from social evils to scientific thoughts in a society.
2. Degressive/Negative Social Change, i.e., in a well-going society, new social evils are emerging like prostitution, alchaholism etc.

Need for Social Change

- Social change saves society from being static and makes it flexible, liberal and adaptable.
- Civilized society/community welcomes social change.

If man would have still remained in the primitive stage there had been no changes/developments.

Characteristics of Social Change

- Social change may be planned or unplanned. Family planning programmes and new traffic rules are planned changes. Change by a natural calamity is unplanned.
- Changes are inevitable.
- Changes may be rapid, drastic or slow.
- Changes can be predicted with an appropriate understanding of the social process e.g., five year plans.
- Changes can take different forms:

1. *Evolutionary*. Example—use of mobile phone.
2. *Wave like*. Example—The flow of the dress style, churidar from North India to South India.
3. *Cyclic*. Example—The cyclical change of feudalism to capitalism, socialism and then again to capitalism.

Factors Affecting Social Change

Cultural Factors

Cultural change leads to social change. Max Weber says, "At the same time of cultural change social change also occurs." The mingling of societies/cultural groups also caused to social change. The social evils like—sati, casteism etc., are up to an end removing from the society.

Science and Technology

Discoveries and inventions are leads to change in life style. Changes in agriculture, production, transportation and communication sectors are also accelerate social change. 24 × 7 services are the result of developments in the science and technology sector.

Urbanization

Migration from villages to cities caused for changes in life styles, increasing number of crimes and emerging of slums etc.

Tension and Conflict

Karl Marx, "Social class is the basis of conflict between unequally advantaged segments of population and that provides energy for social change."

Population

The fluctuations in population like change in male female ratio, difference in ratio of different age groups are the factors of social change. The progress in medical sector, decrease the rate of epidemics and increase the number of elderly people. Population growth caused unemployment, poverty, prostitution begging etc., change in male-female ratio cause to marital, family relationships and status of ladies.

Environment

Environment, geography of particular area are influencing society. Famine, earthquake, drought, flood, Tsunami etc., also caused to social change.

Economic and Financial Set-up/Condition

Undeveloped countries are more chance to social change than developed nation. According to Karl Marx, "The cause of the social change is the economic system of the country." He explains this on the basis of the deviation of feudalism to capitalism and then to socialism.

Ideals

Ideals, politics, ideologies made change in society and life styles. The intensity of social evils like slavery, casteism etc., are reduced because of the works of social, religious organizations and institutions. New ideals like democracy, socialism, freedom, equality of opportunity, rule of law etc., are incorporated to social life that leads to social change. French revolution, Russian revolution, the doctrines of Abraham Linkon, Lenin, Mahatma Gandhi, Karl Marx, Nelsen Mandela, Martin Luther King etc., made changes in the view, perspectives of human beings.

Visual-Print Medias

The mass medias like newspapers, journals, periodicals, books, film, radio, T.V., they develop critical thinking, progressive thoughts/ views, visions, opinions among the layman. This develops a scientific attitude among common man. This made a awareness on new life styles, life equipments, achievement in science and technology etc., among peoples.

Psychological Factors

Generally human mind welcomes changes. Most of them embrace changes easily. The quest for discover and enjoying new ethos, belief, art, morals, laws, customs are human nature. Indoctrination also caused for social change. But some people those who bound with traditions, customs, beliefs and rituals they less chance to affect by social change. Migration, modernization, industrialization etc., also the factors attending social change.

Nature of Social Change

- Social change is a universal phenomenon.
- The spread of social change is not uniform. It is vary society to society, religion to religion and nation to nation.
- Nature and speed of social change is affect by and related to time factors.
- Definite prediction of social change is not possible.
- Social change results the interactions of a number of factors.
- Social change are chiefly those who modifications or of replacement.
- Social change sometimes shows a chain reaction sequence.

Obstacles in Social Change/Constraints of Social Change

- Superstitious beliefs
- Conservative nature
- Cultural inatia
- Habits
- Ideological narrow mindedness
- Sensate culture
- Vested interests
- Caste
- Ethnicity
- Classism
- Religion
- Regionalism
- Parochialism

The Role of Education in Social Change

- Education playing a important/major role in social change.

- Education controls, chanalize, modifies new generations thoughts and behaviour patterns.
- Schools are the 'Kalaris' (workshops) for citizenship training and democratic values.
- For social change, scientific vision/outlook is necessary. Those who bound with the chains of superstitious believes, misconcepts, false notions, wrong beliefs, the care-taker is only education.
- For spreading a awareness against 'sati', child marriage, dowry, casteism, untouchability, such social evils, education is necessary. No one educated man want ready to encourage this kinds of social evils. Aren't you?
- Education makes a national/emotional understanding among peoples.
- Economic progress in a inevitable factor for social change. Through agricultural education, technology education, working classes education, management education etc., the productivity of the state should increased to its meridian.
- Modernization is another essential factor for social change modernization is the main characteristics of social change and it is an evident for social change.
- Growth, and popularity of printing/visual media made drastic changes in our life style. It is because of science and technology education.
- Equality among men and women, the apex social status of ladies, and equality of gender etc., upto an end come to reality because of the spread of education.

SOCIAL CONTROL AND EDUCATION

The survival and smooth functioning of the society is possible only where is exist in it social harmony, social solidarity and social order. This only possible when the members conform to certain accepted standards of behaviour or norms. Soci al control refers to the control of society over the individual.

Definition

"Social control refers to the system of devices whereby society brings its members into conformity with the accepted standards of behaviour."

—E.A. Ross

"Social control refers to the patterns of pressure which a society exerts to maintain order and established ruels."

—Ogburn and Nimkoff

"Social control means the deliberate institutional means of making individuals and groups in a society observe and conform to the avowed social means." It is the informal pressure exerted by a group over an individual by norms of certain techniques such as gossip, ridicule and praise. The group interaction itself which functions to channel behaviour into certain paths is also a kind of social control, quite apart of any deliberate methods.

A society must have harmony and order, individual members must strive to attain these by conforming to the norms or accepted patterns of behaviour in society or else there will not be any social organization. So in order to exist and progress, society itself exercises a certain control over its members since any marked deviation from the established ways is considered a threat to its welfare. Such control has been termed by sociologists as social control.

Nature of Social Control

- The influence is universal; where there is society, there is social control. It is there even in the premitive and so-called uncivilized societies.
- Social control denotes some kind of influence: the influence may be exercised in various ways by public opinion, religion, morality, ideology and leadership.
- The influence is exerted by the society or community, i.e., the entire society influence over all the smaller/sub-groups/individuals, or dominant group(s) over smaller group(s).
- The influence is exercised for promoting the welfare of all the individuals or of the group as a whole. Social control is not aimless. It is there to serve general interests of all and to curb the dangerous selfish interests.
- The influence of the society has been there since time immemorial. Social control is old as human society. It is an essential condition of the human society because in the absence of social control no society can ever hold together its members for a length of time.

Purpose of Social Control

The main purpose of social control is to exercise control over people in an effective manner. Social control is very much necessary so as to bring about conformity, solidarity and continuity of particular group or society. The purpose of social control according to Kimball and Young.

Social Control About Social Conformity

Present-day modern complex society is multi-group society, differential norms will have co-exist. As a result, behaviour patterns of different groups differ significantly. But these differences shouldn't allowed to exceed the limits of tolerance. Then only people will feel secured. For the sake of security they are obliged to accept conformity. Social control thus for conformity.

Social Control Bring About Solidarity

Social control creates the feeling of identity and of solidarity in the minds of people. For the proper and smooth functioning of society, different organizations and institutions of the social system must be properly integrated. It is necessary for the society to establish a balance or equilibrium between different groups and institutions. Society does this through various means of social control.

Social Control Assures the Continuity of Social Group or Society

Continuity is the back bone on which the future of the society depends. Society maintains its continuity by controlling effectively its people and their groups. Due to the continuity the means of social control become part of the culture. As a part of culture they are transmitted from one generation to other. Thus, various means of social control function endlessly to maintain the continuity of society.

Kinds of Social Control

Positive Social Control

Certain positive mechanism such as persuation, suggestion, education and rewards are useful in influencing people to practice the behaviour and hold the attitudes that are socially approved.

Negative Social Control

Negative mechanisms like threat, orders, commands, compulsion etc., are called negative social control. They are employed to prevent people from anti-social behaviour and attitudes.

Positive and negative controls appear to operate together in the concrete order towards the goal of social conformity. Human motivation is complex and the individual may act in approved ways either because she/he seeks rewards or because of both kinds of sanctions simultaneously.

Formal Social Control

Public enactments, ordinance, law, constitutional regulations, commandments of church, official rules of an institution, etc., are the examples of formal social control. They called formal because, they are carefully planned and obligatory on all persons who submit to the authority of law makers. There is also some sort of enforcement procedure of an official kind in formal control.

Informal Social Control

These are not purposefully created but deep rooted with people. Informal controls are equally effective. They are employed to enforce the kind of behaviour "Everybody knows." There is no punishment for the violation of informal social controls. The informal controls operate positively through applause, gestures such as a nod of approval or a pat on the back. Negatively they operate through sneering, hissing and ridicule. Faith in religion, moral convictions, public opinion etc., are some agents in informal control.

Group Control

Group control achieves conformity through conscious voluntary and deliberate action on the part of both controller and the controlled.

Institutional Control

Institutional control is the sub-conscious often non-rational response of the individual to the cultural environment.

Direct Social Control

Direct social control is from parents, play groups, neighbours and other primary groups.

Indirect Social Control

Indirect social factors such as customs, traditions, changing situations. Whenever, the group/society becomes larger and complex the informal devices of control become less effective.

Folk Ways, Mores

The concept folkways and mores were developed by William Graham Sumner in 1906. According to Sumner, folkways refer to the expected ways of behaviour. But they are not compulsory. Example: saying 'good morning', 'thank you' etc. Those approved standards of behaviour passed on from one generation to the next as "the way we do things" are called folkways.

H.W. Odum, "The folkways are in general the habits of the individual and the customs of the group, arising naturally and spontaneously and growing up slowly around different phases of life." The ways of eating, talking, dressing, playing, walking etc., represent folkways.

Example: Taking 3 meals a day and eating with hand is Kerala folkway. Americans and Europeans are use knife and fork in different ways. Trival folkways do express cultural themes.

Mores: Mores are compulsory way of behaviour, that are consider vital to the welfare of the society. Mores are regulations of behaviour. They are used to denote behaviour patterns which are not only accepted but prescribed. Gillin and Gillin says, "mores are those customs and group routines which are thought by the members of the society to be necessary to the groups continued existence."

When 'folkways' act as regulations of behaviour the become 'mores'. Since folkways and mores differ only in degree, it is sometimes difficult to tell them apart. Folkways and mores provide guidelines for citizens to live in society and make them understand that there is a time and place for everything. They are shared attitudes of what is legitimate or what is normal behaviour for a given individual in a given situation.

EDUCATION OF NATIONAL INTEGRATION

National integration is national unity. It is unity in diversity. It means unifying all the forces in the country so as to give the idea of one nation. The problem national integration is very complex. On achieving independence we become pledged to built India in to a secular, democratic, republic based on the principles of social and economic justice.

In spite of our best efforts made in this sphere, India is still faced with many disintegrating. The foundation of our national life is common citizenship, unity in diversity, freedom of religion, secularism, equality, justice and fraternity among all communities. This foundation can be laid through education.

"India is my country, all Indians are my brothers and sisters. I love my country, and I am proud of its rich and varied heritage. I shall always strive to be worthy of it. I shall give my parents, teachers and all elders respect and treat everyone with courtesy. To my country and my people, I pledge my devotion. In their well-being and prosperity alone lies my happiness." The echo of our unity is blowing in the pledge. A nation is said to be integrated if its citizens, may be belonging to any caste, community, religion, language and state have a feeling of oneness, share each others joy and sorrows, smiles and tears and have an interest in the welfare of the nation as a whole.

The citizens of an integral/integrated nation must have

- mutual understanding.
- tolerance.
- respect for the culture.
- traditions.
- ways of life.
- common national ideas.
- common objectives, common interest, above all, and profound confidence in the future of the nation.

View of Indian Education Commission (1964-66)

According to Kothari Commission, National Integration means:

- Confidence in nations future.
- Continues rise in the standard of living of masses.
- Reduction in unemployment.
- Provision of equal opportunities for social, economic and political development.
- A deep sense of obligation of citizenship.
- Identification of the people with sectional loyalties but with nation as a whole.
- Good and impartial administration.
- Respect for cultural traditions and ways of life of different communities of the people and mutual understanding.

National Integration – Involves

1. The sentiments of nationalism
2. The feeling of oneness
3. Unity-especially unity in social, political, economic, emotional, linguistic and cultural fields.
4. Common ideals of life, common code of behaviour.
5. The ability to subordinate sectarian and parochial loyalties to loyalty of the nation.

Need for National Integration

National integration is vital for India's survival at a time of when the country under the threat of foreign aggression as well as the internal centrifugal forces of:

- regionalism,
- communalism,
- linguism,
- racialism, and
- ethnicity.

It is necessary to meet the challenge of the present times.

Emotional Integration and National Integration

National integration is the end whereas emotional integration is the means to achieve the end. The basis of national integration is emotional integration. It is through training of mind and heart that a sense of oneness among the people of the country can be inspired. Emotional integration in this particular sense means a feeling of national pride and faith in the nations greatness. When the emotions are conditioned by the idea of national loyalty and directed towards national welfare, the result is national integration.

Education can play a significant role on promoting national integration. The national unity was most conspicuous during pre-independence days. When the whole nation stood united to over-throw the foreign yoke and also when the security of the Indian boarders was threatened by Pakistan and China. But, in recent years there has been general weakening of this unity. Definite steps have to be taken to promote national unity. Education can play a very significant role here.

Hurdles in the Way of National Integration

Communalism

There are many communities in India. The British tackled the problem by the policy of 'Divide and Rule'. As a result of this policy India partitioned. It is natural for different communities to look after their own selfish interests. But it shouldn't be at the cost of other communities.

Casteism

Casteism, it prevents people from getting a reasonable opportunity in all fields only because of accident of birth. The system widens the gulf between the people of different castes and prevents their coming closer. The recent issue from Rajasthan i.e., the Meena V/s Gajjars riot also read with this.

Religious Prejudices

It is related to communalism and casteism. India is a secular state but still there are sudden outbreaks of violence in the name of religion. Religious feelings are also aroused and exploited in elections.

Provincialism

People think themselves as Gujarathi, Marathi, Bangali, Punjabi, Mayalali etc. But they doesn't think themselves to be Indians. Some states do not even admit students from other states in their institutions of higher learning. This provincialism should be curbed because it tends to disintegrate our country.

Regionalism

Two factors have given rise to this feeling.

1. The urge of the people speaking a single language to form distinct linguistic state.
2. The urge of economic development.

Then there is a dangerous disruptive ideology propounded by certain political parties, regarding the question of north and south. This feeling hinders integration.

Linguism

Language, which is considered to be a great uniting force become a disruptive factor in India. Some people make language a cloak for their ambitious designs particularly in politics and employment. One can understand the desire of linguistic minorities to provide education to their children in their mother-tongue. But when this question is mixed up with other matters it become a disruptive factor.

Economic Conditions

Economic conditions affect integration. Frustration felt by educated young people who do not find employment makes them prone to indiscipline and easy victims of anti-social and anti-national ideas. The provision of employment opportunities to those young men is shall prove helpful to national integration. Unemployment leads to terrorism.

Foreign Language as a Medium of Instruction

Importance of English as an international language and its rich literature can't be denied, but to adopt it as a medium of instruction and expression has resulted into disintegration of people to some extent. This hampered the development of Indian language and consequently the people of different states shouldn't come close to one another. Similarly English as a medium of instruction has created and widened the gap between the educand and non-educated people.

Defective Education System

Our defective education system is also responsible for lack of national and emotional integration. Our system of education was changed after independence. But particularly nothing has been done. (Several factors of our present educational system given promotion to divisive tendencies). Dr. Daulat Singh Kothari remarked, "Instead of promoting social and national integration and making an active effort to promote national consciousness, several features of the educational system promote divisive tendencies."

Educational and National Integration

Dr. S. Radhakrishnan's View

"National integration cannot be built by brick and mortar or with chisel or hammer. It has to growth silently in the minds of hearts of man by process by which it can be achieved is education."

A Matter of Feeling and Attitude

National integration is a matter of feelings, it is matter of attitude with the individual. Feelings and attitudes developed during the impressionable period (usually school life) of ones life, continue to influence his life up to the last breath.

Mudaliyar Commission, "If education doesn't strengthen the forces of national cohesion and solidarity we are afraid that out freedom, our national unity as well as our (culture) future progress will be seriously imperilled."

National Integration Through Education

Education can definitely play a vital role in strengthening national integration. By its deliberately planned programme, education can develop all aspects of a students personality by broadening his outlook, fostering a feeling of oneness and nationalism so that his narrow group interests surrendered in the larger interests of a country. This programme can be undertaken by adopting the following measures:

Re-Stating the Aims of Education

Education should aim at creating a feeling among rising generations. It also should aim at encouraging all these studies and activities which lead to a understanding between different communities and different states thus fostering a feeling of national unity.

National System of Education

We must have a national system of education. At present unfortunately the pattern of education varies from state to state. Though education is a state subject the responsibility of the Central Government cannot be undermined. Effective co-ordination between the centre and state is an essential condition for evolving on effective programme of national system of education.

Courses of Study

The textbooks are not written from the national point of view. They do not give the idea of a state. These textbooks should include an account of the heritage of each region in art, industry and literature. Map reading should be include compulsory so that the pupils become familiar with the whole of the country these will help in inculcating national outlook in our children.

Method of Teaching

Method of teaching, in school should aim not merely at the imparting of knowledge but also at inculcating desirable values and proper attitudes in the students. Student should given adequate opportunities to work in groups and to carry out group projects so that the qualities which are most essential for group life and co-operative work are developed in them.

Role of Language

A nation head a national league. Hindi is our national language. Besides studying mother tongue and national language should learn a number of languages. Steps have been taken in our schools to teach a number of language of the nation.

Emotional attachment is strengthened when we speak in their own language to people of the neighbouring states. The significant role of English in bringing for national integration cannot be denied.

Co-curricular Activities

An extensive programme of co-curricular activities can help to inculcate national feelings in our students. Such activities should include –

1. Singing of National Anthem and National song.
2. Saluting the national flag.
3. Celebration of national days and birth anniversaries of national leaders.
4. Film shows on national importance.
5. Inter school debates on topics concerning national integration.
6. Celebrating festivals of other communities.
7. Conducting social service programmes.
8. Functioning of National Service Scheme (NSS) and National Cadet Corps (NCC).
9. Students participation in dramas depicting glorious events in our Indian History.

Educational Tours and Trips

Through this students get first hand experience about our nation and also know the life styles of various areas of the country.

Exchange Programmes

The Government should arrange exchange programmes so that teacher and students will get in another part of the country and appreciate the ways of life that area. Their acquaintances and friendship in that area will help to bring national integration, government is do a lot in this direction through its scheme of scholarships. The conference of state education secretaries held in October 1968 recommended exchange of students, teachers, and educational administrators at the secondary and university level to promote national integration.

Projects for Improving Knowledge About Other States

Knowledge about other states is essential for National Integration. The Committee on Emotional Integration (1963) suggested that: "Schools may conduct several projects which improve their students general knowledge about the country," e.g., "Know your country" like titled projects.

Teaching of Religion

India is a secular state. Religion is a handicap for National Integration. Secularism doesn't mean irreligious/anti-religious. It implies impartiality and religious tolerance. Religious crusades cannot be allowed here. Celebration of different religious festivals in educational institutions must form a breeding ground for the attitude of tolerance. Good points/values/stories from the teaching of different religions should be taught to pupils.

Organizing National Integration Camps

It is useful in inculcating feeling of oneness among the students and teachers. The main object of such camps is to enable school students understand and appreciate the social and cultural life of pupils in different states.

Encouraging Inter-State Pen Friendship

The exchange of letters, E-mails, SMS etc., facilitate traveling among students and teachers. Inter-state friendship help them to for accommodation and guiding.

Role of Teacher

Children are the most sensitive section of our community. They look to us for guidance and imitate our ways of life. Millions of children's eyes are focused on us and there are no eyes more observant, keen and perceptive than the eyes of a child. So if we really wish our children to be good, honest, brave, national minded and patriotic, we should have to get our example before then. Let you act up to brotherhood among your pupil.

Re-orienting Instruction in Social Science

History should reveal India's unity in diversity. Through geography the students may be made to realize the variety of peoples that inhabit it, their ways of like, their food habits etc.

Civics should be taught with a view of creating desirable attitudes for national unity and Emotional Integration. The study of art, literature and music also help to develop national consciousness.

Re-designing the Curriculum

One of the aims of secondary education itself is national integration. The destiny of India is being shaped in her classrooms. Every subject must be taught from the point of view of national needs and achievements. There is a need to re-interpret the contents of various subjects in the light of larger interest of the nation.

National integration is vital for India's survival. It is the cry of the moment. In the words of our former Prime Minister Mrs. Indira

Gandhi, "The question of national integration is serious enough to be studied calmly. It needs a deep conviction that this is the most urgent question of the day and also burning passion to summon all strength and will to surmount it by fighting all that leads to injustice, in equality and discrimination. Let us not degrade the very name of Indian citizenship.

EDUCATION FOR INTERNATIONAL UNDERSTANDING

The term international understanding implies mutual understanding, faith and respect among the various nations or countries of the world. With the means of supersonic transport and communication, all the countries of the world have come to each other and no country can stand alone and unconcerned from other countries because whatever is happening in one country has its reflection in another country. This has necessitated mutually good and cordial relation among the countries of the world, which is termed as international understanding. Thus international understanding implies respect for human rights and dignity, a sense of solidarity of mankind, international co-operation and to live together in peace with one another that is, international understanding is equaled with world citizenship.

Definition

Internationalism is one idea of the 20th century and it came into prominence after the 2nd World War. The term international understanding defines as:

- "International understanding and internationalism is a feeling that the individual is not only a member of the state but the member of the world."

  —***Oliver Gold Smith***

- "International understanding refer to friendship and harmony amongst different nations of the world and also includes co-operation amongst them—each one maintaining its identity and sovergnity as usual."

  —***Dr. Atmananda Mishra***

Importance of International Understanding

The very survival of humanity depends on international understanding and hence internationalism has assumed importance in the present world. The concept of international understanding aims at securing ever lasting peace amongst the nations of the world which has become the most significant need of the present world.

The last 2nd World War have made it clear to all nations of the world that another war may wipe out the entire humanity from the earth. That is, the development of modern scientific weapons for destruction another war may mean the end of present civilization and humanity.

Thus, the feeling of internationalism/international understanding is important because of the following reasons:

- To prevent world wards.
- To maintain ones sovereignty.
- To strengthen democratic principles.
- To develop backward nations.
- To develop contact with other countries.
- To promote human welfare.

Now-a-days, science and technological development have completely removed the barriers of time and distance and the entire world has become one unit. Events in one country affects other parts of the world and it necessitates the collaboration and co-operation of different nations in the world. No country can be said to be economically self-sufficient and the prosperity of one country depends on the other and hence that is the importance of international understanding.

International Understanding and Education

Modern and ancient philosophers in India have supported the notion of internationalism and advocates that education is powerful force in developing internationalism.

In the words of Berttrand Russel, "Education may not bring internationalism from political point of view but education is the only agency through which it is possible to develop the feeling of internationalism."

The UNESCO rightly remarked that "Since war begins in the minds of men, it is in the minds of men that the defense of peace must be constructed." Thus as a tool for promoting international understanding, education should be so organized and formulated.

Education for International Understanding Should be Based on Some Principles. They are:

Developing the Capacity of Independent Thinking

The first and for most principle on which education for international understanding should be based in the developing and cultivation of the power and capacity of independent thinking in our young men and women, so that they may be able to understand that above all, the world needs peace today, which leads to progress and happiness and war leads to destruction and misery.

Developing Tolerance and Mutual Co-Operation

One of the great principle that all nations of the world should follow in their everyday relationship with other is 'live and let live'. Lack of mutual understanding, distrust and suspicion leads to frictions in the international sphere and hence education should stress the idea of co-operation and tolerance.

Inter-dependence.should be Stressed

Education for international understanding should stress the idea of inter-dependence of nation. No country in the modern world can afford to live in isolation and has to depend upon others for the satisfaction of its physical, social and economic needs. Thus, the needs of all nations can be better satisfied if there is international co-operation and understanding.

Re-defining Patriotism in the Modern Context

The term patriotism shouldn't be conceived in its narrow sense, as the narrow concept of the term patriotism is very dangerous for the world peace. The love of one's own country shouldn't stand in the way of wider loyalty to humanity and therefore the term patriotism should be re-defined and re-interpreted so that it is wide enough to consistent with internationalism.

Elimination of Fear

Fear is the basis of mutual suspicious of nations which leads to a race for armaments. Being afraid and suspicious of one another, the nations. prepare themselves for war. Proper education based on the principle, 'Live and let to live' can help in removing the fear.

Belief in Universal Freedom

The period of imperialism, colonialism and capitalism has gone and no nation is allowed to sub-judge and exploit politically and economically. Thus every nation should have firm belief in the brotherhood of man and fatherhood of God.

Emphasizing Correct Values

Education for international understanding should be based on the principle of emphasizing correct values. Democratic values, group responsibility, co-operation, tolerance, and mutual understanding should be stressed and impressed upon the students.

Inculcate Corporate Responsibility

Education for international understanding should be based on the principle of corporate responsibility. The children should be taught to believe that they are the citizens of the world, which is one and invisible. If there is anything ugly in the world, they all are equally responsible for it.

Practical Use of Knowledge

Mere theoretical knowledge is not enough and all the principles of understanding will be useless and futile if they are not translated into action. Hence, education should train and educate young generation to use the theoretical knowledge of principles of international understanding for doing something practical in the service of international unity and friendship.

Means to Spreading International Understanding

In order to encourage the growth of international understanding, it is necessary to make suitable amendments and modifications in the objectives of education, in the syllabus and method of teaching.

The following are some of the ways and means of organizing education for promoting the feeling and thought of internationalism.

Re-orienting Curriculum and Textbooks

For promoting the feeling of internationalism, the first step should be the re-orientation of the educational curriculum and the textbooks. It is through the right type of curriculum and textbook that the children's mind can be re-oriented in the direction of peace and international understanding. Hence, the aim of developing international understanding among students must be kept in mind while re-designing the curriculum. All the school subjects like history, geography, science and literature should initiate the students into the wider world of which they are the members. Similarly the teaching of different school subjects should be remodeled in such a way that the students may develop a wider and cosmopolitan outlook, realizing the basic unity of the world. The whole curriculum should be re-oriented with the object of promoting international understanding.

Proper Co-curricular Activities

The various types of co-curricular activities organized in the school can considerably promote and cultivate the ideas and feelings of international understanding in the minds of the students.

The activities include the celebration of birthdays of great men and women belonging to different countries/ religions, celebration of international days, lectures by foreign scholars etc.

The school should also keep the students informed of the latest developments in the world through newspapers, magazines, journals, lectures and discussions. The school should also try to cultivate world-mindedness among students by co-operating with the UNESCO in all activities.

Cultural Exchange

In order to broaden the mental outlook of the people and to establish cultural ties among various nations, the schools should co-operate and actively participate in the programme of sending cultural missions, consisting of teachers poets, scholars, artists and writers etc., to different countries of the world. The face-to-face contact will rectify the wrong notions and will create sympathy and affection for the peoples of other countries.

Pen Friendship

A few of the contemporary magazines and the magazines meant for adolescents publish the readers interests, age, hobbies and other relevant information of the persons interested in pen friendship. This friendship leads to exchange of pictures, stamps etc. Thus pen friendship is the means of promoting the feeling of international understanding.

Exchange of Gifts

Exchange of gifts, a diplomatic act by the politicians and heads of the states. The sending of gifts from one country to another helps in strengthening the international feeling by attracting one country to another.

International Competitions and Exhibitions

Now a days, cultural competitions such as display of dance, drama, art, music etc take on an international colour because, people from many countries participate in them. This brings people into contact with the result that the world seems like a vast home. Exhibition also play an important part in promoting international understanding because they help to acquaint people with the art and culture of different countries.

Celebration of International Days

- UNO Day — October 24
- World literacy Day — September 8
- World population Day — July 11
- World environment Day — June 5
- Common Wealth Day — May 24
- Red Cross Day — May 8
- World Health Day — April 7.

Films, Radio and Television

Peoples derive a lot of information from the films, television, radios etc., and it also encourages the feeling that human beings are the same everywhere in these happiness, pain, pleasure, problems and joys. This will help in developing international understanding.

Contribution of Universities and Institutions of UNO

Universities are the most important medium for propagating international understanding because they provide for the meeting of artists, scientists, literary figures etc. This creates international understanding at very high levels. In addition to this many institutions of UNO, more particularly UNESCO, are engaged in directly and consciously promoting international understanding and the growth of international feeling.

Role of UNESCO/Functions of UNESCO in Promoting International Understanding

The role of UNESCO in spreading internationalism is noteable. In order to achieve its goal of spreading international understanding, it performs the following functions:

- This organization transmits knowledge of literature, art, science, etc., of one nation to all other nations.
- It provides many opportunities to thinkers, scientists, teachers and artists to meet each other and exchange ideas and put forward creative plans for promoting world peace and justice.

Efforts are also made to prevent the people from being influenced too much by narrow parochial thinking.

- UNESCO also seeks to improve the mutual relationship between various nations and remove fear, suspision and lack of confidence between them.
- Considerable financial aid is given by UNESCO to improve the teaching facilities in backward countries.
- UNESCO also provides guidance in modifying texts prescribed in various syllabi in order to make the book more internationally oriented.
- In order to promote international understanding UNESCO provides facilities to students and teachers to visit abroad and to exchange views and also gain experience in international.
- It also organizes art, literature exhibitions at the international level to promote feeling of love and friendship.
- Research is also encouraged by UNESCO by providing financial help and assistance to researcher.

Conclusion

International understanding is the need of the day. Education is a strong and potent agency for promoting international understanding. It is rightly say that international understanding will not emerge from the science laboratories but from the school and college where human energy is directed into useful channels. Hence, the spirit of peaceful co-existence and international harmony should pervade the whole of school and college life and learning. The process of developing international understanding is rather slow and difficult, but the effort is worth doing. Not only the progress and prosperity but the very survival of mankind is depend upon promoting internationalism.

MODEL QUESTIONS

1. What is meant by transformation of culture?
2. Why is education regarded necessary for national integration.
3. Outline a programme for promoting internationalism among students.
4. Can education follow as an effect of social change? If so, in what manner? What would be the educators role in this process?
5. Show how home and school are complementary to each other in educating a child.

REFERENCES

1. Bhatt, B.D. and Sharma, S.R. (1993). *Sociology of Education*, Kanishka Publishing House, New Delhi.

2. Entwistle, Harold (1997). *Class, Culture and Education*, New Fetter Lane, London.
3. Gerald L. Gutek. *Philosophical and Ideological Perspectives on Education.*
4. J.C. Aggarwal. *Theory and Principles of Education*
5. Koushik, V.K. & Ravi, Prakash (1996). *A Sociology of Educating– Teaching and Curriculum*, Kanishka Publishers, New Delhi.
6. Meigham, Roland (1996). *A Sociology of Educating*, Cassell Educational Ltd., London.
7. Rai, B.C. (1997). *Sociological and Philosophical Theory of Education*, Prakashan Kendra, Lucknow.
8. Sataya, Raghunath, (1993). *New Thoughts on Education*, The Indian Publications, Ambala.
9. Srinibas Bhattacharya, *Foundations of Education.*

10

Education from Economic Perspective

NATURE OF ECONOMICS

The word 'Economics' is partially derived from the Greek term *Olkynonmia,* which means household management.

Definitions of economics are categorized as

- *Wealth centred definitions,* regard economics as science of wealth in relation to man.
- *Welfare-centred definitions,* regard economics as the science of material welfare.
- *Scarcity centred definitions,* regard economics as the science that studies human welfare as a relationship between ends and scarce means which have alternate uses.
- *Wantlessness-centred definitions,* regard economics as the study of human behaviour concerned with changes and growth in capacity to produce in relation to demand.

Economics studies the activities of mankind in an objective and scientific manner. It has the elements of both science and literature. Its main aim is to study the material aspects of man's life. It teaches man the lesson of material utility. Economics is an integral part of practical problem. Economics studies the resource allocation or resource utilization, size, distribution and stability of national income and fascinating subject of economic growth. Economics is a social science which studies the way the society chooses to employ its limited resources that have alternative uses, to produce goods and services for present and future consumption.

Basically economics deals with aspects like

- What to produce
- How to produce and
- For whom to produce are related to
- Resources economically used
- Problem of full employment
- Problem of growth etc.

The study of economics divided into two major areas:

1. *Micro-economies* deals with the analysis of behaviour of any particular decision-making unit like a firm, an industry, a consumer etc.
2. *Macro-economics* deals with the analysis of the problems of the economy as a whole.

Though economics is regards as science, it cannot predict and future course of events as is done by other sciences like physics and chemistry because prediction of human behaviour is just impossible. Thus economics presents a continually changing doctrine.

Characteristics of Economics

- *Fulfillment of Wants:* It studies man's wants and attempts to fulfill these wants and achieve the maximum benefit on the minimum investment.
- *Material Science*: Being a material science, it has very little to do with the spiritual aspect of human life. It deals with man's activities connected with wealth, earning or livelihood.
- *Science as Well as Art:* As a science as well as art; economics is a systematized body of the knowledge of human activity in regard to wealth also practical application of the knowledge acquired.
- *Welfare:* It brings about human welfare, making man happy.

Economics of Education

Economics of education, one of the youngest branches of economics probes the various sources of educational finance, cost-effectiveness, direction of development and similar issues. The phrase first coined by Prof: Theodore W. Shultz (noted economist of the university of Chicago) in 1960 while addressing the American Economics Association.

In 1965, 'The World Year Book on Education' (1965) carried an article on economics of education giving the subject legitimacy and recognition.

Adam Smith, the father of economics and the author of *Enquiry into the nature and causes of the wealth of nations* (1776), was the first to recognize the relationship between economics and education. Pleading for raising the quality of education, he said, "The money of the parents, the time and talents of children are not lost or injured from the inexperience and ignorance of those to whose care they are entrusted."

Ricardo and Malthus argued, education can do much good under a good government. John Stuart Mill, advocating public education.... "Education is one of those things which a government should provide for the people." Alfred Marshall treating education as a national investment. "Education is the most valuable of all capital that is invested in human beings." Karl Marx asserted, "When the working class come into power, as invariably it must, technical instruction both theoretical and practical will take its proper place in the working class schools."

Meaning of Economic of Education

Education seeks the help of economics to achieve national development in all fields of national life and all spheres of national development including—

- Economic prosperity and
- National security.

Because of an intimate relationship between education and economics, the economy of a particular country influences it education, while the return on education affects the planning of education of that society. Thus education and economies are integrally correlated as two sides of the same coin.

The Universalisation of Elementary Education (UEE) requires vast out lay of funds. It is natural for people to think of returns of this huge expenditure on education. It is precisely this thinking that led to the study of economics of education. Economics of education studies the expenditure on education in-depth with the corresponding return it brings to the nation which spends so much on education for its own good.

Scope of Economics of Education

- Determining the relationship between educational expenditure and increases in income or physical capital over a period of time in a country.
  Analyzing this relationship between education expenditure and growth in income/physical capital formation, Shultz revealed that in the USA the resources allocated to education in the period of 1900-56 rose three and half times... In fact, it is the massive investment in education that made USA superpower.
- Assessing and determining the contribution of education to Gross National Product (GNP) of a country.
- Estimating the return from educational investment.
- Undertaking inter country correlation of school enrolment ratio and GNP.
- Formulating man power planning and programming model for educational planning.
- Estimating educational wastage and suggesting methods to avoid them.
- Synchronizing the education system with the social system.
- Identifying the priorities in the National Policy on Education and their implications.
- Re-distribution of resources and re-arrangement of priorities.
- Promoting the needed changes in education and making it socially relevant and economically productive.
- Improving the techniques of educational planning and management.

Economic Aspects of Education

Education as an Economic Good

There are two types of economic goods. i.e.

- Material goods – Soap, Car, Bike
- Non-material goods – Service of Doctor, Lawer, Teacher, Education, etc.

Education is regarded as a producer's good and consumer's good. While the producer's good is used in the process of producing other goods, a consumer's good is used by a consumer to satisfy his or her wants.

Education is both a producer's good and a consumer's good as it gives satisfaction to the person who consumes it (producers good) and helps in the production of more goods, through acquisition of skills (consumers good).

Education as Industry

Just as a government spends its Gross National Income on different sectors and also to education. Education is considered, as 'growth industry' that provides employment and provides employment producing services needed by the total economy.

Just as any other industry, education contributes substantially to the total economy of the country.

Education as Human Capital

Capital is anything that involves costs and yields steady income over period. According to H.G. Johnson's classification of capital, education is classified as human capital.

Impact of Economics on Education

1. *Aims of Education*: Aim of education determined by economics. Example – Vocational aim is one of the primary aims of education.
2. *Importance of Education*: Economics clarifies the importance of education, as the economic growth of a country is largely dependent on educational development.
3. *Education as a Means*: Education makes man a better producer, both for his own good as well as the good of the country.
4. *Education as an Investment*: Education, being an investment in economic terms, remover poverty, because it produces skilled labour and creates the right attitude toward work and development. It creates awareness for better living.
5. *Education Guarantees Economic Security*: Education has an impact on professional values, the wage structure and guarantees the economic security of the people.
6. *Education and Economic Status*: Education determines the economic status of a person as it helps him in possessing a good earning capacity and leading a good economic life.
7. *Education and Economic Prosperity*: Education influences the economic development of a country, with the economic development of a country being directly proportional to the educational attainment of the people.

Economic Order and Education

1. *An Agrarian Economy*, people are engaged in agriculture and allied occupations like dairy, cattle breeding, poultry and other minor vocations. People can do with primary education often without formal schooling.
2. *Education in Trade Economy*: In trade economy production of goods is considerable whereas the supply of goods produced in the country for home consumption is meager.
   In this economic order higher education of various types is necessary and therefore more and more institutions are established for secondary, higher and specialized education for the benefit of trading community, selling agents and marketing personnel.
3. *In the Capitalistic Economic Order* only the rich have access to education in all fields.
4. *In Socialistic Pattern* all the children are able to get the desired education according to their needs, aptitudes and capacities.
5. *In a mixed Economy* education is provided to all children by both private and public institutions and agencies.
6. *In the Industrial Economy* primary, secondary and often vocational and specialized education made free, compulsory and universal. Higher technological education is made available to those who need it, providing ample opportunities for research.

Education and Economic Growth

G.U. Papi lists the following ways by which education increases the productivity of labour and entrepreneurship:

- Makes people more receptive to inventions and innovations.
- Promotes the division of labour and use of machinery.
- Permits increasingly advantageous combination of factors of production (land, labour and capital) as compared with those in which the human factors are of less quality.
- Makes it possible for any new technical discovery to be brought into operation with little or no delay.
- Promotes both in the domestic economy and on international scale a far-reaching mobility of labour and entrepreneurial ability.
- Education ensures that those individuals who are responsible for making major technical, economic and

political decisions possess the width of knowledge and the breadth of view, which associated with a high moral sense, enable them to avoid potentially dangerous mistakes.

- Development of educated and skilled man power in the long run reduces risks and costs.

Education and Economic Development

The process of development in the country is determined by a harmonious functioning of the triangular of economy, education and polity.

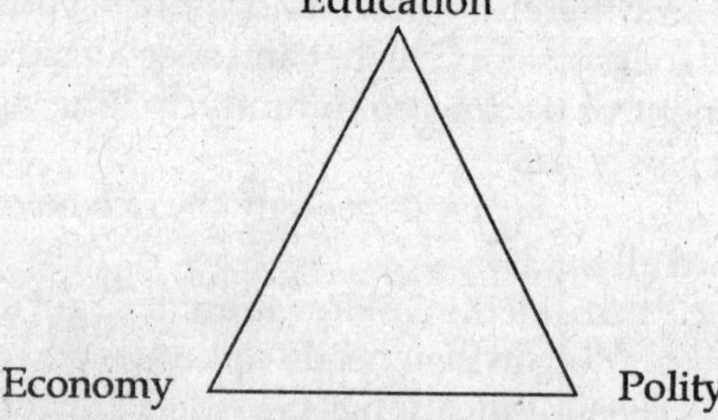

The triangle, are extremely potent tools for the development of the people provided they are utilized to the maximum.

Education is conceived as a critical participant of a triangular process which cumulatively leads to change, development and progress in a society in a planned manner.

What are the indicators of educational development of a particular country?

- Literacy Rate and
- Enrolment Rate.

The relationship between educational development and economic development, it is observed that some of the economically developed countries are also educationally advanced, example—Japan. They have almost cent percent literacy and all children of school-going age are enrolled in the schools.

As opposed to this there are some countries which are not economically much developed but they have registered tremendous educational progress. Example—Sri Lanka, China, Myanmar and Philippines.

Further, there are countries which are economically well-off but they are educationally backward. Example—Gulf Countries.

India is neither economically advanced nor educationally advanced.

The over all situation which emerges is that generally the countries having higher levels of income or economically advanced also have higher level of educational attainment. The economically poor countries are likely to remain educationally backward if they do not give importance to education and/or do not allocate more funds to it and ensure optimum utilization of the available resources.

Factors Influencing Economic Development of a Nation

1. Natural Resources: Soil, climate, water resources, forests, rivers, sea coasts, hills, mountains, mines, wild life, mineral resources.
2. Population.
   - Huge population leads to imbalance between demand and supply and
   - Large section of immigrants/new settlers may be adversely/favourably affect economic development.
3. Scientific and Technological Progress.
4. Capital.
5. Organisation and Specialization.
6. The social factor implies the general desire and aspiration of the people for accelerating the speed of prosperity.
7. Ratio between capital and production.

The Role of Education in Economic Development

In India, we have a mixed economy public (Government controlled) and private. Agriculture and industries, the principal base of economy of India. Specialists needed for both public and private sectors. Accordingly education should be planned.

- Education develops the various techniques of production which may revolutionize the entire area of production.
- Education may increase the efficiency of workers.
- Education may help in creating new avenues in the rural areas of production.
- Education expands the use of natural resources towards ensuring economic prosperity.
- Education may help in removing the defects of economic system in the country.

- Education provides us new way for thinking in the area of economic production.

Education as an Good Investment

Through education and training we may develop knowledge and skills which may help the development of economic prosperity.

It has been found through research in Russia by Strunnilin that if workers are given at least primary education, the production will be increased by 44 per cent.

After 2nd World War there has been great development in the spirit of materialism. So the various nations of the world diverted their major resources for ensuring economic prosperity. This spirit led to the increasing demand for all types of education. The fulfillment of this demand has confirmed the belief that education is an investment towards greater production.

The educationists and economics of today are of the firm conviction that investment in the spread of all types of education is as productive as in industries of iron and coal mines.

In addition to an investment, education is also a *consumption,* because we find that there is generally a great rejoicing when one begins to obtain education, later on after having obtained the required education, there is also realization that education has provided an ability to spend life in happiness.

A great delight in the process of obtaining education. After having obtained education the hope of happy life. Is it right? Is education provide an ability to spend life in happiness?

It appears quite pertinent to mark the difference in investment in education and in other areas of production. Investment made in various industries generally show expected positive results (in 3 or 4 years time). But the investment made in education may show positive results after a few years when the individual gets education as he desires or as he is capable of.

Private Cost and Social Cost of Education

Under the private cost, mainly come the tuition fees and the allied inevitable waste in the process of obtaining education. The social cost is quite comprehensive. This includes the salaries of teachers and other types of workers engaged in educational institutions, costs of organizing libraries, laboratories and other expenditure which are done in any kind of functioning of the place of education.

EDUCATION AND MODERNIZATION

Meaning of Modernization

The most important function of education is modernization. Modernization is a comprehensive concept aimed at capturing and describing the transition of a society from medieval to modern culture.

- It stands for progress beyond tradition.
- Modernization, according to some sociologists, is based upon European and American models.

As compared to Urbanization, Industrialization, Westernization and Europeanization, Modernization presents a more complex process and a more complex result.

In the intellectual sphere it is an awareness that it is possible to see a rational explanation of physical and social phenomena. Thus, it is represented by positivism, empiricism and rationalism.

In the field of religion it is expressed in secularism. Its approach is multiple. In philosophy it is expressed in humanist thought. The implications of science based technology over social and cultural life broadly described as modernization. (*NCERT, 1970,* p. 31)

Thus modernization is a process of change from traditional and quasi-traditional order to certain desired types of technology.

In the words of William, E. Moore, "Modernization is a revolutionary change leading to transformation of a traditional pre-modern society into the type of technology and associated social organization that characterizes the advanced, economically prosperous and relatively politically stable nations of the western world." (*Social Change,* p. 89)

It includes social mobilization and differentiation and specialization in individual and institutional activities. In political field it stands for democratization. In ecology it is characterized by advancing degree of urbanization.

In social set-up we change to under family from joint family. Our traditional married life change to 'free sex'. In production sector agricultural based economy transit to specialized industrialized one

Symptoms of Modernization

- Growing differentiation of the major secular or cultural system. The spread of literacy and secular education (*A.R. Desai*).

- Emergence of new cultural outlook, characterized by emphasis on progress and improvement on the happiness and spontaneous abilities and, feelings, on the development of individuality as a value, and efficiency.
- Emergence of a new personality orientation.
- Greater ability to adjust to the broadening societal horizons.
- Ego-flexibility.
- Widening sphere of interests.
- The ability of society to develop an institutional structure capable of adjusting to continually changing problems and demands.

Modernization Through Education

How we promote modernization through Education? Education is the most important instrument of modernization since modernization includes,

1. Directed change in the system of attitudes, beliefs and values and also in the institutional complex to enhance the acceptability of modern technology and its organizational and operational framework.
2. Growth of the infrastructure essential to the adaptation to technology of foreign origin to specific national needs.
3. Laying the foundations of institutions and organizations which could, in time, assume responsibility for independent innovation and technological growth to the country's needs and problems.

Functions of Education Related to Modernization

Alternatives to Tradition

By enlarging the cognitive map of those exposed to it, education suggests alternatives to attraction, bringing into focus the rewards implicit in them and indicates roughly at least the paths through which the new goals with their attendant regards can be achieved. It broadens mental horizons, raises expectations and predisposes people to make experiments.

Socialization

It can be help in obliterating attitudes and behaviour patterns that are dysfunctional programmes of modernization.

National Consciousness

By providing ideological articulation it can be promote the development of national consciousness and can help people see their needs and their problems in a national perspective.

Educated Elite

Education provides a highway to elite on the educated. The educated provide a reference model to the masses, who in imitation of the former, take the first steps away from tradition.

Problem-Solving Leadership

Scientists and technicians, management experts and administers with the requisite knowledge and still, can only be expected to emerge out of the educational system.

Mobility Multiplier

Although its impact is on the immobility of thoughtways in the long run it does alter rigid forms of social stratification. Modernization requires both types of mobility. i.e.,

(a) *Horizontal Mobility:* It is the transition of an individual from one status to another. Example—a farm labour become an industrial labourer.

(b) *Vertical Mobility:* It is the move of an individual from downward status to an upward status. Example—son of a sweeper get a government job.

Young and Mack, "Social mobility means movement with in the social structure." Education as one route to vertical mobility. It is through education that one can hope to replace the ascribed status by achieved status.

Modernization and Educational Process

Modernization is the process by which fundamental social and cultural changes take place as a result of the adoption of science-based technology. It is the movement of society from the traditional order to a more rational and scientific order.

It implies three things:

1. A wide explosion of knowledge.
2. A rapid social change.
3. A re-orientation of moral and spiritual values.

A Wide Explosion of Knowledge

The main task of education to enable children to keep pace with the rapid growing knowledge, and to help them discover knowledge by themselves.

This would require a deliberate effort on the part of teachers to acquaint themselves with the new concept of educational technology which includes,

Programmed instruction, Audio-visual aids, Action research... etc.

A Rapid Social Change

Another task of education is to make children aware of the challenges they have to meet in the rapidly changing society. Imparting knowledge is only a fragment of education. Real education strives to awaken curiosity of children, develop creative and critical thinking in them and inculcate desirable values.

A Re-orientation of Moral and Spiritual Values

Modernization doesn't mean a refusal to recognize moral and spiritual values. Education should strive to make our children inheritors of all that is nice and noble in our culture. The knowledge and skill gained by science and technology should be balanced with the moral and spiritual values gained by religion and ethics.

Conclusion

Modernization is the process which indicates the adoption of modern ways of life and values. In India context if we combine moral, spiritual, education with general and vocational education, people can achieve both self realization an self expression. The emerging Indian society can more rapidly towards modernization through an ideal system of education, both on the principle of dynamism and synthesis.

CONCEPT OF EDUCATIONAL PLANNING

Meaning of Planning

Planning is an attempt to shape the future by deliberate action. This clearly implies that we should understand the present in its relationship to the past as a basis for understanding the future trends. The basic problem is the understanding of the present social conditions and their relationship to the past social conditions.

Objectives of Planning

The main object of educational planning is to get the most and best educational results for the effort expended, and to maximize education's contributions to each individual and to the whole society. According to Philip, H. Coombs, Educational Planning is nothing more than a rational process of setting clear objectives, choosing the most efficient and effective means for pursuing them, than following through with practical action:

General Principles of Effective Planning

1. A development plan is a collective task. It is the result of co-operative endeavour of experts in a wide variety of subjects i.e., statistics, economic development, agriculture, industry, manpower, public works and building, etc.
2. The preparation of educational development plan should be passed on accurate directions from the responsible political authorities.
3. A choice has to be made between what is possible and what is desirable.
4. Once a decision has been taken, an order of priority must be drawn up among those educational activities that might be desirable.
5. The responsibility for educational planning must be undertaken by the government as a whole.
6. The bodies responsible for educational planning should be closely linked as possible with those responsible for its implementation.
7. Educational planning is a continuous process which finds expression in a succession of plans, each subsequent plan based in the light of the results of the plan preceding it and the new demands.
8. Usually the plan period covers 5 years.
9. A suitable machinery should be evolved for the implementation of the plan.
10. Splitting the plan into operational stage facilitates the implementation of the plan.
11. A reasonably efficient administrative machinery should be evolved.
12. A periodical evaluation at the level of bodies responsible for implementation.

History of Educational Planning in India

India has now a record of over 50 years of educational planning, i.e., since 1951, the birth of the National Planning Commission. Every State and Union Territory has its plan. The Central Government actively assists the states in formulating their plans. The plans of the Central and State Governments and the 'public' and the 'private' sectors are co-ordinated and finalized after detailed discussions with the Planning Commission, at the central level. These plans are approved by the National Development Council which comprises *inter alia* the Prime Minister and the Chief Ministers of states. The approved plan thus becomes the highest policy declaration of what is proposed to be achieved during the next 5 years and how. The Five Year Plan specifies the allocation for education like other sectors, chalk out the polices and the programmes and set targets of achievement.

LIBERALIZATION AND EDUCATION

Liberalization, the process of elimination of licensing and quota restrictions, which began in 1991, was completed in 2001-02, with the removal of all import restrictions. The General Agreement on Trade in Services (GATS), one of the WTO's agreement that came into existence in January 1995, is the first and only set of multilateral rules covering international trade in services.

The GATS agreement has two parts:

- The framework agreement containing the general rules and disciplines; and
- The national schedules agreement, which envisages individual countries' specific commitments on access to their domestic markets by foreign suppliers.

While the commitments apply on a non-discriminatory basis to all member countries of the WTO, the member countries have complete freedom to choose which services to commit, in addition to the services committed. The schedules limit the degree to which foreign-service providers, in this case foreign universities and colleges, can operate in the market. GATS covers all internationally-traded services with the following exceptions:

- Services provided to the public in the exercise of governmental authority; and
- In the air transport sector, traffic rights and all services that are directly related to the exercise of traffic rights.

Modes of Supply

The WTO has divided all services in to 12 sectors. Education in one of them. GATS has categorized the supply of service under four modes:

Mode 1: *Cross Border Supply*

In this mode, the services flow from the territory of one member-country into the territory of another member country.

Example: A faculty member of an educational institution can send teaching material and exercises to students in any other country.

Mode 2: *Consumptions Abroad*

In this mode the consumer of a service moves into the territory of another member country, to secure the services.

Example: Students moving to another country to obtain education in any field, come under this category.

This mode also includes students who attend a part of the programme as a twinning arrangement and obtain a degree from another country.

Mode 3: *Commercial Presence*

In this mode, service suppliers of a member country establish a legal presence in another member-country in order to provide their services. In this situation, the service supplier establishes a legal presence in the form of a university, a joint-venture, a subsidiary, a legal representative, or a branch office in a host country and starts supply of services.

For instance, Sloan School of Management in the USA can set up a business school in India in a strategic location like Delhi and start offering MBA programme with degrees being provided from their mother institutions in the US. They can adopt their own methods of costing, employ their faculty and teach a curriculum designed by them.

Our national bodies like UGC, AICTE, MHRD, etc., have no control on the same.

Mode 4: *Presence or Movement of Natural Persons*

This mode, which covers only export of man power, covers a situation in which a service is delivered through persons of a member-country who temporarily enter the territory of another member-country.

Example: Faculty of various university who move to another member-country and work in the academic institutions situated there, for a specified period.

GATS covers only temporary movement of the personnel and not permanent residence or citizenship.

Does GATS imply that India would lose its ability to pursue its own national policy objectives and priorities like costing of education and ensuring social equity through provision of access to the socially disadvantaged? Is this kinds of foreign universities are meet with India's culture? Is this institutions consider our constitutional provisions? Is they bothered about the marginalized *daridra narayans* of India? Is they felt the education of SC/ST, Tribal, OBC's and Aborigines?

Recognizing this concern, GATS established a framework of rules to ensure that member-countries administer their services and regulations in a reasonable, objectives and impartial manner, while at the same time not acting as a deliberate barrier for trading services.

For instance GATS gives India the right to decide the condition under which a foreign university can establish a subsidiary business school in India.

Flexible Regime for Developing Countries

Some critics of GATS feels that, GATS has imposed many restrictions on developing countries GATS provides the following flexibilities to the member countries:

1. Member countries can choose those service sectors or sub sectors on which they will make commitments guaranteeing the right of foreign suppliers to provide the service.
   Example: In the education service sector, India can make commitments guaranteeing the right of the foreign educational institutions only to the higher education sector.
2. For those services that are committed, the member countries may set limitations specifying the level of market access and the degree of national treatment they are prepared to guarantee.
   Example: In airline sector, we give freedom to internal transportation at first. Now international also.
3. Member-countries can limit the commitments to one or more of the four modes of supply (above said), through which

educational service is traded. They may also withdraw and re-negotiate commitments.

4. In order to provide more favourable treatment to certain trading partners, member-countries may make exemptions, in limited to 10 years duration, from the Most Favoured Nation (MFN) principle, which is otherwise applicable to all services, whether scheduled or not.

Obligations Under Liberalization

The obligations under GATS, which a member country has to discharge as a party that signed the agreement, are categorized into two groups:

General Obligations

These apply automatically to all member countries of the WTO (India is a signatory) irrespective of the commitments made for each sector.

Conditional Obligations

These apply only to those sectors where a member-country has assumed market access and national treatment obligations.

Suppose India decides not to open its services in primary education and secondary education under the GATS. While it has the full liberty to do so, India may also choose to open only technical education under GATS.

Under the General Obligations, India is also can Provide

(a) *MFN/Most Favoured Nations Treatment:* If India allows foreign sector competition in technical education, it should give equal opportunities in that sector to all the WTO members, even if the member in question has made no specific commitment to provide foreign companies access to its market under WTO.

(b) *Transparency:* All member countries have an obligation to publish all measures of general application and establish national enquiry points to respond to the requests of foreign countries for information.

(c) *Other Conditional Obligations:* These include the establishment of a mechanism for review and appeal, grievance redressal procedures and discipline in providing services.

Under the conditional obligations, each member-country identifies the service sector or sub-sectors in which it prepared to make commitment. This is followed by member-countries inscribing the conditions under which it allows services and foreign countries to access its markets. This means, national treatment is not mandatory in GATS, but is negotiated on a sector-to-sector basis.

Market Assess

If India makes a decision to open its market to the technical colleges of foreign universities in the country, the commitment regarding access to such universities can be made after necessary negotiations. India can impose one or more restrictions like the location, the intake etc. Including the legal form of the foreign universities as well as the degree of foreign capital participation in the venture.

National Treatment

This means treating one's own nationals and foreigners equally. For instance, if one or more foreign technical colleges offer B.Tech programme in India, then the graduates of these technical colleges should be treated equally with the graduates of the Indian technical colleges. GATS allows limitations on national treatment to be taken fully or partially, but these should be clear during negotiations.

Advantages of Liberalization

- Good service infrastructure, which includes education, is a pre-requisite for the economic success of any country, in fact, a number of countries are banking on open and transparent environment for the provision of services.
- Access to world-class education helps the educational institutions in the host country to increase their competitive strength. Liberalization in the service sector has thus become a key component of many development strategies.
- Countries with liberalized educational sector see greater product and process innovations. This can be seen in Indias Information Technology sector.
- Commitments to the WTO, in the educational sector, encourage Foreign Direct Investments (FDI). This brings with it new skills and technologies that spill over into the wider economy in different ways.

Conclusion

The public spending on education worldwide is now more the 1 trillion US dollars. This includes the cost of 50 million teachers, 1 billion students and thousands of educational institutions.

In India, as a consequence of liberalization in recent times, the role of the government in higher education has been reduced and the degree of privatization has gone up. With the liberalization of education, the countries with better skills and knowledge will set-up institutions in our country.

The liberal policy of the government in providing foreign exchange and easy loans for educational purposes has made India a prime destination for the educational institutions in the developed countries.

Is there any way for India, having signed the GATS, to stop the foreign educational institutions from invading India?

One strategy could be to include education under the Article 1.3 of the GATS in which case it comes under the services provided by Government, with out any commercial angle attached to it.

But for this, education at all levels in the country must be completely financed and administered by the Government. Since this is not true as far as India is concerned the inclusion is not possible.

Only 49 out of 143 WTO member-countries have agreed to include education sector under GATS. i.e., remaining 94 countries treats as a national subject. No government has so far opened up its educational sector without any restrictions.

India must give a serious thought to this issue, especially in view of the policy of the USA to restrict outsourcing of Jobs to India— a step that is against the spirit of GATS. India must put in place proper restrictions in order to safe guard our social priorities, identity and culture. We have to initiate reforms internally so that the competitive edge of the foreign universities to establish branches in India can be relatively reduced. As a part of its effort to meet the emerging threat of the foreign universities to Indian higher education, the UGC is all set to identifying 500 colleges in the country, with *potential for excellence*, they get Rs. 1 crore each in addition to the existing development grant from the UGC. The UGC has already identified 30 universities as universities with potential for excellence and granted Rs. 30 crore to these universities.

PRIVATIZATION AND EDUCATION

What is Privatization?

The term 'privatization' has come into widespread use in the 1980's because of the economic reforms. During this period, thousands of state-owned enterprises or public sector units were privatized in many countries.

What Exactly is Privatization?

In a sense, privatization is the process of transferring the ownership of an organization or enterprise from the public sector to the private sector.

For the purposes of education, privatization implies the withdrawal of the state intervention from this sector. Privatization has other implications too, like the initiation of the process of private ownership in a sector that is controlled by the State.

In a broader sense, privatization is the induction and control of private management in the public and state sector in the case of education.

Definition of Privatization

"Privatization is the general process of involving the private sector in the ownership of operation of a state owned enterprise. Thus, the term refers to the private purchase of all or part of a company. It covers 'contracting out' and the privatization of management-through management contracts, leases or Franchisee arrangement." (Barbara Lee and John Nellis)

Purpose of Privatization

- Privatization is intended to improve the efficiency of an organization or educational institutions.
- The main objective is to reduce government control over education.
- It is used as an important strategy of economic rejuvenation by many developing and developed countries including Britain.

When Privatization Succeeds?

- The political leadership of the country should be committed to privatization. As privatization cannot be sustained unless the ideologies of the ruling party/opposition are included towards the privatization process.
- These should be no room for private monopoly.
- As competition is the key to the success of privatization.
- The Government should encourage multiplicity of private players.

- The Government should provide freedom to entry to private players in education.
  Restrictions on entry will reduce/ limit the competition and consumer choice. The public will be better served if more number of private educational institutions is encouraged to avoid the ill effects of monopolism. What are the ill effects of monopolism? If only one tea stall in your locale, what happened? We compel to cope with the service of that tea stall.
- The Government should facilitate the consumer to link the benefits they receive from a particular educational service to the costs they pay for it, as the consumers will then take a proper decision on the service they are paying for.

Benefits of Privatization

- Privatization will release the huge amount of capital that is locked up in the higher educational sector and the same can be diverted to the elementary educational sector where there is a dearth of funds to meet the goal of Education For All (EFA).
- It enables the government to downsize the administrative machinery.
- Higher economic growth can be secured by privatization.
- It results in better management of the educational institutions.

Need for Privatization

To Achieve UEE

India in its bid to achieve UEE, has targeted the enrolment, 14 millions children in schools by 2007-08. The government alone cannot achieve this target, as the total cost involved is too much for any government. It is now evident that the government with its not-so-encouraging allocation of funds for school education in the country will not be able to provide quality school education to all the children in the country.

To Attain the Goal EFA

Without the active involvement of the corporate sector or private players, the goal of EFA will continue to be elusive.

Relax the Governments Regulatory Regime

If the corporate sector or the private enterprises are to participate in the school education sector on the desired scale, the Government should relax the regulatory regime that is discouraging the corporate sector from participating in it.

To Expand Higher Education Access

To be successful and competitive in the emerging global market with its products and services, India has no choice but to expand its higher education and associated training. Even after 60 years of independence, the access to higher education in India is still very low.

Today more than 7 million students are enrolled in the formal system with another 2 million in the distance education programmes.

This works out to the access parameter of 6 per cent of the relevant age group i.e., 18-24 years of age, excluding the distance learners.

This compares very unfavourably with the access figures of 70 per cent and above in countries like USA, Japan and Finland, 30-50 per cent in the West European countries like France, Germany and the UK and about 20-25 per cent in some of the Asia-Pacific countries.

Privatization in Educational Sector—Indian Picture

In a way, the process of corporate sector participation in school education is already on though in a limited way in states like Andhra Pradesh, Karnataka, Madhya Pradesh and Gujarat, where the governments have tied up with large companies and Rotary Clubs to raise the necessary funds. One such instance is the initiative of the Azim Premji Foundation of WIPRO corporation, where the states are providing the infrastructure, teachers and are implementing the plan while the foundation has been setting up schools and motivating children to attend schools.

In several Asia-Pacific countries about 80 per cent of the students are in private educational institutions. In countries like Korea, Japan, Philippines, Taiwan and Indonesia, Private Universities enroll as much as 80 per cent of the students.

In fact, before independence, India too was dominated by private educational institutions, until the leaders in authority after independence nationalized education and brought it under public domain. The process now being reversed, i.e., a trend of privatization to nationalization during 1947-90 and nationalization to privatization since 1990 onwards.

The above said facts are not scale down Indian educational sector. Now-a-days the emerging favourable conditions for exporting

Indian higher education to the third world countries. The trend is already get by the IIT Chennai (Indian Institute of Technology) which is all get to establish campus in Sri Lanka to train and offer technical assistance to give shape to an institute as par with the IIT's in that country. The India-Sri Lanka Foundation has initiated work in this regard. In fact, the Birla Institute of Technological Sciences BITS PILANI has already set-up a campus in Dubai knowledge village. So the export of educational services from India becoming a reality, many private players will enter this sector to take advantage of the situation. In fact, privatization is being given a tremendous push with the establishment of private universities in the country, example ICFAI.

Though the Chattisgarh experience in this regard has not been good, what with 100s of private universities being established in that state in less than a year. Some of the other states, like Andhra Pradesh are all set to enact a law to regulate private universities in the state. Orissa, Uttaranchal, West Bangal, Madhya Pradesh, and Punjab are also thinking similar lines.

GLOBALIZATION AND EDUCATION

The term 'Globalization' means integration of economies and societies though cross-country flows of information, ideas, technologies, goods, services, capital, finance and people. Cross-border integration is multi-dimensional including cultural, social, economic and political dimensions.

The IMF (International Monetary Fund) defines globalization as "The growing economic inter-dependence of countries world wide through increasing volume and variety of cross border transactions in goods and services and of international capital flows and also through the more rapid and wide spread diffusion of technology."

Globalization is the shift towards a more integrated and inter-dependent world economy. Globalization has two components.

1. The globalization of markets, and
2. The globalization of productions.

—Charles Hill

Today, the driving force behind globalization is the WTO, which has established in 1995. WTO is the successor to the General Agreement on Tariffs and Trade (GATT).

The WTO has 142 members accounting for 90 per cent of the world trade. About 30 others are negotiating the membership. The

WTO's objective is to ensure smooth, free, fair and predictable flow of trade by

- Administering trade arguments.
- Acting as a forum for trade negotiations.
- Settling trade disputes.
- Reviewing trade policies.
- Assisting developing countries in trade policy issues, through technical assistance and training programmes.
- Co-operating with other international organizations.

Factors Contributing to Globalization

- Widening Markets/Increase in Market Size Companies/manufactures are not depending upon the market in a single country for their products and services.
- Ability of countries with surplus resources to optimally utilize their surplus.
- Facilitating the movement of a company from a recession hit economy of a country to the boom economy in another country.
- Exploring the untapped potential markets.
- The process of cultural transformation and integration.
- Reduction in production costs through utilization of cheap labour in other countries.

India and Globalization

The process of globalization in India started with the economic reforms initiated in 1991. These economic reforms were aimed at integrating the Indian economy with the world economy.

The Narasimha Rao Government (1991), was forced to go in for globalization for the following reasons:

1. The Public Sector Undertakings (PSUs) were becoming sick and there were no adequate returns on the investments made in the PSUs.
2. Because the Gulf War and the poor performance of the export sector, the foreign exchange reserves were at their lowest level and the country was on the verge of de faulting on foreign debt payment.
3. While there was a need for huge investments in the different sectors of the economy to increase the growth rate, the domestic capital investment was inadequate.

As such India had no choice but to opt for globalization to save the country's economy.

Advantages of Globalization

- Movement of the capital ensures that the total savings of the world are distributed among several countries.
- Flow of latest technologies from developed countries to the developing countries.
- Development of the capital markets take place, as it is one of the pre-requisites for the international flow of capital.
- Development of foreign exchanges market is ensured as it is also one of the pre-requisites for the international flow of capital.
- International trade is developed with allocation of resources in tune with the comparative advantages.
- Industrial development gets a boost because of new technologies, huge capital and managerial expertise that is made accessible to the domestic companies.
- Companies no longer depend upon markets in a particular country, as the market is world wide.
- Cultural exchange takes place among countries making people demand a variety of products that are consumed in other countries.
- The consumption levels go up. Because of the availability of products of high quality at lower prices.
- Because of the shifting of manufacturing facilities to the low wage developing countries, employment opportunities increase manifold.

Disadvantages of Globalization

- As globalization is closely related to the structural adjustment programme of the IMF and World Bank, it curtails public expenditure resulting in cut in subsidies and the, marginalizing of the poor.
- Public sector enterprises including public utilities like water and electricity are privatized.
- The gap between the rich and poor widens with skilled and competent people getting huge incomes and the common people struggling to get even the minimum wage.
- The foreign aid comes with strings attached to it and the economy becomes over-dependent on external assistance.

- Unfair trade with the products of the developed countries invading the markets of the developing countries.
- The entry of the MNC's will force the closure of the local companies as they cannot compete with the MNC's and this results in increasing unemployment.

Globalization and Education

We understand the impact of globalization on the countries economy. Now let us discuss the impact of globalization on education.

Globalization has transformed the world into a global village. Under the provisions of the GATS, Indian education is bound to face formidable competition from foreign players. In fact a number of foreign universities and colleges are making intensive efforts to enhance their presence in India by offering alluring packages of academic programmes. The Gullible Indian students who unfortunately, have a craze for foreign degrees. Surprisingly, many of these universities and colleges are not accredited in their own countries.

To check this abuse of the 'Globalization of Education' process, the All India Council for Technical Education (AICTE) has, in September 2003, has decided to regulate the entry of foreign universities into India as some sub-standard foreign universities are cheating thousands students in the country.

Very often, even the parent bodies of these foreign universities are refusing to recognize the degrees awarded by these universities stating that the courses are not equivalent to their courses.

In view of this, the AICTE stipulated that no foreign university could start a programme in India without its approval. The franchisees offering these programmes must get approval from the AICTE for continuing their programmes within six months.

Taking advantage of the Indian students craze for foreign degrees, some of the universities based in US, UK, Canada and Australia are appointing franchisees in India and are offering courses charging huge sums of money. When the students who enrolled for these courses go to the countries where these universities are based, the parent universities reject these degrees on the ground that the courses offered by the franchisees are not equal to their programnmes.

To check this menace, the AICTE is framing a new regulation for foreign universities. Under this, every university intending to set-up shop in India should get the approval from their embassies and must be accredited by their country's regulating authority.

Apart from this, the universities should either set-up their own campuses in India or must collaborate with an AICTE approved college. The AICTE has decided not to allow any foreign university to run the courses through franchisees.

Objectives of Globalization of Education

The stated objectives of globalization of education, as put forth by the proponents of globalization are:

- The motives of the foreign education provides are altruistic
- They want to help the countries by moving into those countries.
- The foreign education provides are interested in supplying the same quality of education to the host countries that they maintain in their main campus in their own country.

That these objectives are more in paper than in practice. The truth of the matter is that the developed countries are keen on globalization of education to maximize their share of profit.

Supporters of Globalization of Education

Threats and opportunities in the globalization of education can be assessed only when one is clear about the motives. Those who subscribe to the economic perspective of the education are the strongest proponents of globalization of education. They opine:

1. the job opportunities and the needs of the economy are the driving forces for the globalization of education.
2. knowledge, skills and competency required for the vocations and professions in demand are the major focus of the globalization of education.
3. all jobs, vocations and professions will acquire the same character world wide demanding similar skills, professional competencies and knowledge.
4. the work, success in career of profession is the ultimate aim of human life.
5. the educational packages being offered by foreign universities and colleges being only job related have neutral value and as such cannot have negative socio-cultural, psychological implications.

6. human beings are essentially self-centered and are motivated to work only for personal gain.

The Opponents of Globalization of Education

Education in every country aims to develop people who are capable of, and have the commitment for contributing to the achievement of national goals. In the process of globalization of education, a problem may arise with reference to the incompatibility between the national goals of the host country and the aims and objectives of the foreign university and colleges. How this conflict can be resolved?

This conflict can be resolved only when the national goals of the host country match the national goals of the country in which foreign educational institution is head quartered. Is it possible?

The opponents of the Globalization of education opine:

1. The difference between the national goals of the foreign educational institutions and the host countries, lead to a conflict of values.
   Example: Secular countries cannot have goals that are common to theocratic countries. Dictatorship cannot share the goals of democracies.
2. Value systems and beliefs vary across cultures.
3. Western education may lead to unforeseen social disorganization, conflict and serious disruption of culture.
4. Education is integral to culture and foreign educational packages may prove to be disruptive in another culture.
5. Students who receive education through the process of globalization of education may prove to be misfits in their own culture resulting in serious psychological repercussions.
6. Globalization of education promotes competition and its nature of individualistic and this will be dysfunctional in a culture and society that seeks greater social harmony, community spirit and social advancement.

Conclusion

While proponents and opponents of globalization education have their views that cannot be brushed aside, a serious thought should be given to the socio-cultural implications and impact of globalization of education.

Education, however innocuous it may appear to be, certainly transmits culture. Foreign education is no exception. This may ultimately result in homogenization of the society.

While leaving globalization of education to economists and politicians, its socio-cultural implications can be ignored only at the risk of world peace, social harmony, disappearance of community feeling, and of course, diversity.

MODEL QUESTIONS

1. "Education is an investment for the future" comment.
2. Enumerate the relation between education and economic development.
3. What is the impact of privatization of education.
4. What is the implication of modernization of education.
5. 'Modernization is not westernization' explain.
6. In what ways does economic development affect education?

REFERENCES

1. Aggarwal, J.C. (2003). *Teaching of Economics: A Practical Approach*, Vinod Pustak Mandir, Agra.
2. Ganta, R. and Dash, B.N. (2005). *Foundations of Education*, Neelkamal Publishers (P) Ltd., Hyderabad.
3. Virendra Kumar, M.P. *Gattum Kana Charadukalum* (Mal) Mathrubhumi Books, Calicut.
4. Yogendra, K.S. (2006). *History and Problems of Education*, Kanishka Publishers, New Delhi.

11

Teacher Education

Teaching as a Profession

Dr. Radhakrishnan has aptly remarked, "The teachers' place in society is of vital importance. He acts as the point for the transmission of intellectual tradition and technical skill from generation to generation and helps to keep the camp of civilization burning."

Teaching is an art. This art has to be learnt by undergoing a specific training. In the beginning of the present century, the general belief was that "teachers are born not made." But old belief has changed now. The whole concept about teacher and teacher education has undergone a tremendous change.

Importance and Need of Professional Education of Teachers

Importance

- Important for Qualitative Improvement of Education Teaching is a highly skilled job and cannot be done satisfactorily without a sound preparation for it.
- Important for achieving the desired goals of education.
- Important for raising the standards of education.

One question that has perennially been asked is teaching a profession? Is it, like other professions, be considered exclusively as a means to a livelihood? A glance at the pages of history dispels this notion. It tells us that it has ever been an ideal vocation. Speaking about Brahmanic education, Lord William said that these places of teaching were constructed out of ordinary mind. Generally it was the teacher who made these huts at his own expense, and the teacher begged, not merely to made the hut, but even to feed his students.

This shows that teaching has always been a profession which makes human beings, a profession with its own unique traditions. In this connection, the regional service/extension department of the National Educational Organization has put forward the following eight points:

1. A profession should be necessarily equipped with intellectual tendencies.
2. A profession should have opportunities for various kinds of specialized skills and abilities.
3. A profession should also possess opportunities for regular and systematic promotion during the period of service.
4. A profession should possess opportunities for the necessary special training and preparation of those engaged in it.
5. A profession provides as an occupation and a permanent membership for the entire life of the participant.
6. A profession generates its own standards.
7. A profession generates the desire for service even more than for personal gain.
8. A profession possess strong professional organizations associated with it.

On the basis of these points/elements, T.M. Stinnet and Albert. J. Huggett have established that education is not merely one of the professions, but the creative source or mother of all professions. Having accepted that education is a profession, it is essential to realize the programmes that are essential for making it a success. The Education Commission has offered numerous suggestions for making this profession attractive and interesting.

Education is a profession which, keeping itself completely away from black-marketing, corruption and other evil practices, gives rise to healthy traditions and thus helps to make concrete the dream of national development. When we accept that education is a profession, we must also accept its responsibilities and its burden. Dr. Carr's view is that an analysis of the existing circumstances and the potential for he future makes it evident that there is a universal tendency towards changing the new power and energy of the teacher.

1. People think that education and school are synonymous with each other.
2. Seeking education means becoming a victim of the fad prevailing in education.

3. The greatest fear is that the public loses faith in the teacher.

Today conditions have changed. The teacher will have to win to his own cause all those who believe him to be maker of the nation. How can the teacher be the architect of his country? In the absence of a national educational policy, who will make the nation? The low salaries of the teacher are dispensed by the administration, the exploitation is done by the administration, the conditions of work are made in sufferable by the administration, and yet it is claimed that it is the teacher who will build the nation. For this, the reason is that the teacher's objections make no dent upon the mind of the legislators. In view of this, it is necessary that the administration and the community must change its attitude towards the teacher who is being grounded to dust between the two grinding stones of the administration and management.

The first of the administration is to nationalize education. It generate a sense of equality. It should also modify the declared national educational policy to bring it into consonance with national requirements. It must also make every effort to isolate education from parochial politics so that education may devote itself to the building of a future society instead of seeking immediate and personal gains.

The following suggestions are taken from the 21st conference of the universal teachers council, for the improvement of teaching profession:

1. Teachers should be given professional training and the latest knowledge.
2. Teachers at all levels should be treated as equal.
3. Teacher trainees should be kept in contact with actual conditions.
4. All teachers should be given equal opportunities for developing and improving themselves.
5. Unions of teachers should be established to safeguard the interests of the teachers.
6. The administration should seek the co-operation of teachers in its work.
7. Educational programmes should be planned properly.

The profession of teaching should be developed as a technical profession. Teachers should get equality in such matters as scales of pay and facilities. They should also be remembered when posts with social status and awards are being distributed. If these steps are not taken, the poor teacher, who is living in an atmosphere of distrust and neglect, will once again have to take to revolutionary means to win for himself what society owes him.

Objectives of Teacher Education

- To develop great values of education such as non-violence, truthfulness, self-discipline, self-reliance and dignity of labour.
- To perceive his role as an agent of social change in the community.
- To perceive his role not only as a leader to the children but also that of a guide to the community.
- To act as a liasion between the school and the community and employ suitable ways and means for integrating community life and resource with school work.
- To help in the conservation of environmental resources and preservation of historical monuments and other cultural heritage.
- To possess warm and positive attitude towards children and their academic, socio-emotional and personal problems and skills to guide and counsel them.
- To develop competence to teach on the basis of the accepted principles of learning and teaching.
- To keep abreast of the latest knowledge of the subject-matter he is teaching and the techniques teaching the same.
- To undertake action research and investigatory projects.

Need of Professional Education

- For giving knowledge of child psychology.
- For making teaching on interesting process.
- For giving knowledge of learning and teaching process.
- Essential for planned education.
- For development of different qualities of a teacher.

What is Teacher Education ?

According to Good's Dictionary of Education, Teacher Education consists of "All formal and information activities and experiences that help to qualify a person to assume the responsibilities as member of the educational profession or to discharge his responsibilities more effectively.

From Teacher Training to Teacher Education

Teacher Education is institutionalized educational procedure which aims at the preparation of teachers. Previously, it was known as Teacher's Training Institutions/Training Colleges. But now 'Teacher Education' has been adopted in place of 'Teacher Training'. W.S. Kilpatrick, the famous American Educationist once remarked, "One trains circus performers and animals but one educates the teachers."

Meaning of Professional Ethics: Commitment to Teaching Profession

"If a teacher has not an ideal aim he had better to take to shop keeping at once, he will there doubtless find an ideal within his capacity." —Laurie "They (teachers) will not look upon their work as an umpalatable means of carrying a scanty living but as an avenue through which they are rendering significant social services as well as finding some measure of self-fulfillment and self-expression."

- Secondary Education Commission (1952-53)

If a teacher takes to his work just to make his living because nothing else is available, he will lack the essential zeal required by the teaching profession. He must be a teacher first and the teacher last.

The professional ethics demands that a teacher doesn't try to exploit school influence for private gains. He realizes that if he/she does it, he/she signs his moral death-warrant. The result is that no amount of pressure can wean him from the path of duty and justice. Authority cannot coerce him, nor can temptation reduce him into any course of conduct, not conductive to the highest interests of the school. He fights all temptations to pad his purse with money to which he is not entitled. He does not indulge in tuitions. He doesn't prescribe/recommend books/guides on some consideration.

Need and Significance of Professional Ethics for Teachers

Teachers are called the makers of man, the makers of a nation, and the real makers of history. It is therefore, essential that teachers should have professional ethics. The following points indicate the need and significance of professional ethics for teachers:

1. Norms and ethics provide credibility to the teaching

profession.

2. They help in developing a sense of commitment among the teachers to the teaching profession.
3. They serve as beacon light to the teachers in adhering to certain important ideals and values.
4. They serve as warnings to teachers not to fall upon unscrupulous methods.
5. They are constant remainders to teachers for discharging their responsibilities with a sense of purpose.
6. Adherence to the norms enhance the prestige of teachers.

General Attitude Acceptable to the Society

A teacher is a member of the society. He lives and works in the society. In view of his special responsibilities and role, he is expected to rise above the average member of the society. His general attitude in the society should be enthusiasm and optimism. He should be a man of co-operative attitude, he should be sensitive to the needs of the society. He should be guided by the ideals of democracy, secularism and socialism.

Work Ethics

It is rightly said, "Dignity consists in being helpful and doing the right things in the right manner and at the right time. "A teacher would do well to prepare his lessons daily. Bagley has said, "However able and experienced the teacher he could do never with out his preliminary preparation." Efforts should be made to ensure that all the work done is neat and clean, systematic and in time.

Ethical Code for Teachers

1. Every teacher shall remain punctual in attendance and in respect of his classwork and also for any other work connected with the duties assigned to him by the head, of the school.
2. Every teacher shall abide by the rules and regulations of the school and also show due respect to the constituted authority.

No Teacher shall:

3. Knowingly or willfully neglect his duties.
4. Propagate through his teaching lessons or otherwise, communal or sectarian outlook, or incite or allow any student to indulge in communal or sectarian activity.

5. Discriminate against any student on the ground of caste, creed, language, place of origin, social and cultural background or any of them.
6. Indulge in, or encourage, any form of malpractice connected with examination or any other school activity.
7. Make any sustained neglect in correcting class-work or home work done by students.
8. While being present in the school, absent himself (except with the previous permission of the head of the school) from the class which is required to attend.
9. Remain absent from the school without leave or without the previous permission of the head of the school.
   Provided that where such absence without leave or without the previous permission of the head of the school is due to reasons beyond the control of the teacher, it shall not be deemed to be a breach of the code of conduct, if on return on duty, the teacher has applied for an obtained, ex-post facto, the necessary sanction for the leave.
10. Accept any job of a renumerative character from any source other than the school or give private tuition to any student or other person or engage himself in any business.
11. Engage himself as a selling agent/canvasser for any publication or trader.
12. Ask for or accept any contribution, or otherwise associate himself with the raising of any funds or make any other collections, whether in cash or in kind, in pursuance of any object whatsoever, except subscription from the members of any of my association of teachers.
13. Enter into any monitory transactions with any student or parent; nor shall be exploit his influence for personal ends; nor shall be conduct his personal matters in such a manner that he has to incur a debt beyond his means to repay.
14. Accept or permit any member of his family or any other person acting on his behalf to accept, any gift from any student, parent or any person with whom he has come into contact by virtue of his position in the school.
15. Practice, or incite any student to practice casteism, communalism or untouchability.
16. Cause, or incite any other person to cause, any damage to school property.

17. Behave, or encourage or incite any student, teacher or other employee to behave, in a rowdy or disorderly manner in the school premises.
18. Be guilty of, or encourage, violence, or any conduct which involves moral turpitude.
19. Be guilty of misbehaviour or cruelty towards any parent, guardian, student, teacher or employee of the school.
20. Organize or attend any meeting during the school hours except where he is required, or permitted by the head of the school to do so.

Ethical Oath for Teachers

I solemnly affirm that I will uphold the dignity of the profession and that I will devote myself to the best of my capacity to the all-round development and well-being of any students.

ACCOUNTABILITY IN EDUCATION

Meaning

The word 'accountability' is a concrete and matter-of-fact expression of what the schools owe as duties and responsibilities to their establishing/employing organization, to the student community and the society at large, with the ultimate aim of doing good by their performance. The idea of accountability should not appear as objectionable of foreign to the institutions and teachers if they could open mindedly look at their own everyday activities and programmes relating to their responsibilities.

Definitions

1. "Educational accountability is the theory that teachers and school systems may be held responsible for actual improvement in public achievement and that such improvement is measurable through tests of teacher effectiveness, constructed by outside agencies."

   ■ Good's Dictionary of Education (1973).

2. The International Dictionary on Education by Terry Page and J.B. Thomas (1987) explains the term accountability as:

   (i) Educational technology term for the extent to which student performance is attributable to instruction rather than ageing, selecting admission etc.

   (ii) Extent to which a state college or university is publicly

accountable for its actions and expenditure. The same authors define educational accountability as, "Assumption of responsibility for bringing about specified results in students." Again it describes teacher accountability in these words, "Theory that teacher and school systems should take responsibility for improvement in public achievement and that teacher effectiveness by this criterion should be measured by external agencies.

3. The International Dictionary of Management (1980) by Itano Jo Hannse and G. Terry Page (1980) defines accountability as "Accountability for action carried out and performance achieved to other, e.g., by a manager to his superior or by the board of directors to its shareholders. Also used more loosely to describe responsibility.
4. The Concise Dictionary of Education (1982) gives the following meaning of Accountability "Educational accountability is a concept in which the school system and especially teachers are held responsible for the learning and academic progress of students."
5. The Blackwill Encyclopedic Dictionary of Organization Behaviour (1995) edited by Nigel Nicholson explains term 'accountability' as "The term denotes responsibility for particular activities, results or outcomes specification of the person(s) or group(s) who hold such responsibility in an organization."

Need for Account Ability in Education

Accountability would make us work hard. We would remain conscious of the fact that we are responsible for our performance. In case our performance is not in accordance with the norms fixed, we are likely to face consequences of our actions, we would tend to become more diligent conscientious and duty bound. A policy of 'Laissez faire' i.e., let us work as we please is hardly conducive to the working of any social institution. School is no exception.

PROFESSIONAL DEVELOPMENT OF TEACHERS PRE-SERVICE AND IN-SERVICE EDUCATION

American President Johnson in his presidential message (1965) emphasized the dynamic role of the teachers. "We must demand that our schools increase not only the quantity but the quality of

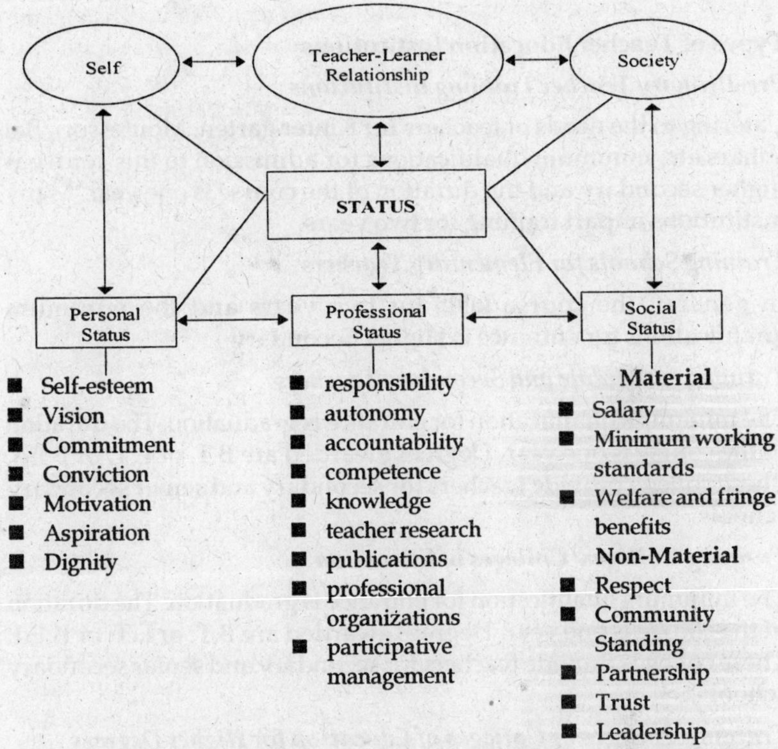

Self
Teacher-Learner Relationship
Society
STATUS
Personal Status
Professional Status
Social Status
■ Self-esteem
■ Vision
■ Commitment
■ Conviction
■ Motivation
■ Aspiration
■ Dignity
■ responsibility
■ autonomy
■ accountability
■ competence
■ knowledge
■ teacher research
■ publications
■ professional organizations
■ participative management
Material
■ Salary
■ Minimum working standards
■ Welfare and fringe benefits
Non-Material
■ Respect
■ Community Standing
■ Partnership
■ Trust
■ Leadership

Figure 11.1: Status of Teachers.

American Education. For we recognize that nuclear age problems, cannot be solved with horse and buggy learning. The 3R's of our school system must be supported by the 3Ts – teachers who are superior, techniques of instruction that are modern and thinking about education, which place it first in all our plans and hopes." For the realization of these objectives, proper education of teachers is the first requisite.

Pre-Service
In-Service
Discussions
Seminars
Workshops
Talks
Seminars
Summer camps
Comprehensive Colleges and Regional Colleges
Pre-primary
Primary
Training Colleges for Special Subjects
Graduate and Secondary Teacher Training
Post Graduate
Training for Supervisors
Correspondence Courses

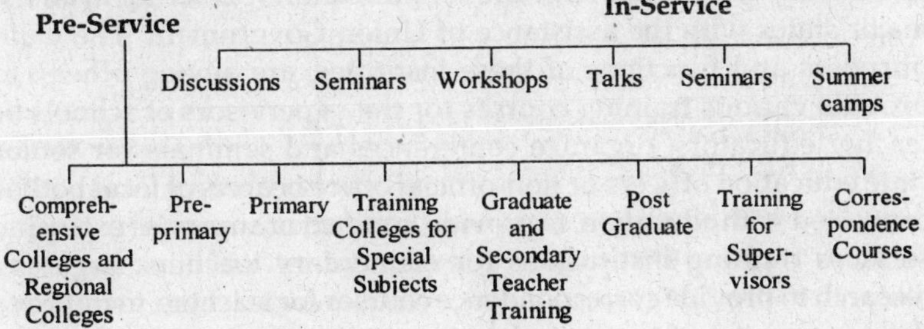

Types of Teacher Education Institutions

Pre-Primary Teacher Training Institutions

Catering to the needs of teachers for Kinter garten, Montessori, Bal Vihars etc, minimum qualifications for admission to this course is higher secondary and the duration of the course is one year. Many institutions impart training for two years.

Training Schools for Elementary Teachers

In general, the course lasts for two years and the minimum qualifications for entrance is Higher Secondary.

Training for Middle and Secondary Teachers

The minimum qualification for entrance is graduation. The duration of the course is one year. Degrees awarded are B.T. or L.T. or B.Ed. These college provide teachers for secondary and senior secondary schools.

Training Colleges/ Colleges of Education

The minimum qualification for entrance is graduation. The duration of the course is one year. Degrees awarded are B.T. or L.T. or B.Ed. These colleges provide teachers for secondary and senior secondary schools.

Training Colleges or Colleges of Education for Higher Degrees

These provide opportunities to take up Master of Education and Ph.D. courses.

Training College for Special Subjects

These are separate classes or colleges for preparing teachers in certain subjects like physical education, home science, crafts, language, etc.

State Institute of Education

In 1964, a chain of State Institutes of Education was set-up in all the major states with the assistance of Union Government. The main purposes and functions of these institutes, are among others, to provide various training courses for the supervisors of schools or teacher educators, organize conferences and seminars for senior state education officers or non-official office bearers of local bodies connected with education, to provide, conduct or supervise extension services training institutions for elementary teachers, organize research to provide correspondence courses for teachers, to improve the programme of teacher education in the state and to assist the

State Education Departments in the preparation and implementation of educational plans.

Regional Colleges of Education

Another important project for teacher education in the diversified system of secondary education relates to the setting up of the Regional Colleges of Education and their attached demonstration multi-purpose schools at Ajmer, Bhubaneshwar, Mysore and Bhopal. The first-three were started in 1963 while the latter in 1964. These colleges are designed to represent a new enterprise in teacher education to train competent teachers and teacher educators in certain critical areas like science, technology, industrial crafts, commerce and agriculture so that they can function in their selected subject fields, in any system of education like technical, commerce and agricultural schools and not only in multipurpose schools. These programmes are four-years bachelor's degree programmes in science, technology, commerce, agriculture and English, one year training programmes in science, commerce and agriculture, industrial crafts programmes of one, two and three-year duration, and two-year master's degree programme. The colleges have undertaken a crash programme of training teachers to clear the backlog through correspondence –cum-summer schools, which may be regarded as sandwich course.

Comprehensive Colleges

A comprehensive college of education prepares teachers for several stages of education and/or for a number of special fields. Some institutions of this type already exist and have shown good results. The education commission recommends that planned attempt should be made to develop more institutions of this type and add sections for training primary and/or pre-primary teachers to training colleges that now prepare teachers for secondary schools only.

Summer Schools-cum-Correspondence Courses

An important step taken in this direction has been the organizing of summer schools-cum-correspondence courses leading to B.Ed. degree at all the four regional colleges of education. This course includes full time training at the summer vacations (4 months) and instruction through correspondence during the ten months period between the two summer vacations.

National Council of Educational Research and Training (NCERT)

NCERT established in 1961 to offer high level teacher education and to investigate in to the problems of education and suggest solutions for them. Its objectives, among others, are to examine, evaluate and co-ordinate the programmes of teacher education conducted by the state departments of education and the universities and to take all such measures as will lead to an improvement in teacher education at elementary and secondary levels (*see also unit 6*).

National Council for Teacher Education (NCTE)

The NCTE has been established as a national level statutory body by the Government of India vide its notification dated 17.08.1995. The main objectives

- To achieve planned and co-ordinated development of the teacher education system.
- Regulation and proper maintenance of norms and standards of teacher education.

Number of Teacher's Training Institutions

In 1946-47, the input of teacher training schools was about 20,000 teachers. In 1998-99, it had risen to about 1,28,700 (68,100 males and 60,600 females). For the secondary teachers' training, these were only 41 training colleges. In 1998-99, the number was 818 with the input of nearly 1,14,200 (65,640 males and 48,560 females).

District Institutes of Education and Training (DIET's)

In pursuance of the directions contained in the National Policy of Education, it is planned to set-up about 400 DIETs for providing pre-service and in-service training to elementary school teachers. About 292 such institutes were in operation in 1998.

STEIs, IASEs and CTEs

The proposed plan also includes the strengthening of about 250 Secondary Teacher Education Institutions (STEIs) , development of about 50 of them as Institutions of Advanced Study in Education (IASEs) and the rest as Colleges of Teacher Education (CTEs).

In-Service Teacher Education

Importance of In-service Education

Rabindranath Tagore thinks, "A teacher can never truly teach unless he is still learning himself. A lamp can never light another lamp unless it continues to burn its own flames."

The eminent teacher at Rugby, Thomas Arnold who said, "I Prefer that my students should drink from a running stream rather than a stagnant pool."

Meaning of In-Service Teacher Education

It refers to the education a teacher receives after he has entered the teaching profession and after he has had his education in a teachers' college. It includes all the programmes, educational social or others in which the teacher takes a vital part, all the extract education which he receives at different institutions by way of refresher and other professional courses, and all the travel and visits which he undertakes.

The commission on teacher education in USA explained this dearly as, "The continued education of teachers means much more than making up defects in preparation. It means continuous growth in the capacity to teach. It means broadened understanding of human development and human living. And now more than at any previous period in school history it means growth in one's capacity to work with others, with classroom teachers and principals in a variety of activities, with parents and community leaders and with children of different age groups.

The true teacher is a student to the end of his life. In-service education is not the responsibility of the teacher alone. It is a co-operative enterprise. It has to be promoted by several agencies. The agencies are:

- Schools,
- Teachers' colleges,
- Government, and
- Teachers' organizations.

Self-development of professional competencies by individual teachers has a large part to play in in-service teacher growth.

Institutions for In-service Teacher Education

1. State Institutes of Education.
2. State Institutes of Science.
3. State Institutes of English.
4. Extension Service Department of Teachers Training.
5. State Directorates of Education.
6. Voluntary Organizations.
7. NCERT.
8. NCTE.
9. UGC.
10. NIEPA.

Programmes for In-service Teacher Education

1. Seminars.
2. Extension Lectures.
3. Refresher Courses.
4. Workshops.
5. Study Groups.
6. Conferences.
7. Experimenting.
8. Professional Writings.
9. Discussions and Debates.

Suggestions for Improving In-service Teacher Education

1. Need for expanding facilities.
2. Co-operation of various agencies.
3. Encouraging role of heads, inspectors and education officers.
4. Well-planned programmes.
5. Well-qualified and trained resource persons.
6. Follow-up programmes.
7. Encourage Research.
8. Incentive to Teachers.
9. Subject teachers associations.
10. Appointment of subject experts at district level.

MODEL QUESTIONS

1. Which is meant by pre-service and in-service education of teachers.
2. What are the Aims and Objectives of Inservice education.
3. The competence and character of teacher influence the quality of education. Elucidate.
4. 'Teachers are born and not made'. Discuss.
5. Show your acquaintance with the teacher's organizations in India.

REFERENCES

1. Aggarwal, J.C. (2003). *Development and Planning of Modern Education*, Vikas Publishing House (P) Ltd., New Delhi.
2. Ahuja, B.N. & Bhatia, R.L. (2004). *Modern Indian Education and Its Problems*, Surjeet Publications, Delhi.
3. Bhatia, K.K. et al. *Modern Indian Education and Its Problems*, Tandon Publishers, Ludhyana.
4. Rao, D.B. (Ed) (2003). *Teachers in a Changing World*, Discovery Publishing House, New Delhi.
5. Singh, U.K. & Sudershan, K.N. (2003). *Teacher Education*, Discovery Publishing House, New Delhi.

Bibliography

Aggaral, J.C. (2003). *Teacher and Education in a Developing Society*, Vikas Publishing House (P) Ltd., New Delhi.

Aggarwal, J.C. (1992). *Theory and Principles of Education*, Vikas Publishing House (P) Ltd., New Delhi.

Aggarwal, J.C. (2002). *Theory and Principles of Education*, Vikas Publishing House (P) Ltd., New Delhi.

Aggarwal, J.C. (2003). *Development and Planning of Modern Education*, Vikas Publishing House (P) Ltd., New Delhi.

Aggarwal, J.C. (2003). *Development and Planning of Modern Education*, Vikas Publishing House (P) Ltd., New Delhi.

Aggarwal, J.C. (2003). *Teaching of Economics: A Practical Approach*, Vinod Pustak Mandir, Agra.

Ahuja, B.N. & Bhatia, R.L. (2004). *Modern Indian Education and Its Problems*, Surjeet Publications, Delhi.

Ahuja, M.C. (1997). *Glimpses of Some Indians*, Vikas Publishing House (P) Ltd., New Delhi.

Amala, Annie, *et al* (2006). *History of Education*, Discovery Publishing House, New Delhi.

B.C. Rai (1997). *Theory of Education-Sociological and Philosophical Bases and Education*, Prakashan Kendra, Lucknow.

Basu, D.D. *Introduction to the Constitution of India*.

Belock and Green, J.L. *Philosophy and Education*, Any Prakashan, Meerut.

Bhatia, K.K. *et al. Modern Indian Education and Its Problems*, Tandon Publishers, Ludhyana.

Bhatt, B.D. and Sharma, S.R. (1993). *Sociology of Education*, Kanishka Publishing House, New Delhi.

Bhattacharya, S. (1996). *Foundations of Education*, Atlantic Publishers and Distributors, New Delhi.

Botia, B. & Bhatia, K. (1992). *The Philosophical and Sociological Foundations of Education*, Doaba House, New Delhi.

Bourai, H.H.A. (1993). *Indian Theory of Education*, B.R. Publishing Corp, New Delhi.

Butler, J.D. (1966). *Idealism in Education*, Harper and Row, New York.

Chakraborty, A.K. (2003). *Principle and Practice of Education*, R. Lal Book Depot, Meerat.

Chandra, S.S. & Sharma, R. (1996). *Philosophy of Education*, Atlantic Publishers, New Delhi.

Chandra, S.S. (2003). *Adult and Non-Formal Education*, Surjeet Publishers, New Delhi.

Chaube, S.P. & Chaube, A. (1987). *Foundations of Education*, Vikas Publishing House (P) Ltd., New Delhi.

Chaube, S.P. *History and Problems of Indian Education*, Vinod Pustak Mandir, Agra.

Chaube, S.P. *History of Indian Education*, Vinod Pustak Mandir, Agra.

Conner D.J.O. (1957). *An Introduction to the Philosophy of Education*, London: Routledge Kegan Paul.

Das, P.N. (2004, May). *Mathrubhumi Thozhil Wartha*, p. 36.

Development of Indian System of Education. Dr. Ramashakal Pandey.

Encyclopaedia of Sociology (Vol. I) – Laxmi Devi.

Entwistle, Harold (1997). *Class, Culture and Education*, New Fetter Lane, London.

Ganta, R. and Dash, B.N. (2005). *Foundations of Education*, Neelkamal Publishers (P) Ltd., Hyderabad.

Gerald L. Gutek. *Philosophical and Ideological Perspectives on Education*.

Gerald, C. G. *Philosophical and Ideological Perspectives of Education*.

Ghanta, Ramesh & Dash, B.N. (2006). *Foundations of Education*, Neelkamal Pub (P) Ltd., Hyderabad.

Hospers, John (1953). *An Introduction to Philosophical Analysis*, Prentice Hall, London.

Aggarwal, J.C. (1995). *Teacher and Education in a Developing Society*, Vikas Publishing House Pvt. Ltd., New Delhi.

Jayakar, P. (1986). *J. Krishnamurti : A Biography*, Penguin Books India (P)Ltd., New Delhi.

Kamala Bhatia and Baldev Bhatia (1992). *The Philosophical and Sociological Foundations of Education*, Doaba House, New Delhi.

Kashyap C.S. (2005). *Our Constitution – An Introduction to India's Constitution and Constitutional Law*, National Book Trust, India, New Delhi.

Kneller, G.F. (1971). *Introduction to the Philosophy of Education*, John Willy and Sons, New York.

Kornblum, William (1998). *Sociology the Central Themes*, Harcourt Brace College Publishers, New York.

Koul, Lokesh (1997). *Methodology of Educational Research*, Vikas Publishing House, Pvt. Ltd., New Delhi.

Koushik, V.K. & Ravi, Prakash (1996). *A Sociology of Educating – Teaching and Curriculum*, Kanishka Publishers, New Delhi.

Krishnamurti Foundation India (1991). *Krishnamurti to Himself His Last Journal*, Auther, Madras.

Land marks in the History of Modern Indian Education—J.C. Aggarwal.

Learning without Burdon—Report of the National Advisory Committee Appointed by MHRD, Government of India.

Manuel, N.V. *Reading and Challenges in Philosophy of Education*, Unpublished Material.

Mathur, S.S. *A Sociological Approach to Indian Education*, Vinod Pustak Mandir, Agra.

Meigham, Roland (1996). *A Sociology of Educating*, Cassell Educational Ltd., London.

Monroe, Paul (2001). *Encyclopaedia of Philosophy of Education*, Cosmo Publications, New Delhi.

Murty, S.K. (1992). *Contemporary Problems and Current Trends in Education*, Parkash Brothers, Ludhyana.

Nanda, S.K. (2000). *Indian Education and its Problems Today*, Kalyani Publishers, New Delhi.

Pandey, R.S. (1991). *A Survey of Educational Thought*, Horizon Publishers, Allahabad.

Pandey, Ramshakal. *Teacher in Developing Indian Society*, Vinod Pustakmandir, Agra.

Pathak, C.K. (2003). *Adult Education – Millennium Challenges*, Rajat Publishers, New Delhi.

Pylee, M.V. (2003). *Indian Constitution*, Bhasha Institute, Thiruvananthapuram: Kerala.

Pylee, M.V. (2005). *An Introduction to the Constitution of India*, Vikas Publishing House (P) Ltd., New Delhi.

Rai, B.C. (1997). *Sociological and Philosophical Theory of Education*, Prakashan Kendra, Lucknow.

Raò, D.B. (Ed) (2003). *Teachers in a Changing World*, Discovery Publishing House, New Delhi.

Rao, V.K. (1999). *Vocational Education*, Rajat Publishers, New Delhi.

Reeba, K.R. (2002). *Educational Contributions of Jiddu Krishnamurthi*. Unpublished P.G. Dissertation, Mahatma Gandhi University, Kottayam.

Roand Meigham. *A Sociology of Educating*.

Robert R. Rusk. *The Philosophical Base of Education*, University of London Press.

Ruhela, S.P. *India's Struggle to Universalize Elementary Education*.

Sataya, Raghunath. (1993). *New Thoughts on Education*, The Indian Publications, Ambala.

Saxena, S.N.R. (2006). *Foundation of Educational Thought and Practice*, R. Lall Book Depot, Meerut.

Sharma, R. (2000). *Textbook of Educational Philosophy*, Kanishka Publishers, New Delhi.

Sharma, R.K. and Chandra, S.S. (1996). *Principles of Education*, Atlantic Publishers and Distributors, New Delhi.

Sharma, R.N. (2000). *Textbook of Educational Philosophy*, Kanishka Publications, New Delhi.

Sharma, R.N. *History and Problems of Education in India*, Surjeet Publications, New Delhi.

Sharma, S.R. (1997). *Practice of Philosophy of Education*, Mohit Publications, New Delhi.

Sharma, Y.K. (2003). *The Doctrines of the Great Indian Educators*, Kanishka Publishers, New Delhi.

Shivarajan. K. (2006). *Education in the Emerging Indian Society*. Calicut University Central Co-operative Stores.

Singh, U.K. & Sudershan, K.N. (2003). *Teacher Education*, Discovery Publishing House, New Delhi.

Singh, U.K. and Sudharshan, K.N. (2004). *Adult Education*, Discovery Publishing House, New Delhi.

Singh, U.K. and Sudarshan, K.N. (2004) *Vocational Education*, Discovery Publishing House, New Delhi.

Sloss, R.R. (1991). *Lines in the Shadow with J. Krishnamurthi*, Bloomsburg Publishing Ltd., London.

Srinibas Bhattacharya (1996). *Foundation of Education*, Atlantic Publishers, New Delhi.

Taneja, R.P. (2000). *Dictionary of Education*. Anmol Publishing Ltd., New Delhi.

Taneja, V.P. (2003). *Educational Thought and Practice*, Sterling Publishers (P) Ltd., New Delhi.

Taneja, V.R. (1987). *Educational Thought and Practice*, Sterling Publishers (P) Ltd., New Delhi.

Vekateswaran, S. (1993). *Principles of Education*, Vikas Publishing House (P) Ltd., New Delhi.

Venkataiah, S. (2002). *Vocational Education*, Anmol Publishers (P) Ltd., New Delhi.

Vidya Bushan and Sachdeva (1995). *An Introduction to Sociology*, Kitab Mahal, Allahabad.

Virendra Kumar, M.P. *Gattum Kana Charadukalum* (Mal), Mathrubhumi Books, Calicut.

Yogendra, K.S. (2006). *History and Problems of Education*, Kanishka Publishers, New Delhi.

URL's

1. www.edu.gov.
2. www.cde.ca.gov.
3. www.oneworld.net
4. http://groupsgoogle.co.in/group/bangalore

Index